Hard to Believe!

The incredible game-by-game story of the
2008 World Champion Philadelphia Phillies

Michael McNesby (signature)

D1417710

Michael McNesby & Jason Weitzel

with Michael Radano

Copyright © 2009 by Michael McNesby and Jason Weitzel
Published by Lulu Publishing Press, a division of Amazon.com. Distribution, marketing, publicity, interviews and book signings handled by the author.

All photography by Michael McNesby unless otherwise noted with permission. This book is
not affiliated with or endorsed by the Philadelphia Phillies or MLB.

No part of this book may be reproduced, stored in a retrieval system, or transmitted in any
form or by any means, electronic, mechanical, photocopying, recording, or otherwise without
the prior permission of Michael McNesby.

Front Cover Photo by: Bob Moules Photography
Back Cover Photo by: Michael McNesby
Cover Design by: Dave Mortlock
Edited by: Paul Mroczka - E-Right
Typeset by: Raheel Ahmed and Muhammad Rehan Ul Haque - Emage Graphic Studio

Michael McNesby can be reached at mikemcnesby@hotmail.com

ISBN: 978-0-557-09436-3

Printed in the greatest nation on God's green earth, the United States of America

September 2009

First Edition

To my best friend and the greatest love of my life, my wife Jennifer

Proverbs 31:10 An excellent wife, who can find? For her worth is far above jewels.

CONTENTS

Acknowledgments

You don't chronicle a World Series Championship season without a lot of help. I had plenty, beginning with Phillies' Beat Writer Michael Radano and Phillies' Vice President of Alumni Relations Larry "The Baron" Shenk. Their faith in a book from "a Phillies fan with an idea" and their steadfast commitment to allow a fan like me into the seldom traveled halls of Citizens Bank Park and the Press Box were the primary cause that this book exists today. Without their direction, guidance and input I could never have pulled it off in a million seasons. I particularly would like to thank Mike for the use of the quotes that he provided throughout this book. They really helped tell the story of the Phillies' World Championship season the way it happened. I would also like to offer my humble thanks to the following truly good people, all of whom had a hand in the completion of this book:

- Jason Weitzel for jumping in and providing incredible written insight across the pages of this book. Not only is his website Beerleauger.com the best Phillies blog on the web, but he personally is a man of tremendous kindness and encouragement and truly one of the best sportswriters in town.
- Phillies' Public Address Announcer Dan Baker for the many, many, many introductions that he did on my behalf before, during and after all of the ballgames. A gentleman of gentlemen, Dan is one of the kindest and most selfless persons that I have ever met.
- Phillies' Director of Broadcasting and Video Services, Mark DiNardo for giving me an incredible education on how the ballpark operates as well as for allowing me to use the Phanavision room for a base of operations for a number of games.
- Phillies Director of Baseball Communications, Greg Casterioto and his staff for their outstanding support and their in-depth knowledge of every and anything that has to do with the Phillies.
- Comcast's Leslie Gudel and Phillies' announcer Jim Jackson for treating an outsider such as I like an insider who belonged in the press box ... even though I didn't belong! Leslie is as kind in person as she is on camera and one of the hardest working, most talented professionals in the country. Jim has incredible insights to the game of baseball and is one who makes listening to the Phillies Pre and Post Game show a treat to enjoy.
- Phillies' Security Guard and good friend John Heath for his tremendous humor and for helping me fine-tune many of the ideas for this book before I had even lent finger to keypad.
- Dave Mortlock for his incredible design skills and for being one of the best neighbors anyone could ever possibly hope to have.
- Bob Buchan, my daughter Nicole McNesby and photographer Bob Moules for their help with the Phillie Phanatic lockeroom photo shoot.
- To all of my great friends and fellow fans in Section 144 Row 1 ... Mark & Moriah Liachowitz, Sam and Trish Sweet, Geoff, Jessica, Maren, Andrew, Jim and Cathy Attanasio, Harry Erney and his daughter Frances ... We all have the BEST seats in the entire ballpark and each of you made it a joy to watch our

Phillies win it all in 2008! Let's be sure to pass down our seats to our children's children's children!

- Mrs. Edith Cutler for her relentless kindness and for teaching me the finer points of English while she was still here on the earth with us.
- My entire family and church family for always laughing at my stupid jokes all of these years and for putting up with my rants and raves about the Phillies. Whomever said that some of the most important things in life are family and friends was one wise individual!
- My Father and Mother (Ken & Dorothy McNesby) for raising me to love God and to follow my dreams.
- Most importantly, none of this would have been possible without my wife Jennifer, my son Michael and my daughter Nicole, who handled the two year journey of this writing with exceedingly gracious support and extraordinary care for my wellbeing while I was pursuing the opportunity of a lifetime. All of you are such an inspiration to me and one of the greatest reasons that I wake up every morning with a smile on my face.

Finally, In an age where political correctness rules throughout the media, individuals sometimes find it difficult to express some of their deepest and most private thoughts publicly, however I couldn't think of a better acknowledgment for this book than to give praise and thanksgiving to my Lord and Savior Jesus Christ. It is through Him that all things are possible. He is the reason as to why I have hope for today and hope for my future. What a privilege it is to serve such an Awesome God!

- Michael McNesby

Prologue

Back in April of 2007 the Phillies were off to another slow start to their season. Twelve games in the Phils were 3-9 and in the basement of the NL East. After being pummeled 8-1 by the New York Mets they looked anything but Jimmy Rollin's self-proclaimed "Team to Beat". During Charlie Manuel's post game press conference 610 WIP's Howard Eskin suggested to the skipper that possibly a bit more anger on the part of the manager towards his players might create some urgency in his team to play better.

Charlie defended his team for a few moments but when Eskin challenged him on his answer, what originally started out as a smile on Charlie's face quickly turned to anger. "I think they see me angry more than you think they do. I think you don't probably see me angry," said Manuel. With his temper building Manuel invited Eskin to "Drop by my office so you can (see my anger) … I'll be waitin' on ya!"

Eskin did make the trek into Charlie's office and the fireworks began. Reporters and players alike were able to hear the yelling going on in the manager's office where at one point Eskin was heard yelling at Manuel, "You shouldn't be mad at me Charlie, you should be mad at the players. It's not fun coming to games and seeing the Phillies lose." While being physically restrained from going after Eskin by coach Milt Thompson Manuel yelled back to Eskin, "We're gonna win … We're gonna win!"

Whether the play of the team was affected by the Eskin/Manuel conflict is up for debate, one thing for sure is that the team turned the corner soon thereafter and began their march to the NL East title. The 2007 season ended with one of the most exciting division wins in decades with the dramatic collapse of the New York Mets and the resurgence of the Phillies to the top of the NL East for the first time since 1993.

After the Phillies clinched the NL East on the last day of the season, I walked with Charlie out to his car interviewing him along the way. It was an interesting few minutes as Charlie reflected on winning the pennant and how thankful he was for his players, his coaches and for the great fans of Philadelphia. It was during that conversation where he pointed out that he not only believed that his team could win, but that his team had finally proven it to themselves.

During the off season Pat Gillick did his magic adding some of the major pieces to the World Championship puzzle with the additions of Brad Lidge, Rudy Seanez, Pedro Feliz, So Taguchi and Geoff Jenkins. Later on in the season he added Joe Blanton and Scott Eyre to fill out the starting pitching as well as the bullpen. At long last Charlie had everything that he needed to make a run for a World Series Championship.

This is a book about the 2008 Philadelphia Phillies season. What initially started out as a day-by-day chronology of the behind-the-scenes activities that take place at Citizens Bank Park ended up turning into a book about the Phillies unexpected trip to the World Series and to their first World Championship in 28 years.

- Michael McNesby

"We're the World Series Champions! ... Hard to Believe!"

– *Charlie Manuel in an interview with Comcast's Leslie Gudel following the Phillies' first World Series Championship in 28 years*

April - All Things New...

Fans in Section 144 Row 1 provide the Opening Day direction for the 2008 Philadelphia Phillies

Quotable: "It wasn't my day ... You definitely don't want to start that way." – Reliever Tom Gordon on getting blown out the first game of the season.

Monday, March 31st - Nationals 11 Phillies 6 (0-1) 1½ GB Nationals

Philadelphia: Jimmy Rollins hits a game tying homerun in the 7th but with Brad Lidge starting the season on the DL, Tom Gordon gets the nod to close out the game in the 9th. He gets rocked, allowing five runs on four hits in 1/3rd of an inning and ends the day with an ERA of 135.00 ... The sellout crowd boos him off the mound. Stuff: Chase Utley starts the year 2 for 3 with 2 runs scored and a solo homer in the 6th... It was the Phils first Opening Day game during the month of March in the history of their 126 year old franchise.

In a game that unfolded in a painstakingly similar fashion as last season's Opening Day, 44,553 fans sat through a windy, drizzly afternoon watching a mini-meltdown by starter Brett Myers in the 5th , followed by a two-out, two-run homer given up by reliever Ryan Madson in the 6th. Down 6-2, the Phils battled back thanks to a Chase Utley solo shot in the bottom half of the inning. A shutout top half of the 7th by Chad Durbin, followed by a three-run rally in the bottom of the inning, capped by a Jimmy Rollins two-

Opening Day Top of the Order
- photo courtesy of Leslie Gudel

run blast, allowed the Phillies to tie the game at six. After J.C. Romero blazed through the 8th, it was Gordon's turn to prove all his skeptics wrong from his poor performances last season. However, as if Gordon himself personally hung each ball from a string right over the fattest part of the plate, the Nationals relentlessly pummeled him into submission. Four hits, three of them doubles, and a walk later the game was essentially over.

The game featured everything hardened skeptics could ask for from this team. A poor outing from the recently crowned "Ace" of the staff in Myers, the "Why can't you just pitch a 1-2-3 inning for crying out loud?!" appearance by Madson (1 IP, 2 H 1 HR, 2 ER), the offensive black hole redux at third base in Pedro Feliz (0-4, 2 Ks, 3 LOB) and the crispy toasted arm of "Flash" Gordon. A very ugly game. It didn't take long for fans to get that sour feeling of walking a tight rope right out of the gate. About the time Romero came in you realized they were up against a wall: they either luck out with Gordon in the 9th or fall to their death ... Spilsh!

Don't get too comfortable with Myers in the rotation if the bullpen breaks in the wrong direction. It's all riding on injured former Astros closer Brad Lidge. All hopes in the bullpen rest on Lidge being the effective closer that the Phillies so desperately need. If he's not, it's going to be a long season.

Quotable: "It's a little frustrating right now to get shut out on one hit. We're going to get shut out. But just one hit? It's kind of unexpected with the kind of offense we have." - Outfielder Shane Victorino after the Nationals Tim Redding shut down the Phillies offense

<u>Wednesday, April 2nd - Nationals 1 Phillies 0 (0-2) 2½ GB Nationals</u>

Philadelphia - In a classic pitchers dual, the Nationals' Tim Redding out pitched starter Cole Hamels (0-1) with Hamels only run coming off of a solo home run by Ryan Zimmerman in the 6th. The Phillies managed one hit, a single in the 2nd inning by Pedro Feliz ... Redding goes 7 innings giving up one single and 3 walks with no Phillies reaching second base the entire game. Stuff: The Phillies bolstered their bullpen by signing veteran reliever Rudy Seanez who pitched a career high 73 games last season for the Dodgers. This is Seanez's 17th season and his 9th major league team. To make room for him the Phils designated Wes Helms for assignment. They have 10 days to trade him or give him his outright release.

Wes Helms was a bust. Not a cataclysmic bungle like other recent signings but nonetheless a miss by GM Pat Gillick. They'll get over this one. The Phils become just another in a growing list of clubs cutting bait and eating contract. Gillick and company opened up and swallowed $2.15 million with Helms on top of Thome's $7 million already lodged into their collective esophagus's.

Helms' legacy is that of a moderately expensive stopgap who failed to deliver on promises of "18-20 home runs at Citizens Bank Park." Five homers were

Charlie Manuel fielding questions during his pre-game press conference

all they got. Others wondered all along whether the Phils were asking a lot from a player who never stayed in a starting lineup for very long. Many projected him to be another David Bell. That's selling Bell short. Helms seemed to lose Charlie Manuel's confidence out on the West Coast last season committing two costly errors in San Francisco. After that, his playing time diminished and he was swapped for a steady stream of Greg Dobbs and Abraham Nunez.

The Phils had more than ample time to strike up a deal for Helms in the off season, but the cost of his guaranteed contract ($2.15 million this season with a $750K buyout in 2009), and the signing of Pedro Feliz, basically meant that anyone who wanted him could simply wait the Phillies out. Be that as it may, Helms joins a growing list of ex-Phillies who neither gave anything, nor netted anything for the team.

Quotable: "With this offense, we're never out of a game, especially in this ballpark" - Starter Jamie Moyer

Thursday, April 3rd - Phillies 8 Nationals 7- 10inn. (1-2) 1 ½ GB the Nationals

Philadelphia - *First win of the 2008 season. Down 6-1 in the 6th, the Phillies string together seven straight singles and score six runs to take a 7-6 lead. After the Nationals tied up the game in the 8th, the Phillies rally in the 10th with Jimmy Rollins going from 1st to 3rd on a sacrifice bunt by Shane Victorino. The Nationals intentionally loaded the bases on walks to Utley and Howard but unintentionally walk in Jayson Werth for the winning run. Stuff: Jamie Moyer gets smacked around as he is tagged for 6 runs (3 earned) in only 3 2/3rd innings of work ... Horrible fielding by the Phillies as they commit 4 errors ... Ryan Howard doesn't get charged with any of the errors but his poor fielding at first base is a primary cause for the mishaps ... The Phillies introduced their alternate home jerseys at the first Business Person Special of the year ... they are the same styled uniforms that were used by the 1946-49 Phillies. Brad Lidge made his final rehabilitation appearance at Single A Clearwater and will join the team in Cincinnati.*

It wouldn't be an official Opening Day series in Philadelphia without all the gala and pageantry that comes with the start of every new season. It also wouldn't be an official kick-off to a season without ensuring that Citizens Bank Park's playing field was in spectacular fashion. That's the role of Phillies' Head Groundskeeper, Mike Boekholder. He is in charge of making sure that every blade of grass and every grain of dirt is just right — a job he doesn't take lightly.

Groundskeeper Mike Boekholder keeping the outfield grass at a consistent height of 1 1/8th inches

I've been working on ball fields since I was in high school when my dad and I practically rebuilt our entire field from scratch. I enjoyed it so much that I started doing it professionally with the Dodgers "A" team in Yakima, Washington. During my freshman year of college the Yakima team moved into a new stadium and they hired a local landscaping guy to take our place and get the stadium ready for the first game. The guy really didn't know a whole lot; he was kind of just going by the seat of their pants. Needless to say, Opening Day comes and they were playing Spokane. The first guy up for Spokane gets on base and he takes a lead at first base and he tries to steal 2nd base and the infield is so loose that the guy just totally blew a 4 inch divot in the dirt and he fell flat on his face. The infield was too soft and it just went downhill from there. The poor Groundskeeper stayed at the ballpark trying to fix everything until about 1:00am in the morning. From what I understand he went home that night and passed out on his living room floor from exhaustion. He then wakes up the next morning, calls the team owner and says, "I'm done." The guy lasted one day into the regular season.

So the owner of the team called my old boss from the old stadium and within three days myself and the entire crew were rehired to fix everything. After that season my old boss decided he couldn't do the job full time so he asked me if I wanted the job and I said "yes". I ended up running that field through three years of college and loved it so much that it was then that I decided that I wanted to do this for the rest of my life.

After Yakima I went to Durham, North Carolina, and worked for the Durham Bulls for two seasons. After my second year in Durham a job opened up with a AAA team in Indianapolis. So my family and I (wife Karla and children Sarah & Erin) moved up to Indianapolis and stayed there for 4 ½ years. During those nine years in the minors I actually won eight *"Groundskeeper of the Year"* awards.

I started with the Phillies in July of 2003. I found out about the job in Philadelphia from Paul Zalosko who used to be the Groundskeeper for the Baltimore Orioles. He and I had gotten to know one another though various seminars and conferences that all the groundskeepers would attend over the years. One day I get a phone call from Paul and he says, "Hey Mike, Philadelphia is looking for somebody to be their groundskeeper. Do you know anybody who might be interested?" so I give him a couple of names. He then says, "You think you'd be interested in talking to them?" I end up telling him, "Well you know Philadelphia is probably not exactly the place I'd want to move to, but it never hurts to talk." So I told him to go ahead and throw my name into the hat and I guess the rest is history.

The keys to having a great playing field is to have owners that are willing to spend the money to do it correctly and to make sure you have someone who knows what they are doing. There are a lot of things that go into this job. Managing moisture and your infield skin is probably the most important thing we do during the day. The Philadelphia area is kind of challenging area to do this profession because our weather changes so much during the year. The easiest jobs in this business are in California. They've got consistent weather that never changes, it never rains, they never tarp, I mean everything that causes us problems they don't even have to worry about.

The Phillies did everything right with this ballpark. The way that the surface was built we can take 10 ½ inches of rain an hour on the grass. They first put down 16-20 inches of crushed concrete underneath the field to act as a base. They then put in 6" drain tiles every 15 feet all across the entire field, which are all tied into one another without any dead ends in the system. On top of the drainage system they then put in a 4 inch layer of pea stone over everything. We then put in a 12 inch mixed layer of sand and peat on top of the pea stone. There's no topsoil on the field at all. It's 90% sand and 10% Dakota Red peat.

We installed Kentucky Bluegrass sod across the entire field. It came from Tuckahoe Turf Farms in Hamilton, NJ. Sand-based sods are the best surface you can put down for a baseball field. Tuckahoe Turf Farm has got one of the sandiest farms in the entire country. The worse thing you can do to a sand based field is come in and put soil based sod on to the field. It has to be sand-based sod. We had them cut the sod to less than a ¼ inch thick when they delivered it to us. It was almost falling apart when we laid it. The thinner you cut the sod when you first lay it the faster it will root. So we laid that field in October of 2003 and by Opening Day the sod had 10 inch roots.

During the summer the root structure will shrink back to 3 inches or so. Kentucky bluegrass struggles to hold on to itself through the summer months. Last August Pat Burrell put a ½ foot divot in left field sliding to catch a ball during a game. It took some time to repair it but you have to expect that with the growth curve of that type of grass. By the time September and October come around the root structure will grow much deeper into the sand. If it happens again this year we would be ready to go for the October playoffs. At least that's the idea anyway.

Working on a grounds crew is tough work. We have 8 full time members during the season and for an average game we have a total of 20-25 to help out with the tarp and anything else that needs to prep the field for a game. If we have a 7:05pm game and the weather is good we'll usually be in by 10:00am. We'll work on the field as soon as we get here and keep going until about 2-3:00pm. That's when Charlie likes to get his team out here to start hitting or doing infield practice. Everything though is driven by the weather. If you got rain we might have to get in very early and get the tarp down at 7:00 in the morning. The weather can make for some very very long days. But typically if we have good weather, we'll get everything mowed in the morning and then work the details of the field until the team comes out to warm up.

When we mow the grass we keep the outfield grass 1 1/8th inches high. In the infield we keep it at 1 1/16th inches. We don't do any patterns here like they do at other ballparks. We like the feel and look of a traditional field. It works well with the entire ambiance here.

We tailor the dirt to player specifications more than anything that we do with the grass. When David Bell was playing here he liked his area of third base very very very wet. Probably wetter than any guy I've ever seen. We would literally have that thing muddy by the time the game started. I mean it's to the point where sometimes you get guys from the other team saying things to us like "Why is this so wet over here?" I said "Look, go talk to Bell. That's the way he likes it.".

We fight a lot of the same problems that a homeowner will come across with their lawn. We have grubs. You know every year it's something different. The most tantalizing problem we probably come across are the patch diseases that you get in this part of the country. They can be very persistent and it is something that happens every year.

Patch disease is actually a fungus. It's very difficult to get rid of because it's a soil-borne pathogen. If you have a problem on the grass it's easier to kill the leaf type fungus because you can just spray it on the grass. When you start dealing with pathogens that attack the root structure, getting the material effectively into the field enough to get it treated can be a bit of a challenge and summer patch is one thing we know that we're gonna deal with every year. You develop a whole program to combat it. Some years it's worse than others.

What does my lawn at home look like? It's not bad. When we first moved into where we live in Delaware it was ugly. The entire yard was practically crab grass. It was so bad that the realtor didn't even want to show us the house. We ended up killing the entire lawn and starting from scratch. There wasn't any grass left in it, just crab grass and weeds. My wife and I sprayed it and reseeded the whole thing. Three weeks later we had that greenest lawn in the neighborhood.

My advice to fans is if you don't have 50% viable turf in your yard and its all nasty weeds and stuff you're just better off just to get rid of it and start over. It's kind of a rule of thumb with landscapers. Kill the yard with a non-selective herbicide and start over. That's what I did. Use a tall fescue grass seed where you have more shade than sun. I use a blend of fescue and bluegrass in the front yard and it's worked out pretty well. It's come along better than what I could have expected. It's not embarrassing anymore.

The best thing I like about my job is that I get to be outside all day. It definitely beats sitting behind a desk, plus its fun. Anyway you cut it you get to go to work at the ballpark every day. Some of my favorite times are when nobody else is in the ballpark and you walk out on to the field. I look around and see how peaceful everything is and all the work that we've done and I think, "This is a really cool deal!"

Quotable: "The bats are starting to come around. We caught a couple on the screws tonight. This is a nice park to play in." – Manager Charlie Manuel on his team's victory

Friday, April 4th - Phillies 8 Reds 4 (2-2) ½ GB the Mets

Cincinnati- *The Phils jump on Red's starter Josh Fogg early as Chase Utley hits 2 homeruns and Pat Burrell launched a 434 foot upper-decker, his 1st of the season, to help get the Phillies to .500 for the first time this year. Kyle Kendrick gets his first win of the season in a shaky start in which he gives up 4 earned runs in 5 innings of work. Stuff: Utley's homerun was the 100th of his career … Burrell goes 2 for 3 with 2 RBIs and now leads the team with a .385 average … The Phils bullpen shut down the Reds for the final four innings allowing only 1 hit … The start of the Red's season opener was delayed an hour and thirty four minutes because of rain … once the game started it was a chilly 46 degrees.*

In January, Forbes.com ranked the Phillie Phanatic as the #1 sports mascot in the USA, besting many of the familiar mascots in baseball including the San Diego Chicken, Mr. Met and the Racing Sausages in Milwaukee.

"One of the earliest baseball mascots, the Phanatic became an instant smash when it debuted for the Phillies in 1978. Leading fans from the top of the dugout, riding around on a motorbike and heckling opposing players … Players and purists hated it. Dodger manager Tom Lasorda got into a scuffle with the Phanatic, while broadcaster Joe Garagiola once lamented that "baseball is being invaded by the Muppets." - Forbes.com

It's a rare occasion when Philadelphia is lauded as The Best in anything on a national scale, but what the rest of the nation might just now be formally recognizing is something that Phillies fans have known for years. The Liberty Bell and Independence Hall are an ever-drawing presence to the city of Philadelphia, but it's the Phanatic that has helped continued to draw in millions of fans to Veterans Stadium and Citizens Bank Park over the past three decades.

We caught up with Tom Burgoyne, who has been the Phanatic's best friend for the past 19 years, to get his take on the Forbes.com honor and to take a quick peak into the world of the Phanatic.

The Phanatic's best friend Tom Burgoyne

What are your thoughts on being honored as the #1 mascot in the USA?
The Phanatic is the biggest idiot out there I guess. Honored by Forbes! I guess the Phanatic really wished that he was being honored in the Forbes 100 Richest people in the world. That is the list that he really wanted to be on. He wanted to be on the list with Oprah, Tiger and Bill Gates and be jet setting around and power lunching with all of the big moguls. So when he heard he was on the Forbes list he just
thought that he was getting a big raise.

Did that happen? Did he get the big raise?
No, no … he was excited but it was really good and something that the organization can really share in. We have always prided ourselves over the years in being very marketing driven with the promotions, the Phanatic and the food … that whole experience is "A+". So to be recognized for that is not only good for the Phanatic but also good for the entire organization.

Who are your favorite mascots in the nation?
Let's see … I'm a fan of Slider out in Cleveland. He has been doing it for a long time. He's real good. Then you have Raymond in Tampa Bay who is really good. I've also been a big fan of NBA mascots like Hip-Hop and the Phoenix Gorilla because they have all the talent. They do all the flips.

Do you think that the Phanatic will pull out the trampoline and start doing jumps?
Nah, the Phanatic isn't much of a flipper. Those guys have the real talent. They all know how to spin. The Phanatic just knows how to fall down.

The Phanatic turns 30 on April 25th of this season. Are the Phillies going to do anything special to let the fans know that the furry green monster has now been around for three decades?
Not really. We kind of keep the Phanatic's age kind of young. We always have a big day at the park when we celebrate the Phanatic's birthday. This year we will have lots of special events going on including handing out a "Paint your own Phanatic" figurine to all the kids at the ballpark.

Anything else special going on?
Well, next year the Phanatic is going to be immortalized all over the city of Philadelphia. We're teaming up with the city to create "Paint the Phanatic Public Art Project". Artists from around the region will be chosen to paint approximately 20 five-foot fiberglass statues that will be displayed throughout the city in March and April of 2009. All of the statues are going to be auctioned off with the proceeds going to Phillies Charities.

How much does that costume weigh?
35 pounds. It's not that bad. Just hot and smelly

So how do you get it washed?
Soak it in the bathtub. That's why they gave the Phanatic a bathtub in Citizens Bank Park. That's a little known fact. The Phanatic has the only bathtub in Citizens Bank Park because my wife complained that every time I washed the costume at home, I would get green fur in the drain. So she said, "Is there any place there in the Vet where you can do it?" When we were planning to move to the new ballpark I talked to the project manager, John Stranicks, and said to him on a whim, "Hey, you know I could really use a bathtub." And he said, "I'll work on it". And sure enough when we came in the new ballpark the bathtub was down here to wash the costume and there was a shower in there for me!

Why do you think the Phanatic is so popular with fans?
There are a couple of factors. First, it's a funny looking costume. It's hard not to laugh when the Phanatic is mocking an overweight player by rolling his huge belly around in circles or sticking his tongue out at an umpire. I think another reason the Phanatic is popular, especially in opposing cities, is that the Phanatic has a great relationship with the players. When other teams come to Philly, they love messing with the Phanatic. They'll steal his keys to the 4-wheeler, wrestle him and in some instances, they bring their own Super Soakers to the ballgame just to start a water fight with him. It can be total mayhem before the game between the Phanatic and the players and that interaction always keeps the act fresh and exciting.

Give me one of your routines that the players enjoy.
Every time the San Francisco Giants come to town, I do a pre-game routine on Bruce Boche (the Giants manager). He has a REALLY big head. So the Phanatic has a routine in which he mimics Boche with a huge head. I bend over and try to pick up an invisible head and put in my shoulders and now I'm all wobbly and then the Phanatic goes down on the ground and is trying to pick his head off of the ground and pick himself up and then as his head is almost straight it slams down to the other side and I end up slamming my head back and forth and the players (on the Giants) just die for it.

What does Bruce Boche do when you're performing it?

He tries to hide out in the dugout but he kind of laughs about it. That interplay with the coaches and the players before the game really sets the stage for the Phanatic for the rest of the night. During a three game series, you throw it out there in the first game and see who responds. By the second game the players might get a bit bolder and go after the keys (of the ATV).

Do managers who don't appear to have a sense of humor like Lou Piniella or some of the others ever get engaged in your routines?

You'd be surprised, Piniella is good. He laughs at everything. Jim Leyland is another guy … serious, serious, serious but he would love it when the Phanatic would mock him smoking cigarettes in the dugout. Puffing away on a cigarette … put it out, stomp it out, and then walk away saying that he quit smoking and does the hand gestures for "No More." Then the Phanatic starts shaking a little bit; he then starts reaching into his pocket. Nah! I'm not going to do it any more. But then he rips a cigarette out of his pocket and starts to smoke, smoke, smoke and Leyland would love it. Jim would then pull out his own cigarette and hand it to the Phanatic.

The Phanatic's famed run in with Tommy Lasorda was well documented. Have there ever been any other "issues" with other players or coaches?

Nothing nasty … probably more playful than anything else. Luis Castillo of the Mets is probably a good one. He's always up to no good on the Phanatic trying to push him over and things like that. He's usually organizing somebody like Delgado or Reyes with "Hey, kneel behind the Phanatic and I'll push him over." You have to keep your head on a swivel when Castillo is out there.

The Hot Dog Launcher … it looks really dangerous!

Yea, it is. You should see the huge nitrogen tanks that we use on the Hot Dot launcher. We've launched hot dogs out of the ballpark. It's the best. The fans love it and go wild.

The Phanatic has been at this now for over 30 years! What does the future hold for him?

There is no doubt that the Phanatic will still be doing what he does best 10 years from now - taunting opposing players, flirting with the pretty girls in the stands, dancing with umpires and shining bald heads. The only difference will be that he will have 10 new World Series rings on his fingers to go with the one that he has from 1980! In 50 years, he'll own the club. I can see the headline now - "Phanatic Goes From Being Team Mascot to Team Owner!" If that ever happens, we're all in trouble!

Quotable: "He did a hell of a job. Once he got on track, he had some quick innings ... It's been a long time since we've seen him have his pitch count down like that. He had a good rhythm going."
– Charlie Manuel on Adam Eaton's first outing of the season.

<u>Saturday, April 5th - Reds 4 Phillies 3 (2-3) 1 GB the Marlins</u>

Cincinnati - *Adam Eaton pitches a solid game but can't hold on after going 7 2/3rd before allowing a homerun by Cory Patterson to tie the game in the bottom of the 8th at 3-3. Chad Durbin pitched the 9th and walked the first two batters he faced before surrendering an infield single to Red's catcher Paul Bako for the game-ending run. Chase Utley continued his hitting rampage going 2 for 3 while Ryan Howard hit his first homerun of the season, a mammoth 479 foot solo shot to take a 3-2 lead in the 8th. Stuff: Eaton started off the game with a four pitch walk and one could only envision TV sets being turned off all over the Delaware Valley as fans remembered his continuous poor pitching performances from the 2007 season ... Howard's homer was the 6th longest in the history of "Great American Ball Park" ... The Phillies traded Wes Helms to the Florida Marlins for cash considerations. Brad Lidge was activated prior to the game but didn't see any action. To make room for Lidge the Phils sent pitcher Tim Lahey to AAA- Lehigh.*

You think your job is difficult? Try putting together a schedule for 30 major league baseball teams that play 2,430 games against one another over the course of six months. Add on top of that all of the special scheduling requests that each team wants you to fulfill, interleague play in which you have to rotate amongst the other league's divisions each year, and then make that schedule unique every single season and you got yourself one heck of an unenviable task that would even make a NASA flight director cringe.

Welcome to the world of Katy Feeney. The daughter of former National League President "Chub" Feeney, Katy

Chase Utley's 100th career homerun ball

is the Senior Vice President in charge of scheduling for the Commissioner's office and is often in the crosshairs of team executives, ballplayers and the fans. Taking a look at this season's Phillies' schedule we were able to spend a few minutes with Katy to find out some of the peculiarities and issues that go into creating a 162 game schedule that will try to make everyone happy.

The first rule of this job is that nobody is ever completely happy. We work hard to make the schedule as fair as possible for each team but it's next to impossible to make everyone happy.

There are a number of things that are built into the Players Union contract that we must consider when building the schedule. All the games must be played within 178 to 183 days, each team's schedule can not include more than two day-night doubleheaders and teams that fly from coast to coast must have a day off before their next game. This year was also a bit challenging because we kicked off the season with the A's and Red Sox in the Tokyo Dome in Japan. A lot of complaints in trying to get that finalized mostly because of all of the travel that we had to take into consideration.

We also have to consider events outside the scope of Major League Baseball as well. This year Pope Benedict will be having mass at Nationals Park in Washington, D.C., on April 17th and in Yankee Stadium on April 20th so we have to plan the teams around those dates.

One interesting aspect of the Phillies' schedule is how we plan each team's "natural rivals". Every season we have a National League team play their American League team's natural rival. The Mets play the Yankees, the Cubs play the White Sox, each team actually lines up quite well with an opposing league's team … except for the Phillies.

Back when the Nationals were still the Montreal Expos their natural rivalry was with the Toronto Blue Jays. The Phillies' natural rivalry was with the Baltimore Orioles and the Boston Red Sox's was with the Atlanta Braves. It worked out really well for everyone. However when the Expos moved down to Washington, D.C. it only made sense for us to change the National's natural rival to the Orioles so that they could play each other every season and build the rivalry up between the two teams.

The problem with that was that we then didn't have any natural rivals for the Phillies and the Blue Jays. So to make it more "fair" for both of those teams we began interweaving them each season so that we had the Phillies play the Blue Jays as their natural rival one season and the Red Sox as their natural rival the next year. In 2009, the Phillies will go back to the Blue Jays and keep on switching with the Red Sox for the foreseeable future.

Naturally the Red Sox are a huge attendance draw for whatever team they are playing. So are the Yankees. So that's why we try to balance them between the Braves and the Phillies in some kind of a fair manner.

What I think fans really do enjoy is how we've managed interleague play across all the divisions. This season the National League Eastern Division will be playing the American League Western Division. We've gotten it to a point where we have almost had every team play in all other 29 ballparks across the country.

Right now we are in the midst of putting the finishing touches on to the 2009 schedule. By June we will deliver our first draft of the schedule to all the teams so we can then work out all the issues so that we have a fairly stable schedule completed before the season ends and so that teams can begin marketing the following season to their fans.

The TV networks also have some input into the schedules along with the Players Association. Fox and ESPN won't select their games until December but that won't impact series, just starting time changes for the teams that they want to have on their broadcasts.

The schedule is really never locked in throughout the year. Even as we speak I know that there are going to be some time changes for the Phillies this year. There are also rainouts and other events that we can't foresee.

Many teams, including the Phillies, will push for specific dates on the schedule. Some dates, like Memorial Day and Labor Day, teams may not want to have at home because fans are doing other things than going to baseball games. A lot of teams want July 4th at home but obviously not everybody can be home July 4th so for the holidays we sort of alternate them between the teams.

You'll also notice this season that there are a few two-game series on the schedule. I believe the Phillies have three 2-game series this year (During April at Colorado & Milwaukee and at home with the Mets in August). Ultimately it comes to how to best fit all the teams into each others schedules and to balance it out to make it fair for every team. Like I said, nobody is ever completely happy.

Quotable: "I just couldn't put anybody away. I was throwing every pitch as hard as I could. I was pretty irritated at myself with not being able to put people away." - Starter Brett Myers

<u>Sunday, April 6th - Reds 8 Phillies 2 (2-4) 1 GB the Marlins & Braves</u>

Cincinnati - Brett Myers (0-1) struggled with his velocity throughout the game as he gives up 4 runs in 5 innings of work, including two homeruns: one of them to Ken Griffey Jr, his 594th of his career. Myer's fastball is usually in the 92-95 mph range but only registered in the 88-91 mph range throughout the game. Brad Lidge looked good in his Phillies debut pitching a solid 1-2-3 8th inning. The offense was flat and once again the team made a number of mental mistakes on the field and on the base paths. Stuff: Jimmy Rollins stole his 250th base of his career putting him into 7th place on the Phillies all-time stolen base list. Hall-of-Famer Billy Hamilton (1890-1895) is first with 508 steals as a Phillie ... The Phils have now been held to three or fewer runs three times this season ... Chase Utley hit his 150th double of his career.

Brett Myers and Charlie Manuel may have different views on the quality of his stuff yesterday. The real problem was getting behind batters because he was trying to be too tricky, and missing when it mattered.

Someone needs to introduce Brett Myers and Carlos Ruiz to a first-pitch fastball, a hard strike with which they can get ahead of the batter. Instead, we saw too much tinkering and trying to be too fine, getting behind batters until he had to come over the plate, or getting ahead - as he did with Paul Bako in the 4th - then noodle around until ball four. Myers allowed four runs on eight hits over five frames, including two homers and three walks, almost the same exact line as Kyle Kendrick, only Kendrick kept the Reds balls within the park. It's a below-average start, even for a Kendrick. For a No. 1 starter like Myers, it's downright unacceptable. He's

better than this.
One of Myers' greatest strengths is that
he is a strike thrower. He can command his fastball beautifully when he
isn't overthrowing. Unfortunately, his
command wasn't there, either. Myers
threw 95 pitches, and only 59 went
for strikes. If you want to blame something, blame smarts, then command,
then all the other stuff Myers and Manuel talked about in the reports. On the
rare occasion he threw a regular-old
fastball, it sailed high.

Yes, it's very early. But after two starts,
Myers resembles a closer who's trying
to mix in to the starting rotation.

Brett Myers playing ball with his son Kolt

*Quotable: "We started swinging the bats like we're capable of. It takes the pressure off the pitchers. If
you consistently have good swings, you'll produce good results." - Phillies left fielder Pat Burrell*

<u>Monday, April 7th - Phillies 5 Reds 3 (3-4) 1 GB the Marlins</u>

Cincinnati - *Cole Hamels (1-1) wins his first game of the year behind the power of four Phillie
homeruns. Two by Burrell and solo shots by Jimmy Rollins and Geoff Jenkins (Jenkin's first as a
Phillie). In what ended up being a white-knuckle experience, Brad Lidge picked up his first save as a
Phillie. Starting the 9th inning, Lidge gave up a walk, saw So Taguchi drop a ball off the heel of his
glove for a two-base error, walked Ken Griffey Jr. to load the bases and then uncorked a wild pitch,
allowing the Reds to get within two before retiring the side. The win gave the Phillies a split of their
four-game series ... Hamels goes 7 innings giving up only 1 earned run while striking out four. His
ERA is now 1.20. Stuff: Pat Burrell collected his 750th RBI of his career. With his two homeruns
today Burrell now has 17 multi-homerun games in his career. Jimmy Rollins' leadoff homerun was*

the 27th of his career.

"I think there are only three things that America will be known for 2,000 years from now when they study this civilization: the Constitution, jazz music and baseball. They're the three most beautifully designed things this culture has ever produced." – Gerald Early, American Scholar and Philadelphia native

When our founding fathers gathered in Philadelphia to write the Declaration of Independence during the summer of 1776, baseball wasn't on the minds of Jefferson, Franklin nor Adams as the game was not to be invented in the form that we know it today for another 60 years. However, somewhere on our country's way to our "pursuit of happiness" and our attempt "to form a more perfect Union", the beautiful and wonderful game of baseball was invented.

Cole Hamels explaining to Comcast SportsNet how he throws his change-up

Two blocks north of Independence Hall in center city Philadelphia is one of the finest museums in the country, the National Constitution Center. A highly attractive and interactive museum dedicated to increasing the public understanding of the U.S. Constitution. "Baseball as America," the first traveling exhibit featuring the entire holy grail of baseball artifacts from the National Baseball Hall of Fame Museum in Cooperstown, NY, allows fans to see how baseball and our Constitution have helped form us into a great nation.

The exhibit itself is a baseball memorabilia collector's dream. Some of the Crown Jewels on display in the exhibit include the baseball used in the "supposed" first game ever played by Abner Doubleday in 1839, an honest to goodness Honus Wagner T-206 tobacco card in which a similar one recently sold at auction for $2.8 million. The bat used by Babe Ruth to slug his 60th homerun during the 1927 season, and the actual Brooklyn Dodgers uniform worn by Jackie Robinson during the 1947 season when he became the first African-American to break the color barrier in the Major Leagues. The display of over 500 such artifacts leaves all true baseball aficionados drooling.

Upon arriving at the center, I was greeted by Gina Romanelli, the National Constitution Center's Public Relations Coordinator. A former Customer Service Representative intern for the

Phillies, Gina walked me through the exhibit explaining how the exhibit was put together.

Once everything arrived it took about two weeks to put the Baseball as America exhibition completely together as you see it here. The crates arrived in the beginning of February and we had everything ready in their cases by February 14th. The exhibition opened to the public on Friday, February 15th.

The National Constitution Center follows the ideas and suggestions of the lending institution, which, in this case, is the Baseball Hall of Fame. The *Baseball as America* exhibition has a theme for each section of the exhibit. Each case was positioned in the Center based upon the content that it contained, the story or timeline that it told as well as the size and configuration of the actual case. A big consideration in the layout was also the anticipated visitor flow.

After a quick tour through the exhibit Gina brought me back to the beginning to meet with the National Constitution Centers President and CEO Joe Torcella. A lifelong Philadelphian, Torcella was the driving force in the creation of the Constitution Center. He is also a huge Phillies fan.

I love the Phillies so one of the more fascinating items to me on display in this exhibit is a jersey worn by a 10 year old girl by the name of Edith Houghton. Edith played baseball for the Philadelphia Bobbies, an all-female team that barnstormed across the United States and Japan playing against men's teams back in the 1920s and 30s.

Houghton grew up in North Philadelphia and played ball as a young girl at 25th and Diamond Streets before joining the Bobbies (named so after the way the ladies "bobbed" their hair back in 1922). She was so small when she joined the team that she had to pin her cap in the back just so it could fit on her head. Her uniform was so big that she had to punch new holes in her belt just so she could keep her uniform pants from falling down.

Edith was supposedly an incredible talent who was an outstanding hitter and fielder and was able to play any position in the field. She continued to play baseball on various all-female baseball teams up until the start of World War II.

After the war the all-female baseball teams completely vanished and it left Edith without work in baseball for the first time in her life. Undaunted, Edith contacted Phillies owner Bob Carpenter in 1946 and asked him for a job as a scout. Carpenter decided to give Edith a chance and signed her making Edith Houghton the first female scout in Major League Baseball History.

According to Phillies historian Rich Westcott, Houghton stayed on as a scout for the Phillies until 1952 but never did sign any players that made it to the big leagues. Today, Edith is 96 years old and living in Florida and can lay claim to being the first female to break into the all boys club in Major League Baseball.

One of the defining pieces of the *Baseball as America* exhibit is a case that is completely dedicated to all things Philadelphia. There are a number of Phillies items in it that are usually kept up in Cooperstown, NY.

Included in the case was:
- Chuck Klein's 1932 National League MVP trophy (complete with the bat broken off the batter at the very top of the trophy).
- The spikes worn by center fielder Richie Ashburn during the Phillies 1950 National League championship season.
- Jim Bunning's cap from his perfect game against the New York Mets on Father's Day in 1964, the first in the National League since 1880.
- Commissioner Bowie Kuhn's 1980 Phillies World Series ring (Author's note: I didn't know that the Commissioner was given a ring!)
- The ball hit by the Phils' Pete Rose that broke Stan Musial's record for the most hits by a National Leaguer in a career (3,631) on August 10, 1981.
- A batting helmet worn by Jimmy Rollins when he ended 2005 with a 36-game hitting streak exceeded only by Pete Rose (44) and Paul Molitor (39) since 1945.
- The spikes worn by Chase Utley during the final game of his 35-game hitting streak in 2006, which tied him with Luis Castillo for the longest hitting streak by a second baseman in the history of Major League Baseball.

The *Baseball as America* exhibit captures a huge slice of Americana. Baseball has been so integrated into our culture that one can't imagine that the game will ever fade from our national pastime.   This great game has been an incredible reflection of our country since the mid 1800's. It captures our hopes, our dreams and our joys.

So thank you Mr. Jefferson. Thank you Mr. Franklin. We the people of the United States, in order to form a more perfect union … have our game of baseball.

Quotable: "As long as we whip 'em, we don't have to make a big deal about it. They'll talk. We'll hit." - Charlie Manuel on the growing Phillies-Mets rivalry

Tuesday, April 8th - Phillies 5 Mets 2 (4-4) ½ GB the Marlins

New York - The Phillies picked up where they left off last year as they beat the Mets for the 9th consecutive time dating back to June 30th 2007. It is the last home opener for the Mets at Shea Stadium as it will be torn down at the end of the season to make way for their new ballpark "Citi Field". Jamie Moyer, the only active pitcher in baseball who is older than Shea Stadium (Randy Johnson is on the DL), pitched a solid outing giving up only 2 runs in 6 innings. It was Moyer's first win of the season and the 231st of his career. Stuff: Chase Utley set a franchise record and tied a major league record the hard way as he was hit by a pitch three times during the game. He led the majors in HBP last season with 25 … The Phillies had previously lost seven straight Home Openers at Shea before today's victory … 56,350 fans packed the stadium making it the largest Opening Day crowd in Mets history … Jimmy Rollins sprained his left ankle in the 8th inning and had to leave the game.

He is day-to-day ... Jerry Seinfeld and Larry David sat 10 rows behind the Phillies dugout ... is George Costanza going to get a shot as the Phils new GM when Gillick retires?

Bangor, Pennsylvania, is located in the Lehigh Valley about two hours north of Philadelphia. It's a sleepy, old-fashioned town that reminds one of any number of the small mountain towns that are scattered across the northeastern part of the state. However, Bangor stands out from these other towns in an extraordinary way as it is the headquarters and manufacturing home of Majestic Athletic, the official provider of every major league baseball uniform, including the Phillies.

Majestic Athletic started its humble beginnings back in 1950 when Mary Capobianco opened up her own sewing mill in Bangor. She started out making women's clothing, mainly blouses. Maria Rose Fashions, as it was called back then, eventually became known

A seamstress at Majestic Athletic puts the finishing touches on Chase Utley's away jersey

as a premier manufacturer of high-end clothes for the well-dressed woman from coast-to-coast. In 1976, Faust Capobianco III, Mary's son, took over the business and created an athletic apparel arm of the business that he called Majestic Athletic. The company started their relationship with Major League Baseball in 1982 but didn't sign their first licensing agreement with the league until 1984. They have continued to grow with the league ever since and today they provide the uniforms, jackets and many other items that Ryan Howard, Chase Utley and Cole Hamels wear every game.

Nicole Capobianco, the daughter of founder Faust, is the Director of On-field Outfitting for Majestic Athletic. She and her team ensure that every major leaguer is properly fitted with a tailored uniform before they walk on to the field of play. It all begins in their cutting facility in an old shopping center in downtown Bangor.

I initially started working in the cutting facility because this is where all the orders come in from the teams. I have production associates in the back of the building that talk to the team's equipment managers that take and fill all the orders that come into Majestic. My team is able to process the orders and issue them right out to the cutting room floor. We actually pull the fabrics of the team right off the shelf, cut their garments, and deliver a tailored-made uniform to any of the teams in the league in a matter of days.

When I talk to the Phillies we mostly work with their Clubhouse Manager Frank Coppenbarger. Sometimes we'll talk directly to Dave Buck, the Phillies VP in charge of Marketing. Most of the conversations with him deal with uniform changes or that type of thing. But Frank is our main contact there and a great supporter of ours. He was the first clubhouse manager to agree to let us make their on-field uniforms. He was one of three clubs that we started with.

We'll get anywhere from 200 to 300 calls a month from the teams around the league. The Phillies usually call a couple times a week. A lot of the times we'll get a call from them when they'll ask us to take an inch off of someone's pants or give another player some additional room in their thigh. There are some guys on the Phillies that are on their 5th or 6th pattern. They change for any number of reasons. Sometimes it's personal preference. Sometimes it's gaining weight, losing weight. You never know.

All the uniforms are made right here in Bangor. We do import some of the materials here but the cut and sew for the uniforms, batting practice jerseys, pants; they're all made right here.

Michael Panuccio is the head pattern maker at Majestic and in charge of Product Development. At last count he had over 750 different pant patterns and 100 jersey patterns in his computer system. His job is to measure each and every major league player in Spring Training and to keep them happy through the remainder of the season.

Each year we send two measuring groups down to Florida and two to Arizona for Spring Training. It's usually during the last two weeks of February when all the players are in camp and they haven't started traveling to play games. We have about a week to hit all 30 clubs.

We measure everyone that's in the camp. It could be 90 players plus coaches and managers that we measure. That's when we collect all of our sizing and pattern information going into the season. That's also when we establish all of our sizing so that we can begin cutting uniforms for Opening Day as soon as we get back to the shop. Usually it takes us between 2-3 hours to measure everyone. Things might change throughout the year though. A player might change his waist size or decide he wants to wear his uniform differently, but that is our primary opportunity to lay the groundwork for the entire season with them.

When we're with the players in Spring Training they tell us how they want their uniform tailored. When you see a Pat Burrell or Jimmy Rollins wearing their uniform they are built to their exact specifications. If you see them skin tight or real baggy, that was at their request. We give them exactly what they want. We start off with what we call a size run. We'll take down about a dozen jerseys, from size 40 to about 56/58. The players will try them on for fit and then we work on the customization. They might add to the body length, they might add to the sleeve length. The guys that are really working out might taper the jersey. Some request the bottom opening to sweep for more room. Jerseys are relatively simple.

After the jerseys we then work on the pants. The pants consist of three measurements: the actual waist size, the pant size and the inseam. With today's trends, what you'll notice is the pants are a lot bigger and have a baggy look. It's all personal style these days. Years ago, people used to wear regular pants or a husky. Now what they're doing is they're going up 4, 5, 6, 10 sizes bigger.

We're in there with tape measures with each and every guy. Some like it tighter in a certain place, some like it shorter … it all depends on the player. But every player has the benefit of custom tailoring should they choose to spend the time. Not everybody is that concerned about their uniforms. Most guys are thorough and most will spend the time with us to get it right.

Typically the average player starts the season with two complete home jerseys and two complete away jerseys, plus any special jerseys that they club has ordered from us. This year we sent the Phillies 234 pair of pants for Opening Day. That includes the home and road uniforms. Throughout a season we will ship hundreds and hundreds of uniforms to each team.

In the event that there are some last-minute roster changes or a trade each clubhouse manager has a few sets of extra uniforms with numbers and lettering if something has to be created immediately. However, we're required to have all new uniform requests to the team within 24-72 hours after a transaction is made. It's very rare if we don't have it to them within 48 hours. With Philadelphia being so close we've sometimes have hand-delivered them a uniform the day that they gave us the order. It's nice being in their own back yard.

Many times we will find out about a trade before the average fan does. But sometimes we'll see it pop up on ESPN and we hadn't heard anything about it. So it really varies on how hyped a trade it is. We certainly know some of the bigger trades when we think they might happen or could happen. Since many of us around here are Phillies fans we're especially interested when they're involved.

Quotable: "We've got to catch the ball"- Charlie Manuel on the Phillies' early season fielding woes.

<u>Wednesday, April 9th - Mets 8 Phillies 2 Record:(4-5) 1 ½ GB the Marlins</u>
New York - With Jimmy Rollins sitting out the game due to a sore ankle, fill-in Eric Bruntlett made two huge errors early on in the game to help the Mets end a nine game losing streak against the Phillies. Overall the Phillies committed four errors on the day and now have 13 errors in their first 9 games. Kyle Kendrick didn't help the cause too much allowing 6 walks and 7 runs (only one of them earned) in 2 1/3rd innings. Stuff: Sitting out today's game broke Rollins consecutive game streak of 230 straight games. It was the 3rd longest active streak in the majors behind Grady Sizemore (Indians – 366 games) and Jeff Francoeur (Braves – 334 games).

"I have a lot of respect for Philadelphia fans. Imagine rooting for teams that never really win."

– Kevin Kernan, NY Post Sports Columnist September 8, 2007

Back in August of 2007 New York Post sports writer Kevin Kernan wrote the following lead: *"Memo to Jimmy Rollins: The best team won. Yes, it's still the dog days of August and the Mets have to travel to beautiful Philadelphia tomorrow, but the NL East race is over ... the Mets are merrily on their way to another October."*

The Mets, then 6 ½ games up on the Phillies with a month of baseball to play, were flying high at the end of August. The Phillies were mired in a slump and in the minds of the New York media, its fans and the Mets themselves, this race was over.

"Sure, there are magic numbers ahead and the official champagne clinching, but the Mets have no worries until October." wrote Kernan.

The Mets were at the top of the NL East by a full 7 games on September 12th with 17 games to play in the regular season and appeared on their way to wrap up their second consecutive division title for the first time in their franchise history.

Eric Bruntlett committed two of the Phils four errors against the Mets

"The Mets biggest challenge is to stay interested in the final five weeks of the season and to have the eye of the tiger when they get to the postseason."

Three days before the regular season ended Kernan wrote an article on his blog in which he said the following:

"Memo to me: Was I ever wrong about the NL East and the Mets and the Phightin (sic) Phils. In August I wrapped up the NL East in a nice little package for the Mets and said the race was unofficially over. I wrote these words: Memo to Jimmy Rollins: The Best Team Won. Here we are three days to go in the regular season and the race is just beginning. The Phillies have overcome numerous injuries and no matter what happens these final three days, they have shown the hearts of champions and for that they should be congratulated. It was Rollins who said the Phils were the team to beat in the NL East over the winter. He was right. I was wrong."

The Mets went on to lose the NL East title to the Phillies on the last day of the season to complete the greatest collapse in the history of Major League Baseball. No team had owned a lead of seven games or more with 17 to play and failed to finish in first place. Not even the 1964 Phillies! The collapse was historic and for Phillies fans it was sweet!

Phillies fans that regularly read Kernan unmercifully hammered him.

I received a ton of emails, and I responded to a few early on, but it became clear that it was really just a loop of emails so that's why I wrote the blog congratulating the Phillies. I understand fans, I'm a fan of the game, and I wanted those fans who were not just into name-calling to feel good about what the Phillies had done. I could have easily written, the Mets simply collapsed, the Phillies didn't win it. However, the Phillies did a great job, especially in the head-to-head competition, they won it.

As the wheels eventually came off of the Mets' bus and the season ended, Kernan reflected on his feelings about the Phillies beating his hometown Mets.

I was happy for people like Charlie Manuel, a baseball good guy, and the Phillies' staff. And I've always had the utmost respect for Jimmy Rollins, back to the days when Larry Bowa told me they had a kid shortstop coming up who was going to be good. I think Rollins talks the talk, and walks the walk, which is rare these days. He's a true leader and a wonderful player. I never get tired of watching him play.

The Mets collapsed for two reasons, they thought they had it, but even though I wrote that several times well after the column that generated so much interest -- which is a good thing, by the way -- the Mets still really thought they had it. Earlier in the year, I pointed out the Mets' weaknesses and as they began to fall apart I also wrote that they were losing their grip. It wasn't like I was just Mr. Met the whole time. When I wrote The Column I thought the Mets had finally gotten their act together. When I saw they had not, I wrote what I saw and questioned them. The game comes down to pitching and that failed the Mets, too. Jose Reyes had a bad second half and Carlos Delgado never got it together. Put it all together and there is a collapse. One other point, the Phillies were the better team in the head-to-head competition as well and deserved to win the division. They owned the Mets. When the Phillies got to the playoffs though, they had nothing left.

I think the Mets were in denial right to the end … I write what I see. Most times I see it right, once in a while I get it wrong. If I'm going to be wrong, it had to take the greatest collapse in the history of the game to be wrong. So be it. But I felt the Mets were losing their grip and that's why I wrote what I wrote in that blog and that the Phillies had come together as a team. Another huge factor is that Rollins did a wonderful job leading the Phillies down the stretch. No one stepped up for the Mets. We'll see what happens in the future. This is now one great rivalry.

Jimmy Rollins is right; the Phillies are the team to beat this season. They own the MVP in J-Roll, they financially satisfied young slugger Ryan Howard, and they have a total pro in Chase Utley. Cole Hamels continues to be the best-kept pitching secret in the league and Houston escapee Brad Lidge must stay healthy so Brett Myers can remain a starter. I pick the Phillies to win the NL East and play the Chicago Cubs for the National League title with the Cubs winning the World Series for the first time since 1908.

Quotable: "The final play when we came back in here the guy was out. If you go look at it (the replay) he was out. Didn't make it. He was out. Maybe Ted (Barrett, home plate umpire) wanted to go home. He told me, he said he got there first. Maybe he ought to go look at it." - Charlie Manuel on the final play of the game

Thursday, April 10th - Mets 4 Phillies 3 - 12 in.   (4-6) 2 ½ GB the Marlins

New York - *Umpire Ted Barrett calls Jose Reyes safe on a close play at the plate in the 12th to hand the rubber game of the series to the Mets. The video replay shows that Reyes was out before he touched the plate. Jayson Werth threw a perfect strike from center field to catcher Chris Coste who had the entire plate blocked. Starter Adam Eaton allowed 3 runs in 6 innings for his second consecutive quality start ... Although the Phils came back from a 3-0 deficit, the offense continues to struggle as they stranded 13 runners, 10 in the final seven innings ... Pedro Feliz knocked in two runs including his first homerun as a Phillie... The Phillies bullpen threw 5 innings of shutout ball until Angel Pagan's 2 out single in the 12th . Stuff: After ten games, the Phillies team ERA is a solid 3.96. Ryan Howard continues to struggle at the plate batting .189 and having struck out 14 times in the first ten games. Phils' starter Cole Hamels was used as a pinch hitter in the 11th and got a bunt single ... Rollins didn't start for the 2nd game in a row but did pinch hit in the 9th striking out in his only plate appearance. The Phils only have 3 stolen bases this year (13th place in NL).*

In a tight game officially decided on a bang-bang play at the plate, the Phillies sealed their fate by going 0-for-12 with runners in scoring position, falling to the Mets 4-3 in extra innings.

A well-pitched night for both sides, the game carried a familiar, April theme for the Phillies: Too many ducks left on the pond (13 total), poor execution of fundamental plays, in this case, dropping down a bunt. The team wasted a solid effort from Adam Eaton who, next to

Even friendships have their limits

Cole Hamels, has been their best starter through two turns. John Maine was even better on the opposite side. In the opening series between these two rivals this was probably the best pure ballgame. Despite the incorrect ruling at home, the Mets did enough to earn the win and take the "Eric Bruntlett" Series.

Quotable: "I definitely felt a lot more aggressive today. It definitely felt like I was letting it go better today. I felt like I had a good cutter today and when I have a good cutter usually the fastball falls in line" - Starter Brett Myers

Friday, April 11th - Phillies 5 Cubs 3 (5-6) 2 ½ GB the Marlins

Philadelphia – *Brett Myers (1-1) gives up 3 homeruns but pitches 8 strong innings for his first win of the year. His fastball was consistently in the low 90s. The Phillies are now 7-1 versus the Cubs in the last eight games that Myers has pitched against them. Burrell goes 2 for 4 knocking in 3 with a 2-run HR and a RBI double. He's now batting .400 (4th best in the NL) with 4 HRs and 13 RBIs. Lidge makes his first home appearance and gets his 2nd save of the season. Stuff: The Phils got their first look at Cub's Japanese phenom Kosuke Fukudome. He looks a lot like Ichiro Suzuki but doesn't hit like him as he goes 0 for 4…his first hitless game since playing in the major leagues …Rollins sits out his 3rd straight game. Manuel says, "I'm very concerned about him".*

Baseball writers live in paradise!

Sitting in a Press Box is like making it to baseball's Promised Land. Soft, cushioned seats, a climate controlled environment where writers can either experience the open fresh air of a cool summer evening, or close it up to an air-conditioned 72 degrees. The food that they get to eat from the media cafeteria would shame ¾'s of the restaurants in downtown Philadelphia, plus they get to eat all the ice cream and free soda that one can squander in one evening. It truly is the utopia of how one should be able to watch a ballgame at the park.

So what's the Press Box like behind the "Media Only" elevator doors on the main concourse behind home plate?

One's journey starts having to get through Security. Rich Hodges is positioned in front of the Media Elevator throughout the length of every Phillies home game. His job is to make sure that only credentialed media and au-

Press Box Security Guard Ed Deal filling out the starting lineup before a game

thorized Phillies employees go into the elevator. *"Every once in a while I'll get someone who tries to sneak by, but for the most part the fans respect that its only for the Media. Sometimes we'll get fans who will wait by the doors to see Harry Kalas or Larry Anderson but that only happens every so often."*

Once the elevator doors open you are greeted by Bill Atkinson. Bill's job is half security guard, half elevator operator. *"Lots of times we'll get visiting media and they don't have a clue to where they are going so part of my job is to make sure that I get them to the right location. Basically I'll either take them up to the Press Club or down to the Media Room in the basement."*

Today Bill is taking me to the Press Club. He presses the button marked "2-Press Club" on the elevator controls and we're on our way.

As you walk out of the elevator into the Press Club you walk into a hallway where the first door on your left are the offices of the Phillies' TV and radio broadcasters. The door is slightly opened and I see Larry Anderson and Scott Franzke talking to each other. Anderson has his feet propped up on his desk and Franzke is standing in the middle of the room and appears to be telling Larry an entertaining story.

At the end of the hallway begins the row of broadcast booths. There are five booths in the Press Club. Going left to right they include the Visiting team's radio booth, the Phillies' Spanish-broadcasting radio booth, the Phillies' regular radio booth, the Phillies' TV broadcast booth and finally the Visiting team's TV broadcast booth.

Right out in front of the Phillies' radio booth are two six foot tables. Each of the tables holds numerous copies of various PR-related information that both the Phillies and the visiting team put out for the media every game. The Phillies have a 10-12 page legal sized document that's titled *"Phillies Game Information."* It's a complete listing of any possible statistic or piece of trivia that one would most likely never venture to wonder about. The Chicago Cubs have their own version of the same titled *"Cubs Game Notes."* However they have it printed in both English and in Japanese as there are a number of Japanese reporters that are following Kosuke Fukudome at every game.

There are also other documents on the table today as well. A copy of the up to the minute MLB statistics for both the National and American leagues. There's also a blank lineup card for writers to keep score during the game, a two page "op note" on newly acquired right-hander Rudy Seanez (still pictured with his LA Dodger cap on) and finally a copy of "Citizens Bank Notes" which lists all of the activities taking place throughout the ballpark for the evening's events.

Walking past the last booth, one then walks directly into the Press Box. Two signs immediately pop out in your face when you walk in. The first is an old beat-up sign from Connie Mack Stadium that reads "NO BOTTLES OR CANS IN PRESS BOX". The second is a sign letting everyone know that they have entered "THE BARON'S BOX". Affectionately named after the long time and newly retired VP of Phillies Public Relations, Larry Shenk.

Immediately upon entering you are greeted by Security Guards Ed Deal and Alex Sermarini. Both asked to see my credentials and then Alex let me know which seats I could sit in for today's game.

The Press Box is quite large. Located slightly off-center of home plate on the Phillies' dugout side of the ballpark, there are three rows of seating with each row tiered above the other so that one can walk in front of a row of seats and not block the view of those seated behind them. In total there are 119 fixed workstations for the media plus additional seating along the back wall in the event that all the workstations are filled.

The Press Box is conveniently set up with all the modern amenities that one would expect in a new ballpark. Huge comfortable blue seats that swivel and have rollers on them and twelve TVs that are always tuned into the ball game. There is wireless Internet access and electrical outlets for each station.

The Media Dining Area is located directly behind all of the seating. Reporters pay $10.00 a game to have complete access to their choice of a wide variety of food and beverages. Although alcohol is not available in the Press Box or in the Media Dining area there are plenty of stories of when this wasn't the case back during the Connie Mack Stadium days. Rumor has it that there were plenty of shriveled-up livers at the end of each season.

Tonight Alex has me seated between Channel 6's Jamie Apode and Comcast's Leslie Gudel. Throughout the game they give me the low-down on who sits where in the Press Box and what the written and unwritten rules of the Press Box are…

Seating Arrangements:
Row One is the prominent seating section in the Press Box. The first two seats are assigned to the Official Scorer and the Assistant to the Official Scorer for Major League Baseball. Tonight these belong to long-time scorer Bob Kenney and his daughter Nancy Kenney. The next four seats, 3-6, are assigned to the Phillies' PR staff. Media Relations assistant Kevin Gregg, son of ex-Major League Umpire Eric Gregg, sits in seat #3. Scott Palmer, retired Channel 6 reporter and now the Phillies' Director of Public Affairs sits in seat #4. Greg Casterioto is the Phillies' Director of Baseball Communications and most directly responsible for coordinating all player and coaches interviews sits in seat #5 and Jay McLaughlin, the Phillies' Baseball Information Analyst sits in seat #6.

The remaining seats in Row One are assigned to the newspapers and radio stations that regularly cover the team. Each major newspaper is usually given two seats: one for the Beat Writer and one for the paper's Columnist. Tonight it appears that all the columnists are covering the Flyers' playoffs series against Washington so the game is only being covered by the Beat Writers. Seats 7 & 8 are assigned to the Associated Press. Tonight long-time AP reporter Jack Scheurer is covering the game along with Rob Maadi. The *Philadelphia Inquirer* is assigned seats 9 & 10 with Todd Zolecki as tonight's lone representative. Seats 11 & 12 are for the *Bucks County Courier Times* with beat writer Randy Miller representing the paper. Next is the sports heavy *Philadelphia Daily News* with Marcus Hayes and David Murphy. Bob Grotz of the *Delaware County Daily Times* has seats 15 & 16. Geoff Mosher is in seats 17 & 18 for the *Wilmington News Journal* (sitting in for regular beat writer Scott Lauber) and Kevin Roberts and Mike Radano of South Jersey's *Courier Post* are in seats 19 & 20. The remaining seats in Row One include the *Trenton Times, Allentown Morning Call, Press of Atlantic City, Gloucester County Times, Easton Express Times,* the *Metro,* the *Northeast Times, KYW News Radio, DM communications and KSIS.*

Row Two starts off with the Cubs' Public Relations staff and 11 additional seats which are assigned to the Chicago media that are covering the Cubs. ESPN.com is assigned seats 49 & 50. Jason Stark is reporting tonight. *USA Today* has seat #51 but no one is reporting for them. Seats 52 – 55 are assigned to MLB.com. The two representatives for MLB.com this night are Andy Jasner, son of long-time *Daily News* reporter Phil Jasner, and Ed Kenney. Andy is writing the game information that will be on MLB.com and Ed is working the game day datacaster which is an in-game service that MLB provides to Yahoo and other internet sights that provides a pitch-by-pitch account of the game.

Row Three is for the "rest" of the media. This row is usually reserved for TV and Cable media, but tonight the first nine seats are occupied by Japanese reporters covering the Cubs and Fukudome.

Rules of the Press Box:
There are "official" rules and unofficial rules. First the official rules:
- You must be appropriately credentialed by Major League Baseball to be in the Press Box.
- No photography. Don't ask why though. Nobody seems to know. It appears that it is a long-time rule that started back in the early days of baseball when reporters didn't want flashes going off in their faces as they wrote their stories.
- Do not talk to the Official Scorer. It's best that you let them do their job but if you do have to speak to them it must be between innings.

The unofficial rules? That's easy. Sit in the seat that you are assigned and most importantly, No cheering in the Press Box!

Pat Burrell hit a two-run homer in the fourth inning and the crowd went wild. It was funny watching all of the reporters. They didn't clap, yell, pump a fist or even smile! While the fans are going crazy the reporters are all heads down furiously typing away. It's a different world in here.

Quotable: "I've definitely been lucking out a lot. I haven't really hit that groove. It's nice to know I'm still able to go out and challenge guys. I have guys so fooled and off-balance that it can allow me to get away with a poor game." - Starter Cole Hamels

Saturday, April 12th - Phillies 7 Cubs 1 (6-6) 1½ GB the Marlins
Philadelphia - Cole Hamels (2-1 0.82) pitched 7 shutout innings of one hit ball while walking 2 and striking out 5. Pedro Feliz and Ryan Howard both hit 2-run homers off of Cubs starter Ted Lilly. Stuff: Jimmy Rollins was presented with his 2007 NL MVP award before the game and received a standing ovation from the sellout crowd of 45,072 at Citizens Bank Park. Rollins also

received his 2007 Silver Slugger Award (best offensive player at shortstop in all of baseball) along with Chase Utley (best offensive player at second base). Shane Victorino had an incredible catch off the fence in center in the 2nd inning but had to leave the game in the 6th with a right calf strain. He was placed on the 15 day DL after the game. With Rollins still day-to-day and Victorino out the team will be struggling for speed at the top of the lineup ... Chris Snelling was called up from AAA–Lehigh to replace Victorino.

This is the same injury that sidelined Shane last season, and one begins to seriously wonder whether his body can withstand a full season. There is now significant evidence it cannot. His game is almost entirely predicated on speed, and this is his second blowout in only a few months. Manager Charlie Manuel said he planned on starting him only 125 times, but so far he's been plugged into the starting lineup every game. Jimmy Rollins' injury may have been a factor in the manager's decision to stick with Victorino because although his hitting is only just starting to come around, the center fielder's sterling glove work has already bailed them out on a number of occasions.

In the meantime, outfielder Chris Snelling's contract was purchased from the 0-10 Lehigh Valley IronPigs, where he had a .643 OPS. A left-handed hitter, Snelling figures to be a marginal improvement over the departed Chris Roberson, who would have gotten the call last season in this situation. Snelling's MO is nice swing, versatile outfielder, but can't stay healthy. Snelling, So Taguchi and Jayson Werth figure to

Jimmy Rollins' unsuccessfully tests his sprained ankle out with the team doctor prior to today's game

split time in center while Victorino recovers. Taguchi's defense so far has failed to inspire much confidence.

While Rollins is expected back Tuesday, this is a significant setback for a Phillies team just starting to get into a good rhythm.

Quotable: "You have your offensive slumps, your pitching slumps and defensive slumps, and right now we're not catching the ball and throwing the ball that well." - Chase Utley, who has committed four of the team's 15 errors this season.

Sunday, April 13th - Cubs 6 Phillies 5 - 10 innings (6-7) 1½ GB the Marlins

Philadelphia - *Third base umpire Adrian Johnson blows a call in the 6th inning when a ball hit foul by the Cub's Mark DeRosa is ruled a homerun. Replays clearly show the ball going foul by at least three feet but Johnson signaled a homerun to the angst of Phillies fans and Charlie Manuel. Manuel was thrown out of his first game of the season by Johnson... "I tossed some profanity at him ... I was ticked off because he missed the play," said Charlie after the game. The call was a turning point for the Cubs who went on to win in extra innings on a throwing error by Chase Utley, the Phillies' 15th error of the season. Only the Pirates (18) have committed more errors. Stuff: With Rollins and Victorino out, Manuel had Geoff Jenkins bat leadoff where he goes 2 for 6 and Jayson Werth hit second where he goes 2 for 4 with 2 RBIs. Dropping to 6-7, this is the third time this season that the Phils have not been able to get over the .500 mark. In 2007 they didn't get over .500 until May 26th.*

There are tens of thousands of young teenage boys across the Delaware Valley whose dream is to one day play for a major league baseball team. Most likely though that dream will not come true. Sure there are the Jamie Moyer's from Souderton, the Johnny Marzano's from South Philly and the Orel Hershiser's from Cherry Hill, but the vast majority of players in the majors come from warm climate areas across the United States and the Caribbean where they can play year round and even then you have to be an incredible athlete and be able to hit the curve ball.

Phillies' Batboys Mike Chernow (Cubs uniform) and Rob DeClementi (Phillies uniform)

However, there is one shortcut where a teen or two can not only be on a major league baseball team but do so while they are still in high school! One only has to become a batboy for the Phillies. A once-in-a-lifetime job ... a kid's fantasy come true.

So how does one become a batboy for the Philadelphia Phillies? The man in charge of answering that question is Phillies clubhouse Manager Frank Coppenbarger.

I look for a number of qualities when I hire a batboy for the team. I first look to see if the young man is a good citizen. I actually check into how they are in school, how they are at home. I also ask them to bring one of their parents in with them for the interview, because it's a lot more work and time than people realize. It's a lot more than what one will see when you see the batboys in the ballpark; it's a lot more than you see on television. It's not just wearing a uniform and chasing the bats and balls during a game. It's a lot of stuff before and after the game. The hours are longer than people realize and the commitment is definitely a big one.

When they are interviewing for the position we're looking for someone that's polite and someone whose appearance is neat. They're representing our organization out on the field. As far as I'm concerned the batboy job to me is a critical job, it's very important. They're wearing our uniform out on that field. They're on television all around the world. They're in the newspapers sometimes. They're within full view. I need people that are neat, clean, I have to know that they have their act together. We don't have any room for people that are not like that. We can't put them out there representing us and we don't want to. We need someone that's mannerly. That's why generally when they're a good student in school they're a good student away from school, or a good citizen all the way around.

A young person that's a ball player in high school won't work well for us because they cannot give us the commitment we need. We need a guy who loves baseball and can give us their commitment for half a school year and an entire summer. If you're a ball player you should go play (for your school) because you have the rest of your life to work and you only have a short window of opportunity to play. Every kid that comes in here that's a player, I encourage them to go play. But even if you're a football player we can't use you because in the fall you start having practice after school. I need you here. We got a job for you to do when the Phillies are in town and we can't work around that. It doesn't work.

When I interview a potential batboy they need to have a clear picture of what the job really is like and sometimes a 16 or 17 year old kid can't make that decision by themselves. I want their parents to be there when I interview them. What we don't want to have happen is 3 or 4 weeks into the season have somebody's mom or dad come in or send a note in with their kid that this was more than they thought and they're not going to be able to do it anymore and then we're back to square one again. So we like to paint the worst picture we can of what the job might be like. If everybody's agreeable and all the other factors work out then we probably have ourselves a good kid.

My biggest rule for the batboys is to be on time. They have to be here. That's not necessarily a duty it's just part of their job. For a 7:05pm start they have to be here by 4:00pm. They put their work clothes on as soon as they get here and then get the dugout laid out. The helmets and bats and the towels and the drinks down there, the PowerAde and the water and the cups and gum and seeds. And then basically they sit there and keep their eyes on the stuff in the dugout. We have a lot of visitors down on that field and in the dugout and people come from upstairs and the sponsors and guests of the ball club and what not, people we don't know. So they are kind of like the security guy down there for us.

Rob DeClementi and Mike Chernow are our batboys this season. Rob is the batboy for the Phillies clubhouse and Mike is the batboy for the visitor's clubhouse. Rob's a very quiet kid, which I think is good for a batboy job. He's a behind the scenes type guy, just does his job, doesn't try to get noticed in the clubhouse. He's very polite; he's well spoken. He minds his own business. I think he's an excellent batboy for us. Mike actually reports directly to Kevin

Steinhour (Manager, Visiting Clubhouse). Kevin personally hires all of the batboys for the Visiting Clubhouse and he interviewed Mike himself. From what I can tell about Mike, he appears to be a very polite kid and he gets his job done.

Both Rob and Mike really are excellent at what they do. I couldn't be happier with the two of them. With regards to their future, I suspect that Rob and Mike will go on to college and graduate and be pretty special no matter what they decide to do in life.

Quotable: "I guess at USC they never taught (Jenkins) to look twice." – Phillies Third Base coach Steve Smith on Geoff Jenkins running through his stop sign after Feliz's double in the 9th.

Tuesday, April 15th - Phillies 4 Astros 3   (7-7) 1½ GB the Marlins

Philadelphia - *Erasing a three run deficit, the Phillies come back to win a wild one with 4 runs in the bottom of the 9th. Chris Snelling had his first hit as a Phillie, a homerun, to start the rally in the 9th. Pat Burrell then followed with a 2-run blast of his own to tie the game at three ... Geoff Jenkins then reached first on a strikeout/passed ball and was doubled home by Pedro Feliz for the game winning run. To the chagrin of Phillies third base coach Steve Smith, Jenkins ran right through his stop sign and fortunately scored the winning run. Adam Eaton pitched another solid game with his third straight quality start of the season without a decision. Stuff: The Phillies starters now have 8 quality starts in 14 games. That's 3rd best in the NL so far ... not bad considering that pitching was the primary concern coming into the season. Astros' starter Shawn Chacon shut down the Phillies for 8 innings and left the game with a 3-0 lead ... This was Ed Wade's first time back to Philadelphia as a GM with another team. Burrell's homerun tied him with Greg Luzinski for fourth place on the Phillies all-time HR list with 223.*

Rob DeClementi is a 17-year-old senior at Lindenwold High School in New Jersey and has been the Phillies Clubhouse batboy since the start of the 2007 season. As it goes with teenagers in the Philadelphia area, Rob gets the most face time on TV since Frankie Avalon and Bobby Rydell as he runs balls back and forth to the umpire, chases a broken bat down the first base line or stands on the dugout steps waiting to complete his next duty.

What's it like being a batboy for a Major League team?
It's unbelievable. It's kind of like a dream. I've been following baseball all of my life and to be a part of a Major League team is like one of those "out of world" experiences that you'll remember forever.

How did you become the Phillies batboy?

I was reading about batboys in ESPN Magazine and it kind of got me inspired to want to be one. I called up the Phillies, they told me how to apply and then I submitted my application to them. I guess I was good enough for them because they hired me.

What's the most surprising thing to you about being a batboy?

Probably how up-close you can get with the players and what not. I mean, I didn't know that I could actually be on the field, catch fly balls, and have catches with major league players. It's kind of really cool.

What do you like best about being a batboy?

Just being on the field, watching every single game from the dugout. How many people can say they did that? I

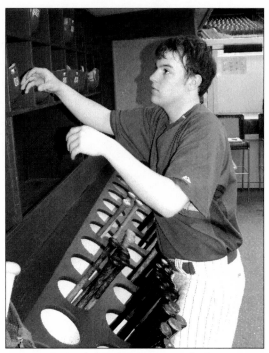

Batboy Rob DeClementi getting the dugout ready before the game

also get an opportunity to travel with the team on a road trip once a year. Last year I went to Washington and Pittsburgh. I'm not sure which road trip I am going on this year.

What are your responsibilities on a game-to-game basis?

For a typical night game I try to get here by noon. I hang up the players' jerseys and help with the laundry and then get ready for the game. Before every game I have to fill up and take the coolers out to the dugout, set up all the bats, put the batting helmets out and then get ready for batting practice. Once batting practice starts my job is to gather the batting practice balls and run them into the pitcher and dump them into the ball container. It's like running the gauntlet sometimes trying not to get hit with a ball.

What is your role once the game starts?

Basically you spend most of your time running balls to the umpire but I also go out and pick up each players bat if they get on base.

Of all of your responsibilities, which ones do you least like to do?

Probably on the hot days running back and forth giving water to the umpires. I'm not complaining about it but it's really hot out on the field and it gets tiring.

What has been your greatest experience so far in this job?

Being in the locker room celebration last year when the Phillies won the NL East. It was really fun being a part of it. Getting drenched in champagne and everything like that. It was really cool. Hopefully we can do it again.

Mike Chernow is the Phillies Visiting Clubhouse batboy. He is 17 years old and attends Timber Creek Regional School in Erial, New Jersey. Mike is the batboy that gets to wear the visiting club's uniforms whenever a team comes into town.

Phillies visiting clubhouse batboy Mike Chernow retrieves a broken bat during a game against the Nationals

Why did you become a batboy?
Primarily because I love the Phillies and I love baseball and because there isn't a better job anywhere on the planet for someone my age to work at then here.

What do you like best about doing your job?
I like everything about it. Probably the neatest thing is sitting in the dugout and hearing how loud the fans can get. When Ryan Howard hits a bomb or Burrell hits one the crowd just goes crazy. I actually get goose bumps. Being in the visitor's dugout I'm not allowed to cheer for the Phillies so sometimes it can get pretty hard not to jump up and yell but inside I'm really cheering.

You get to meet all of the players that come to Citizens Bank Park. Who is your favorite?
All of the players have been really cool. They're just normal guys like us. I really don't have a favorite player but I thought it was pretty cool to meet Ken Griffey Jr. I always watched him on TV when I was growing up so it was pretty weird when I met him the first time which, strangely enough, happened to be my first game as a batboy last season. Bobby Cox is really nice as well. One time I lost my baseball glove and I guess he found out about it. He ended up sending me one of his. That was great!

Do you ever get booed wearing the opposing team's uniform?
When you're wearing the Mets uniform you hear it pretty loud. But the fans really aren't too bad with me. The worse I've ever had anyone say to me is "I HATE the Mets". Nothing that would be that bad. One time though I had to run some baseballs out to the Mets bullpen between innings of a game because they ran out of them and I dropped the balls right in the middle of center field. The crowd gave it to me good and really booed me. That was pretty funny.

Quotable: "The last guy I want to give up a home run to is him (Michael Bourn), but he put a good swing on it and I have to give him credit. I'll give him a sinker next time." – Kyle Kendrick on Bourn's 5th inning homerun

Wednesday, April 16th - Astros 2 Phillies 1 (7-8) 2½ GB behind the Marlins

Philadelphia - *A classic pitching dual ... The Astros' Ray Oswalt (1-3) goes back to his vintage self throwing 7 innings while giving up only 1 run to the Phillies ... ex-Phillies speedster Michael Bourn is the hitting star of the game for the Astros as he goes 2 for 4 with a homerun, a stolen base (he leads the NL with 8) and two runs scored ... The 23-year-old Kyle Kendrick (1-2) goes 7 innings, retiring 13 of the last 14 hitters that he faced and giving up a total of 4 hits ... Burrell's hot hitting continues as he goes 2-for-4, raising his average to .362. Stuff: This was Oswalt's 6th straight win against the Phillies dating all the way back to 2003 ... It was the Phillies fifth time this season that they failed to get over .500 mark ... Jimmy Rollins missed his 7th straight game with the sprained left ankle.*

When Al Gore invented the Internet he must have been thinking about blogging. A perfect match for a nation that can't seem to get enough information about their favorite team, baseball and blogging go together like Chase Utley and Jimmy Rollins. Even after watching the pre-game show, the game, the post-game show and the highlights on Comcast and ESPN it still isn't enough information to satisfy the hunger that Phillies' fans have for their team. Instant analysis and second guessing necessitates baseball blogging for the myriads of armchair GMs that crave the need to express their opinion on the "coulda, woulda, shoulda" of every game.

BEERLEAGUER

Beerleaguer.com , the #1 rated Phillies blog on the Internet

There are literally dozens of blogs that cover the Phillies. Some are written by the Beat Writers (*The Zo Zone* – Todd Zolecki of the Inquirer, *High Above Home Plate* – Mike Radano of the Courier Post, *High Cheese* – David Murphy of the Daily News and *Phollowing the Phillies* – Ryan Lawrence of the Delaware County Daily Times), but most are written by everyday fans that just have a passion for the team and a desire to express that passion to those willing to stop by and read their musings and even leave their own comments.

The most popular Phillies blog on the Internet is *Beerleaguer.com*. A site run by 30-year-old Jason Weitzel of Pottstown, Pennsylvania. Weitzel, whose "real" job is as an Editor and Designer for the Reading Eagle, has been running Beerleaguer non-stop since 2005. He was most recently voted the Best Sportswriter in Philly by *Philadelphia Magazine* ... *"Jason Weitzel is the man behind Beerleaguer, the best Phillies blog out there. Great mix of analysis, detailed info that obsessive Phillies fans die for, and fairly intelligent comments from diehard fans."* Quite an honor when you consider you are up against some of the best sportswriters in the country.

Ah, yes. The thrill of victory and the agony of reading about Ryan Howard's slump the next day. Beerleaguer is happy to oblige. – Beerleaguer April 16, 2008

I think longevity plays a big part as to why Beerleaguer.com is recognized as one of the best Phillies blog. The site has been up and active for three-plus years, which makes it ancient in blog years. For every blog that survives a year, there are dozens of others that go black. You have to be patient, a little nuts and obsessed to write every day, which I do, even in the off-season. Readers log on to Beerleaguer and expect fresh content yet something distinctly Beerleaguer, which means it must be Phillies related and something that hasn't been covered in quite the same way. I try to inject personality into the entries when it applies. Although I'm not on a traditional beat, I try to maintain journalistic integrity and remain pragmatic, and that example is reflected in Beerleaguer's comments section, home to some of the smartest baseball fans on the Internet.

Beerleaguer can expect close to 20,000 unique visitors a month, a level that stays pretty constant. There's a drop in the off-season, obviously, although trade speculation and the winter hot stove keeps the site very active. Baseball, more than any other sport, lends itself very well to the Internet, with access to stats and outside markets.

I started Beerleaguer because I needed a creative outlet and figured Phillies baseball was a good subject to tackle since its familiar and a passion of mine. In 2005, blogging was still in its infancy and there weren't many Phillies blogs, and almost none maintained in official capacities like the dailies and the MLB Web site. So there was a real need for something like Beerleaguer as an alternative to sports talk radio and print. That hunch turned out to be correct. The thing that still excites me most about Beerleaguer is knowing it was on the cutting edge. Now, I see many blogs where Beerleaguer has had a clear influence.

You really don't get many "famous" people participating on the site because it's not what the site is intended to do. I write from a fan's perspective and attack issues on their level. I've done interviews with players and coaches in the past and they generated surprisingly little interest or reaction. Behind the scenes, I suspect many players frequent the site as "lurkers" but never comment. I know Chris Coste has read it since he has a link to it on his Web site.

My favorite Phillies blogs are *"Balls, Sticks and Stuff "*and *"Swing and a Miss".* They broke into the blogging scene with Beerleaguer and I've had a connection to them ever since. *"We Should Be GMs"* is an outrageous site that's good for a laugh and posts a lot of things I don't have the courage to post. *"The Good Phight"* is well-done and offers a unique take. *"Phillies Flow"* is a very thorough source and has a dry sense of humor that I like.

My favorite Beat Writers that cover the team would include David Murphy of the Philadelphia Daily News, who has done a great job in his first season covering the team; Scott Lauber for the Wilmington News Journal is another great source; and the one guy who doesn't get the respect he should is Ken Mandel of Phillies.com. He's been on the beat since 2002 and isn't just some puppet for the Phillies. He knows this team inside and out and has written more than anyone over the last five years.

I do not believe bloggers should be given the same access to the team (clubhouse/field/press box) as the major newspapers. Logistically, a press box and clubhouse can only accommodate so many people. Papers like the Inquirer are institutions and are treated as such. However, if you ask me should a blog site like Beerleaguer be granted access above someone like a fifth stringer or blogger for ESPN.com or SI.com or Sporting News, who would only attend a game or two a season? I say yes. However, the process of picking and choosing could prove difficult as the coverage of baseball continues to grow into alternative media, such as online video, pod casting and the continued growth of blogging. It's all great exposure for the Phillies, who've seen attendance grow tremendously, in large part because of all the attention they've received from bloggers across the globe.

Quotable: It's frustrating (to be at .500), but we've definitely been a lot worse. To look at our team the last couple years ... it's been tough for us to put anything together let alone have days like today where everything worked together. We can build on it, and, hopefully, once we get above .500, we don't go back." - Left fielder Pat Burrell on the Phillies ability to get over the .500 mark

Thursday, April 17th - Phillies 10 Astros 2 (8-8) 1½ GB the Marlins
Philadelphia - *The Phils pound out 16 hits including 4 home runs ...one each by Coste, Howard, Burrell and Utley. Brett Myers (2-1) pitches the Phillies 10th quality start of the season as he goes 7 innings giving up 1 run. Stuff: Coste goes 4 for 5 with a double, home run and 3 RBIs. ... 7 of the 8 starters had at least 2 hits except for shortstop Eric Bruntlett who takes a goose egg and goes 0 for 5 ...Phils Assistant GM Rueben Amaro denies rumors that Jimmy Rollins is headed to the DL "We believe he will be ready to play Saturday or Sunday ...he's progressing towards that."*

Walking through the left field gates one can't miss one of the cooler features of Citizens Bank Park, the Topps Starting Lineup. Prior to every game the Phillies starting lineup is displayed on large Topps Baseball Cards that gives the fans a visual of the players that are starting and in what order they are batting in that day's action.

Phillies interns' Amanda Grant and Craig Solomon are working together to hang tonight's starting lineup. Amanda is on the ground reading the lineup to Craig ensuring that he has the right player in the correct order of the lineup. Craig, having somewhat the more difficult job, is trying to put Geoff Jenkins into the number six hole of the lineup while fighting against a steady 10 mile per hour breeze with an occasional gust to 15 or so. He's having a hard time getting the card into position and lock it into place as the wind is pushing him and the huge cards on

Craig Solomon installing the Topps starting lineup cards at the Left Field entrance to the ballpark

top of his twenty foot high self-propelled scissors lift around. Craig finally gets the 5' x 7' effigy of the ex-Brewer into the metal slot that holds the card, looks down and asks Amanda who's batting seventh. "Chris Coste," Amanda yells up. Craig then uses the steering mechanism on the lift to move himself down to the next slot.

Amanda appears to be enjoying the task much more so than Craig so Amanda gives the low-down on how it's all done.

We usually get the starting lineup around 3:45pm before a 7:05pm start. Craig and I will walk down to the clubhouse and copy down the lineup off of the whiteboard that's directly outside the clubhouse. We then go to the storage closet that's located in the basement underneath the stands and we pull out the starting players and put them into the scissors lift. Tonight's lineup was a bit more difficult to put together because there are a few more bench players starting tonight like Taguchi, Jenkins and Dobbs.

If a player is called up and we don't have a card for him we will put in a generic card that just shows a picture of Citizens Bank Park. Last year Tadahito Iguchi was acquired by the Phillies after Utley was hurt and we had to use the generic card for him for a few games before they finally got a card made up of him in a Phillies uniform. I think the fans want to see the actual player and not a generic card so the Phillies go about getting a Topps card made of a new player as soon as feasibly possible.

The cards are made up of some kind of canvas. They're pretty light. The only thing that keeps them together is the metal frame in the back. You can see that they aren't the easiest to handle in a strong wind. If Craig doesn't hold on to them tight they will take off like a kite.

We have photos of all the players on the team except the relief pitchers. We still even have some of the players that left the team over the past few years. I guess we're hanging on to them in case they come back one day.

We leave the cards up overnight but then the next day we have to rearrange them to match Charlie's lineup. The biggest number of cards that we have had to swap out happened last August (2007). We had to move Pat Burrell from 6th to 3rd, we replaced Iguchi's generic card with his real one, we moved Dobbs over to 7th, put Kyle Kendrick in as the pitcher and then we had to make two other changes. I can't remember who they were but it took a long time. Usually it takes us about 25 minutes to make the changes but that day it took us close to 50 minutes.

They might take even longer today as the winds are still playing tricks with Craig as he tries his best to get Chris Coste's photo into the seven hole before the winds turn the card into a projectile hurtling down Ashburn Alley.

Quotable: "Not at all. Philadelphia fans hate New York fans and New York fans [hate Philadelphia fans]. I don't have any problems with any of these guys. I mean, they'd like to take me deep, not because they hate me, but because it's part of the game. If I'm out there, you have to beat me." - Mets Closer Billy Wagner when asked if the Mets players hate the Phillies players.

Friday, April 18th - Mets 6 Phillies 4 (8-9) 2 GB the Mets

Philadelphia - *Staff Ace vs. Staff Ace with the Mets Johan Santana (2-2) out-pitching Cole Hamels (2-2) in the Mets first visit to Philly this season in front of a sellout crowd of 45,156. Through the first seven innings Santana/Hamels brought back strong memories of the Seaver/Carlton match ups in the 1970s with Santana striking out 10 and giving up 1 earned run. Hamels equaled the effort with 2 earned runs but only striking out 4 Mets batters. Unfortunately for the Phillies the 8th inning proved to be Hamels downfall as the Mets put 4 runs on to the board and the Phillies were unable to answer them. Stuff: David Wright, who previously was 1 for 11 against Hamels, goes 4 for 4 including 2 RBIs. Phils pinch hitter Greg Dobbs did get the Phils back into striking distance in the bottom of the 8th with a 3-run pinch hit homerun but it wasn't enough as Billy Wagner shut down the Phils with a 1-2-3 9th inning ... Jose Reyes smashed his head into Chase Utley's knee during a head first slide as he stole a base in the 3rd inning. Mets Manager Willie Randolph said that Reyes was disoriented and dazed but after a few minutes was able to stay in the game ... Shane Victorino will go to extended Spring Training this Saturday to start rehabbing his strained right calf. Hopes are that he will be back in Philly on April 29th against the Padres. No new news on Rollin's status.*

As a Phillies fan, today's start by Santana should terrify you. Not only the prospect of facing Johan head-to-head perhaps three more times this season, but the fact the Mets can feature exactly what we saw last night every fifth game against the rest of the league through 2013 with a vesting option in 2014. Granted, it won't be 10-strikeout, zero-walk phenom start every time out but to rationalize his overall impact boarders on denial. Historically, the left-hander becomes even more beastly as the season rolls along. Santana alone could be enough to tip the scales in a mediocre NL East.

The shame of it was, the Phillies had a chance to be the ones left standing, not to detract from the terrific games Santana and David Wright had. Cole Hamels wasn't brilliant keeping it close. It was their defense that let them down again. Carlos Ruiz, considered the smoother defender of

Fans Dave Mortlock and his daughter Trish display their contempt towards the Mets prior to the game

the two catchers, allowed a crucial passed ball in the first moving Ryan Church into scoring position. In the third, Ruiz's throw would have been in time to get Jose Reyes had it not sailed seven feet over the bag. He wasn't alone. Jayson Werth misplayed a ball in center, which turned into an RBI triple. Ryan Howard booted one in the 7th. The Mets capitalized on all these gaffs.

Quotable: "We were always confident against the Phillies. There was no doubt in this team's mind. When a team is really on you, and you know you can't beat them, you know that. We lost some games last year against the Phillies in that so-called streak that everyone likes to bring up where we knew we should have won some of those games. If you know that, then you don't lack confidence against a team." - Mets Manager Willie Randolph

Saturday, April 19th - Mets 4 Phillies 2 (8-10) 3GB the Mets

Philadelphia - The Phillies dropped their fourth straight game to the Mets in 2008, all without Jimmy Rollins, as the offense continues to stall, this time leaving 12 men on base. The Mets pieced together a solid pitching performance by Oliver Perez and six relievers as they hold the Phils to 2 runs on 7 hits. Jamie Moyer pitched well, 2 earned runs in 6 IP. Chase Utley is the lone bright spot as he goes 2 for 4 and homers in his third straight game (6 on the season) to break up the Mets shutout in the 7th.   Stuff: After going 0 for 5 with three strikeouts Ryan Howard, who is now hitting a paltry .182 (he now has struck out 26 times in 66 at bats), said the following: "Obviously I'm not comfortable and I'm not seeing the ball well. Once I get comfortable I will be all right." said Howard.

Trouble with the gloves, bats and bullpen means the 8-10 Phillies aren't much better than they were last April (7-11). Yesterday, it was the attack of the killer "0-fers": Ryan Howard: 0-for-5, 4 LOB, 3Ks; Jayson Werth 0-for-5, 5 LOB, 3Ks (Werth has really cooled off); Pat Burrell: 0-for-4, 3Ks. As a team, they stranded 11 runners!

Offensively, you can point the finger at two primary areas: first and third. Catcher and shortstop earn dishonorable mention. Since Scott Rolen left it is as though the Phillies have been eternally cursed at third and have had to settle for bottom-rung production players every season. With Pedro Feliz basically starting every game, the hot corner has produced little (.603 OPS.). The National League average at third is .774. Feliz's last hit was Tuesday's game-winner against Houston. How much longer can he ride out

The Mets have turned the tables and are now dominating the Phillies in '08

that moment? Actually, he's the team's worst offender with runners in scoring position, hitting just .067. Compared to National League clean-up hitters, Howard is last in average (.182) and fourth from the bottom in slugging (.394). His 26 strikeouts are six more than Adam Dunn and the most in baseball. Over the last seven days, he has three hits.

Thanks to Chris Coste, the catching stats are respectable compared to the rest of the league. Ruiz alone, just as Eric Bruntlett alone, comes up far below the average. But with guys like Russell Martin producing little out in LA, few catchers have produced, and Bruntlett could be back on the bench shortly when Rollins returns.

Then there's the bullpen. For the second game in a row, middle relief couldn't hold it; this time it was Ryan Madson. Between Howard, Feliz, Madson and the defense, it's enough to drive one nuts. Or in my case, not write another depressing word about it, and end it at that.

Quotable: "I don't want to keep going back to last year, but we proved to be a very resilient club. We knew we didn't have Jimmy (Rollins), but we never worry about who we don't have and that's a really strong part of our club." - Charlie Manuel after placing Rollins on the 15 day DL

Sunday, April 20th - Phillies 5 Mets 4 (9-10) 2 ½ GB the Marlins
Philadelphia - *ESPN Sunday Night Game of the Week ... Chase Utley remains on fire as he hits 2 homers and knocks in 4 RBIs. He has now homered in four straight games and leads the majors with 8 on the season ... Pedro Feliz hits a pinch-hit homerun in the 8th to put the Phils on top for good ... Adam Eaton pitches five outstanding innings but then gets clubbed for 4 runs in the 6th before being lifted ... Brad Lidge pitches the 9th for his 3rd save of the year. Stuff: The Phillies and fans honored the life of Philly favorite John Marzano before the game with a moment of silence ... Jimmy Rollins was officially placed on the 15 day DL with a left ankle sprain. It is the first trip to the DL in his 8 year career ... Both Manager Charlie Manuel and Assistant GM Ruben Amaro Jr. admit that keeping Rollins off the DL till now was a mistake but stated that Rollins didn't know how bad he was hurt ... The Mets series sets a Citizens Bank Park record for the highest attendance for a three game set with 135,478 fans coming through the turnstiles.*

"Lost too young, too soon. A funny guy with a heart of gold. RIP." – A Blogger on MLB.com on the death of John Marzano

SOUTH PHILADELPHIA (AP) - April 20, 2008 -- Former Major Leaguer and sports broad-caster John Marzano has died at the age of 45. Marzano, a native of South Philadelphia, was found dead inside his home on Passyunk Avenue.

As the news filtered out today that John Marzano had died, my family and the rest of Phila-delphia were deeply shocked and saddened. "Johnny Marz" was a special part of the baseball community in Philly as well as a special part of our own family. One could easily tell that John was an extraordinary man whose passion for baseball and the Phillies was reflective of his passion for life and his daily desire to live it to the fullest. He was Rocky, Richie Ashburn, Frank Rizzo and the Liberty Bell all wrapped up into one. John Marzano was a special gift to the city, his friends and to his family.

John Robert Marzano was born on February 14, 1963. A standout ballplayer from Central High School he went on to play college ball at Temple University in the

Johnny Marzano talking up a storm with his ex-skipper Lou Piniella

city that he loved. In 1984 he was drafted in the first round by the Boston Red Sox and was also selected to play on the silver medal-winning Olympic baseball team. He loved playing baseball and was one of the few fortunate ones to play in the majors for an extended period of time (1987 – 1998). Once he retired from professional baseball, Marzano's natural gift of gab and likeability drew him into the media spotlight. Phillies fans know him mostly from his time on *Phillies Post Game Live* where he spoke from his heart every night what the Fightin's were doing right or wrong. Later on he became a regular guest on 610-WIP sports radio, *Daily News Live* and *Comcast SportsNet*.

Unfortunately John's success stole him away from Philadelphia as he was destined for bigger and brighter things. For two years Marzano worked for MLB.com as the co-host of *"Leading Off"*. I missed not seeing him on Comcast or on the radio, but you just knew that Marzano personality was too rich and infectious to be limited to the Philly market. Everyone knew that Marzano would one day rule the baseball airwaves across the county.

The closest I ever came to meeting John in person was last week before the April 11th game with the Cubs. As I was taking pre-game photos for the book I saw Marzano standing around the batting cage talking to a few of the Cubs players. A few minutes went by when Cubs manager Lou Piniella came in from the outfield and walked directly over to John with outstretched arms and a huge smile on his face. "Sweet Lou", best known for his swings with his bat and his fists, gave his former catcher with the Seattle Mariners a bear hug that would have taken the breath out of any one of us. They embraced for a few moments and then exchanged pleasantries. Not many people can get Piniella to smile but John Marzano ain't just any people. One could tell that Piniella, the prototypical crusty old manager, loved being around Marzano. They laughed and talked for a good ten minutes and then went their separate ways. Lou, walked away with a big smile on his face and Marzano walked away looking for his next "victim" with an outstretched hand and that face-wide grin that he always seemed to be wearing.

Leslie Gudel, a co-host with Marzano at *Comcast SportsNet* said the following: *"I worked many a nights with John Marzano and there wasn't one that went by that wasn't full of laughter. There also wasn't a night that I didn't learn something about baseball from him. John loved the game, he loved people and he loved Philadelphia. He epitomized Philadelphia sports. You knew when he entered a room and when he left... it's just a terrible tragedy that he's now gone forever."*

Phillies President Dave Montgomery released a statement shortly upon hearing of the death of John. *"The Phillies family is saddened by the news of John Marzano's untimely death. John was an endeared member of the Philadelphia sports community who not only represented our city well as both an athlete and a broadcaster, but also had incredible passion for the games we play. Our deepest condolences go out to the Marzano family at this difficult time."*

While the wound is still fresh and the grief is great, we will mourn for John and his loss for a time and then move on with our lives. But we will be the poorer for having lost one of Philadelphia's treasures. The entire city of Philadelphia and baseball fans everywhere give their heartfelt condolences to his wife Terri, his daughters Dominique and Danielle and his two grandchildren. They love him as we do too.

Someone once said "You don't get to choose how you're going to die or when. You can only decide how you're going to live." John Marzano chose to live his life with an unmatched passion for his fellow man and the game of baseball.

Quotable: "Chase Utley is a very, very, very tough player. I've been in the game a long time, and he's as tough as any player I've seen. I'm talking about old throwback players, guys like Pete Rose and Kirby Puckett. You could put Utley in that category. He could play with any of them." - Charlie Manuel before last night's game

Monday, April 21st - Phillies 9 Rockies 5 (10-10) 2 ½ GB the Marlins

Denver - *Carlos Ruiz hit a bases-loaded double in the 8th inning that scored two runs and put the Phils in front for good. Chase Utley hit his 9th HR of season and in doing so tied a Phillies team record with homeruns in five straight games. He is the third Phillies player to do so joining Mike Schmidt (July 6-10, 1979) and Dick Allen (May 27-June 1, 1969) ...Pat Burrell goes 3 for 4 raising his average to .364. He hit his 7th homerun of the season and now has 19 RBIs ... Jayson Werth belted his first career inside-the-park homerun ... Kyle Kendrick pitched poorly allowing 5 runs on 8 hits in 5 innings however, a late offensive rally and four scoreless innings from the bullpen picked him up as the Phils win the first game of the series against the team that swept them three games to zero is last year's playoffs. Following the game Charlie Manuel stated, "Pay back! Any time when you get into the playoffs and a team wins three games in a row, you've got to prove you can beat them!"*

As Director of Entertainment, Chris Long is responsible for all of the on-field programming that happens each and every night at Citizens Bank Park. Getting the right singer for the National Anthem, coordinating any special events on the field, recognition ceremonies, throwing out the first ball. If it's happening on the field and it's not directly related to Charlie Manuel's team then Chris is the one in charge.

It's a stressful job but one that also seems to have a lot of perks. She gets to talk to all of the recording artists, celebrities, athletes, coaches, broadcasters, high school students and any other special guest stars that go on the field. Kind of like the person in charge of the green room of the Jay Leno show but tougher because she does it in front of a live audience of 40,000+ Phillies fans almost every night.

Chris Long preps the Phanatic during pre-game activities

I've been fortunate enough to meet literally hundreds of famous people since I started with the Phillies back in 1971. There are a few that really stick out to me over the years.

Charles Barkley is probably one of the ones I think that I've really enjoyed meeting the most. He has a reputation in Philadelphia that isn't necessarily a positive one, but I was very impressed with him. I never saw him turn down an autograph request. He took every picture that was asked of him. He was friendly and very outgoing. He never said no to anybody about anything when he was here. He's also very funny and it was kind of fun just hanging around him.

I was able to meet the entire Happy Days All-Star softball team when they came to the Vet back in the mid-70s. I think the TV show was near the peak of its popularity back then. I really enjoyed meeting Henry Winkler (The Fonz), Ron Howard (Ritchie) and Erin Moran (Joanie). They were all friendly and down to earth people. You could tell they just enjoyed being with each other and playing softball. They ended up playing a Philadelphia media celebrity team. I don't remember who was on the media team or who won the game but the fans really enjoyed it and I did as well.

Danny DeVito was here last season and he was an absolute joy. He's on the TV sitcom *It's Always Sunny in Philadelphia* (FX Network) so he and the show's creator, Rob McElhenny were in Philly filming for their show and we had them come over to throw out the first pitch. Nothing was too much trouble for DeVito. He was game for everything that we asked him to do. He had fun. He danced on the Phillies dugout with the Phanatic. He was just pleasant and a joy to be around the entire time.

Meatloaf. What an especially nice man. As a matter of fact the last time he was here his agent contacted us about having him come and asked if he could sing the National Anthem. I told them he couldn't since we had already had it booked. So I said what we could do is have him sing *"Take Me Out To The Ball Game"* during the 7th inning and he could have some fun with that. They agreed and everything was set. So we went out and started publicizing his coming to the ballpark to sing. However, when they got to the ballpark his agent told me that he couldn't sing because he had laryngitis. I wouldn't have cared if we hadn't told the media about it but fans were going to be coming to the game to hear him sing. So I finally said to the agent "Could we at least just introduce him? He doesn't have to sing, but can we just let people know he's here because we talked about it on air and I don't want it to appear as though we were falsely advertising, talking about it." So his agent goes over and talks to Meatloaf who then turns around and waves me over. We sit down together and he says, "Now tell me what the situation is". So I told him and I said, "You know we thought it was so definite that we wanted people to know that you were going to be here and they are looking forward to it." And I said, "If you wouldn't mind just being introduced." And he said, "What do you want me to do?" I said "I want you to feel comfortable." And he said "What do YOU want me to do?" I said "I would love to have you sing "Take Me Out To The Ballgame"." He said "Well, then you've got it". So he went down on the field in the 7th inning and he sang a little bit of the song and then he would talk a little bit of the song then start singing it again so that he wouldn't strain his voice anymore than it was. But he kept the commitment and it turned out just fine.

Last season I was able to met Billy Paul and he came out and sang "Me & Mrs. Jones". I absolutely enjoyed seeing him perform it live. We've also have had a lot of the singers that helped make Philadelphia famous. We've had the Soul Survivors, Boyz II Men, Bunny Sigler and of course Kenny Gamble and Leon Huff who were the pioneers of Philadelphia Soul. We are fortunate to have some incredible performers in our own backyard.

Most of the time everything works out well with the entertainers, the singers and with the other events that we have on the field. But I think the biggest flub that I ever experienced was back in the early 1980s. We used to have a lot of individual singers performing the anthem back then and many of them came from community and corporate groups who purchased a lot of tickets and they would have a person from their organization come to the game and sing the anthem. One corporation had this lovely, lovely woman who had sent us an audition tape that sang just beautifully. So she gets out on the field and she sings "Oh say can you see…" and then she took a breath and she looked at me and she says "Oh Lordy I forgot the words!". So she then says to me "Can I start again?" And I said "Sing, just sing!". So she started again and she was still having problems and I can see she was like a deer in headlights so I began to sing with her hoping that she would remember the words. Then the crowd must have recognized that she was in trouble so almost in unison began to sing with her as well. Eventually she finally got past the stage fright and was able to finish the song on her own but the crowd finished it with her and gave her a huge ovation. She was wonderful but it was definitely a moment.

Quotable: "Usually that happens in June." – Pat Burrell on the team going over .500 for the first time this season.

Tuesday, April 22nd - Phillies 9 Rockies 6 (11-10) 1 ½ GB the Marlins

Denver - Great come from behind victory as Pat Burrell hits a bases loaded, 3-run double in the 9th that gives the Phillies the win and the sweep of the two game series at Coors Field … Chase Utley drove in 2 runs on 2 hits but failed to hit a homerun breaking his consecutive streak of homering in 5 straight games … Brad Lidge pitched the 9th and recorded his 4th save of the season. Stuff: It was the team's sixth come-from-behind victory of the season. Last season the Phils led all MLB teams with 48 come-from-behind victories … Burrell leads the National League in RBIs with 22, which tied him for the most RBIs in the month of April in Phillies' team history … The Phils are over .500 for the first time this season. It marked the first time since April 21, 2005, that the team was over .500 in April. Last season the team didn't go have a winning record until May 16th.

Somewhat lost after Pat Burrell's 9th-inning heroics last night was the key run the Phillies scored in the 8th to cut the Rockies lead to 6-5. It was driven in by Greg Dobbs' pinch-single, which continued a remarkable April run by Phillies pinch-hitters.

Through 21 games, Phils' pinch-hitters have put up the following line: .316/.381/.579. They've blasted three home runs (Snelling, Dobbs, Feliz) and knocked in 8. Dobbs (4 for 9, HR, 5 RBI) is leading the charge, but eight Phillies have hits off the bench, including Cole Hamels and, alas, Jimmy Rollins.

Pat Burrell's assets has made him a fan favorite for many of the ladies in left field

The Phils lead the league in pinch-hitting by an absurd margin. The next-best team in terms of triple-slash numbers is the Braves, with a .219/.306/.406 mark through the early going. The rest of the NL has four pinch-homers to the Phils' 3. Dobbs has as many or more pinch-hits than five NL teams.

In today's *Inquirer*, Phillies subs give Charlie Manuel--a bench guy himself in his playing days--credit for knowing which late-game buttons to push. But Manuel's late-game "strategery"

--never previously considered one of his strong suits as a manager--has another dimension as well.

The Phillies' bullpen leads the NL with a 2.76 ERA, 32 points better than the Marlins, who have the next-best figure.

Now, they haven't been perfect, as four losses clearly indicate. And they've walked 35. And I'm pretty sure the collective relief ERA won't stay below 3. But there's also reason to believe this early success represents something real, not just early-season illusion. Collectively, the Phils' relievers have pitched 65.1 IP, the third-fewest in the league. The starters--who, as a group, have been middle-of-the-pack--generally have gone deep enough into games not to overburden the bullpen. Chad Durbin (10 games, 14 IP) and J.C. Romero (10 games, 9.2 IP) have borne the heaviest workloads, but Durbin as a former starter and Romero as a situational guy are probably better prepared to handle that than any other players in the 'pen.

Manuel's deployment of these relievers has been superb. After Tom Gordon got crushed on Opening Day, Manuel didn't lose faith in him, and since that inauspicious season debut, Flash has been mostly excellent (2.45 ERA, 10 K/3 BB in 7.1 IP). Brad Lidge--whose injury the Phillies handled as well as they botched Rollins'--has started to show why he was considered the league's most dominant closer three years ago. New pickup Rudy Seanez has walked seven, but still has a spotless ERA.

The line on Manuel, and certainly my take on him, has been that he's a good manager overall for his work in the clubhouse, but that he's far from a master strategist between the white lines. His use of the bench and bullpen through the early going in 2008, though, suggests that either he's been very lucky through the first 21 games, or that we've severely under-rated him.

Quotable: "In his last at-bat, I got him out with pitches away. I wanted to avoid his strong zone. I was hoping that he would roll over or miss. But I hung it up there. He's a great hitter." - Cole Hamels on Milwaukee's Prince Fielder, who entered the game with only one homerun in 68 at-bats this season, got two today off of him today

Wednesday, April 23rd - Brewers 5 Phillies 4 (11-11) 2 ½ GB the Marlins
Milwaukee - Prince Fielder's 2nd homerun of the game off of Cole Hamels in the 8th gives Milwaukee the come from behind victory... Hamels (2-3) gave up 3 runs in the 1st inning and then went on to retire 20 of the next 25 batters, striking out 11 in 7 1/3rd innings until Fielder's 2-run blast ... Hamels had started the 8th inning after having thrown 120 pitches, leaving some to question Manuel's decision to keep him in after the 7th; however Manuel made the decision to leave him in the ballgame to face the heart of the Brewers lineup. Stuff: Utley's homerun was his Major League leading 10th of the season. With 21 RBIs and a .368 average, Utley is the early-on favorite to win the NL MVP ... Pat Burrell's Major League leading 23rd RBI of the season set a Phillies franchise

record for most RBIs by a batter in the month of April ...Utley and Burrell's combined HRs, RBIs and Slugging Percentage are the highest amongst any teammates in the majors this season. Through 22 games the pair have combined for 18 HR, 44 RBIs, and a 1.582 slugging percentage ...Greg Dobbs continued on his own hitting tear, going 2 for 3 with a homerun and 2 RBIs and is now batting .379 on the season ...Last November, Geoff Jenkins took out a full page ad in the Milwaukee Journal-Sentinel thanking Milwaukee fans for 10 good years with the Brewers. Before his first at bat in today's game the fans gave Jenkins a standing ovation. Classy guy. Classy fans.

Considered the lesser half of the right-field platoon before the season, outfielder Jayson Werth is making a strong case to remain in the starting lineup once Shane Victorino returns. Will Charlie Manuel forgo his lefty/righty system?

Werth is a little like "Pat Burrell Light." He's fleeter of foot, but shorter on power. Aside from that, the similarities run deep. They're both patient hitters. Werth leads the team with 4.7 pitches per plate appearance, and his blend of .391 OBP and speed makes perfect sense at the top of the lineup, especially against left-handed

Shane Victorino working his way back off of the disabled list

pitching. Like Burrell, he's a big, imposing threat from the right side. His four homers and nine RBIs put him well on pace for a career year.

Charlie Manuel faces a tough decision once Shane Victorino re-enters the mix. Vic figures to return to the top of the lineup since Manuel values speed there, but which Victorino will we see? His defense has been brilliant, but he's stumbled at the plate. Meanwhile, Geoff Jenkins, who figured to start most games in right field, has so far knocked in only three runs this season, sinking the offense with his low 55 OPS. The fact of the matter is Jenkins has been nothing special offensively since midway through the 2007 season.

The other developing situation is at third where Manuel may be starting to weigh the offensive limitations of Pedro Feliz and his early 67 OPS. Greg Dobbs, who appears to be more handicapped against left-handers than Werth against right-handers, is a fastball hitter and poor defender who benefits from the anonymity of irregular playing time. However, the book on Feliz, a high-fastball hitter himself, is a mile long, and he's totting an early .608 OPS against righties. Meanwhile, Dobbs has made the most of his 34 plate appearances, reasserting himself as one of the league's top pinch hitters.

Quotable: "He looks like the guy I saw as a starter in Kansas City eons ago ... and the guy that I saw as a teammate in Boston ... and the guy that I saw as an opposing pitcher when he was in New York. He's locked in. He's healthy. He's working hard pre-game and he's got a lot of confidence." - Jamie Moyer on Tom Gordon who bailed Moyer out of a two-on, no out jam in the 7th inning.

Thursday, April 24th - Phillies 3 Brewers 1 (12-11) 1 ½ GB the Marlins

Milwaukee - Pat Burrell continues hitting like Ted Williams going 1 for 2 with the game winning two-run double in the 8th, his 24th and 25th RBIs of the season ... Chase Utley goes 3 for 4 raising his average to .385 ... Jamie Moyer goes six strong innings allowing 1 run on 8 hits but gets into trouble in the 7th. Entering the game with runners on first and third, Tom Gordon helps Moyer out by shutting down the Brewers with a gutsy performance as he strikes out two and gets Brewer's center fielder Gabe Kapler to ground out to end the inning. Gordon's ERA since his Opening Day melt down is 2.16 in eight appearances ... Lidge allows one hit in the 9th and gets his 5th save of the season. ... Stuff: Ryan Howard doesn't start the game in the midst of a major slump in which he is batting .181 with 32 strikeouts through the first 22 games of the season. However, Manuel pinch hits him in the 8th and he ends up going 0 for 2 striking out both times and ending the day even lower with a batting average of .176 ... In talking about his slump after the game Howard says, "You know, you can call my mom and she'll tell you that I've never hit good in April." ... Jimmy Rollins is taking batting practice in Florida as he continues to rehab his ankle. Shane Victorino continues his rehab on his right calf strain as he is assigned to the Reading Phillies (AA). He hit .400 (2 for 5) in Single A Clearwater in two games.

"One of the very nicest things about life is the way we must regularly stop whatever it is we are doing and devote our attention to eating." ~Luciano Pavarotti

Back in the days when Steve Carlton still occasionally pitched a complete game or two, dinner at a Phillies game consisted of a few cold hot dogs, a stale box of popcorn and some semi-congealed cheese that covered about 15 tortilla chips. We would all wash it down with a flat soda and then baby-sit our stomachs with Mylanta for the rest of the ballgame because that was the best that we were going to get with regards to eats at the ballpark.

Tony Luke IIIrd sizzles up the best steaks in Philadelphia on Ashburn Alley

For better or worse, those days back at the Vet have gone the way of the screwball and the twi-night doubleheader. When the Phillies were planning out the new park they not only placed their efforts into ensuring that the field dimensions and the look of the stadium were right, they also focused on improving the food experience as well. They realized that fans just didn't want a great ballpark, but they wanted a complete experience centered around a great team and great food.

In Chicago, the cornerstone food is their deep dish pizza. In Pittsburgh it's their pierogies. In Milwaukee it's the sausage. In Philly ... the food that helped put us on the map. The cheese steak!

The best cheese steak in the ballpark, let alone Philadelphia, comes from Tony Lukes'. A winner of *Philadelphia Magazine's* "Best of Philly Award" so many times that the magazine inducted them into the Best of Philly Hall-of-Fame, Tony Lukes still continues to impress palettes across the city and the country. Located smack dab in the middle of Ashburn Alley, Tony Lukes is to cheesesteaks as Jimmy Rollins is to major league shortstops. None are better. With its "mother" location less than 5 minutes from the ballpark on Front & Oregon Avenues in South Philly, Tony Lukes has brought its magic over to Citizens Bank Park under the care and direction of 27 year old Anthony Lucidonio 3rd or "LT (Little Tony)" as he is known to his friends.

Little Tony was born and raised in South Philadelphia at Front and McKean Street. After spending his high school years in Glassboro, NJ, Tony moved back to Philly and helped his family open up Tony Lukes in South Philly in 1992. He's been running Tony Lukes at Citizens Bank Park since it opened in 2003.

What's on your menu at the ballpark?
We keep it very limited here. You can get a cheese steak with American cheese, sharp provolone or Cheez Whiz. You can also get our famous roast pork sandwich. You can get that plain, with sharp provolone or Italian style with the broccoli rabe on the side. We also sell some finely seasoned curly French fries.

What's the most popular way the steaks are ordered?
It's actually kind of a toss up. It's a different mixture every day. I want to say that people tend to always go with the same thing, but some days I find that it's the American cheese steaks that are moving, and then another day I can't stop selling sharp provolone steaks. The other day I ran out of Cheez Whiz. It all depends on what kind of mood the customers are in, but the steaks are the big seller for us.

Let's say tonight you have a sellout at the ballpark. How many sandwiches are you going to sell, cheese steaks and roast pork combined?
On our busiest nights we sell up to 1400 sandwiches. Our record for a game is 1,525 sandwiches. There was a rain delay and it made the game a little bit longer than usual but that was our record. That was a very long day. On average though we probably sell about 1,200 of them. 80% of them will be some type of cheesesteak and the other 20% will be our roast pork sandwich.

Anybody from Philadelphia knows that the secret to any good sandwich or steak are the rolls. What type of rolls does Tony Lukes use?
We get all of our rolls from Liscio's in Glassboro, NJ. The big difference in what we do with the rolls that others don't do is that we actually bake our bread at each of our locations. Every

15-20 minutes we're baking bread in our stores. For the ballpark, the bakery does bake it prior to the game for us and they deliver it right to us. It's just easier that way because we don't have any ovens here in the stadium. But if we need rolls I just pick up the phone and have the guys at Oregon Ave ship a load of fresh hot bread for us so we can keep the customers filled.

Why do you think Tony Luke's has the best steaks in Philadelphia if not the world?
We're really crazy about our steaks and I know we have a lot of devoted fans. I think it's the quality and the love we put into our sandwiches. We don't pre-make our food. When you come to our store you might have to wait 5 minutes for a sandwich but that's one of the differences between us and the other cheesesteak places. We're not McDonald's. You don't pull up, get your sandwich and go. When you place your order you get exactly what you ordered and we give it to you the way you want it, fresh and hot.

Who is the most famous customer you ever served here at the ballpark?
Kevin James from the King of Queens TV show. He came here last year with his fiancé. He was such a great guy. Apparently he's the biggest Mets fan in the world so he came up to our window during a Mets game and sat right next to the store and ate his cheesesteak. He loved it. What was really nice to see was that he came up and ordered it himself just like any normal guy would. He didn't send anybody to go get it for him.

Do any of the Phillies ever eat your cheesesteaks?
We actually do feed the bullpen a lot. A lot of the players in the bullpen really like our sandwiches. We sometimes get orders during the game! A good friend of mine works security. He lets me know if somebody wants something and as soon as they want something we deliver. Whatever helps our Phillies go all the way, I'll gladly feed them. Ryan Madson orders them a lot. Occasionally we will do a special run up to Harry Kalas and the guys in the Press Box. They told me that they enjoy them immensely.

Any comment on Dollar Dog Nights at the ballpark?
I think Dollar Dog Nights makes the ballpark very exciting. The crowd comes and they really know how to have a lot of fun. They really enjoy themselves. As far as for us it might affect us a little bit at the cash register but not drastically. It doesn't affect us enough where we're like "oh no, its Dollar Dog Night." We don't feel it that much because there are so many people in this ballpark. There's enough food in here for everybody. I mean every food location in the park can sell out everyday if they wanted to, that's how many people come to see the Phillies play.

What do you like best about your job?
I love dealing with the people and I love seeing people enjoy our food. You wouldn't think someone could get so much enjoyment out of seeing people eat but I do. If somebody's having a bad day and all they're looking forward to is getting a Tony Luke's sandwich and then they come here and bite into that sandwich ... you can see the happiness on their face ... I love seeing that!

What one thing would your customers be surprised to find out about Tony Luke's?
That we're only 15 years old. Customers can't believe it. I actually have people come up to me

and they tell me how much they enjoy the food and how they've been eating here for 25 years. I don't say anything because I really appreciate the fact that they like eating with us. I think it's because they appreciate the quality of the food. It's that reason why we've become such a Philadelphia landmark.

Quotable: "I felt like, at the start of the game, he didn't have a whole lot. Through three innings, he did make a pitch when he had to. In the fourth, they were hitting the ball hard, and I thought they were catching up to him." - Charlie Manuel on why he pulled Adam Eaton in the 4th inning.

<u>Friday, April 25th - Phillies 6 Pirates 5   (13-11) 1 ½ GB the Marlins</u>
Pittsburgh - The Phillies hung on to win their 5th game in their last 6 decisions at PNC Park in Pittsburgh ... Adam Eaton was hit hard, lasting only 3 2/3rd innings and giving up 3 runs on 5 hits ... The bullpen was able to hold off the Pirates allowing 2 runs in the final 5 1/3rd innings. ... Tom Gordon (2-2) earned his second win in as many nights and Brad Lidge recorded his 6th save of the season ...Chris Coste, back from a bout with the flu, went 3 for 5 with 3 RBIs ... Jayson Werth hit a solo homerun, his 4th in the last 5 games. Stuff: Australian native Brad Harmon made his first major league start at second base and got his first hit and RBI of his career as he went 1 for 3 on the day. Harmon was called up from AA Reading when Rollins went on the DL.

Located directly behind the Phillies Press box on the Hall of Fame Level of the ballpark is the Media Dining facility. It is a state-of-the-art cafeteria that caters to the hungry hoards of press, visiting team employees and full-time Phillies employees that work at the park each game.

The media pays $10 for an all-you-can eat buffet that includes a salad bar, two to three main entrees, veggies and sides. And when you are done with your meal you get to down as much hand-dipped

Heidi Alexander (far right) and her team have been noted as one of the best media kitchens in all of baseball

Turkey Hill ice cream that your stomach can hold. For 10 bucks no one is going to find a better selection of incredibly tasty food than what is served out of Heidi Alexander's kitchen.

Heidi is the Wolfgang Puck of her domain. Originally from Heidelberg, Germany, Heidi moved to the United States with her husband when she was 24 years old. Today she runs the kitchen with an iron hand and an extremely tender heart. You can't miss Heidi. She's the one in the back with the spatula in her hand ensuring that everyone is getting a great tasting meal and taking on anyone who has anything bad to say about it!

A lot of people get mad at me. I'm very outspoken. What you see is what you get. And I know when somebody is bulls***ing me. A lot of people don't want the responsibility. They sit there and complain all the time. I try to make it a little fun. And then I look at the people… they eat and their plates are clean. I guess we're doing a good job.

I've been in the press kitchen for 27 years now. Boy could I tell you about some stories but I'm not going to get into those now. There used to be another German lady that ran the kitchen whose name was JoAnna. She was looking for somebody part-time that would work five hours a day so I applied for the position and got the job.

Never in my life would I have thought that I might wind up working in a kitchen. Never. I hate to cook. I swear it's the truth. My mother was always a good teacher. She would say to me, "Heidi, come over here to the stove, look and listen." She always was trying to get me to cook but I would tell her that I couldn't and that I was going to be sick. But now I love what I do here. My mother is probably laughing now saying, "Oh I got you!"

Richie Ashburn used to love my pork chops. I knew him for a long time. He was one of the nicest people you could ever meet. He always treated everybody the same. In the old place (at the Vet) he would come in and order and tell us it was such an honor to eat here.

I've been told that some say that this is the best media dining room in baseball. I don't know if that's true. I just always tell everybody we have to treat everybody the same. I don't care this one has more money or if this one has less. I don't kiss anybody's behind. We're all equal. I mean you have to treat people nice. You don't necessarily have to like them. You can go in the back and tell them to go s*** on themselves.

But people like it here. It's like home to them. My old boss used to tell me that I'm too fussy when it comes to cooking the meals. I don't like this and I don't like that. But I told her you have to consider everyone who is eating their meals here. You have to cook a little bit of what everybody likes because a lot of people have (medical) problems. We use a lot of season but don't use a lot of salt. The only time we use salt is when we cook the spaghetti or if we drop something on the floor.

We have six ovens in the back. Tomorrow I have to cook 100 pounds of ground beef. On average we serve about 300 people a game, sometimes more. It depends what teams are here at the park. When the Mets come to town, we love it. They eat anything. They really clean us out. They tip well too.

For tonight's game we'll probably make 250 pork chops. You won't need a knife to eat them, that's how good we make our food. Some things I make from scratch. Other things do come pre-prepared. But for the pork chops they come in frozen. I'll boil them first and when that's done I'll sear them on the grill. After grilling I put them all in a pan and top them with a chicken-based liquid. I then bake them in the oven. They come out so tender and everybody loves them. We have a lot of good stuff. Another favorite is "Heidi's Barbeque Chicken". It's all made from scratch. They love it.

We have 9-10 people working here each game. We're like a family. We don't like each other sometimes. We get mad but then we're still together. You don't see this too often anymore. When we hire someone we make sure that we teach them how to do everything in the kitchen. It's a big happy family and we have to know how to help each other out. That way if anyone ever leaves and goes someplace else they can say that they had a really good teacher.

After the interview with Heidi we were joined by some of the cafeteria workers that are part of her team. Anita, Nick, Sharon, Carol and Brody spent some time talking about some of their favorite visitors to the Media Dining Facility.

Tommy Lasorda is one of the nicest ones who come through here. He was here for Italian night. He really enjoyed it and loves the food here. I think what he and most of the other people who eat here enjoy is the variety that we give them.

From what I understand some of the media food at the other parks is really bad so when they come here it's a treat for them. A lot of people I talked to said that all they give them is hot dogs, soda and a bag of chips. There are a lot of places that don't have the selection that we have. A lot of places will have spaghetti night and the only choice you get is spaghetti. On fish night you get fish. Nothing else. I guess you had better like what they're putting out because that's all you'll be seeing.

One time the Atlanta broadcast team actually thanked us on the air for the food that we made one night. They said that we were by far the best in baseball. That made us feel good.

We get famous people eating here as well who are at the park. Vanna White and Pat Sajak were here one time from the *Wheel of Fortune*. Vince Papale of the Eagles (and the film "Invincible") was here just the other night.

Bob Uecker is another who loves coming here. He is always so gracious to us. He's probably the biggest tipper. Every time he walks through line he leaves us $20 dollars. He'll come with his sunglasses on and he'll do autographs. He won't turn anyone down. He's also a big teddy bear.

Tony Gwynn enjoys coming here as well. He likes the ice cream station with all the different types of selections that we provide. He'll sometimes come back twice. Bob Gibson was another one who came in here and was surprised at how nice everything was.

John Vukovich is still one of our all time favorite players to come in here. He was always considerate and caring. There was one time that he came here and brought in about 20 Bobby Chez crab cakes for everyone just because he wanted us to try them. He was just a happy guy, a friendly guy. Last year Dallas Green came in and gave everyone corn from his farm. It's nice when other people think about you and do something kind like that.

Quotable: ""It felt pretty good. Today I felt a little better at the plate, seeing pitches and kind of running the count a little bit deep." - Ryan Howard on his 5th homer of the season, his second since April 12th

<u>Saturday, April 26th - Phillies 8 Pirates 4 (14-11) ½ GB the Marlins</u>

Pittsburgh - *After sitting out the past two games Ryan Howard came out in the first inning and ripped a two-run homerun which highlighted a five-run first for the Phillies. It was Howard's 5th HR of the season. He had only six hits in the 12 games since his last homerun. He entered the game hitless in his last nine at bats ... Geoff Jenkins went 2 for 5 with an RBI ... Chase Utley went 2 for 4 and scored two runs. He has now scored a run in 10 consecutive games ... Kyle Kendrick (2-2) pitched seven strong innings allowing 4 runs (3 earned) to secure his first win since April 4th ... Rudy Seanez and Ryan Madson pitched two scoreless innings and lowered the Phillies' bullpen ERA to a National League leading 2.58 ERA. Stuff: Since Opening Day, when the bullpen allowed 7 runs in 4 innings, they have put together a nifty 1.86 ERA (15 ER in 72 2/3rd innings) against their opponents ... Charlie Manuel has used 19 different lineups in the first 25 games of the season ... With the win the Phillies have guaranteed themselves their first winning April since 2003 when they went 15-12.*

For Phillies fans, Tommy "Programs" is the one vendor you won't miss walking through Ashburn Alley or traveling up your aisle late in a game. He's the guy you can easily hear screaming over the crowds of fans at the top of his lungs, "Proooogramms, Scorecards, Yearrrrr-booooooks!!!"

The best hawker of Programs and Yearbooks in the nation, Tommy Payne

The fact is that the self-named Tommy Programs, whose real name is Tommy Payne, also entertains and livens up the Citizen Bank Park crowds with his theatrics and sense of humor. His incomparable selling skills only add to the experience.

I grew up in Olney ... five blocks from the Fern Rock transportation center where I jumped the Phillies Express subway line as a kid. I live in Manayunk now; people joke that I am the unofficial Mayor of Manayunk. I know everybody, shake a lot of hands etc. I also speak very highly of the area; it is one of the best parts of the city.

I started selling programs back in 2001 so I'm now in my 8th season still going strong. I usually lie about my age. Let's just say that I'm too old to be running around in red baseball socks and a uniform selling programs so I don't like admitting my age. I'm old enough to have been alive when they won the World Series but young enough to not be able to stand in front of the TV to watch it.

Usually I'll sell anywhere from 100 to 200 programs per game and probably 20 to 25 year-books. But by far the hottest selling item that I sell are the Phillies team photo cards. One day back at Veteran's Stadium I was tired of lugging around the programs and yearbooks during one of those long dog days of summer. When I went into the stock room to get more programs I noticed a set of what looked like postcards. The Phillies had always produced these over-sized baseball card sets but nobody really promoted them. They were light so I figured I could easily carry a hundred or so of them around with me so I threw them in my bag and started selling them that day. Last season I sold over 10,000 sets.

By far my best day of selling was the last game at the Vet. Everybody wanted a "Final In-nings" program. People were buying cases from me. I actually continued to sell them well after the game was over and literally sold them at the entrance to the subway as fans were going home. It was quite a night.

The most famous person I ever sold a program to was John Ritter (Three's Company fame). He moved his son into a dorm at the University of Pennsylvania and that night he took his family to the Vet to watch a Phils' game. He was sitting on the first base line and I came up the aisle selling the programs. I was in a mood. I was using every line I had in my arsenal that night. After my "Lots of pictures and no big words" line he flagged me over. I didn't realize it was him at first but after he told me who he was I just sat down next to him and talked to him for about a half hour. As I left, I asked him to sign a program for me that I treasure to this day. A week later he passed away. I felt bad for his son. I hope he still has that program that I sold to his father so he can look at it and remember the good time he had with his father that night. He went way too early.

God gives everybody something special; I got a really loud voice. To be able to sell programs at a ballpark you have to have one of those great big booming "barker" voices. Growing up, my mom would attest to the fact that my voice got me into a lot of trouble, but it also gave me the opportunity to play the lead in a bunch of school plays. People ask me a lot at the ballpark if I get hoarse, lose my voice etc. Thankfully I don't, some days I really push it when something special is being promoted and I pull a muscle in my diaphragm, no DL for the program guy though, I suck it up.

Quotable: "I haven't seen a fastball … He topped out at 89 (mph). He's usually 92-94, 92-95. I haven't seen the fastball since the start of the year." - Charlie Manuel, after a ten minute closed door session with Myers after the game.

Sunday, April 27th - Pirates 5 Phillies 1 (14-12) 1 ½ GB the Marlins
Pittsburgh - *Brett Myers (2-2, 5.11 ERA) only lasted five innings allowing 4 runs on 8 hits, includ-ing two homeruns by Pirates' center fielder Nate McLouth. Myers' fastball generated some concern*

with the coaching staff as it only topped out at 89 mph on the radar gun ... Pirates' starter Paul Maholm (2-2 3.26 ERA) pitched a complete game 2 hitter ... Pat Burrell doubled in the 5th and Eric Bruntlett singled him in for the Phillies lone run and the only two hits of the game. Stuff: Rudy Seanez (2-1, 1.00 ERA) gave up his first run of the season in the 6th after pitching 8 previous scoreless innings ... Shane Victorino was activated off of the DL. The Phils sent down T.J. Bohn back down to AAA ... The Phils went 5-2 on their 7 game road trip.

Following another sheepish start, featuring high-80s cheese, Myers was reportedly called into the boss's office for a closed-door session. Then, pitching coach Rich Dubee suggested the right-hander isn't taking the right approach on the mound, but also isn't participating in enough long-tossing, which Dubee believes is an essential step in building and maintaining arm strength. Indeed, Myers' fastball has been MIA this season, rarely hitting 90s on the gun. Myers was hit hard continuing a trend of puzzling starts, rampant head scratching and universal frustration. "When will Myers get it," fans wonder?

Coach Rich Dubee and Gary Matthews discuss the pitching staff as Jamie Moyer stretches his 45 year old body

The Phillies wish it was as simple as having Brett pick up a baseball at 4:30 p.m. on an off day and throw it 90 feet to Mick Billmeyer. Dubee says a better approach and more long tossing are needed. I'm not sure Myers has accepted his reassignment to the starting rotation and all that comes with it – the prep work, the focus. He's a closer trying to cut it in the rotation, content to mix it up with a couple different looks instead of taking a patient approach, establishing a rhythm and setting a tone through seven innings.

His velocity is the other issue. The missing zip is alarming. Myers is a competitor and wants to pitch; if anyone would try to battle through bruises, it would be the former boxer on staff. It would be easy to put the situation squarely on the shoulders of Brett Myers, to make the adjustments and move on. On the other hand, it must be hard to shake the words "premier closer" from your head, especially when the Phillies were the ones repeating it.

Quotable: "That's good, but we're not done yet. What are we? 15-12. I want to do much better than that in May. We want to keep pace if not do better than the rest of our (division) and this is just a start." - Charlie Manuel on the Phillies finally having a winning April.

<u>Tuesday, April 29th - Phillies 7 Padres 4 (15-12) ½ GB the Marlins</u>

Philadelphia - *Cole Hamels (3-3, 2.70 ERA) gives up 2 runs in 7 1/3rd innings while striking out 6 and walking 2 as he picked up his first win since April 12th ... Padres' future Hall-of-Famer Greg Maddox is denied his 350th career victory as the Phillies drove in 7 runs on 12 hits ... Chase Utley goes 2 for 4 raising his batting average to .364 ... Stuff: Victorino pinch hit in the 9th (flew out) in his first game back from the DL ...the Elias Sports Bureau reports that the Phillies now have 15 wins in six straight months for the first time since July 1963 and August 1964.*

Cole Hamels has pitched at least seven innings in each of his first six starts, becoming the first Phillies pitcher to do so since Curt Schilling, who did it 11 times to begin 1998, according to the pre-game notes. In so many words it illustrates what a fine career Hamels has had, and also how long we've been deprived of a pitcher this good. In the past 30 years you can basically tout three stud pitchers in the organization: Steve Carlton, Curt Schilling and Cole Hamels.

Cole Hamels may one day join Robin Roberts, Jim Bunning and Steve Carlton in the Hall-of-Fame

Quotable: "Young pitched a good ballgame and we couldn't get to him. The fact that he's very deceptive and his fastball up has some ride on it, he looks like he's standing on top of you. He's aggressive and he'll give you something to hit, but we had trouble keeping up with him." - Charlie Manuel on Padres' starter Chris Young

<u>Wednesday, April 30th - Padres 4 Phillies 2 (15-13) ½ GB the Marlins</u>

Philadelphia - *The Padres' 6 foot 10 inch starter Chris Young scattered 5 hits in 6 innings of work allowing only 2 runs as the Phillies truly appeared unable to get anything started against the Padres the entire night ... Chase Utley connected for a 2-run homerun in the 1st (his Major League leading 11th of the season) for the Phils' only two runs of the game ... Geoff Jenkins had 3 of the Phillies 7 hits (3 for 4) to raise his average to .265 ... After Utley's homer the Phillies did not move any runners past second base for the remainder of the night ... Jamie Moyer (1-2 4.50 ERA) gave up 4 runs on 9 hits in 5 1/3rd innings of work. Stuff: The Phillies ended April with a winning record and ½ GB of the first place Florida Marlins. This was Charlie Manuel's first winning April in his four seasons as the Phillies' skipper (10-14 in 2005, 10-14 in 2006 & 11-14 in 2007) ... The Phillies set a franchise record by hitting 39 homeruns in April (they hit 2 in March). It broke their previous record of 29 homeruns that was set in 2006 ... The Phillies celebrated the 125th anniversary of their first game today. To commemorate the occasion the team had Maje McDonnell throw out the first ball. McDonnell joined the organization as a batting practice pitcher in 1948 when the team was only 65 years old!*

"It seems like when we make a change or two, it seems like we play a little better. In this period right now ... and I can't explain it ... we're missing Victorino, we're missing Rollins, we've played a lot better baseball. It's not because they're not in there. I can't give you the reason. It just seems like we've picked it up." - Phillies GM Pat Gillick

Behind Pat Burrell and Chase Utley, the Phillies finished April with a winning record and sitting in 3rd place only a ½ game behind the Marlins. With the team coming out of the gates slowly, as they usually do every April, the Phillies somehow managed a winning record even with the loss of MVP Rollins and catalyst Victorino. Much of the success in the first month of the season can directly be attributed to Charlie Manuel's timely moves in the lineup and pitching staff as well as with Pat Gillick's uncanny ability to pick up cast-off players that somehow manage to play to their original expectations.

The next 30 days could generate a whole new list of heroes and goats as the weather begins to warm up and teams learn more about their strengths and weaknesses. Don't be surprised when underachievers, like Ryan Howard, start hitting, and when overachievers, like Pat Burrell, cool off. (Burrell has already quietly cooled since the Pittsburgh series.)

Areas of legitimate concern: it looks like Carlos Ruiz can't hit left-handed pitching, and Pedro Feliz hasn't hit lefties since 2005. Ruiz is hitting

Pat the Bat is one of the main reasons the Phils ended April with a winning record

.167 against southpaws in 2008, dropping his career line to .197, and Feliz has an OPS below .670 against southpaws for the third year in a row. Eric Bruntlett is only a temporary measure (overstaying his welcome more than we'd like), but Ruiz and Feliz could literally and figuratively put the 'Zs' into the everyday lineup all season long.

Then there's Geoff Jenkins. It's been a good, long while since Jenkins got hot for a prolonged period of time, and at 33, that's a problem. Actually, since June of last season, he's been an average or below average hitter. But between Ruiz, Feliz and Jenkins, expect slight improvement over their terrible starts, especially Jenkins, who will definitely contribute more than four RBIs.

That leaves Rollins, Utley and Jayson Werth and Greg Dobbs and Chris Coste, in part-time roles, as the players I look toward for more of the same, Werth being the biggest surprise of this group. His discipline, clean bill of health and age lead me to believe this could be a breakout season. Coste isn't going to hit .400, but why shouldn't we expect .280-.300 with some pop? And as for So Taguchi, he's going to help this team sooner or later.

And maybe, just maybe, healthy, aggressive, studly Burrell, the one who earns my vote for Phillies' MVP so far, can keep up this torrid pace, or at least something close to it.

May - It's Hittin' Season...

Quotable: "He's eventually going to get hot, and maybe this is the start of it. It's just a matter of time before he gets to .200, then .250. He's too good of a player to be kept down too long." – Padres manager Bud Black on Ryan Howard

Thursday, May 1st - Phillies 3 Padres 2 (16-13) 1st Place - ½ GA of the Marlins & Mets

Philadelphia - Ryan Howard starts off the month of May with a bang hitting a game-winning solo homerun in the bottom of the 8th inning, helping to move the team into first place for the first time this season. He ends the night going 2 for 4 with 2 RBIs, raising his average up to .186 ... Brad Lidge came into the 9th and nailed down his 7th save in seven opportunities ... Adam Eaton came back from a poor pitching performance his last time out to throw 6 effective innings, giving up 2 runs ... The bullpen came through again with 3 scoreless innings with J.C. Romero pitching another 1/3rd inning of scoreless ball. He has now thrown 28 1/3rd consecutive scoreless innings dating back to last season. It's the longest streak in the majors and the 9th longest in Phillies' history. Stuff: Randy Wolf made his first appearance against his former team since leaving for free agency at the end of last year. He pitched well, going 6 innings, giving up 2 runs and striking out 9. Yes, the Wolf Pack was in attendance ... The Phils have now won 7 of their last 10 games

"As we look for role models for our nation's youth, we need to look no further than to Jerry Coleman and Ted Williams—heroes of the baseball diamond and the battlefields of the skies. Each was asked to interrupt his or her private life to serve in harms way." - Commissioner Bud Selig

Jerry Coleman is truly one of the precious gems that make up this great country of ours. A former infielder with the New York Yankees (1949-1957), Coleman won the Rookie-of-the-Year award in 1949 and the 1950 World Series MVP award for helping the Yankees sweep the Phillies in four straight games. His playing career was interrupted twice because of the call of duty from his country as a Marine pilot during World War II and Korea. He flew 120 combat missions, received two Distinguished Flying Crosses, 13 Air Medals and three Navy Citations while eventually earning the rank of Lieutenant Colonel.

*Padres Hall-of-Fame Broadcaster Jerry Coleman,
A Phillies killer and an American war hero – Photo courtesy of Jerry Coleman*

Coleman was born and raised in San Jose, California, but he has made San Diego his home since 1972 as the play-by-play announcer of the Padres. He began his broadcasting career in 1960 for CBS Radio, and in 1963 he began a seven-year run in which he was an announcer for the Yankees. After broadcasting for the Angels in 1970 and 1971, Coleman began his Hall-of-Fame announcing career with the Padres in 1972. Except for a one year stint as the Padres' manager in 1980, Coleman has been behind the microphone ever since. In 2005, Coleman was inducted into the Baseball Hall-of-Fame as a Ford C. Frick Award winner, honoring him as one of the premier announcers to ever sit behind a microphone.

The 1950 World Series against the Phillies was a fun time for me. Every time I was up something was happening. During Game 1 of the Series, Bobby Brown was moved over to third base and I came to the plate against Jim Konstanty. I hit a fly ball to deep left field; it was almost out of the park. (Dick) Sisler caught it and Brown scored for the only run of the game. We won 1-0. In the second game, I scored one of the two runs. DiMaggio won the game in the 10th inning with a homerun. The third game I drove in the winning run in the 9th inning and we won 3-2.

I rested in the fourth game. I think I went 0 for 3. I just didn't have anything to do with that one. We were ahead 5-0 going into the 9th. (Whitey) Ford was pitching. He had a shut out going and someone on the Phillies hit a ball that went right through his hands. Rolled on to the grass, two runs score. Casey Stengel was furious. He wanted Ford to get that shutout. Anyway, every time I came up to the plate during the Series it was a crazy situation where I could drive in a runner or score a run. That's how I got the MVP award in the 1950 World Series. I think of the ten runs that we scored; I was responsible for five of them.

I joined the Yankees in September of 1948. My first full year was in 1949. I played with the Yankees for 9 years (1949 –1957) and played in six World Series. I missed '52 and '53 because of Korea. I actually got back in time for the '53 Series but I just sat on the bench. Couldn't play.

World War II started when I was a senior in High School. 17 years old when I joined. Of course, we were all young kids back then. What are we going to do? Our country's at war. We didn't know what we were going to do in the military. Are we going to be commandos, going to be this, going to be that? One day they called all the senior boys into the auditorium. We're sitting there waiting and all of a sudden from the back of the auditorium walked in two Naval Aviators with huge wings on their chest. They come in and talk to us and are pushing a thing called the V5-Program that trains Naval Aviators. I immediately said, "That's for me." Now I'm 17 years old at the time but you got to be 18 to get into the flying program. I won't be 18 until September. This is in like March or something like that. So I'm thinking, how I am going to make it all the way to my 18th birthday? I originally was going to go to USC on a baseball and basketball scholarship, but I ended up signing with the Yankees once school ended. Joe Devine was the Yankees' scout who signed me.

So before I went off to war I left and started playing professional baseball. I had to kill the summer. I played Class D Pony League in Roseville, NY. We played teams from Pennsylvania, Ontario and New York. That's how they got the name PONY. The season ended on September 6th and I got home on the 10th. I went to the Federal building and joined up on the 14th. It took about three weeks to process the whole thing. There was a line from here to Poughkeepsie to get in. Everybody wanted to get in. At the end of the processing to get into the flying program you were interviewed by a Commander. He's looking over all my paper work and then gets to my high school transcript. "I can't sign this." He said. "Why?" I asked. He said, "You know how much it costs to train a pilot?" I said "No sir." "It costs $300,000. You're going to fail because your grades aren't good enough." I said, "I'm going to tell you sir, studying wasn't what I was focusing on in school. I thought if I brought my baseball and basketball shoes to school that's all that's necessary to graduate." I really didn't study much. I wasn't a student. I had actually scored good grades on my entrance tests to the military and my physical was fine; so he said, "Well, you'll never make it." I wish I could've found him when I got my wings. Actually, flying was something I really wanted, and I did quite well to be honest with you.

My goal was to sink a Japanese carrier. We had a choice when we went in. You can choose to either fly with the Marines or the Navy. In the Marines you would be a 2nd Lieutenant or an Ensign if you joined the Navy. At that time Joe Foss and Pappy Boyington were Marines who were knocking planes out of the sky. They were the big heroes of the war. I wanted to be Joe Foss Jr. Then when I got into it, in June of '42, the type of plane that I would end up flying, the SPD dive bomber, sunk the four carriers at Midway. I chose the Marines.

So this in 1942 and my idea was to sink a carrier. Stupid thinking for a young kid. Anyway, what happened, I get into the service and I'm interviewed by a guy named Mangler. I think it was Richard Mangler. He was the first man that ran a plane at Guadalcanal's Anderson Field, which I flew off of later in the war. He interviewed me and asked, "Why do you want to be a Marine?" He scared the daylights out of me by the way he was talking. I forgot what I said, but they end up making me a Second Lieutenant and off I went to Cherry Point, NC, for training. After I was commissioned I went to Jacksonville, Florida, and then back to Cherry Point. Anyway, I was at Cherry Point with several hundred other pilots trying to get out of there. They put them in ferry duty, but before you did that they sent you out to the boondocks for three weeks. Simulated landings and all this sort of stuff, being bitten alive by mosquitoes. One day they lined us all up and said, "The following officers, step forward, … Coleman 36103, step forward." I thought they were going to shoot me or something. I don't know what the hell they were doing. They pulled six of us guys out and then told us that we were going to California for advanced flying training. Twenty days after getting to California I was overseas. When I got there it was July or August of 1944. I was only 19.

I was assigned to Marine Torpedo Bombing Squadron 341 … VMSB-341. The Torrid Turtles. It's heavier than an air scout bomber; it's a dive bomber. I joined them in a place called Green Island, which was actually a Japanese island called Nissan Island. We called it Green Island. It had a landing strip and that was about it. We flew missions against bypassed Japanese bases in the Solomon Islands and Bougainville Island. Then MacArthur was going to hit the Philippines. We were the first squadron designated for close air support. You had to be within 50 yards of your target. If you missed you'd blow up your own guys. When we'd come in troops would back off 50-100 yards. We'd go in there with 1,000-pound bombs. They made a pretty good pop!

We ended up going all over the place back then. In July 1945, senior pilots, and I don't mean in rank, senior pilots overseas were called back. They wanted to bring all of the carrier qualified pilots back to train in the U.S. to hit the Japanese mainland in November. So I was sent back home to the states to begin carrier landing training. When I was home they dropped the atomic bomb and the war ended. Otherwise, I wouldn't be talking to you right now. Maybe 100,000 other people too.

When the war ended they sent me to Cherry Point again. I finally got out at January 1946. Which is now almost 3 ½ years later since I was last there. Eventually they made our squadron "inactive". So you think to yourself that you've been to war for four years and that was it. Now we fast-forward and I go into play pro baseball. I go to Bingham, Kansas City, New York and on to the Yankees. I'm with them, '49, '50 and '51. We won the World Series my first three years in the big leagues.

At end of the '51 season, I go home to San Francisco and I get a phone call from some Major. I thought he wanted to go to lunch or something. He said, "What do you think about going back into the service?" I said," Well, I haven't given a lot of thought to it to be honest with you." The Marines trained almost no pilots from 1945 – 1950 and then the Korean War started. He said, "Well, we're going to get you." I said, "How long?" He said, "One year and a half." I said, "Why don't you do me a favor, take me right now, in October 1951. Let me out in March 1953. I'll miss one year playing for the Yankees." But the military has a mind of its own. They end up taking me in the beginning of '52 season and let me out at the end of '53 season. That basically was the end of my baseball career.

I get sent to Korea in 1952 along with Ted Williams. He flew jets and I flew in an old Corsair that they turned into an attack bomber for Korea. I flew with the DMA-323 Death Rattlers. We did everything in those planes. Close air support, whatever they wanted. We'd sit in the ready room all day long waiting for the call if they needed us. They usually had us in groups of four pilots. When the siren went off it would scare the shit out of you. It went off all the time. Sometimes you'd sit in the ready room for eight hours. Sometimes you'd be up bombing in an hour. It depended on what was going on.

The military played an important role in my life. It really made me grow up quick. The teamwork, the way you feel about groups. I recall one mission we had in Korea we heard, "Mayday, I got a Mayday, I got a Mayday." over the intercom. At that time we knew that everybody flying in North Korea was a Marine. Every pilot instantly became your brother when they ran into trouble. So anyway, we're listening to this and some guy pulls up next to the pilot who's having troubles and he says, "I got you, I got you. You got flames out of your pipe so we're taking you over to K-55 for an emergency landing." It turns out the Mayday pilot was Ted Williams. No one knew it at the time, but it was his plane that was in trouble. He's lucky he's alive. He landed hot and on fire. He had no wheels, had no flaps and he ended up doing a controlled crash landing on the runway. You can easily blow up that way. But, that was Ted Williams.

My biggest memory from being in the military were the friendships that I made during World War II. There were four of us in a tent. Art Mallard, Bud Madden, Bob Means and myself. We played bridge everyday when we weren't flying. We became very good friends. Art was married. I didn't see him much after the war, but Bob and I still see each other from time to time. Bud's dead now. I think Art is dead too. Developing those friendships in time of war are bonds for life. They never stop. We had a lot of fun together; we really did. We had a good time. Of course we were all young and stupid. Hell, I was 20 when I got home. I wasn't even 21 when I got back to the Yankees.

I really don't think much back on the wars. It's behind me. I'm one of these people, when it's behind me, it's behind me. I don't think about all the six World Titles, all the pennants and all this stuff. I don't think about that. That's behind me. It's what's up front that's important. I have a 22-year old daughter. My first wife died. I was married to her for 35 years. I'll be married to my second wife for 26 years. We have a beautiful young daughter. That's my life now. Maggie and Chelsea, that's my life.

How do I want to be remembered? I don't even know how to answer that question. Probably as the guy that could work with the team. A good teammate, because that's what it takes in life to make it through anything. You know Alex Rodriguez went to Texas at $25 million a year and they ended up in last place every year. A cohesive unit is what makes things happen. Not individuals. I said this several times and I mean it ... there are only two important things in your life: The people that you love and who love you and your country. The rest is a lot of you know what.

Quotable: "All machine. There's not a human bone in him." - Brad Lidge after Burrell's walk-off homerun. After the game Lidge raced to his locker and threw on his Pat Burrell "Man or Machine" T-shirt. The shirt depicts a shirtless Burrell pumping iron. A photo from his earlier days that once hung on a billboard near the park.

Friday, May 2nd - Phillies 6 Giants 5 - 10 in. (17-13) 1st - ½ GA of the Marlins & Mets
Philadelphia - *Playing his first game back in Philly since joining the Giants, Aaron Rowand hit a solo homerun in the top of the 10th to give San Francisco the lead, however the Giant's bullpen was unable to hold the lead ... With a 3-2 count and two outs, Pat Burrell hit a dramatic game-winning two-run walk-off homerun for the victory. It was Burrell's 9th homer of the season and his first walk-off homerun in six seasons and third of his career ... Chase Utley went 2 for 3 with a HR and 2 RBIs ... Pedro Feliz also went 2 for 4 with a HR and 2 RBIs ... Kyle Kendrick game up 3 runs on 6 IP, striking out 6 and walking none ... J.C. Romero (2-0) got the win even though he gave up the go-ahead run to Rowand. The run stopped Romero's scoreless streak at 28 1/3rd innings. Stuff: Chase Utley was named the National League's Player of the Month for the month of April. He batted .352 (38-108) with 10 HRs and 21 RBIs. The last Phillie to win the award in April was Von Hayes in 1989 ...Burrell's homerun now gives him 227 on his career which puts him 4th on the Phillies' all-time list behind Mike Schmidt (548), Del Ennis (259) and Chuck Klein (243).*

When the greatest third baseman in the history of Major League baseball stepped up to the plate during the course of his 18-year career, National League pitchers cowered in having to face one of baseball's most prolific homerun hitters of all time. 548 times Schmidt cleared the bases for the Phillies. 548 times the Phillies broadcast team got to give one of their signature homerun calls. 548 times put Mike Schmidt into the record books and into the Hall-of-Fame.

Today Schmidt lives in Florida. It's been 19 seasons since he has hit one out of the park but today Michael Jack is doing it again by lending his name and his 548 homeruns to help raise funds for the Cystic Fibrosis Foundation.

CharityWines.com is a non-profit organization whose sole goal is to take advantage of the drawing power of celebrities and raise as much money as possible for the celebrity's charity. They have raised well over a million dollars for charities including $350,000 in Boston alone with the sale of their wines for Manny Ramirez, Curt Schilling and Tim Wakefield's charities. In an effort to capitalize on the popularity of Mike Schmidt in the Philadelphia region the two came together to create Mike Schmidt 548 Zinfandel: a red-wine from the Eos Estate Winery in Paso Robles, California. A bottle is priced to sell at $19 in hopes to raise a serious load of cash for Cystic Fibrosis. Not a dime of it goes to Schmidt with 100% of the proceeds going directly to help those with this terrible disease.

Mike Schmidt turned his 548 lifetime homeruns into a charitable venture with the creation of "Mike Schmidt 548 Zinfandel wines"

I've been working with Cystic Fibrosis for about 10 years now. Every year I do a couple of big events for them down in Florida. Recently, I was approached through the 500 Home Run Club (a marketing company sponsored by MLB and the Hall of Fame that markets products for the select few who have ever hit more than 500 homeruns in baseball) to get involved with this project with Charity Wines. When I saw what they were doing with charity wine sales in Boston I was very impressed, and I said, "Yeah, count me in."

$1.25 off of every sale of the wine will go to Cystic Fibrosis. I don't like to put a goal on the amount of money that we will raise, but I'll be unhappy if it's not 6 figures. If they can do that in Boston, we can do it in Philly right?

Their art people did a great job with their logo for the bottle and I think it brings together the homeruns, Phillies' history and me, and it fits quite nicely. They helped me pick a wine. They didn't say, "Here's the wine, we want to put your name on this bottle." No, they let me pick the wine and a quite extensive dinner and wine tasting and we picked it and I'm quite proud of it. I can't wait until I can have a couple of cases around the house.

I got involved with Cystic Fibrosis back in 1999. We had a very close friend of our family lose their 21-year-old son to the disease. We watched the young boy actually die waiting for a set of lungs at Duke University Hospital in North Carolina. They never got to do a transplant, and he ended up dying in his mothers and father's arms. His and his family's very courageous battle and the opportunity to raise funds to look for a cure for Cystic Fibrosis so families didn't have to go through what they did got me started working for the Foundation.

What have I been doing with my life since I retired? Well, I have a wonderful life. I've been living in Florida and I do a lot of golfing, fishing and working on events. If you look at my calendar, I do some speaking; a lot of traveling with the family. I now have a nice relationship with the Phillies so I work with them in Spring Training and do some marketing work for them throughout the year. I've got to pinch myself. I do pinch myself once a day actually to realize how lucky I am.

My thoughts on Chase Utley … hmmm. He sure is a good one. I marvel at him as a player; I really do. He's a throwback guy; he can play in any era. I often refer to Chase Utley as a baseball rat. If you've heard of a gym rat in basketball, you know the type of guy that hangs around the gym? Chase gives me the impression he only really wants to be at the ballpark, and he really wants to do is play baseball.

What a breath of fresh air he is for the Phillies and for the sport. Chase is a unique hitter in that he doesn't have an ego. He has no fear as a hitter, so many great qualities. He doesn't overreact to striking out; he doesn't overreact to home runs. He's just a machine; he's an offensive machine, and I'm saying all these good things at a time when he's probably the best player in the league right now. Nobody can keep that pace up for 6 months, nobody will. There will be times throughout the year where Chase will level out a little bit but in the end he'll be that kind of a player, probably the leading candidate right now for MVP.

It has to be in God's plan for Chase Utley and the Phillies' plan for Chase Utley to make it all the way through the season without injury. If he does, he'll be right there in the top 2-3 players in the league. I just love watching him, when I'm home, I won't go to bed if he's coming up. I just love being around him and watching him.

My work with Pat Burrell a few years back? I think my work is finally effecting what he's doing right now on the field (to an assortment of laughs). I told him to hit like this years ago, what the heck has he been waiting on? Pat Burrell and everybody else have always hoped that his hitting would surface and stay the way he is hitting right now. He's a big key to what the Phillies are doing so far.

He's had a lot of big hits so far this season. If it weren't for Chase Utley, we'd be talking about Pat Burrell being the best player in the league right now. He's aggressive now; he's confident; he doesn't waste swings. He covers plays; he shoots to right field. He still hooks the ball a little bit to left field when he should be going to right field, but that's his nature. He's become a really complete hitter, and I'm hoping he'll hold on to this for the rest of the year.

How many homeruns would I be able to hit in this ballpark? I think everybody is well aware that homeruns are a little bit easier to come by today for a lot of reasons … maybe 5-10 more a year. You reach the opposite fields a little bit easier today with the ballparks and the bats so a lot of the old warning track fly balls and those hits to the opposite field track are now homeruns. Even the players that are playing today would admit to that.

Quotable: "I noticed it warming up before the game. He wanted to prove to himself, not just everyone else, that he still had his fastball. He had that extra zip. I told [pitching coach] Rich Dubee after about six or seven throws, 'Man, he's got a little attitude on the ball tonight.'" - Chris Coste on Brett Myers fastball

Saturday, May 3rd - Giants 3 Phillies 2 - 10 in. (17-14) 1st - ½ GA of the Marlins & Mets

Philadelphia - *Brett Myers appears to have rediscovered his fastball as he goes 7 strong innings giving up 2 runs and striking out 10. He threw close to 93 mph throughout the game, a significant difference from his last outing when he hit 89 mph on the radar gun only a few times ... However, the Giants' Matt Cain and the Giants' bullpen were better as they shut down than the Phils on 3 hits, two of them homeruns, while striking out 8 ... Rudy Seanez (2-2) took the loss after giving up 4 hits and a run in the 10th ... Chase Utley had two of the teams 3 hits raising his average to .369. Utley's homerun in the 4th inning was his 13th of the season, which leads all Major League players.*

Baseball and the Star Spangled Banner go together like bread and butter. They are inseparable. The earliest references to our nation's anthem being played at a baseball game was back in 1897 during Opening Day ceremonies in Philadelphia. It was also documented being performed during the 7th inning stretch of the 1918 World Series. But it wasn't until World War II that the tradition of playing the national anthem before every baseball game became a core part of the experience.

Baseball fans are a fickle lot. Probably a good reflection of how patriotic the nation is at any given time. They can sing the song at the top of their lungs or they might honor the nation through the simple gesture of just removing their hat and standing quietly while the anthem is sung. After the horrific events of 9/11 unfolded, the bowels of Veterans Stadium and baseball stadiums everywhere across the country were filled with the voices of thousands of men, woman and children singing

Folk Singer John Flynn belts out the Star Spangled Banner before a Phillies' home game

every last note of the song. Today, however, many fans are less vocal during the playing of the anthem. Not a criticism of the fans of the game, nor our nation, but merely an observation of the times in which we currently live.

Being that fans spend more time listening to the anthem then singing it these days, we are afforded scores of opportunities throughout the season to listen to various performers sing the anthem. Singing the National Anthem isn't an easy task, even for the most heralded of singers. Forgotten words, notes that somehow never get hit and renditions that would probably make Francis Scott Key spin a few times in his grave. But that's not the case for singer/songwriter John Flynn.

A graduate of Temple University and a resident of Philadelphia, Flynn is well known throughout the world as one of the premier folk singers of our time. His powerful songs of humanity and hope are deeply rooted in the traditions of Woody Guthrie and Phil Ochs. A lifelong Phillies fan, John has sung the National Anthem at Citizens Bank Park numerous times. His clear and simple rendition of the song is a work of poetry that the fans always enjoy.

I usually sing the song in the key of A. I'm a tenor so it definitely works best for me to be able to sing all the notes in the song.

The first time I can remember singing the song in public was probably in grade school. Or it might have been in church. I grew up in Ridley Park and have been a Phillies fan for as long as I can remember. I still remember sitting around the radio with my grandfather listening to the games. My dad's actually here tonight to watch me sing. It's his first he has ever come to see me sing at a ballpark. He's never been a really big Phillies fan until Chase and Ryan started playing for them.

My manager at the time, Biff Kennedy, actually got me started with singing the National Anthem. He met John Brazer of the Phillies and worked it out so they were kind enough to tell me to pick a date and a team that you'd like to go see. So I picked the Montreal Expos because I figured I'd get to sing two anthems and double up on my stage time.

I've never forgotten the words of the song ... I just pretend that the microphone is out. I don't think it's the most difficult song to sing. I think probably because of what it means to people it puts a little extra emotion into the moment and so you can sweat that or you can ride it. You know you can make it carry you through the entire song. I never found it to be a real difficult song. The reason that melody endured was because it was an English drinking melody. Francis Scott Key didn't write the melody, it came over from England.

I've been singing the song with the Phillies since 1995. I lost count to the number of times that I've done it, but I've had some real special moments. I got to sing the first game after 9/11... It was September 17th and the Braves were in town. We did *"God Bless America"* from the roof of the dugout instead of *"Take Me Out To the Ballgame"* and it was just amazing. I mean 40,000 people were singing at the top of their lungs and tears were on their faces and...I actually wrote a song that was on an album that came out shortly after that and it was called *"I Will Not Fear"* because there was a guy in the crowd that night that had a big piece of cardboard with those words on it. And it just captured that moment for me and for the nation.

I got booed once by a sold out crowd at the Vet during *"Take Me Out To The Ballgame".*
It was Harry Kalas tribute day and I think, it's never really has been explained to me, but they
booed as soon as I was introduced so it wasn't the performance they were critiquing, and I
think they may have been expecting Harry to come out and sing, that's the only thing I can
think of. So I sang it all the way through and then I yelled "One more time." Because I was
like I'm not gonna let them see me back me down… so they just cranked it up to a level and
the boos were just raining down. So finally afterwards they take me down the tunnel and I
got to meet Dick Allen for the first time and I'm thinking, "Of all the people to meet at this
moment." So Allen is laughing at me and he says, "Man, where I come from we call that a
standing ovation!"

The echo in a stadium when you are playing can sometimes be tricky. I had gotten to the
point that I was doing it so often at the Vet that I didn't notice it, but I haven't yet figured it
out here. It throws me a little bit more here in this park and I don't know why that is. I've only
sung here four times. I don't know, you just kind of really have to concentrate and especially
with the guitar notes because the guitar notes are like separate little missiles that zing in, you'll
hear it and I guess that's why people don't do it on the guitar too often.

I never tried singing it a cappella. I guess my guitar is my security blanket. I always perform
with a guitar wherever I work. Even in the recording studio, I like to sing holding the guitar
because it's more natural for me.

*Quotable: "I was thinking score all the way. I had a good jump. A lot of it had to do with the shoes.
I had lighter-color shoes on today, so I was a little faster." - Ryan Howard on his game winning run
from second base to home*

<u>Sunday, May 4th - Phillies 6 Giants 5 (18-14) 1st - ½ GA of the Marlins & Mets</u>
Philadelphia - *Ryan Howard scored from second on an infield error hit off the bat of Geoff Jenkins
in the bottom of the 9th to give the Phillies the walk-off win and the series victory over the Giants
… It was the Phillies 2nd walk-off in three days and their Major League leading 4th walk-off win
of the season … Carlos Ruiz hit a solo homerun in the bottom of the 8th to tie the game at 5 …Pat
Burrell went 2 for 3 with 2 RBIs and now has 30 on the season while raising his average to .330
…Shane Victorino went 2 for 4 with two doubles …Cole Hamels surrendered 4 runs in 6 innings
while walking none and striking out 5 … Brad Lidge picked up his first win as a Phillie pitching
a scoreless 9th. Stuff: After the game the Phillies presented Manuel with a jersey with the number
"500" on the back. He now has a lifetime 500-428 record and is 280-238 as the Phillies' manager-
When asked about the significance of 500 victories Manuel said, "Five-hundred wins means I've
had some great players along the way. I told the guys in there I want to win at least 500 more. The
manager is only as good as the players he's had."*

The first-place Phillies took two out of three from the Giants via walk-off wins, made possible by a surprisingly good pitching staff. The lesson here is if you pitch well, you can win pretty (Friday) or win ugly (Sunday). There's no mystery behind their success this season. None. The starters have been able to go relatively deep in ballgames and a shutdown bullpen has kept it close for the offense to pull it out. They're four deep with late-inning arms they can trust, none better than Brad Lidge and his spotless ERA. The results have seen comeback wins in 10 of their 18 victories; this from the team that led all of baseball with 48 come-from-behind wins a year ago, with a much worse bullpen.

Joette Cuomo-Evers shows her Phillies pride at the Sausage Stand on Ashburn Alley

The merits of good pitching were also illustrated on the other side. The Phils entertained the weakest offensive links of the West and nearly every game was tit for tat. From Greg Maddux on Tuesday to Tim Lincecum today. The home stand demonstrated just how good the West will be and serves as a preview of what the Phils will encounter as they begin a seven-game road trip tonight in Arizona. As good as they've been, the Phillies' pitching staff could be asked to kick into an even higher gear inside parks that will neutralize their long-ball threat.

Quotable: "It's amazing how that 98 (mph fastball by D'Backs Max Scherzer) gets hit and that 78 (mph fastball by Jamie Moyer) wins, isn't it? I think the law of gravity gets it." - Charlie Manuel on the 20 mph difference on the two starter's fastballs.

Monday, May 5th - Phillies 11 Diamondback 4 (19-14) 1st - 1 GA of the Marlins
Phoenix - *The Phillies started their 7-game road trip throwing 45-year-old Jamie Moyer against D'Backs rookie Max Scherzer. Moyer (2-2, 4.15) was the star of the game on the mound and at the plate, throwing 7 innings and giving up 2 runs while walking none and striking out 5. At the plate, Moyer went 2 for 3 with a double and a RBI ... The Phillies get a season-high 17 hits with Jenkins and Ruiz both notching 3 hits apiece and Victorino, Bruntlett, Utley, Feliz and Moyer each smacking 2 hits ... The 11 runs was also a season high for the team. Stuff: With his two hit performance, Moyer became only the 4th pitcher in the history of Major League baseball to have two or more hits after turning 45 years old. The other three pitchers were Jack Quinn (3 times), Satchel Paige (3*

times) and Charlie Hough (once). It was Moyer's 558th start of his career while the Diamondback's Max Scherzer (0-1, 5.10) started his first game.

The Diamondbacks were no match for Jamie Moyer and the Phillies, who topped their highest run total of 2008 without hitting a single home run. The concern coming into this series was finding ways to score against the tough Arizona pitching staff in a large park and without relying on the long ball. Once again, the Phils are finding new ways to surprise us. Story of the night: unexpected contributions from the top and bottom of the lineup. Shane Victorino, Eric Bruntlett and Chase Utley combined to reach base nine times. Bruntlett knocked in three. The bottom – Geoff Jenkins, Pedro Feliz, Carlos Ruiz and Jamie Moyer – combined for 10 hits and four RBIs.

Obviously, this was a nice way to start a road trip, and a good game for Ruiz, Feliz and Bruntlett to keep up appearances by raising their batting averages to more palatable levels.

Jamie Moyer signing autographs for the kids as is his usual practice before every home game

Quotable: "To walk the pitcher on four pitches is pretty pathetic, I [bleeped] up. I don't think Arizona beat us. I think I beat ourselves." - Adam Eaton on his performance in the 4th inning

Tuesday, May 6th - Diamondbacks 6 Phillies 4 (19-15) Tied for 1st with Marlins

Phoenix - The fourth inning was the story of the game. Defending a slim 2-1 lead, Adam Eaton once again fell apart, giving up five runs in the bottom of the inning. He walked three in the inning, including D'Backs pitcher Randy Johnson on four straight pitches ... After posting a 4.12 ERA in his first three outings, Eaton (0-1) appears to have regressed to his 2007 form once again with a 7.23 ERA in his past four games ... The bullpen pitched well after Eaton exited the game. Seanez, Gordon and Durbin threw four scoreless innings and scattered just two hits. Eric Bruntlett and Jayson Werth both went deep off of Johnson. Stuff: 44 year old Randy Johnson won his 286th career victory. He is now 10-3 lifetime against the Phillies ... The Phillies lead all of baseball with 50 homeruns. Last season the Phils didn't hit their 50th homerun until their 49th game of the season ...Ryan Howard didn't start for the third time this season. He did pinch hit in the 8th, striking out and is now batting .168. Since his game winning homerun last week, Howard is 1 for his last 16 with eight strikeouts …Pat Burrell didn't fair much better today against Johnson. He went 0 for 3, striking out twice to the "Big Unit". He is now 4 for 22 lifetime against Johnson with 14 strikeouts … Jimmy Rollins continues his rehab assignment in Florida. He has gone 6 for 8 with Clearwater and should be back with the team on Thursday.

In the world of weather, meteorologists issue "watches" when conditions are favorable for certain weather to occur. Adam Eaton probably has one more shot to prove himself before an official "watch" is issued and the storm chasers of fantasy baseball can begin tracking his potential replacement. If the minor league picture wasn't so cloudy, a fifth-starter watch might have already been issued. Remember, a "watch" wouldn't necessarily facilitate a change, not like a "warning" would. A "warning" means Eaton is in the eye of the storm. In other words, right now, conditions are favorable for conditions to be favorable for something to happen. Got that?

Nevertheless, don't underestimate the team's frustration with Eaton. The team made offers to several free agents this off-season aimed at replacing the beleaguered right-hander, who pitched himself out of the rotation and onto the imaginary DL at season's end. In the past, Pat Gillick, who was the one

Adam Eaton's poor performance on the mound may ultimately force Pat Gillick's hand to have to go acquire a 5th starter

who courted Eaton out West, has demonstrated a willingness to play the hot hand ,and reportedly made a special trip to scout rising Double-A right-hander Antonio Bastardo (what a great last name!). J.A. Happ has also pitched well at Triple-A Lehigh Valley and could eventually be a replacement for Eaton.

Quotable: "That was the worst collision I ever saw at first base. It got ugly." - Geoff Jenkins on Shane Victorino's collision with Conor Jackson on a play that eventually led to the Phillies tying the game in the 8th.

Wednesday, May 7th - Phillies 5 Diamondbacks 4 (20-15) Tied for 1st with Marlins

Phoenix - *The Phillies assembled their 11th come-from-behind victory of the season on back-to-back RBI hits in the 8th inning by Eric Bruntlett and Chase Utley ... Bruntlett doubled home Shane Victorino, who got to first on a wild play that included him striking out but being able to run to first on a wild pitch by Chad Qualls. Unfortunately the ball, Victorino and D-Backs first baseman Conor Jackson all arrived at the bag at the same time, causing a massive pileup with Victorino being called safe. Jackson had to leave the game with a mild concussion. Victorino then went on to steal second base on the next pitch and then was doubled home by Bruntlett to tie the game at four. Chase Utley followed up with a single that scored Bruntlett for the game winning run ... Ryan Howard continued his slump going 0 for 4 with three strikeouts ...Kyle Kendrick pitched well, going 6 innings and giving up 3 runs while scattering 10 hits ... J.C. Romero picked up the win in relief. He is now 3-0 ... Brad Lidge continued his perfect season pitching a 1-2-3 9th for his 8th save in 8 opportunities. He still has a 0.00 ERA.*

Brad Lidge, running in from bullpen, has been perfect so far this season

The following are a number of quotes from those that posted on Beerleaguer.com after tonight's game:

"Lidge is nasty, those batters looked totally overmatched. While we're praising Chase and Pat for their incredible play thus far and contribution to the Phils' success, I think it's also fair to say Lidge is playing at that level as well so far. Some of these ninth innings are almost Mariano-esque." – *Bob*

"In my memory we've never had a closer as dominant as Lidge. Whatever mental issues he might have been having in Houston seem to have gone away." – *sifl*

"Good win by the Phillies. Bruntlett with a big hit. Feliz with the tying run shot. Victorino going Pete Rose on Conor Jackson. Chase MVP. Nice job by Romero/Gordon/Lidge. Good job by KK for keeping the game close enough to tie. I wouldn't call this game a "grand theft". This is what the Phillies do." – *mike cunningham*

"One thing which is absolutely beyond dispute is that Howard needs to be hitting lower than fourth in the order. He looks utterly defeated mentally and he needs at least two or three *full* games off. I can't remember a hitter struggling as mightily for this prolonged a period as Howard in the last two Aprils, except possibly Burrell in '03." – *RSB*

Quotable: "I can't put together back-to-back good starts, and I don't know what the problem is. I made some good pitches they hit. I made some bad pitches they crushed. I don't know. I've just got to try to get through it. Every time I get my rear end kicked it's frustrating. It's definitely not fun, going out there and feeling real good and getting beat up like that." - Brett Myers on giving up 7 runs

Thursday, May 8th - Diamondbacks 8 Phillies 3 (20-16) 2nd - 1 GB the Marlins

Phoenix - *Brett Myers (2-3, 5.33) once again pitched poorly in the series final game with the Diamondbacks allowing 7 runs in 5 innings pitched ... D'Backs ace, Brandon Webb won his 8th game against no losses on the season. He stifled the Phils offense on three hits through the 8th inning before giving up two runs and three hits in the 9th. Stuff: Eric Bruntlett was 7 for 18 with 8 RBIs in the four game series ...Jimmy Rollins is expected to join the team tomorrow in San Francisco.*

For four decades Bill Conlin has covered every major sports story in the city of Philadelphia. A Beat Writer for the Phillies starting back in 1966, Conlin has seen it all and has written it all. He is known across baseball as one of the most talented craftsmen to have ever covered the "World of Perspiring Arts". He can be caustic, rude, incredulous, enlightening or just downright funny. But no matter what one might think of Bill Conlin as a writer there are few if any who could ever hope to climb to the heights of his career.

The Philadelphia Daily News' Bill Conlin in his younger days as a lifeguard on the beaches of the New Jersey Shore – photo courtesy of Bill Conlin

Many may not know this about Bill but well before he became the "King of the World" he had already been nicknamed the "King of the Beach". In 1952 and 1955 he won first place in both the long-distance swimming and Doubles Ocean rowing championships of New Jersey. In 1983, he was inducted into the Ocean Rowing Hall of Fame in Margate joining – among others – Jack Kelly, brother of famed movie actress Grace Kelly.

I got involved with life guarding back in the 1940s. I became a mascot for what was probably the best beach patrol ever assembled. All these guys that came back from WWII, they were mature. Most of them were in their 20's. They were battle-hardened. One guy, who was an idol to everyone there, was "Whitey" Thomas. He was an Ace in WWII flying Corsairs in the Pacific. He was also a world-class ocean rower. The best ocean rowing crew I ever saw was Whitey Thomas and the guy by the name of Joe Herron. I saw them in Ocean City in 1949. I saw them beat Jack Kelly Jr. and a guy by the name of Frank Regan. They beat them by almost 200 yards in a flat ocean, which was just unheard of back then. Usually flat ocean races are very close. These guys were so good they just absolutely killed them. In 1948, they had a National Life Guard championship; beach patrols from all over the country and it was held in Atlantic City. Ventnor ran against all the beach patrols that came in from all over the United States. They crushed them all. Whatever their score was they just doubled whoever came in second. That's how good that beach patrol was.

Before I started entering competitions I worked with a bunch of guys down at the Jersey Shore. They taught me a lot about being a lifeguard and about the sport of rowing. You really had to be an athlete to be even remotely capable of going out on to the surf. There was one guy who I consider to be the best athlete nobody ever heard of. A guy by the name of Billy Howarth. He weighed maybe a buck 55 soaking wet. He was about 5 foot 9 or 10, and he could throw a football 60 yards with either hand. We'd be on the beach near the lifeguard stand, and he'd through the football over the boardwalk right into the storage shack 50 yards away. With either hand! He was an athlete. Sometimes he'd jump down off of the lifeguard stand, run to the boat, grab an oar out of the boat and he would turn around and sprint toward the boardwalk and he would pole vault up, right up onto it to talk to a chick. It was about 11 feet high! It's a fluffin' oar not a pole! He was just amazing. I just enjoyed doing it so much, but I knew I eventually had to get a real job.

My first job was writing for the Evening Bulletin. I started in 1960. My salary as a summer replacement was $65 a week. I got married that October and by then I had been put on full staff and they gave me a $10 raise. So when I got married in 1960, I was making $75 a week, which is the same exact salary that I had made in 1954 as a member of the Ft. Lauderdale beach patrol during Summer Breaks when I was bumming around.

I spent my first six months on the night re-write desk. I really didn't enjoy it all that much. I didn't like doing obits. When you're on the night re-write desk, somebody's always on obit duty. I didn't like calling people and ask if they had a picture of someone who just died. I could never disconnect with the grieving people the way a good obit writer needs to do while at the same time expressing sincere regrets over the loss of somebody you wouldn't know. So I didn't like that part. My first bi-line was doing a piece on a gal who just had quadruplets.

I think I was the first reporter to do a mainstream newspaper feature on Bill Cosby. The headline was something like "Temple footballer Bill Cosby is knocking 'em dead." I think it was at a comedy club in Greenwich Village. I didn't even go see his act. I was two years ahead of him in school. I think when I graduated he was a sophomore. Going to work for The Bulletin right away, he was still there playing football. I wrote the story when he had his life decision. Temple was playing Toledo and Peter, Paul and Mary were having a concert at The Academy of Music. He was approached by whoever was promoting the concert to be the warm-up act for Peter, Paul and Mary. Cosby was supposed to do a stand-up comedy bit in front of them and this was a tremendous opportunity for him obviously. He went to Ernie Cassal, who was the Athletic Director at Temple at the time. He said, "Ernie, I've got a chance to appear on the same bill as Peter, Paul and Mary at the Academy of Music Friday night. I want to do it and I would be very happy to fly to Toledo Saturday morning first thing at my own expense." The game was at 1:00pm. He could've gotten there. He probably would have to fly to Cleveland. I don't even know if there were flights into Toledo at that time, but he could have gotten there easily. Ernie Cassal said, "No, we travel as a team. We don't permit anybody to make their own travel arrangements. Your option is go with the team or go to the concert and give up football." He wrestled with it for about 12 seconds and said, "Well, I'm going to give up football." The rest is history.

I ended up writing about that scenario where he had to make his choice between football and, you know he was a second string running back and not very good. What he was though was tough and he was dirty. He was a 3 yards straight ahead runner, no moves. Wasn't all that big but he was not afraid to gouge an eye or kick you in the groin.

I've never spoken to him about the story. In fact, I'm on the anti-Bill Cosby bandwagon because of the way he has consistently supported what has become the worst football program in the history of Division 1 football.

I usually got along with most of the ballplayers on the Phillies. I did have my problems with Steve Carlton, and they've been well documented. Actually when we spoke he was a good interview and we had a good rapport up until the middle of the 1973 season when it became obvious that there was something seriously wrong with him. He was on his way to becoming a 20 game loser after winning 27 games the year before. I thought that maybe this was kind of a fake sports story and the readers deserved to know what was going on with the guy. I wrote 10% of what I actually knew what was going on. He was having arm problems, he was drinking his ass off, he didn't like his catcher and he hated the manager.

They were trying to break in Bob Boone behind the plate at the time. Carlton was just violently opposed to the way Bob Boone setup behind the plate. He needed a catcher that sat still. He told me once that he told Boone, "Let me worry about where the ball is going. I'm visualizing where I want the pitch to go. I'm looking at a spot on the shin guard. That's my target. I'm looking at his shoe tie if I want to bounce a slider in the dirt.

So in 1972, the second half of that season, his catcher was John Bateman. He loved Bateman. John would say "Ok. Whatever you want Lefty." So Bateman would go setup behind the plate and wouldn't move. That was easy for him. Bateman's a big, lazy son of a bitch. He didn't want to be jumping around back there so he just gave him a target and Lefty just pitched like that through the whole year.

I really haven't spoken to Carlton since 1973. But now that I think about it, we did talk a bit in 1976. Spring Training got started late that year because there was a strike that lasted through about half of Spring Training. Tim McCarver, Carlton and I were all in the same condo complex. I pulled up in my car my first day there and he was out in the parking lot. We talked for a bit and after some time we shook hands and said lets bury the hatchet.

As the strike went into the second week, I wrote a very sarcastic column about how the tough life of the ball player. It was actually brutal. These guys, the toughest days they would have was getaway day on the road, which means they had to carry their suitcase from wherever it was in their room to the door and place their suitcase outside the door. That was the last time they would see their suitcase until they got to their room where they were traveling to at which time, a knock would come on the door, a bellman would come in and would set the suitcase up wherever he was instructed to set it up. And now horror of horrors, I outlined a day where it was an open date and they were flying from Atlanta to San Diego, and they were not flying charter that particular day. They were flying American Airlines out of Atlanta and the flight was delayed. The flight was coming in from someplace else and it got weathered in from wherever it was coming in from and they announced the flight would be delayed by 2 hours.

Lefty was very tight with Joe Hand, the boxing promoter, who hates me and the feeling is mutual. Whenever I wrote anything even remotely negative that mentioned Carlton's name, Hand would call him and read him selective passages from the column. The column could be 90% favorable, but if there was one negative graph in there, he would read him the negative graph. He called him and read him that whole column. Carlton came storming out of his unit one day. I was sitting poolside with McCarver. Carlton saw me, muttered something obscene under his breath and went and sat on the outside of the pool. I asked, "McCarver, what's that about?" He said, "Well, you wrote something that really pissed him off. You wrote something about a Bloody Mary hour at the airport last year." That was game, set, and match for my talking to Lefty. By that time, he wasn't talking to any of the writers.

When you are a reporter you have to tell readers what's going on. I went through Richie Allen's whole career. I struggled trying to make him understand that if he broke the law or if he broke team rules and was fined for it, I was obliged to report it. He didn't understand that. He never got that. He thought we had a little bit of a friendship, that I was obliged to protect him. I told him, I can't do it. Too bad things happened the way they did. Allen was one of the best I ever saw play for the Phillies.

Gene Mauch had a few good quotes about Allen. He once said, "The only man strong enough to hurt Richie Allen is Richie Allen." But my favorite Mauch quote was when a guy asked Mauch if Richie Allen was having trouble with the high fast ball? Mauch said, "No, the fast highball."

Newspapers are a dying industry. They're being undermined and circumvented by various other media most of which are accessible immediately: cable TV, radio, call-in shows, blogs. Almost everything out there gets the same basic material that we're given to disseminate to our readers available to those people and available in such a way that a Leslie Gudel can take the same quote you're going to use from Brett Myers in tomorrow's paper and present it immediately over the Comcast airwaves. We've got to do a better job of covering the sport in such a way that we're giving our readers stuff that can be entertaining, maybe a little more subjective and a little less reliant on what a player said 18 hours ago, which has been repeated on radio, on TV. We've got to reinvent ourselves and remember that we are no longer the sole conveyor of baseball news.

I'd never consider doing a blog. No. I take that back. I would do a weather blog. That's what I would do if I weren't writing about sports. I probably would have been a weather forecaster if I had been better at math. I might have gone into it. I might have studied meteorology, but there's no way I could deal with the quantum physics and all that stuff that you have to know.

I'm going to keep on writing as long as they want me to do it. I've been collecting my full pension for some time so as long as they keep paying me, I'll keep writing.

Quotable: "I'm happy we've got everybody back now. It means we're going to play better. We're going to go get the East. We've got a good league, but when we're healthy, we've got a good chance." - Charlie Manuel on getting Jimmy Rollins back in the lineup

<u>Friday, May 9th - Phillies 7 Giants 4 (21-16) 2nd - 1 GB the Marlins</u>

San Francisco - *In his first game back from the disabled list, Jimmy Rollins appeared to be in mid-season form going 3 for 5 with a double, homerun and 3 RBIs while coming up a triple short of hitting for the cycle … Pedro Feliz's 2 out RBI double in the 6th inning tied the game at four … Rollins RBI double in the 8th inning capped at 3-run rally that included a pinch-hit RBI double by Greg Dobbs and the 7th run of the game on a Carlos Ruiz fielders choice … Cole Hamels (4-3 3.36) went over the .500 mark for the first time this season allowing 4 runs in 7 innings …Brad Lidge pitched the 9th, striking out the side and earning his 9th save of the season. Stuff: Tonight's victory was the Phillies' 12th come-from-behind win of the season … Except for a few pinch hitting appearances, the team has been without Rollins since April 8th. During that time Charlie Manuel has used ten different lineup combos with the #1 and #2 hitters … Greg Dobbs leads the majors in pinch hits (7) and RBIs (8).*

Following a productive night by Pedro Feliz, and another spotless ninth from Brad Lidge, it appears Phillies GM Pat Gillick, expected to step down after the season, saved his best for last in Philadelphia.

Jimmy Rollins is finally back from the disabled list and swinging the bat like he never left

Acquiring Brad Lidge in the off-season was the steal guys like Millwood and Garcia were supposed to have been and there's no better way to put it. In 17 appearances, the Phils' closer still maintains a perfect 0.00 ERA to go with his nine saves. Along with recent pickups J.C. Romero, Rudy Seanez and Chad Durbin, it's the best Phillies' bullpen since the Billy Wagner era. Critics will justifiably argue that in Gillick's first two seasons, the bar was set quite low, but in '08, it's a different story, where five of Gillick's hand-selected choices are anchoring a dominant pen.

Moving to Pedro Feliz: the third baseman has 29 hits on the season – not too good – but I'll bet 10 of them were big hits, such as last night's game-tying double. His .244 average isn't pretty, but his addition seems to accomplish the better defense/better bench goal than what wouldn't have occurred with a Wes Helms/Greg Dobbs platoon. Nevertheless, the jury is still out on Feliz.

There's Geoff Jenkins, too, who hasn't impressed, but the impact of Lidge cannot be understated. After a month and two weeks, it appears Gillick has hit the jackpot here, taking a chance on an arm that might have simply needed a change of scenery. Relief pitching isn't the easiest thing to gage, but it looks like Gillick got his man.

Quotable: "Hard, harder, harder," - Pat Burrell on how Giant's starter Tim Lincecum threw to him all night long

Saturday, May 10th - Giants 8 Phillies 2 (21-17) 2nd - 2 GB the Marlins

San Francisco - *Just one of those bad games that a team has every now and then ... Jamie Moyer (2-3, 5.02) only makes it through 4 innings, giving up 6 runs on 9 hits ... The Phillies only managed four hits and two runs off of Giants' starter Tim Lincecum (5-1 1.61) ... Both runs came on solo shots by Ryan Howard (#7) and Chris Coste (#3). Stuff: The Phils are 3-3 on the West Coast road trip even though the team's two best hitters are in horrific slumps. Chase Utley is batting .120 (5 for 25) and Pat Burrell is 1 for 16 with only 1 RBI.*

Did anyone wonder why the Phillies wore those brightly colored green hats against the Padres a few weeks back? Aside from looking like Christmas trees with their red uniforms on, there had to be a reason. Were they celebrating Saint Patrick's Day late this year?

On a team that usually "Paints the Town Red" at the start of every season, the Phillies took the time to mark an important day for them and for the earth, as they went green by purchasing 20 million kilowatt-hours of renewable energy to serve the electric needs of the entire ball park for an entire year.

In an announcement made in conjunction with Major League Baseball, Governor Ed Rendell, Mayor Michael Nutter, the EPA, the Natural Resource Defense Council (NRDC), Green-e Energy and WindStreet Energy, the Phillies are leading the way and making every effort to aid in the effort for a cleaner environment.

"The EPA applauds the Philadelphia Phillies for playing ball and protecting our environment by purchasing green power," said EPA Administrator Stephen Johnson. "By being the first major league baseball team to join the Green Power Partnership, the Phillies have hit a grand slam for the environment."

The purchase of the green energy is estimated to help avoid the equivalent greenhouse gas emissions of nearly 2,800 cars each year. According to the EPA, this is the largest single purchase of 100% renewable energy in professional sports and is equivalent to the planting of 100,000 trees though the purchase of renewable wind and hydroelectric sources. Other "green" initiatives announced by the Phillies at the ballpark to protect the environment include:

(Front to Back) Roxanne Ferrell, Trudy Odgers and Jeanine Hyndman enjoying an afternoon at the park

- The creation of "Red goes Green Team" that will collect recyclable materials from the seating bowl after each game this season.
- The placement of 35 80-gallon recycling containers that will be placed throughout the ballpark.
- Vendors will recycle frying oil so that it can be used as a biodiesel fuel.
- All vendors in the stadium will also be recycling glass, plastic and cardboard
- All carry out trays will be made from 100% post consumer fiber
- Fans buying food at the ballpark are eating locally grown produce and organic foods
- Environmentally friendly cleaning products and a bio-enzyme will also be used to remove grease trapped in kitchen drain pipes
- The Phillies are installing light control systems throughout the ballpark to decrease the amount of energy used
- The entire facility is converting to lighting that uses light emitting diodes, which take 80 percent less power and last years longer than traditional incandescent bulbs.
- The ballpark is reusing rainwater run-off for landscaping and field irrigation.

Governor Rendell said, *"When Phillies fans think of green and Citizens Bank Park, they're not going to just be thinking about the grass on the field or the Phanatic."*

Although it's for a tremendous cause, let's just hope that we retire the green caps on the players' heads and make sure those aluminum Bud Light cans get tossed into the recycling bin!

Quotable: "You hang it, they bang it. It was a bad fastball and he hit it a long way." – J.C. Romero on the Steve Holm's game winning homerun in the 8th inning.

<u>Sunday, May 11th - Giants 4 Phillies 3 (21-18) Tie for 2nd - 3 GB the Marlins</u>

San Francisco - *J.C. Romero (3-1, 1.76) blew a one run lead in the 8th, giving up a 2-run homer-un to Giant rookie Steve Holm. It was only the 7th run that Romero has given up in 69 outings with the Phillies ...Adam Eaton allowed 2 runs in 5 innings but struggled with his control, walking 5 while striking out 4 ... The Giants' bullpen pitched 4 1/3rd scoreless innings, giving up only two hits ... Ryan Howard hit his first triple of the season and his first since 2006 ... Greg Dobbs got his major league leading 8th pinch hit of the season in the 9th. Stuff: The Phils ended the road trip 3-4 ... It was the first time since April 18-19 that the Phillies have lost two straight games ... It was announced today that Pat Gillick has been elected to the 2008 Canadian Sports Hall of Fame, thank you Mitch Williams.*

It could be the weather, or Monday morning or watching the team get beaten by a 28-year-old catcher who spent last season in Double-A; in any event, I sit here, look at the Phillies 21-18 mark and realize they've only been okay. They haven't dug themselves into an early April hole, which is fortunate. They're hovering, and there's nothing wrong with that after 39 games. But I look at how they've managed to win and see a bullpen that needed to be perfect, a rotation that may be getting lucky and an offense that isn't producing.

Phillies' Chief Technical Engineer Dave Abramson displays one of the hundreds of LED boards that make up the large Phanavision screen in left field

The offense part should take care of itself if Ryan Howard and Shane Victorino get on track, and if a few others can show a just a little im-provement over the first month. It's the pitching that scares me. The pitching, quite frankly, could have been smoke and mirrors for a month. Jamie Moyer gets shelled Saturday and J.C. Romero, who hasn't been the spotless pitcher everyone says he's been, gets tagged by Holm. Even Hamels was knocked around Friday night. This against a Giants' lineup generating less than 3.5 runs coming into this series.

The front office understands there's still work to be done. They're looking around and shuffling prospects in hopes of uncovering another lefty to add to the mix.

To take nothing away from Arizona, the Phils have run up against a string of teams that can't hit: San Francisco, San Diego, Colorado are struggling, Milwaukee is struggling, and Pitts-burgh doesn't scare anyone. Now they face Atlanta, a big division opponent, where the heart of the order goes Escobar, Chipper, Teixeira, Francouer and McCann. I can barely recall the Giants' lineup besides Rowand.

This week, we'll start to see what the Phillies are truly made of.

Quotable: "I was just trying to put good ideas together. I had guys on base pretty much every time I went up there and I was just trying to do a job and get the guys in." – Jayson Werth on his 4 RBI performance

Tuesday, May 13th - Phillies 5 Braves 4 (22-18) 2nd - 1 ½ GB the Marlins

Philadelphia - *Trailing 3-0 in the 4th, Jayson Werth drove in 2 runs to bring the Phils within one of the Braves. In the 5th, he came through again as he and Howard drove in 2 additional runs to take the lead ... Brad Lidge (1-0, 0.50) gave up his first run of the season in the 9th but still earned his 10th save of the year ...Romero and Gordon pitched a scoreless 7th and 8th innings ... Tom Gordon has now gone 12 straight appearances without giving up a run. He gave up 5 runs in March, 2 in April and 0 so far in May ... Werth went 3 for 4 and tied his career high with 4 RBIs ... Kyle Kendrick (3-2, 4.87) threw 6 innings, giving up 3 runs for the win. Stuff: Eric Bruntlett was used as a late inning defensive replacement for Pat Burrell over So Taguchi for the first time... Shane Victorino stole his 6th base of season ... To date, the Phillies have swiped 22 bases and have only been caught 5 times, which is 2nd best in the National League*

One of the best kept secrets at Citizens Bank Park is that the Phillies actually have a broadcast team that you've probably never heard of before and if you did hear them you probably wouldn't understand them anyhow.

For the past three years, the Phillies have been broadcasting all of their games in Spanish on 1480AM in Philadelphia through an agreement that they have with the Spanish Beisbol Network, which is a company owned and operated by Bill Kulik, better known to his listeners as "El Gringo Malo", or the "bad-ass white boy".

The Phillies' Spanish language radio broadcast team of Dan Martinez and Bill Kulik

What Kulik does is quite simple. He buys the Spanish broadcasting rights to a major league team, finds local Latino-focused radio stations in the team's area and sells the airtime to local and national businesses. With a Hispanic population booming all across the United States and that loves the game of baseball, Kulik has struck gold.

Today the Spanish Beisbol Network holds the broadcasting rights to the Boston Red Sox, the Washington Nationals, the Oakland A's and the Phillies. With more teams in his crosshairs, Bill's empire is growing one team at a time.

The last census taken around here they said that there were 300,000 Hispanics in the tri-state area. But we know that number is much larger. More than likely there is somewhere between 700,000 and 800,000. It's very difficult to gauge. But what's more important to our business is the nationality they're made up of.

On the East Coast the Latino population is made up primarily of Dominicans and Puerto Ricans. Both nationalities have a great passion for the sport. The census will probably say that there's more Mexicans here than any other group which is true in Philly but most estimates put the Mexican population in close 3rd, followed by Cubans and then South Americans.

Hispanic populations tend to follow the player from their country more so than the team. For example, the Dominicans will listen to an entire ball game just to hear how Pedro Feliz is doing. If the Phillies are playing the Mets, the Puerto Ricans will listen into hear how Pedro Martinez is pitching.

I'll get times when a specific Latino ballplayer comes to town and everyone and their grandmother will call me to see if I can get them tickets. I expect that when Albert Pujols or Magglio Ordonez comes into town but now fans are even getting excited when Claudio Vargas comes to Philly. Who the heck is Claudio Vargas? You couldn't believe how many people called us asking if we knew what hotel he was staying at or if we could get in touch with him and leave him a message.

It's actually quite interesting to think that this is how they get involved with the game but we're beginning to see that change. Over the past three years we have seen a big shift with our fan base in that many of them are truly just becoming Phillies fans. You can see it during all of our call-in shows. They'll tell us that they only used to listen because JC Romero or Carlos Ruiz was playing but now they call and talk about the team, how they're playing; they'll question Charlie's moves. It's been quite a transformation.

Each season the listening audience is growing. I think one of the reasons is because the word is getting out there in the community about who we are and what we do. Danny Martinez (the color analyst on the broadcast) and I give speeches at the Hispanic schools. We go to Little League events; we have hitting clinics for the Hispanic kids here at the park. We do a lot of things with the community

What's been quite interesting and surprising is we're now running into our listening audience all over the place. As we've become more popular we're getting stopped on the streets, in malls, at restaurants. You have to laugh to see it. Latinos are so passionate about the game of baseball. Whereas fans might see Harry Kalas at a restaurant and walk up to him, say hi, ask for an autograph and leave, our fans will literally pull up a chair and sit next to us and watch us eat lunch. We're like, OK, I guess we're gonna talk baseball.

Even the ballplayers are like that as well. If someone on our broadcast team goes down and interviews a player like Pujols or Ruiz, they'll walk up to them and hug and kiss them first before the interview starts. It's just such a different culture and their passion for the game is phenomenal.

I'm not Hispanic at all. I'm a blond hair, blue-eyed guy from Boston who spent nine of my childhood years growing up in Buenos Aires, Argentina and Bogota, Columbia, where my father was an executive with Roman Haas. By the time I left South America, I was fourteen years old and I spoke the language fluently. But then I didn't use my Spanish for probably 15, 20 years. Once I started this company, I basically had to relearn the language, but fortunately it didn't take as long the second time around.

Why did I start the Spanish Beisbol Network? I guess because a family tragedy had entered my life and when that happens you start re-evaluating everything. Maybe it was a midlife crisis or something. At the time, I was with AT&T Broadband and then Comcast came and bought them out. I was Director of Employee Communications, and I was given an assignment that I absolutely hated. I remember telling my boss one day that I would finish the assignment but when it's done, I'm done.

That night after talking to my boss I came home and told my wife that I had an idea for a business. Personally, I think she didn't believe that I was going to do it but the only thing she said to me was, "Well as long as you have benefits for the kids you can do whatever you want." At the time, we had four kids and her comment was basically how I got my first investor to sign on with me. The investor asked me, "Why are benefits listed first on your business plan?" I said to him, "My wife won't let me do this without it." He basically ended the interview and said, "Where do I sign?" Because he knew I was fully committed to making the business work

My first major league signing for the Spanish Beisbol Network was with the Boston Red Sox. When I told my friends and family about talking to the Red Sox they said, "The Red Sox aren't going to listen to you. Who the hell is Bill Kulik?" I remember getting the phone call from Dan Duquette (former GM of the Red Sox), saying that John Harrington (CEO of the Red Sox) would like to meet with you. I remember calling my dad and saying, "Hey, Dan Duquette & John Harrington want to meet with me." And my dad goes, "Oh crap!"

It was like Pat Gillick and Dave Montgomery calling you and asking if they could sit down and talk with you. My dad said, "Alright, you and I have to talk. I want to see your business plan." At this point my dad was just retiring so he's real nervous about me. He was like, "You have four kids; you can't walk away from a steady job," and everything that parents say to you when you're about to do crazy things. So he took my business plan to some of his venture capital buddies and showed it to them, and they're all reading it over. At the time, the money I was looking for was too small for any venture group to handle. I just wasn't asking for enough money to get it going, and they were looking for investments in the tens of millions. I remember my dad's friend said, "This is very interesting. Way too small for us, but Bill Sr., you should do this." And my dad goes, "Really?" So his friend says, "Yeah this is a good business plan." And so my father then puts the money in and off it went. I ended up signing my first contract with the Red Sox right before the start of the 2001 season.

I actually got involved with the Phillies when the Red Sox came here to play in 2004. Back then we had to call in advance to reserve a space and get the telephone lines connected so we could do our broadcast. I remember the Phillies being kind of shocked when they said to me, "The Red Sox have a Spanish broadcast team?" Because you expect it from the Dodgers or Mets but not from the Red Sox. So we're announcing those three games and I remember the Phillies officials kind of always looking in the booth and I finally said to them, "Can I help you?" and they say, "Well, we don't understand how the Red Sox have a Spanish broadcast and we don't. Can we talk to you?" And so we basically started talks right then and there. We started the spring of 2005, and we've been here ever since.

Quotable: "I don't know what else we can do with Brett Myers but to keep on sending him out there" – Charlie Manuel on Comcast Post Game Live

Wednesday, May 14th - Braves 8 Phillies 6 (22-19) 2nd - 1 ½ GB the Marlins

Philadelphia - Brett Myers (2-4, 5.91) is pummeled in 4 1/3rd innings giving up 8 runs (6 earned) while walking 3 and striking out 6 … his numbers this season are dismal. He is tied for the fourth-worse ERA in the NL. He has the highest ERA on the team. He gave up three homeruns tonight to add to his major-league leading total of 15 homeruns allowed, and in his last five starts, he is 0-3 with a 7.62 ERA … Chris Coste went 4 for 4 and scored two runs … Chase Utley hit his 14th HR of the season. That's tops in the majors … Ryan Howard had a bad game in the field again. In the 5th, Howard dropped a double play ball that hit him smack dab in the middle of his glove … Losing 8-0 after five innings, the Phillies did manage to score 6 unanswered runs and actually had the tying run on 2nd in the 9th but Shane Victorino hit a long fly out to the warning track to end the game. Stuff: Today marked a quarter way through the season. The biggest question marks for this team are its inconsistent hitting and its starters. Cole Hamels is the only starter with an ERA under 4.00 (3.36). Kyle Kendrick (4.93), Jamie Moyer (5.02), Brett Myers (5.91) and Adam Eaton (5.40) have all struggled this season. Fortunately, the bullpen has the best ERA in the majors at 2.63. They also have the 3rd lowest opponent's batting average at .226 (lowest in the NL).

The Phillies need to get to the bottom of the velocity issue with Myers, because if he's hurt, now's the time to do something about it. A 15-day trip to the DL would be an excellent option. It's not like they'd miss his starts right now, and they have a replacement throwing well in Happ. A tryout would also allow the Phils to see what they have in Happ, who's 25 and doesn't need any more time in AAA. Myers' strikeout totals - which are still strong - are a little deceiving. Even the game at San Fran was not particularly sharp

Chris Coste signing autographs as he and Clay Condrey commute in for another day at work

and the reported improvement in velocity couldn't have been more overblown. He's barely at

90, and he looks sloppy, too. Sharp contrast in craft between Glavine, who hits his spots, and Myers, who isn't establishing his fastball and gets burned by too many careless mistakes.

Taguchi slumping: A look around the league finds teams starting to cut bait with underperforming players, even players with substantial contracts. It happened recently with outfielder Jayson Michaels in Cleveland. That was on a different team, one with better depth than the Phils, So Taguchi, who grounded into a killer DP last night, might have been out of a job as well. I thought Taguchi would be a nice fit – and still may be – but his last hit came April 25, and he's batting .178. Taguchi, who signed for $1M this winter, will be 39 in July. One has to wonder if he's lost just too many steps to contribute.

Quotable: "It's one of those monkeys that have been on my back. It's definitely the best I've pitched so far this year. Any time I'm able to keep my pitch count under 110 after the eighth inning, I think I'm capable of pitching the ninth." - Cole Hamels on the first shutout of his career

Thursday, May 15th- Phillies 5 Braves 0 (23-19) 2nd - 1 GB the Marlins

Philadelphia - Cole Hamels (5-3) threw his first career complete game shutout, scattering 4 hits and two walks while striking out 6 Braves. From the 1st through the 6th inning, Hamels retired 15 straight batters … Hamels also did damage at the plate going 2 for 4, raising his average to an incredible .320 … Pedro Feliz (6), Ryan Howard (9) and Shane Victorino (1) all homered to generate all five Phillies' runs. Stuff: The win was Charlie Manuel's 285th as manager of the Phillies tying him with Terry "Mulligan" Francona for 11th place on the Phillies All-Time Wins list.

Following the first complete-game shutout of Cole Hamels' career why not sign Hamels to a multiyear contract right now? This comes on the heels of another deal to a rising star, as the Brewers signed Ryan Braun to an 8-year, $45 million contract yesterday, which buys out his arbitration years and eats two years of free agency. Elsewhere, the Rays agreed on a three-year extension with left-hander Scott Kazmir worth $28.5 million, which includes a team option for 2012. So why not offer the same type of long-term deal to Hamels? Phillies GM Pat Gillick had the answer.

"Right now, it isn't going to happen," Gillick told Dave Murphy of the *Daily News*. Ok, then. So, when do the Phils start thinking about it?

"If at some point, if [Hamels is] performing to the level, you're going to have to talk multiyear at some point," Gillick said. "These guys, maybe they are smarter giving guys 8-year deals. I don't know."

Cole Hamels is as dangerous with a bat as he is with his arm

Quotable: "It was a blessing in disguise I guess (coming to Philadelphia). Now I'm here with this group of guys, this team, this organization. I can't say enough about this place. This city, these fans, it was special tonight. I never had a curtain call and I had two tonight. That was pretty cool. I'm grateful and I'm thankful.' - Jayson Werth on his 3 HR and 8 RBI performance

Friday, May 16th - Phillies 10 Blue Jays 3 (24-19) Tie for 1st with the Marlins

Philadelphia - *In the first inter-league game of the season, Jayson Werth destroyed the Blue Jays pitching staff, going 3 for 4 with three homeruns in first three at bats - a solo shot, a three-run blast and a grand slam (the first of his career). He ended the game with 8 RBIs, tying a franchise record …Jimmy Rollins and Shane Victorino had two hits apiece …Jamie Moyer (3-3) got the win in 6 2/3rd innings of work while the bullpen pitched 2 1/3rd scoreless innings. Stuff: Werth's 8 RBIs tied a Phillies' franchise record for most RBIs in a game with Kitty Bransfield, Gavvy Cravath, Willie "Puddin' Head" Jones, and Mike Schmidt … He is the 18th player in Phillies' history to hit 3 homeruns in a game … The last player to hit 3 homeruns in a game was Ryan Howard on September 3, 2006 … The Phils now have 62 HRs through 43 games. Tops in the majors.*

Werth, who was plucked from the scrap pile last winter when the Dodgers decided they couldn't wait for his wrist to heal, is turning into the steal of the Pat Gillick era. Although his left/right splits are cavernous, the Phils seem to be drawing more left-handed pitching these days and Werth is playing a significant role, adding a much-needed power bat from the right side to compliment Pat Burrell. They're no longer doomed against a left-hander.

Some thought the outfield would be only a little better than average after Aaron Rowand, but that hasn't been the case. Nine homers by Werth ties Burrell and Howard as he continues to look more like an everyday player and less like a 4th outfielder. He's strong, fast and patient. His defense would show better in right, but that's another subject. His numbers are up with the best at his position and close to very best in baseball.

Jayson Werth's 8 RBIs tied a franchise record

There's a guy in Werth who's very interesting. He's still at a decent age and is probably ready to start making real money. If they believe he can sustain this level, and if they feel they cannot keep Burrell, you have to wonder if the Phils should think about keeping him around a tad longer than the schedule dictates when the two sides meet this winter.

Quotable: "Who can't? People in New Jersey could hear the boos. I heard some screaming, and some cheeseburger comments, but I tuned that stuff out. It didn't bother me." - Former Phillies and current Blue Jays' catcher Rob Barajas when asked his reaction to the chorus of boos that greeted him throughout the game

Saturday, May 17th - Blue Jays 6 Phillies 3 (24-20) 2nd - 1 GB the Marlins

Philadelphia - *Ex-Phillie Rob Barajas' hit two homeruns including a 5th inning grand slam off of Adam Eaton that sealed the Phillies' defeat. Even prior to the start of the game, Phillies' fans began booing their ex-catcher. The vilification came from an incident last season against the Marlins in which Barajas stood up to tag Hanley Ramirez instead of blocking the plate. Ramirez ended up scoring the tying run in a game that the Phils eventually lost. Two pitches later, Brett Myers hurt his shoulder and missed two months of baseball. Phillies' fans, being who they are, ended up taking out their frustrations on the catcher and never forgave him for the rest of the season. To make matters worse for Phillies' fans, Barajas smoked Adam Eaton with the grand slam and Tom Gordon for a solo shot in the 9th. 5 RBIs and a "back at you" to the fans ... Eaton (0-2, 5.59) was pitching fairly well going into the 5th then all things broke apart for him again ...Jimmy Rollins went 3 for 5 with 2 RBIs and is batting .329 ... Greg Dobbs went 2 for 4 with an RBI. Stuff: The Phillies threw out 3 runners at the plate during the game and one at second base.*

You're sitting in your seat at Citizens Bank Park and you hear Dan Baker come over the loudspeakers announcing Shane Victorino as the next batter. All of a sudden you hear a few seconds of some type of reggae song as Shane walks from the on-deck circle into the batters box and then it stops. You're sitting there and wondering to yourself, "What was that song? ... I've heard it before!" Or you're thinking to yourself, "Why in the world did he pick that song?"

Mark Wyatt "spinning" his music for the crowd

To answer those questions one would have to turn to the Phillies' Music Coordinator, Mark Wyatt. He's the guy up in the booth spinning the records ... oops, I mean the MP3s for the Phillies. No matter what recorded music you hear in the stadium, it all starts with Mark.

"Buffalo Soldier" by Bob Marley. That's Victorino's song. Yeah, he picked that out and he's been using that song for a couple of years. Shane loves Bob Marley and reggae music. Marley's from Jamaica. Victorino is from Hawaii. Maybe it's an island thing.

Rollins just changed his song yesterday. It was "Umma Do Me" by Rocko but now he's playing the GEICO song where the Caveman is in the airport and sees the sign that says, "It's so easy a Caveman can do it.". The song is called "Remind Me" by a group called Royksopp. I have no idea why he changed it! A player will sometimes change it to try to snap them out of a slump or just because they found a new song that they like better.

I even get calls from the players sometimes who want to make fun of the other players. Like for example, Jayson Werth. I don't know what the story is behind this one but I got a call yesterday from an unnamed player who told me that if Werth is going to hit in the next day or so they want me to play "Don't Fear the Reaper" and "King Kong". I don't know why, something must be going on in the clubhouse.

Some players have only one song they want me to play. But others will give me a few to choose from. For those guys I'll rotate through their songs depending upon my mood and the amount of time I think they have before they get to the plate. Here's the list I'm currently playing:

Jimmy Rollins: *"Remind Me"* - Royksopp
Jayson Werth: *"Merchant of Death"* – Ramin Djawadi
Chase Utley: *"Kashmir"* – Led Zeppelin
Ryan Howard: *"Dey Know"* – Shawty Lo, *"The Boss"* – Rick Ross or *"The Second Coming"* – Juelz Santana
Pat Burrell: *"Dirty Laundry"* - Don Henley
Shane Victorino: *"Buffalo Soldier"* – Bob Marley
Pedro Feliz: *"Faint"* – Linkin Park
Carolos Ruiz: *"Remedy"* - Seether
Chris Coste: *"La Grange"* – ZZ Top or *"Lover Rollercoaster"* – Red Hot Chili Peppers
Greg Dobbs: *"Megalomaniac"* – Incubus
Geoff Jenkins: *"Kiss Kiss"* – Chris Brown

Some players don't have a song. When they come I'll just play whatever I like at that moment.

I actually do have song lists for the pitchers as well. The starters I play when they come into the game and the relievers when they start jogging to the mound from the bullpen. The pitchers though are pretty superstitious. They'll usually go with the same song unless they are in a really bad slump so they usually don't switch around too often. Here's what they've given me so far this year:

Tom Gordon: *"Flash's Theme"* – Queen
Cole Hamels: *"Thunderstruck"* – AC/DC
Kyle Kendrick: *"Wherever I May Roam"* – Metallica
Brad Lidge: *"Soldiers"* – Drowning Pool
Ryan Madson: *"Blister"* – Down Theory
Brett Myers: *"Enemy"* – Drowning Pool
Adam Eaton: *"Cochise"* – Audioslave
JC Romero: *"Out Here Grindin"* – DJ Khaled

There are definitely rules that we have to follow when we can play the music or sound effects during a game. We can't make fun of the umpires. When the batter's in the batters box the music has to stop, and we can't play music when there's a play happening on the field. Other than that, it's open season.

My biggest screw up ever happened back in 1999 at the Vet. The Phillies had a back-up shortstop by the name of Alex Arias. He got 3 doubles in a game against Pittsburgh and he was coming up to bat late in the game. I think that if he would have gotten another double it would have been a record for the Phillies, or at least a record for him. So right before he come ups to hit, John Brazer (Phils' Director of Fun & Games) comes running into the control room before he comes up and says, "Mark, Mark you have to play Double Vision for him." I said Ok, whatever. So at the time I didn't have Double Vision loaded in my machine, so I had to turn around to get it from my pile of CDs. In the meanwhile there was a really bad call at first base that went against the Phillies, and I wasn't watching. So just as Arias comes walking up to the plate I pop in Double Vision.

So now the entire game comes to a screeching halt. It was being broadcasted nation-wide on ESPN and the guys announcing for them were like, "What's going on? Play has stopped for some reason." What had happened was the umpire thought that I had played the song because of the bad call at first so he stopped the game and went into the Phillies' dugout to call my boss. The umpire ends up getting connected to the Phillies' operator and he wants to talk to the guy in charge of Phanavision. But she can't get anyone on the phone. She's calling all over the place and this goes on for more than 5 minutes. Finally, she connects the umpire to our room and the umpire says, "If you don't stop making fun of the umpires we're gonna shut Phanavision completely down." After he hangs up the phone, the entire room busted out in laughter and I'm still not exactly sure what's going on. I ended up explaining to everyone what happened and my boss, who finally shows up, told me not to worry.

David Montgomery called me later that night. I had to explain to him what happened; he didn't appear to be too upset. I still have my job.

Quotable: "I hate rain delays, they suck. Just stop and get it over with and see you later. I hate rain delays, doubleheaders, and afternoon starts. Today, all of that screwed up our rotation, it screwed up our bullpen." - Phillies' reliever Rudy Seanez on today's 2 hour and 43 minutes worth of rain delays

Sunday, May 18th - Blue Jays 6 Phillies 5 (24-21) Tied for 2nd - 1 GB the Marlins
Philadelphia - Ryan Howard gave the Phils a quick 2-0 lead in the 1st inning on his 10th HR of the season and then the heavens opened up for a 2 hour 4 minute rain delay. Later in the 6th the rains came again and stopped play for an additional 39 minutes ... The Phillies couldn't hold a

3-0 lead as Chad Durbin and Rudy Seanez each gave up 3 runs in the 5th and 6th innings … Pat Burrell hit his 10th homerun of the season in the bottom of the 9th but the rally fell short. Rob Barajas continued his revenge against his former team. He went 2 for 3 with an RBI in helping his team take two of three games from the Phillies.

Baseball Chapel is an international ministry recognized by Major League and Minor League Baseball which has been in operation for over 35 years as a service to those in professional baseball who desire to deepen their Christian faith but who are unable to attend church during the season. Their ministry is directed toward players, coaches, managers, their wives, umpires, team personnel and stadium staff in helping them grow in their walk with Jesus Christ.

Phillies' Chaplain, Rich Sparling (left) spreading the Good News

The Baseball Chapel in Philadelphia is run by Reverend Rich Sparling and his wife Beverly. The two Bucks County residents have been directly involved with Baseball Chapel full-time since 1998. Rich is a full-time employee of the ministry where he is Director of Latin American Ministries. He and his wife have been volunteering their time at Citizens Bank Park to help encourage and build up the faith of those that aren't able to attend church during the season.

My primary responsibility is to share the Good News of Jesus Christ with players, coaches, managers, umpires, their families and stadium personnel. We have chapel services Sunday mornings and also on Wednesdays when we have our weekly bible study. While I'm conducting the services with the men, my wife Bev holds similar meetings with their wives and their children. It has been a joy for us to be able to meet and work with everyone here.

My testimony? Back in the early 1960s, traveling evangelists were still very popular across the United States. We had some traveling evangelists come to our church and presented the gospel message to the entire congregation. During one of the evening services, I clearly understood that I needed my own personal relationship with Jesus to be saved from my sins. So I responded to the invitation at the end of the service.

But my desire to be in ministry really began when I was about ten years old. Back in 1964 there was a terrible rebellion in the Congo in which the rebel army took a number of missionaries and other foreign hostages for well over a year. One of hostages was a famous medical missionary by the name of Dr. Paul Carlson. During a rescue attempt by American and Belgian armies, the rebels panicked and started killing the hostages. Dr. Carlson and another hostage, Al Larsen, tried escaping together but Dr. Carlson was shot and killed while Mr. Larson was able to escape. Mr. Larsen came to our church one day to share his experience in the Congo and told everyone about the incredible faith of Dr. Carlson and how he stood up for his beliefs without denying them. It was during that meeting that the Lord began to draw me to the ministry.

After High School, I went to Northeastern Bible College. Initially, I worked at a Bible Conference for a year after graduation and then I ended up teaching at the Philadelphia College of Bible for five years. Soon after graduating, I began teaching at a Christian School in Pennsylvania. After a few years of teaching, I felt a strong desire to become a full time missionary in Latin America. So my wife and our two kids packed our bags and went to Costa Rico for a year to learn Spanish, and then we moved to the Dominican Republic where we were missionaries for nine years.

In 1998 we came back to the United States and were introduced to the Baseball Chapel. At the time, they were looking for someone to run their Latin American ministries. Vince Nauss, the President of Baseball Chapel, spoke to me about their mission of spreading the gospel within the ballparks and it ended up being a perfect fit so till now that is my full time job.

All baseball chaplains, including myself, are volunteers. We don't get paid to come to the ballpark, but we do this as part of our desire to tell people about the good news of the gospel.

On a typical Sunday we will get to the ballpark by 9:45am. At 10:05, we have our chapel for the stadium workers. I usually then go into the Phillies' clubhouse and talk individually to the players. I then conduct Spanish chapel for the Latinos on the team followed by a chapel in English for the Phillies' pitchers. Each chapel lasts 15-20 minutes. Once that is done, I'll then go over to the visiting clubhouse and conduct their chapel. Afterwards, I will stop in the umpires' room and meet with them and finally after the Phillies finish their batting practice, I will conduct chapel for the position players.

The thing I find most interesting about being a team chaplain is that I have the opportunity to minister to players who, because of their status in society, have the platform and opportunity to become world-changers with the gospel.

The most difficult aspect of being a team chaplain really has nothing to do with baseball. It really comes down to wanting everyone to know Jesus Christ as the Lord and Savior of their lives, whether it's a ballplayer or an usher. I just want everyone to hear the message that changed my life and can change theirs.

JC Romero was 14 years old when he gave his life to Christ. In his testimony on baseballchapel.org he tells how he wanted to stop living in darkness and explained how he dedicated his life to live in His light. The following is from an interview with JC on the importance of the Baseball Chapel in his life.

Baseball Chapel keeps me connected to the Lord. Because of the busy schedule that we have as ballplayers we barely have time to seek God as we would like. But Baseball Chapel provides that opportunity for me to focus on the importance of why I am here on this earth. Even if it's for 15-20 minutes a week, it provides the time in which I can separate myself from baseball and come before the presence of God and learn about Him.

I've been fortunate in my life. I come from a Christian family in Puerto Rico where my mom is a preacher so before I come on to the field I always try to present myself before the presence of God and try to ask Him for guidance because without Him none of this would not be possible.

During the off-season I go back to my hometown of San Juan, Puerto Rico. My mom runs a church so I do a lot of work with the youth in the town. The youth is the future of Puerto Rico and they need Christian role models so the message I try to give them is that no matter what you do in life, no matter how successful or rich you may become in life, God is the most important thing.

My main ministry though is what I do now with the Phillies right now. This is the bridge that God is using for me to speak to the youth, to be an example for them. I want everyone to know that the JC Romero between the lines, who is aggressive and on-fire, is the same JC Romero that uses that same energy to reach the community in a Christian manner.

Each time I meet with the youth I leave them with the verse that I live by which is written inside my baseball cap. Philippians 4:13 says," I can do all things through Christ who strengthens me." So every time I talk to a kid I try to share that with them. It's not about me and what I can do with the Phillies. It's about what He does in my life and can do in their lives.

Quotable: ""We've got to play better. There is a reason why you don't get a play or we don't get a pitch. Getting it done is what we're all about. We want to win. We talk about winning. We have guys on our team out there that talk about winning. How are we going to win? By playing good and hustling and playing hard and getting the job done." - Manager Charlie Manuel on the Phillies recent decline

Monday, May 19th - Nationals 4 Phillies 0 (24-22) 3rd - 1 ½ GB the Marlins
Washington D.C. - The Phillies were shut out for the 2nd time this season, both against Washington,. This time it happened in their first-ever visit to Nationals Park in Washington, D.C. ... Brett Myers (2-5, 5.76) took the loss as he gave up 3 runs in 6 innings pitched. It was the first time that Myers went beyond 5 innings since May 3rd in San Francisco ...Utley, Victorino and Jenkins had two hits apiece ... The Nationals had 6 doubles in the game ...Nationals' starter Tim Redding (6-3 3.16) scattered seven hits in 6 1/3rd innings. Stuff: Even with the shutout, the Phillies are 4th in the National League in scoring runs with 219 ...The Phils have been held to one run or less four times this season and in the game following have averaged 8.3 runs.

Good fortune has been on the Phillies' side for most of the season, as the club emerged victorious in a number of tight contests and comeback victories. But lately, a listless offense has shepherded the yang to April's ying. They're 4 for 32 with runners in scoring position during the last three games. Redding, who still appears utterly hittable to the naked eye, is responsible for leading the opposition in the second shutout against the Phils this season.

On the mound, the outing qualifies as a quality start for Brett Myers, but applying that term feels like grasping at straws, especially against a very weak Nationals club. His improvement in velocity appears marginal at best, and he's still missing his spots.

A Phillies' fan poses with National's mascot, Abe Lincoln at Nationals Park in Washington D.C.

Quotable: "He's one of the elite guys in the league, despite just being up here for barely over two years," - Nationals' manager Manny Acta on Cole Hamels.

<u>Tuesday, May 20th - Phillies 1 Nationals 0 (25-22) Tie for 2nd 1 ½ GB the Marlins</u>
Washington D.C. - *Pinch hitter Greg Dobbs RBI double in the top of the 9th knocked in Eric Bruntlett for the only run of the entire game …Cole Hamels pitched a spectacular game, going 7 strong innings while shutting down the Nationals on 4 hits and striking out 11. He also extended his current scoreless streak to a career-high 19.0 innings… Tom Gordon (4-2) picked up the win in relief … Brad Lidge pitched a shaky 9th (walking two) but managed to get his 11th save of the season …Pedro Feliz's double in the top of the 9th set up the winning run for the Phillies. Feliz went 2 for 4 on the night raising his average to .234. Stuff: Although they scored in the 9th, the Phillies' offense had not scored up to that time in 17 innings. The last time they went that long without scoring was June 20-23, 2006 …Greg Dobbs became only the 2nd pinch hitter in the past 6 years to drive in the winning run in the 9th inning of a 1-0 game. Ex-Phillie Travis Lee did it for Tampa Bay in August 2005.*

Insightful fans emerge from the woodwork every day on Beerleaguer.com and today was no exception as Phillie Phorever wondered what Charlie Manuel was thinking in the ninth.

"Charlie Manuel's mishandling of third base is costing the Phillies, and I seriously doubt he will realize that, tonight, he unknowingly burned three players (Feliz, Dobbs, Bruntlett) as he did time after time last season (Helms, Dobbs, Nunez).

"For the manager to pinch run Bruntlett in place of Feliz -- who was already in scoring position with no one out! -- is ridiculous. Presumably, the reason Dobbs does not start is because he is below average defensively at 3B (note: Dobbs also has a sore back), even though he is clearly a better hitter against right-handed pitching than Feliz. If that is the case, why would you remove your top defender at that position for the bottom of the ninth, when defense matters most?

"Moreover, is Bruntlett that much faster than Feliz? Even if he were Vince Coleman, Feliz is standing on second base with nobody out. As it turns out, Bruntlett winds up trotting home, which, conceivably, Feliz could have done just as well. Thus, Manuel removed his top defensive third baseman for no reason.

Charlie Manuel's strategies during today's game raised some questions from fans

"On top of this, he leaves Dobbs in to run for himself! What the hell is So Taguchi doing on this team if he is not pinch running or catching balls in the outfield? It's almost as if Manuel tries something and it doesn't play out favorably, so he changes his strategy mid-inning. The equivalent would be splitting 8s in blackjack, losing both hands, and never doing it again even though it is the proper statistical play.

"Dobbs gets thrown out at the plate. One, Dobbs should never have been sent (not even with two outs) because Utley was on deck. Thus, your best hitter doesn't have a chance to hit. However, if that run was important enough for Smith to send Dobbs even with Utley standing there, why wasn't Taguchi running for Dobbs? Wouldn't Taguchi have beaten the throw?

"The decision-making on this team by the coaching staff is brutal. What, exactly, would Manuel have done had this game gone to extra innings? Who would he have double-switched Lidge's spot with? It couldn't be Bruntlett, because that would leave them with Coste as their third baseman. Burrell was still in the lineup. Would his second pinch hitter be Adam Eaton? Maybe the guy can handle a clubhouse, but he cannot make baseball decisions." -- Phillie Phorever

Quotable: "It seemed like forever. I don't know if we saved it all for tonight, but it's definitely nice to get the big boy going." – Shane Victorino on the 12 run explosion in the midst of their recent offensive slump

Wednesday, May 21st - Phillies 12 Nationals 2 (26-22) Tie for 2nd – 1 ½ GB the Marlins

Washington D.C. - *Ryan Howard's bat awakens as he goes 3 for 5 with 2 HRs and 5 RBIs, driving him up closer to the Mendoza line. He is now hitting .195 ...Jamie Moyer (4-3, 4.37) pitched 6 innings of shutout ball ... Clay Condrey pitched the final three innings to earn his first career save, although he did give up the only two runs that the Nationals could muster ...Shane Victorino and Pedro Feliz had 3 hits apiece. Each homered as well. Stuff: The 12 runs is the highest scoring game for the Phils this season ...In the 15 hit onslaught, Pat Burrell and Jayson Werth both went 0 for 4. Burrell's average has plummeted from .333 to .271 since the beginning of May. He is 0 for 11 in the last three games ...Ryan Howard's 2 dingers marked the 13th multi-homerun game of his career ... 45 year old Jamie Moyer pitched in his 46th major league ballpark tonight, as he made his Nationals Park debut. That ties Phillies' reliever Rudy Seanez amongst active pitchers.*

The 2006 National League MVP is having a horrifyingly bad season. What are they going to do about it, besides pout?

Prior to today's game Howard was hitting .183 and struck out three times on Tuesday, the seventh time it's happened this season, and no one appears to be in a rush to do much about it. The manager continues to pencil him into the clean-up spot, and Howard continues to swing at everything. "You ground out. You fly out. You strike out. An out is an out," Howard told the *Philadelphia Inquirer* in March. "You don't hear anybody say, 'That guy led the league in groundouts last year.' "

Even with a 3 for 5 performance today, Ryan Howard's .195 average is a major cause for concern

That quote gets right to the heart of the problem. On pace for around 225 strikeouts, we get the point. We also recognize that your .686 OPS is about .300 points below where it needs to be for you to have much purpose batting clean-up. Meanwhile, the entire offense seems to be following the leader with terrible at bats while lineup-wide changes haven't happened.

"Strikeouts may be benign to sabermetricians," Dave Sheinin writes in the *Washington Post*, "but they can still do damage in the bigger picture."

Quotable: "Right now I'm probably pitching the best of my career." – Brad Lidge after recording his 12th save of the year in 12 opportunities while sporting a 0.43 ERA

<u>Thursday, May 22nd - Phillies 7 Astros 5 (27-22) Tie for 2nd - 1 ½ GB the Marlins</u>

Houston- *Pat Burrell's pinch-hit homerun in the 8th inning broke a 5-5 tie, allowing the Phils to win their third straight game. It was Burrell's first appearance as a pinch hitter this year … Rollins, Victorino and Feliz had 2 hits each …Kyle Kendrick pitched poorly, allowing 5 runs on 8 hits in 5 innings. His ERA is now 5.19 …The bullpen picked up Kendrick as they threw four scoreless innings against the Astros, scattering three hits … Chad Durbin (1-1) picked up the win and Brad Lidge closed out the game with his 12th save of the year. Stuff: Since Ryan Howard hit a season-low .163 on May 7th, he is hitting. 304 with 7 HRs and 15 RBIs during that 14 game stretch …Brad Lidge received a text message from the Astros Lance Berkman after the game that said, "I hate you," after Berkman popped up to end the game.*

"Now batting for the Phillies … Number Eeeeeeeeleven …. shortstop …. Jimmyyyyy Rollllllllllinzzzzzzzz!" For the past 37 seasons over 80,000,000 fans have come through the turnstiles of Veterans Stadium and Citizens Bank Park and have been graced with the sensational stylings of the Phillies' Public Address Announcer, Dan Baker.

One of the finest gentlemen in the entire city of Philadelphia, Baker is a true cornerstone of Philadelphia sports. In addition to his role with the Phillies, Dan has also been the PA announcer for the Philadelphia Eagles since 1985 and is the only PA announcer to have worked for all four major professional sports teams, which also includes the Flyers and the 76ers. He has been broadcasting Philadelphia Big 5 Basketball games since 1977 and currently

Phillies' PA Announcer Dan Baker has been with the team since 1972

is the long-time radio announcer for the Drexel Dragons men's basketball team. Dan was inducted into the Big 5 Hall-of-Fame in 1997.

I started working for the Phillies as their Public Address announcer in 1972. Bill Giles hired me but the person most responsible for me getting the interview with Bill was the Phils' former Director of Stadium Operations, Pat Cassidy. Mr. Cassidy knew me because of some of the behind the scenes things that I used to do at some Eagles games and Phillies games. At the Eagles games I would do the statistics or spot for the visiting play-by-play announcers. I tried to learn the play-by-play craft by observing and listening carefully to their styles. But I also did a post game radio show on WFPG in Atlantic City. It was called the NFL Report with Dan Baker, and I would call in and do a report on that particular game and report on scores from other NFL games. So he used to see me in the press box doing my post game show.

Between the 1971 season and the 1972 season Pat Cassidy told me that Bill was contemplating making a change in PA announcers. He came up to me one day and asked me if I would have interest in doing the job. "Oh God, I'd give my right arm!" I told him. He said "I can't promise anything but I work closely with Bill Giles and I'll recommend that Bill interviews you, but after that you're on your own."

A few days late Bill gives me a call and asked that I come in for an interview. So I interviewed with him in November of '71. The interview went very well. During the course of the interview, he told me that that although announcing is a very important component of the PA job at Veterans Stadium I would also be responsible for running the in-game progress report; keeping track of the balls, strikes, outs, hits, run, errors, and the entire line score. He also wanted to make sure that I knew baseball so I told him about my previous experience in Little League, the Camden County Pony League, the Garden State League and as a player at Audubon High School (NJ). I wasn't a big star or anything, but I wanted to make sure that he understood that I was very familiar with the game.

As a child I was a huge Phillies fan and I would lay in bed late at night listening to the game on the radio and keep count of the balls and strikes on my hands. So during the interview when he told me about keeping balls and strikes I immediately told him, "Mr. Giles if you hire me, I will be the quickest and most accurate in baseball." He hired me right after the interview.

My sports heroes growing up were Robin Roberts, Richie Ashburn, Del Ennis and Stan Lopata. Robin Roberts was my favorite. In fact, there's a picture of me introducing Robby in last year's yearbook. It was such a great honor for me.

My father, Edward Baker, was the one who really connected me into the game. He used to take me to ballgames at Connie Mack Stadium. He was a hard worker and enjoyed the Phillies immensely. He used to drive a bread truck for Friehofers Bread and eventually for Wonder Bread. One of my first memories growing up was going to see the Phillies play the New York Giants with my dad. I remember the first time I ever say Willie Mays play and thought he was absolutely terrific.

Pete Byron was the Phillies' PA announcer back then. I thought he was terrific. I think he announced for them for about 15 years. I know Dave Zinkoff (famous 76ers PA announcer) was the Phillies' PA announcer in 1950 for the Whiz Kids National League pennant. I admired The Zink. He was something special.

I've been able to meet a few PA announcers from other major league teams over the years. We've had a few of them come to observe what we do and how we do it. I think we've had the PA announcers from the Mets, Pirates, Indians, Orioles and Nationals come up to meet with me.

I went up to New York City to observe the infamous Bob Sheppard of the Yankees. I learned a lot from him. He has been their PA announcer for 58 years! He started in 1951. He was born in 1910 so he's getting close to 100 years old! I don't think anybody's ever achieved that kind of longevity.

Since I started in 1972, I think I've announced close to 3,000 games. In all those years I missed maybe 15 or 16 games. I missed when my wife Cathy and I went to our son's Darren and daughter's Courtney's graduations. I missed a couple of games in the fall in the 70's and 80's when I was doing Temple football and Penn football. The Phillies were kind enough to give me permission to do the play-by-play for those games. I haven't missed a game at Citizens Bank Park yet. I think the last one I missed was back in 2001.

When I'm announcing the ballplayers I always want to make sure that I pronounce it correctly. We have a "Green Book" that basically lists the phonetic spelling of all the players. There's a high degree of accuracy in the book but sometimes it's wrong or a player may not be in the book. When that occurs, I'll usually go ask the Public Relations manager from the other team what the correct pronunciation is of the player's name. But in some cases where there's a discrepancy over maybe the phonetic spelling or the way someone tells me that their name is said, I'll go ask the players themselves.

I remember this happening one time with one of the Phillies' reserves in the 1980 World Champions, Ramon Aviles. Ramon's last name has been anglicized over time so I went down on the field one time and asked him, "How do you say your last name?" He said, "However you hear it said on the radio is fine." So I said, "Well I'll say it whatever way you want it." Out of respect for every individual that plays the game, I feel that we owe it to them to say their name the way they want it said or the way that their ethnic background or language dictates. He said, "Well in my country my last name is said AV-i-Les." And I said, "Well, then I will announce you as Ramon AV-i-Les." I always love doing Spanish…I took Spanish in high school, and I was pretty good at it. But the Spanish names, the longer last names, lend themselves to a more melodic interpretation. Names of players like Mickey Morandini, Greg Luzinski … they have multi-syllabic words. The really lend themselves to announcing them with some flare.

There is one funny story I like to tell about announcing a batter. Situations dictate whether I try to raise a player's name to a crescendo or not. If Luzinski comes up in a tied game with the bases loaded and one out, I'll give it everything I got … "Now batting for the Phillies, No. 19 leftfielder Grrreg Luzinnnnnskiiiii!". But on the other hand if a player comes up in the late innings of the games when we're losing 10-1, I'm not gonna hit it so hard…because then I'm insulting the fans' intelligence. One day back in the early 90's, I'm standing in the Phillies' dugout at the Vet. Before the game, Larry Bowa is in there with me. He was a coach at the time. Von Hayes comes in and Larry turns to him and he says, "Oh, here he is Von. Tell him yourself." Well Hayes gestures towards me and says, "I think I scored short". I said, "What are you talking about?" He said, "Well if I hit a home run the next time up, you give me that energetic, 'Now Batting … Vonnnnn Hayessssss!' But if I strike out the next time and go up to bat you give me the basic Von Hayes." I told him, " Von, it's the situation. You can strike out 3 times. If you come up with the bases loaded in the 8th inning of a tied game, I'm gonna give it the big Von Hayes and try to get the fans behind you. And make you feel good about it." I said, "On the other hand, you can hit a couple of home runs, but if we're losing 14-4 in the late inning when you come up I'm probably not going to give it the basic 'Von Hayes!' because of the situation."… He all of a sudden says, "Ah, Bullshit!" and then turned and walked away.

There are some favorites that I do like saying. Mickey Morandini is a fun one to say. I also liked announcing Bobby Abreu. Not just because of his name but because he was such a nice player as well. One of my favorites, and this is going way back a bit to the 1970s, was Ted Sizemore. … "Now batting for the Phillies No. 9, 2nd baseman Ted Sizzzze-More." And Ted loved it. He came back for an old-timers game one time and he said to me, "Let me hear you say that name just one more time."

On the current team, I like saying Jimmy Rollins a lot. Pat Burrell is a good one as well. I think one thing that Pat appreciates about how I announce him is that I still give him the big Pat Burrell even when he's in a slump. "Now batting, Number 5, left fielder … Pat Burrellllll" … I don't care if he struck out at 5 times. Boom! I'm gonna give him that hit.

My biggest gaff was with one of the fans most favorite Phillies of all time, Willie Montanez. The Phillies were playing the San Francisco Giants and I must have had a brain cramp or something so I announce him with, "Now batting for the Phillies, No. 27 Willie McCovey." I don't know what the heck I must have been thinking. Anyway Willie…he hears me say that and he stops and looks up to where I am sitting, shaked his head and went into the batters box. The next day, I was down on the field and he comes over to me and says, "Montanez, Montanez!" And I said, "Willie I'm sorry." And I gave him a big hug, told him I was sorry and he hugged me back.

Personally I would like to work for the Phillies for at least 50 years. I've had the privilege to serve and work here and I hope that I'm doing a good enough job that they want to keep me around here for another 13 years or so. If the Phillies will have me until then and my health holds out and I sure hope that I could do 50 years. I would be very honored indeed.

Quotable: "That was the best that I've seen him pitch." - Charlie Manuel on Adam Eaton's 7 inning performance

<u>Friday, May 23rd - Astros 4 Phillies 3 (27-23) Tie for 2nd - 1 ½ GB the Marlins</u>

Houston - *Adam Eaton finally pitched a game that was good enough for a win but the offense disappeared after producing 19 runs in the two previous games. Eaton (0-3, 5.37) gave up 3 runs in 7 innings ... Pat Burrell hit a homerun for the second consecutive game (his 12th) and followed that up with a double in the 9th ... The Phillies had a late rally going against Houston reliever Jose Valverde that included a line drive off of the reliever's head from the bat of Pedro Feliz. The Phils put two on the board but were unable to tie the game up in the end ... Jimmy Rollins went 3 for 5 with an RBI. Stuff: Jayson Werth was placed on the 15 day DL with a right oblique strain. Outfielder T.J. Bohn was recalled from Triple A – Lehigh.*

Phillies manager Charlie Manuel told MLB.com that he believes third baseman Pedro Feliz can maintain his current pace. Feliz went 2-for-4 with an RBI yesterday against Houston after going 5 for 13 in the Washington series. The 33-year-old is hitting .252 with seven homers and 20 RBIs. "When he's aggressive at the plate, I really like his swing," Manuel told MLB.com. "He gets defensive at times, though. He gets kind of passive. But when he gets aggressive, he's a good-looking hitter." Manuel believes 30 homers and 100 RBIs may be attainable.

Vastly improved bench: Remember the days when the Phillies acquired Randall Simon and Jose Hernandez to upgrade the bench in the heat of the playoff race? Seems like yesterday, right? That's because it practically was (2006). Since then, they've come a long way in improving their bench. Led by Greg Dobbs, Phillies pinch hitters are hitting .280 (23-82), 2nd-best in the NL and lead all NL teams in pinch hits, HR (4), RBI (14) and SLG.

Pedro Feliz has been hot at the plate

Quotable: "I send him. I send him, really. Erstad's had a bad arm in the past, and when it was hit, I questioned how good his arm was. He made a hell of a throw. It's a tough way to lose, but I send him there." - Charlie Manuel on Steve Smith's decision to send Pedro Feliz on Victorino's fly ball to left in the 9th

<u>Saturday, May 24th - Astros 4 Phillies 3 (27-24) 3rd - 2 GB the Marlins</u>

Houston - *Ryan Howard generated all the Phils' offense with a 2-run HR (14) and an RBI double … Brett Myers (2-6) picked up the loss, giving up all 4 runs which included a season high 4 walks … The Phils had a chance to tie the game in the top of the 9th. With the bases loaded and one out, Shane Victorino hit a fly ball to left field. Darin Erstad, who had just come in as a defensive replacement for Carlos Lee, caught the ball and fired a perfect strike to home to gun down Pedro Feliz who was tagging from third. That play ended the game. Stuff: Brett Myers has not won a game since April 17th, seven starts ago… Ex-Phil Michael Bourne stole his major league leading 22nd base of the season …The Phillies have now played in 21 games this season that were decided by one run.*

Baseball is by far the most statistically-driven game in all of sports. The practice of keeping records of player achievements was started back in the 1850s by Henry Chadwick. Often called "the father of baseball," Chadwick was a sportswriter and baseball statistician. He served on baseball rules committees and had a strong influence on the game itself. He devised the predecessors to modern day statistics, including batting average, runs scored and runs allowed.

Official Scorer Bob Kenney preparing for a game
– photo courtesy of Bob Kenney

Today there are literally hundreds of different types of statistics. They are referenced by practically everyone that has anything to do with the game. Scouting departments use them to determine the potential of a player in high school and college. General Managers use them to help determine whether or not to sign a free agent. Grown men will sit around a table each spring and use them to draft their fantasy baseball teams. No matter how they are used, they all start with the statistics captured by the Official Scorer.

Bob Kenney works as an official scorer for Phillies home games. A lifelong New Jersey resident and former Beat Writer and Sports Editor of South Jersey's Courier Post, Kenney is officially employed by Major League Baseball. Scorers are paid $135 per game. Most don't do it for the money, but for the love of the game.

I played a lot of ball growing up as a kid. I always liked baseball and knew the game pretty well. As a writer, I started covering the Phillies in 1963 for the Burlington County and Bucks County Times. I moved over to the Courier Post in 1965 to begin covering the team for them.

During that time, I became good friends with Allen Lewis who was a great Inquirer writer and who literally helped write the baseball rulebook. Allen was always fascinated with my interest in rules and stuff. Both he and Ray Kelly Sr. did all of the scoring back then.

Allen mentioned to me that they were looking for a back-up scorer and during the winter of '67 he put together a test for to see how good my knowledge of the game was. I scored a 100 on the test. He put in a lot of trick questions on the rules and stuff like that but I knew the details of the rulebook so I was able to answer all of his questions. It was then that I ended up getting the back-up scoring job.

The first year I was an Official Scorer was 1968. I think I did 3 games that season. They game me Memorial Day, 4th of July and Labor Day. Those three games ended up being pretty basic and I didn't have any problems with them. Thankfully I didn't have any problems with the games and the following season they gave me additional games.

Ray Kelly hated to do the paperwork after the game was over. Back then you still had to write your story at the end of the game and get the official scoring information to the league as soon as the game was over. Ray cut a deal with me in which he would score the game and I would file the paperwork. So we ended up splitting the scoring fee. He was happy to not have to do the paperwork and I was happy to get more involved with the job.

Back then all the Official Scorers in the majors were Beat Writers. It wasn't a separate position until fairly recently. Things have changed so much with all the additional paperwork and electronics that we're using now that I can't imagine doing both roles now, but back then in those days you did.

I became the Official Scorer for Phillies' home games in 1971. As Ray and Allen were getting a bit older, they would come home off road trips and take more and more time off so they decided to give me most of the games. I jumped right in. I was very eager to do it and I've been doing it for 41 or 42 years now.

Why do I do it? Well obviously the money's good number one, but I do it because I love scoring. Till this day I still score games in my hometown of Riverside. I live around the corner from Riverside High School and I do the scoring for them for a bunch of their sports. Every game that I go to I'll score. If I go to a girl's basketball game, I'll score it. I can't just sit there and just watch a game. I see people talking and watching the game but I can't; I have to score the game. My wife Emma usually just shakes her head when she sees me doing it at the games.

We're paid by Major League Baseball. We used to work for the National League but then about 4-5 years ago Major League Baseball restructured it and took control over both the umpires and the scorers.

I share scoring duties now with Jay Dunn and a young guy name Mike McConi. All the scorers in baseball get graded every season, and we are regularly rated as one of the best scoring teams in baseball. Although the League President can overrule an Official Scorer's call, it's never happened with us. The League knows where the problem scorers are in the league but we're highly regarded as one of the best. We pride ourselves in that we don't really think about who's hitting or whether or not a no-hitter is going on. We just call them the way we see them.

I've had a few controversial calls in my career. I had a bad game back in 2006 in which I let Bobby Abreu get away without giving him two errors while he was in right field. I took a lot of heat from my coworkers on those calls. I might have missed them, but in my heart I think I made the right call. There were two balls that were back near the fence. As Bobby did sometimes, he shied away from them and both of the balls were not caught. To me it looked like he was back there fighting the wall so I gave both batters a double on those plays and took a lot of heat for that.

Probably one of the more pressure calls that I was faced with was when Pete Rose was going for the National League hit record. Fireworks were set to go off all around the Vet when he got the record and Bill Giles had a walkie-talkie in his hand and sat down next to me when so he could tell the fireworks guy to shoot them off if Pete broke the record. So Rose comes to the plate batting left-handed and hit a chopper towards shortstop. The ball hits off the heel of the shortstop's glove and it should have been fielded. After it gets booted, Bill looks at me and I shook my head back and forth saying that no, it was an error. So Bill jumps on his walkie-talkie and tells the fireworks guy, "No, No". Well the guy with the fireworks thought he said, "Go, Go!" so all of a sudden the Vet erupts with fireworks and 40,000 fans are going absolutely nuts even though there was a big "E" flashing up on the Phanavision board. It was an error. There was no question about that but the fans wanted to see the record. I remember sitting there looking over to Giles and the fans started booing the shit out of me. He was red-faced, but he's the one who screwed it up, not me!

Another time Manny Trillo had a tremendous errorless fielding streak going on. He used to backhand a lot of the balls hit to him so this one particular game a ball was hit up the middle and the ball hit his glove and the ball bounced out of his glove and the runner reached first base. Manny takes off his glove and throws it to the ground and I charged him with an error. It snapped his streak and all the fans started booing me. It was an error. Manny knew it was an error. Then about three years later I'm in a dentist office and I was reading a *Baseball Digest* and there was a story in a section called, "A Game that I'll Never Forget" and it's written by Manny Trillo. He writes in the article about how the Official Scorer robbed him of his record streak in Philadelphia. He never said a word to me about it but apparently he carried in his craw for a long, long time.

There's another call that I made late in 1980 towards the end of the season. Bill Buckner of the Cubs hits a ground ball down to first base that appears to go off Pete Rose's glove so I charge Rose with an error. So at the end of the game the phone rings and it's Rose on the phone. He says, "Kenney, I don't give a shit one way or another but that wasn't an error. That ball hit the edge of the turf and went sideways on me. Why don't you check with the umpire?" Buckner at the time was in the middle of a batting race but Rose could care less. He just wanted me to get the call right. So I call down to the umpire room and talked to the first base ump that game, Bob Engle. I explained what happened and he told me that it definitely did take a bad bounce and that it was a hit so I changed it from an error to a hit. So now I'm flying with the team on a road trip and we had to go to Chicago for a layover. When we land I grab the *Chicago Tribune* and at the bottom of page 1 there's an article that says "Philadelphia Scorer Gives Buckner a Well Deserved Hit". I think he ended up winning the batting title that year. I never thought I'd make page 1 of any newspaper.

The toughest call that I have to make is the passed ball. Things happen so fast out there. For the past 15-20 years I've had an assistant scorer, Rick Ventura, help me with those and other close plays. So he'll help me with some of the calls but the passed ball happens so quickly and you have to make a quick decision we'll talk about it, sometimes look at the replay but make sure that we get it right.

I thrive on the pressure of being a scorer. I guess it's the sports editor in me. I love pressure. One of the things that I'm proud about is that I'll give the final totals of the game out in the Press Box within 15-20 seconds after the game has ended. I'm very, very proud of that. But it's absolutely the best job in the world. I love it.

Quotable: "It was probably one of the worst games I've pitched all season. I'll try to make it be the only worst game I'll pitch." - Starter Cole Hamels after giving up 6 runs in 4 innings of work

Sunday, May 25th - Phillies 15 Astros 6 (28-24) Tie for 2nd - 2 ½ GB the Marlins

Houston - *A 5-run 6th inning and a 6-run 7th inning helped power the Phillies to a season-high 15 run outburst against the Astros and helped pick up Cole Hamels who pitched his worse outing of the year (6 runs, 7 hits, 1 walk, 0 K's in 4 innings) ... The Phils bullpen was able to shut down the Astros over the final 5 innings, giving up a total of three hits to seal the victory ... Rudy Seanez (3-3) picked up the win in relief ... Utley (14), Burrell (13) and Jenkins (3) all homered ... Greg Dobb's continued his incredible pinch-hitting with a 2-run pinch hit triple in the 7th ... Geoff Jenkins ended the day with 3 hits while Victorino, Burrell, Feliz, Ruiz and Cole Hamels each had two hits apiece. Stuff: Cole Hamels' 19 inning scoreless streak was halted in the Astros' 3-run first inning ... The Phillies are now 17-2 when leading after seven innings ... Home plate umpire Jerry Crawford had to leave the game after getting smacked in the head by a Carlos Lee follow-through swing and miss.*

The Phillies' Phanavision Representative David Akers prepares the right field scoreboard for the Phillies' upcoming homestand

In a game in which the Phillies offense crushed the Astros with 15 runs on 16 hits, Ryan Howard continued his slump by going 0 for 4 and lowering his batting average close to the Mendoza line at .204. Although he appeared to have started to heat up a bit (8 for 18, 4 HRs and 9 RBIs) in his previous four games,

Phillies fans can't really decide whether they are looking at Babe Ruth or the pig from the movie Babe. Either way the Phillies are going to need him to heat up soon if they have any thoughts of winning the Division.

Quotable: "The weather's getting warmer. It's getting into hitting season. From now until August or the first of September is hitting season. That's when the production in baseball should pick up."
- Charlie Manuel prior to the game as he noticed the summer-like weather and soft breeze blowing out.

Monday, May 26th - Phillies 20 Rockies 5 (29-24) Tie for 2nd - 2 ½ GB the Marlins

Philadelphia - *The offense continues its hitting ways, in particular for starter Jamie Moyer. With a 20-run, 19-hit onslaught of Rockies' pitching, the Phillies have now provided double digit offensive support for Moyer in four of his last five starts and an average of 7.3 runs in his last 11 starts ... Moyer (5-3, 4.45) went 7 innings, surrendering 4 runs on 6 hits while striking out a season high 7 batters ... Chase Utley drove in a career-high 6 runs, going 3 for 6 with 2 runs scored and hitting his 16th HR of the season ... Pedro Feliz when 4 for 6 with 4 RBIs ... Chris Coste went 3 for 6 with 4 RBIs with his 4th HR of the year ... So Taguchi, making a rare start in the outfield, went 3 for 5. Stuff: The 20 runs are the most runs scored in a game since a 21-8 win against the Cubs on July 3, 1999 ... They now have scored 35 runs in the past two games, the most since that same series with the Cubs (35 runs July 2-3, 1999) ... The offensive output truly began six games ago against the Nationals when they put 12 runs on the board. Since then they have scored 60 runs and are batting .349 with a .418 on-base percentage ... Pedro Feliz is batting .484 (15 for 31) over his last seven games ... The victory was Jamie Moyer's 235th of his career, one behind Whitey Ford and Clark Griffith for 56th on the all-time win list. With his win over the Rockies, Moyer has now beaten all 30 major league teams in his career.*

Charlie Manuel calls late May through Sept. 1 "Hittin' Season." Right on schedule, the Phillies' offense explodes for 35 runs in two games with a 20-5 dismantling of the Rockies.

Chris Wheeler mentioned Manuel's "hittin' season" quip as the camera caught the Phillies' skipper basking in the glow of another high-scoring affair. Cholly loves hittin' like a helping of mountain trout and cornbread. Their 20 runs eclipsed their previous season

Charlie Manuel believes the warmer weather means that it's time for "Hittin' Season"

high of 15, set Sunday, and it was the most by a Major League team this season. Chase Utley knocked in a career-high six. Pedro Feliz and Chris Coste both plated four. The Phils had one hit through three innings and would finish with a season-high 19.

It was the best the offense looked all season, but it was also the worst showing by an opposing team in ages. Decimated by injuries, the Rockies' lineup and pitching staff is filled with holes. It's a shame; they're nothing close to the team that swept the Phils in the NLDS.

The hubbub surrounding the game masks what was otherwise a so-so showing by Jamie Moyer, who was hittable and terrible before the Phils spotted him all those runs. After that, he picked apart the young, impatient Colorado lineup and finished with seven strikeouts in seven innings.

Watch these averages soar. Feliz is riding a seven-game hitting streak and has his marks up to .271. So Taguchi earned a rare start and made the most of it, going 3-for-5 to raise his average to .204. Coste keeps hitting (3-for-6, .341), Dobbs keeps hitting (1-for-2, .358). Howard and Victorino appear to be heating up and Utley never slumps for very long, lifting his OPS back over 1.000 (1.016, 16 HR, 42 RBI).

Quotable: "He's keeping us in the game and starting to rediscover his confidence. If you look out there, I'm on him all the time to quit nibbling and quit begging for guys to swing at pitches; they're not going to do that." - Jimmy Rollins after stating that Kendrick was more aggressive in his rookie season last year.

Tuesday, May 27th - Phillies 7 Rockies 4 (30-24) 2nd - 1 ½ GB the Marlins
Philadelphia - The Phils beat up on the Rockies again scoring all 7 runs in the first two innings of the game ...Kyle Kendrick (4-2, 4.84) picked up the win with an outstanding start, going 7 1/3rd innings (his career best) while only surrendering 2 runs ... Although the bullpen gave up 2 runs in the final 1 2/3rd innings (Gordon and Lidge one run each), they still lead the NL in ERA (2.86) and wins (14) ... Rollins, Victorino, Dobbs and Jenkins all had 2 hits a piece. Stuff: The 42 runs in the past three games fell 3 runs short of the modern day record that was set in 1900. The Phillies all-time record was 60 runs in three games back in 1894 when Grover Cleveland was president ... Major League Baseball announced that Chase Utley is currently the leading vote getter among all NL players. He has 100,000 more votes than his next-closest player, Chipper "Larry" Jones... Utley also was voted to the "25 Fittest Guys in America" by Men's Fitness magazine.

American Poet Carol Lynn Pearson once wrote, "Heroes take journeys, confront dragons, and discover the treasure of their true selves." Treasures can be found in many varied forms and are different from person to person. The Phillies have a hero who has confronted a dragon and who has found his true self in a 62-year career with one of the oldest professional teams in

America. This true treasure of a man is long-time Phillies' coach and employee Maje McDonnell.

Prior to ever joining the Phillies, Maje had already been part of one of the greatest teams that ever graced our planet. The United States military during World War II. Maje is an Army veteran and a true American hero. This hero took his journey to Europe as part of the 95th Infantry Division, "The Iron Men of Metz", and confronted the Nazi dragon that the Americans laid waste to over the course of four long years. During the 95th Division's time in Europe, they sustained over 10,000 casualties, took over 31,000 German prisoners and were nicknamed "The Bravest of the Brave."

Long-time Phillies employee Maje McDonnell shows Michael Ryan McNesby one of his three World Series rings

For his part in the war, Maje was awarded a Bronze Star (the 8th highest medal awarded in the military), a Purple Heart and 5 Battle Stars for the 95th's campaigns in Northern France, the Rhineland, Ardennes, Alsace, and Central Europe.

How long have you been with the Phillies? I've been with the Phillies now for 62 years. After the war I went back to Villanova and finished my degree in 1947. I was a starting pitcher on their baseball team. A week before I graduated, we played the Phillies in an exhibition game and lost 7-6. I pitched the entire game. The Phillies GM at the time, Herb Pennock, was at the game. He saw me pitch and told me to come by the ballpark the following week. When I met him, he asked if I would come to the team and work with them. I said, "Yes Sir!" and I've been with the team ever since. .

What did you do with the team back then? They had me doing odd jobs for them at first but because I could pitch they put me on the field as their batting practice pitcher. The manager of the team at the time was Ben Chapman. I guess he liked me because he ended up putting me on his staff as a coach. I was a bullpen coach and sometimes I coached beside the manager in the dugout. I ended up coaching for 11 years under six managers. I think my favorite manager during that time was Eddie Sawyer. What a beautiful man he was. I truly enjoyed working for him.

What is your role now with the Phillies? I'm in Community Relations. I help run team try-outs during the summer. I also go out and speak quite a bit for the team. Usually to community groups or school children. I used to speak 75-100 times a year but since I've gotten older I've cut down on that some. I still go to the ballpark every day. I just love being there.

You were part of "The Greatest Generation". You left your home and went and fought Hitler and the Nazis. Aside from being an infantryman, what was your job in your Regiment? I was in charge of the athletic program for the Regiment. I was in a service company because I played basketball and baseball in high school and at Villanova University.

When did you see your first action in the war? We were stationed at Camp Barton Stacey in England for some time and we were ready to get in and battle the Germans. We went to France 2-3 days after the D-Day invasion on Omaha Beach. We were the third infantry division to hit Omaha. The smell of death was horrible. Coming across the English Channel we could smell the stench of death two miles out to sea. Terrible. Absolutely terrible.

How were you awarded the Bronze Star? Our Company's responsibility at the time was to remove the American bodies off of the beach. We were called the "Ghoul Patrol" because one of our jobs was to pick up the bodies and move them to a staging area. On the beach, we found two guys who were still living. We stabilized them and got them to a hospital. They ended up living. It was because of this action that I received a Bronze Star. I have to say as I think back on those days that our guys were incredible … they had no fear.

What are some of your memories of France? I enjoyed Paris. I was there one time on a three-day pass… never slept the entire time! It was great to get away from everything. One of those days, I was in a bar on the second floor of a building. I was so happy to be out of combat that I told the bartender that drinks were on me for the entire house. They poured drinks for half an hour. I snuck out of the bathroom window, hung out the window and then dropped myself to the ground without paying … they're probably still looking for me! … But back then you would do things like that. You're in a war so you figured you get killed the next day anyhow.

What are your memories of Germany? Our Division was the third division to enter into Germany and the first to hit the Rheine River and we were destined to go to Berlin but the war ended before we entered the city.

You also received a Purple Heart. What happened? We were in Saarlautern Germany. I was on the second floor of a building and the Germans were bombing the town. A shell exploded while I was in a building and shrapnel hit me over my left eye. It wasn't that bad. You can still see the scar. Still, if you get wounded in war they give you a Purple Heart.

What was VE day like? We were outside Berlin in a small town. We were given the word that we were going in and then we heard that the Germans surrendered. We went crazy! We were the next division to enter Berlin. Thank God it ended. None of our guys got hurt going into the city. The Germans treated us better than the French did. Probably because we had defeated them and they figured that they had better be nice to us.

Did you play baseball in the service? Yes, back in the United States we were the best Regiment in the division. I was the coach and we had four guys on our team who were in the Minor Leagues. We had some guys in the Regiment that could play. We played thirteen games and we didn't lose one.

Did you play baseball in Europe? No, there were no baseball fields over there. We played some basketball but not much.

What did it feel like coming home after the war? We left Le Havre, France, on a Victory Ship back to the United States. We landed in Boston. It was wonderful! We stayed there a couple of days and then we were sent by train to Indian Town Gap, PA, to out process. The guys being discharged from the Philadelphia area took a train into Philadelphia. We had a ball coming home. We laughed, we cried, we sang … we were so happy. My first stop was at my parent's home. My mother had passed away so I went and saw my father and my two sisters. Everybody just hugged each other and cried for joy. I then went over to see my fiancé, Mildred … honestly the finest person that I have ever met in my entire life. We've been married now for 62 years. I thank God for her every day.

What are your lasting memories of the war? I tell you, the greatest thing about that war was our guys. The soldiers were wonderful. So brave. They didn't care about nothing. They were beautiful, beautiful! No fear at all. We had a guy named Casey from Chicago. A big Irishman. He was always in the brig. Always in trouble. He was the worse thing you would ever want to see in an outfit. But he was the bravest soldier in the Regiment. He had no fear of combat. He was awarded more medals than any other soldier in the entire Regiment. Before we invaded Normandy the officers hated him. He'd always be drunk and causing problems. He'd go out on leave and never come back and they'd have to go out and find him. But, what a soldier … he was so brave in combat! The Captain of his company couldn't stand him but at the end of the war they both hugged each other. I was never more proud of our American soldiers … they were marvelous. Absolutely marvelous!

I had a guy in my arms in Germany who was going to die in a minute or two. Do you know what he said to me? "Maje, go get 'em!" To this day I remember that … I'll never forget that. Isn't that amazing? It was really heart wrenching but that was the spirit of our guys. …"Go get 'em." … I was never more proud of the American solider than I was during the Second World War. I never saw such bravery. I loved them …

How did your time in the military help make you the man that you are today? I tell you, the discipline was so tremendous that you use it for the rest of your life. If you live with it you become well disciplined in everything. If anything comes up in life, good or bad, you have that discipline to think it through and do the right thing. Whether it's death or life … it's amazing what it does for you.

In your 62 years with the Phillies and your time as a hero in World War II, how do you want to be remembered by the people of Philadelphia? That I was a part of the greatest Army that ever walked on the face of the earth, and that I did exactly what I wanted to do my entire life. Ever since I was a kid I wanted to be with the Phillies. And look at me now. I've never worked a day in my life, and I loved every minute of it.

Quotable: "I was nervous, to be honest with you. It was a weird feeling. I've got quite a few wins under my belt, pitched with leads before, but it was definitely nice to get that one [win] out of the way. I mean, it's the last week in May." - Adam Eaton on getting his first win of the season

Wednesday, May 28th - Phillies 6 Rockies 1 (31-24) 2nd - ½ GB the Marlins

Philadelphia - *Finally! After 11 starts Adam Eaton (1-3 4.99) won his first game of the season holding the Rockies to 1 run in 6 innings of work to help the Phillies complete their first 3-game sweep of the season ... The run support came from a 3-run homer by Chase Utley, his major league-leading 17th and Geoff Jenkins 2-run HR in the 5th inning ... Shane Victorino went 3 for 4 with 2 runs scored and 2 stolen bases (his 11th and 12th of the season) ... Madson, Romero and Durbin pitched 3 scoreless innings to wrap up the victory. Stuff: Eaton's win was his first in his last 20 starts ... The Phils have now stolen 38 bases on the season and have only been caught 6 times. Their 86.4% success rate is best in all of baseball... Pat Burrell was unable to play in yesterday's game due to a stiff neck. When asked today as to how he was "injured" Burrell blamed his 115 pound English bulldog "Elvis" saying, "Elvis had the pillow".*

Benjamin Franklin is one of the greatest men in the history of Philadelphia if not in the history of America. His brilliant ideas have survived centuries without even the slightest hint of them disappearing from our society. One of his greater ideas was the practice of developing himself. To help himself grow in his own personal development, Franklin created a list of thirteen virtues which he would read to himself every day and focus on throughout his life. In his list of 13 virtues, his number 10 virtue was "Cleanliness." "Tolerate no uncleanness in body, clothes, or habitation," wrote Franklin.

Bram Reynolds is responsible for ensuring that Citizens Bank Park sparkles

Almost three million baseball fans inhabit Citizens Bank Park every season. Not only is it one of the most beautiful ballparks in America, it's also one of the cleanest. The man primarily responsible for ensuring that it remains that way is Bram Reynolds. Reynolds works for a subcontractor of the Phillies, Global Spectrum. His job is to ensure that Mr. Franklin would be extraordinarily comfortable in the confines of the Phils' ballpark.

Keeping Citizens Bank Park clean is a 24-hour a day job during the season. During a long home stand, we will run three shifts around the clock to make sure the ballpark is as clean as we can possibly make it before the next game begins. We use approximately 220 people around the clock to get it clean once the fans leave. After a night game is done our main cleaning around the park isn't finished until 2:30pm the following day. So it takes us a good 16 –17 hours to clean it up each night. But to be honest, there is always something being cleaned.

A sellout crowd will usually generate anywhere between 18 to 19 tons of trash. You'd be surprised at how much trash people leave from either bringing it to the ballpark or from buying here and consuming it during the game. 3 ½ tons of the trash will just be cardboard alone. We have two trash compactors and one cardboard compactor on site to help us process the trash to get it ready to be either hauled off to a recycling facility or to a trash processing center.

During a game we have what we call an Events Crew. It includes a staff of anywhere between 40-44 people, depending upon what size crowd is expected at the game. We strategically place them throughout the ballpark to address all of the cleaning that we do during a game. We have Policers who go around with a caddy and a broom and just sweep up anything they see on the concourse. We also have trash runners that are constantly checking and emptying trashcans in the bathrooms, on the concourse and even around the outside of the park. For a 7:05 game we will have the entire crew in here working by 5:00pm.

During the game we segment a portion of the crew that is dedicated to some of the tougher assignments in the ballpark. They are responsible for soda and beer spills. Picking up peanut shells. They get to do the throw-up calls, urination calls and on a rare occurrence blood clean ups if there was a fight. They unfortunately get some unpleasant calls that they have to address.

Once the game is over, the Events Crew will do one last trash run on the concourse, the restrooms and all of the premium seating areas in the ballpark. We then have the Overnight Crew come in. The first segment of that crew will get here by 9:30pm for a 7:05pm start. We call this team our Picking Crew. They are the ones wearing the red smocks. It consists of about 40 individuals. Once the game ends the Picking Crew starts in the lower bowl of the stadium and line themselves up from row 1 to row 36: one row for each person. They then start walking their row and pick up any trash that they find in the seating area. As they fill up their trash bags they leave them at the end of their aisle.

Our Trash Crews also come in at 9:30pm. They are responsible for moving all of the trash bags up the steps to the concourse that are left by the Events Crew. Once on the concourse the trash then gets moved to the trash compactors. That crew totals about 7-8 people.

The next crew to come to the ballpark are the Backpack Blowers and Sweepers. We have 15 guys who wear the gas powered blowers and 5 sweepers. Instead of going across the seating bowl, these guys will blow all the debris down from the top seat in a section all the way down to the first row of that section. The sweepers will then be at the bottom of the section and sweep up all of the debris into trash bags.

We then employ around 65 people for our Bathroom Crews. They come in around 11:00am. We have a total of 137 bathrooms that they need clean each game.

For our Club and Suite Crews, we have a crew of about 14 people that start cleaning these areas around 11:00pm. This is the team that gets into those areas and get them sparkling clean.

As the Picking Crew, Trash Crew and the Blowers/Sweepers continue to work their way throughout the ballpark, we then bring in the Pressure Washing Crew. They usually start at around midnight with a crew of 13-15 people. Pressure washing is a very difficult task, probably the most rigorous of all the cleaning tasks that takes place here. They use large hoses; they're dealing with a big pressure gun that has water shooting all over the place. It's a wet job that requires you to move a lot of hose around and over all the seats.

The Pressure Washing Crew usually takes about 8 hours to get all of their sections done. So they are usually done anywhere by 8:00am in the morning. We then bring in a second Pressure Washing Crew that will continue to clean up everywhere else in and around the ballpark to around 2:30-3:00pm. So like I said, it's a 24-hour operation.

The most difficult thing for us to clean is probably a grease spill. Depending upon the severity of the spill, it may need to be absorbed and scrubbed which usually requires a lot of elbow grease to clean. No pun intended.

In a sellout of the ballpark, we will go through a lot of stuff. We'll use approximately 2,200 trash bags, 3,200 rolls of toilet paper and over 50,000 feet of paper towels. Like I said, 40,000 people create a lot of trash!

Quotable: "I'd like to be Big Brown (Triple Crown Race Horse Contender). I'd like to look back and see somebody behind me, chasing. That'd be good." - Charlie Manuel on getting to first in the NL East

I feel bad for anybody that has to pitch against us right now. It's like everybody is seeing the ball well at the same time, and there's no easy out in this lineup." - Brett Myers on the Phillies' offense

Friday, May 30th - Phillies 12 Marlins 3 (32-24) 1st Place - ½ GA of the Marlins

Philadelphia - *The Phillies vaulted back into first place on the strong pitching of Brett Myers (3-6, 5.52) and another double-digit game from the offense ... Myers struck out 11 in 8 innings. It was Myer's first win since April 11th after 5 straight losses ... The Phils batted around in the 2nd, scoring 7 runs on a 3-run HR by Chris Coste (5), a 2-run double by Shane Victorino and a 2-run HR by Chase Utley (18) ... They added 4 more runs in the 4th with an RBI single by Jimmy Rollins and a 3-run blast by Ryan Howard (15) that hit the left field foul pole. Stuff: The Phillies are 8-2 in their last 10 games ... In their current 5 game winning streak, they are hitting .337 with 10 HRs and 60 RBIs, an incredible average of 12 runs per game. They now have scored 10 or more runs in six times this month ... With their 3 HRs tonight the Phils have sent a franchise record for homeruns in the month of May with 41, breaking the previous mark of 39 back in 2006 ... Ryan Howard has 10 homeruns in May.*

It's been a charmed run for the Phillies. Yes it has. Sixty runs in five games. When they play this way, they're humbling. Chase "Pinch Me He's Ours Forever" Utley is in that familiar zone. The baseball looks like a beach ball to Chase, who took over the league lead in homers (18) and RBIs (48). The hitting has been infectious. Your backup catcher, Chris Coste, is hitting .455 with runners in scoring position and provided the key hit in last night's contest. In next week's draft, teams won't give a guy like Coste the time of day. The big innings have been made possible by more base runners and made possible by patient at bats from Shane Victorino. Vic has scored 11 runs in six games and has shown excellent pa-

Chase Utley leads the NL with 18 Hrs and 48 RBIs

tience – yet another case of a player rising to the challenge, in this case, when Jayson Werth went down.

After one inning, I bailed on Brett Myers, but that's okay, because so did the Phillies. They started warming up Rudy Seanez. Then Myers went to his breaking ball ... and his split ... and his change, and was locating all of them. Eighty-nine on the gun, which is where it could be frozen forever, didn't matter. What mattered was that he was throwing his fastball inside for strikes and putting guys away. That's how he handled the young, aggressive Marlins. It's how he should handle everyone.

The Phillies, winners of five in a row, climbed to first in the East and hold the third-best record in the National League (32-24). They're red-hot, fun to watch and appear primed for the long summer haul.

Quotable: "I'm more disappointed in letting the team down. We just started playing well and I let them down." - Cole Hamels on giving up 7 runs against the Marlins

Saturday, May 31st - Marlins 7 Phillies 3 (32-25) 2nd Place - ½ GB the Marlins
Philadelphia - *The Marlins snapped the Phils' 5 game winning streak with 3 homeruns off of starter Cole Hamels ...Hamels (5-4, 3.73) was tagged with all 7 Marlins runs in 5 2/3rd innings ...Chase Utley hit his major league leading 19th homerun and Shane Victorino went 2 for 4 with 2 doubles*

and 2 runs scored. Stuff: Hamels' 7 earned runs tied for the most runs he has allowed in a game. He gave up 7 runs twice during his 2006 rookie season ... Today was the Phillies' 12th sellout of the year with an attendance of 45,261. It was the 6th largest crowd in the history of Citizens Bank Park. Through the end of May, the Phillies have drawn 1,150,190 fans to Citizens Bank Park with an average attendance of 39,662.

When you walk into the Phillies Player's Lounge your eyes immediately fixate toward the huge 3' x 4' neon sign on the wall that reads "Welcome to Swanny's Kitchen." It's the place to be if you are a player. It's one of the few places besides the weight room and the trainer's room where the ball players can just be amongst themselves. No autographs. No interviews. Just the guys on the team and some really good food.

Joe Swanhart keeps the grill cleaned and the Phillies' stomachs full at "Swanny's" in the Player's Lounge

Swanny is Joe Swanhart. A 29 year old native of Saint Petersburg, Florida, who was once the Spring Training batboy for the St. Louis Cardinals at the young age of 12. Today, Swanny is in charge of the game-day meals for the entire team which is an awesome responsibility given that there are anywhere between 35-40 players, coaches and Phillies' staff mouths that need he needs to feed each and every game at Citizens Bank Park.

I'm responsible for providing the Phillies players and coaches with food and making all of the menus for the Pre and Post-Game meals. I pretty much run it all so I'm responsible for ensuring that I have all the necessary food items in stock, I'm responsible for all of the grocery shopping, ensuring that the meals are ready at the proper time, scheduling the caterers, keeping everything clean. It's just as if I'm running my own restaurant.

I've been with the Phillies fulltime now since the 2004 season. Prior to that I did some work for them in Spring Training down in Clearwater for a few years while I was in college. But I basically gained all of my experience doing this when I was the Visiting Clubhouse Manager in charge of meals for the Tampa Bay Rays from 1998 to 2003.

The Players Lounge is where all the players and coaches come for their meals. It's open from the time they get here until the time they leave. For Pre-Game meals, which usually happens right after batting practice, a player can typically go over to the sandwich station and make anything that they might want. We provide them with whole grain breads and have a fully stocked refrigerator with cold cuts like turkey, chicken, ham, cheese and tuna salad. There's also peanut butter and jelly, Nutella, stuff like that. There's also always some type of Campbell's Soup. Chicken Noodle, Tomato, or Vegetable Beef. We stick with their classics.

If the players are just in the mood to snack, we also offer them a wide variety of options. We have everything from organic granola, to fruit to Peppermint Patties or Kettle Chips. Basically I want to make sure that have a wide variety of options.

I stock a lot of drinks as well but we don't provide them with soda. Way too much sugar and no nutritional value. They do have the option of drinking some diet sodas but I basically try to keep every choice as healthy and nutritious as I possibly can. Right now I'm stocking water, PowerAde, teas, lemonade, milk and orange juice.

Before every game, I fill in a huge white menu board for everyone to see that tells them what the feature meals of the day are going to be. In addition to sandwiches, I also provide one pre-game feature meal that they have the option of eating. Today's Pre-game feature is raviolis. Sometimes I'll have chicken & rice or pizza. Believe it or not you can eat healthy pizza.

I usually cook all of the pre-game meals myself. Once in a while I might give them sushi or pizza which I'll order from somewhere close by. For pizza we've been using Buca Di Beppo in the city. They make some really health conscious pizza with wheat dough. We never order pepperonis or sausage because of the fat content so we end up sticking to veggie pizza, chicken, barbeque chicken or even shrimp sometimes. If it's pizza, we'll usually order 6-8 pies. The guys really enjoy it.

During the game the only players still hanging around here are the relief pitchers. Mostly the back-end guys like Gordon and Lidge or a starter that might not be pitching for the next couple of days. There's always some type of food that they can grab but by game time I'm already getting ready for the post-game meal.

The Post-Game meal is almost always catered. It's their big meal of the day that we provide for them. I use our executive chefs here at the ballpark a lot. They do a great job for me; they're very versatile and can do anything I can think up. They'll cook everything up in the executive dining room and then bring it down here before the game is over.

We also use restaurants like *P.F. Chang's, Bone Fish Grill* and *Outback Steakhouse.* One of the keys to healthy eating is to stay away from heavy cream sauces and fried foods. They just aren't good for the players or anyone for that matter.

I used to do cheese steaks before we went to a healthy menu. Now we'll do chicken cheese steaks instead of beef. So there's an alternative. When we have sloppy Joe's now we use ground turkey with a wheat bun. It's all about eating healthier.

Variety is important as well. I try to mix up the catered food that comes in. Some days we will do Mexican, Italian, Latin, Asian, barbeque … we'll also do a Creole theme, you know a little Louisiana kick for some of the guys.

If you'd ask the players what food they like best in the Player's Lounge, I think I'd say it would probably be my breakfast. When we have day games the players come in real early so I cook them a made-to-order breakfast. That's kind of been my big speciality with the players. It seems like every last one of them are waiting in line for it when they come in.

To keep breakfast healthy we only use egg whites now. We do an egg sandwich that we call the "Milt Melt" after Milt Thompson. He's been ordering that since the day we opened the lounge. We'll also do a turkey bacon or a healthy choice bacon, egg and cheese for his sandwich. Pancakes are always a big hit as well. I can do a really nice dark chocolate chip pancake. A lot of the guys really enjoy it.

Chase Utley is a very healthy eater. His favorite food is wheat pancakes for breakfast with peanut butter. He changes it up sometimes but for the most part it's some sort of egg white with turkey bacon. That tends to be his breakfast. He really likes the creamy peanut butter with strawberry jelly.

Ryan Howard likes a very healthy sized omelet. When it's done it takes up about half the plate. It's pretty big ... but it's an egg white omelet so it's good for him. I throw everything in there but tomatoes. He likes mushroom, ham, American cheese, onion and peppers ... he just doesn't like tomatoes at all.

When Jimmy Rollins comes in for breakfast, he'll always say something to me like "Joe, just make me something good with some hits in it." He tends to like waffles but he'll go for a breakfast sandwich every now and then. Lately, I've been making him a turkey sausage egg and cheese sandwich. Brett Myers is a big waffle guy as well.

Charlie Manuel, he's southern so he likes to just eat turkey sausage for breakfast. He'll just kind of sit there and pick through it. He really likes that and every once in awhile he'll let me make him up some scrambled egg whites. Believe it or not he doesn't eat much through the day, he really doesn't. He'll take some stuff home at the end of the night because he usually doesn't have time to eat here and it's so late. But for the most part he doesn't eat too much.

Post-Game meals the players vary their likes as well. Chase tends to go with some sort of chicken-based entree. I tend to feature different meats each day so I'll always try to have a chicken or a pork type meat. Ryan's a big barbeque guy along with Jimmy. Charlie likes all the southern-type foods, meatloaf, chicken, ribs and all the barbeque stuff.

Jamie Moyer is a true Philadelphian. Whenever he pitches he has to have an Italian hoagie from Planet Hoagie for his Post-Game meal.

I really haven't seen too many strange items being eaten here. I have seen Ryan Howard make a tuna sandwich and he'll put honey in it. That's kind of off the wall. Some guys will do the health shakes and they'll put in their health mixes and veggies and stuff and the shakes are green and not very pretty to look at. They somehow suck those down.

Any of the excess meals that we have at the end of the day we end up giving to a charity called Sports Wrap. They're affiliated with Rock and Wrap It Up! It's a national charity that gets food from sports teams, rock concerts, things like that. The two places that the Philadelphia chapter brings our food to is a women's battered shelter in New Jersey or to a soup kitchen in downtown Philly.

Ultimately I take a lot of pride in my job. When the players or coaches come in I really want them to be impressed. I want everybody to have meal options that are healthy and that they can enjoy. It's tough if you go somewhere and you spend the whole day there and then you have to eat poor food. So I want everybody, no matter who they are, to be able to walk in the Players Lounge and have something good to eat.

June - The Swoon...

Quotable: "I spent 17 years of my life and put everything that I had into baseball and into the Phillies. I know I finished [last season] with the Dodgers, but it's definitely an honor to come back here and finish with the Phillies. I was still a Phillie at heart when I was in LA." - Mike Lieberthal explaining why he came back to retire with the Phillies

<u>Sunday, June 1st - Phillies 7 Marlins 5 (33-25) 1st Place - ½ GA of the Marlins</u>

Philadelphia - The Phillies fought their way back from a 5-1 deficit to score 6 unanswered runs and move back into first place as Chase Utley hit his major-league leading 20th homerun of the season and Pat Burrell hit a tiebreaking, two-run double in the 7th to put the Phils ahead for good... Although he surrendered 5 runs in 7 innings, Jamie Moyer (6-3 4.65) extended his unbeaten streak against Florida to 8-0 lifetime. It was Moyer's fourth straight win ..."Lights Out" Lidge, which is what fans are now calling the Phils' ace reliever, pitched a perfect 9th for his 13th save in 13 opportunities. Stuff: Mike Lieberthal signed a one-day contract and retired from baseball as a Phillie today. The contract was with AA Reading and was worth a grand total of $4.00 as there is a rule that states that a player must be paid at least $1.00 per month for the rest of the season. David Montgomery was quoted as saying, "He's the first player I've ever paid cash for!" ... Chase Utley became the fastest Phillie to reach 20 homeruns in a season. He also passed Roger Hornsby as the only second baseman ever to reach 20 HRs in 58 games. Hornsby hit his 20th in 1925 during his 61st game of the season.

For the 900th time this season, the Phillies overcame a rough start by a starting pitcher thanks to an unyielding offense and a merciless bullpen. Will this approach translate into long-term success?

Today's quote comes from Jamie Moyer, who earned the win despite giving up five runs. This is from Sunday's Morning Call, published before yesterday's start: "You just try to ignore the dimensions here (Citizens Bank Park)," he said. "Home runs and balls off the wall here are routine fly balls in other parks. Pitching here, you know you're going to give up runs. You just can't get flustered by it.

Jamie Moyer is now 8-0 lifetime against the Marlins

I don't like to give up runs myself, but if you can minimize those runs, put some zeroes up after you give them up, you can give these guys a chance to win the game."

Sage advice, and words to live by ... particularly for a starting rotation that's been just so-so overall. Lately, their best starts have come after the offense spotted them big leads against clubs that won't be playing October baseball. Yesterday, they found themselves down 5-1 in the third and stormed back again. Indeed, it was great to see so many parts contribute in the comeback cause: Geoff Jenkins off the bench; T.J. Bohn on defense; Chase Utley getting his 20th; Moyer settling in; the back of the bullpen preserving the win, which put them back on top in the NL East.

That division-leader designation makes them subjects of comparison. As defending champs, their sights are set higher. For now, it appears this is their division to lose. But why settle for stacking them up against the Marlins, Mets, Braves and Nats? How do they stack up against the other division leaders? Offensively, it's favorable, pitching-wise, less favorable.

While the offense has earned top billing, and the bullpen has been the solid under card, the rotation will become the focus as baseball rolls rapidly toward July 31.

Quotable: "If we didn't have Chase, we wouldn't be where we're at. He has 52 RBIs, 21 homers, and it's not only that. It's how he plays the game." - Charlie Manuel on the Phils' march into first place

Monday, June 2nd - Phillies 5 Reds 4 (34-25) 1st Place - 1 ½ GA of the Marlins

Philadelphia - *The Philadelphia homerun machine continued tearing up the National League as all five runs were scored on homeruns by Chase Utley (21), Pedro Feliz (8) and Chris Coste (6) … Shane Victorino went 1 for 4 to extend his hitting streak to 14 games … Kyle Kendrick (5-2, 5.00) picked up the victory and Brad Lidge came in again to shut down the "Little Red Machine" in the 9th for his 14th save of the year. Stuff: For the second time this season Utley has hit 5 straight homeruns in as many games …In addition to being a stud at the plate, Utley also made two diving catches in the field in the 7th and 9th innings to rob the Red's Joey Votto of two sure hits … Utley was named the NL Player of the week … The Phils lead all of Major League Baseball with 88 homeruns… To the disappointment of 38,530 fans, Ken Griffey Jr., who's at 599 homeruns lifetime, sat out the game. The reason? "General body soreness."*

Baseball, unlike all other professional team sports, has never been governed by time. It's one of its enduring charms. However over the years the length of time it takes to play a baseball game has steadily increased. At the turn of the 20th century games usually took an hour and a half to play. By the 1920s they averaged a little bit less than two hours. By the year 2000 baseball games took an average of two hours and fifty-eight minutes to play. Today games average around 2 hours and 45 minutes.

Major League Baseball, wanting to take the "dead time" out of ball games, began making efforts to shorten the length of ball games back in 2003. So in an attempt to shorten the game they asked all clubs and umpires to adhere to the following guidelines:

Rob Holiday keeps time between innings to help speed up the game

- Innings must start within two minutes and 5 seconds after the last out is made.
- The umpire will signal the first batter of the inning 1 minute and 40 seconds after the completion of the prior inning.
- Batters are instructed to stay in the batters box. If not, pitchers can throw and each pitch will be a strike.
- When bases are empty pitchers are to deliver the ball to the plate within 12 seconds
- Managers are to have relievers called into the game before they reach the foul line.

In an effort to help keep these rules in effect the umpires and each team are tasked with the job of ensuring that these guidelines are followed. For the Phillies this job primarily belongs to Assistant Director of Scouting, Rob Holiday.

Aside from my scouting duties my game day job includes the role of Official Time Keeper. The role is all about Major League Baseball's effort to try to speed up the game. They came up with this direction a few years ago and they want the umpires and us to help keep the action going between innings.

All PA announcers have to announce the batter a minute and forty seconds between innings. So my job, along with the second base umpire down on the field, is to ensure that we follow this timing. At a minute forty I cue Dan Baker and he announces the batter. This is to let the umpire and everyone else on the field know that there's 25 seconds left before the inning is supposed to start.

When there's a pitching change they allow two minutes before we announce the batter and this gives the pitcher time to get in and get his warm-up pitches. But then they know that they're supposed to start right after that. Fans should take a look at the second base umpire. He has a stopwatch that he uses to watch the time on the field. So as soon as the third out happens we'll both hit our watches at the same time and the clock starts rolling. He will also signal to the home plate umpire to make sure that he doesn't start the game too soon before the television comes out of its break or to tell him to speed it up.

By keeping track of the time in the Phanavision Booth I'm able to help Dan since he is always reading ads over the PA system and has a lot of things going on. So when we have pitching changes or some other delays, I try to help him keep track of who's coming in, what the batting order is. I'm an extra set of eyes for our team in the booth to make sure that everything that we are doing, balls, strikes, announcing of the players, is correct. My job is to try to catch any mistakes before they happen.

What's interesting is that Major League Baseball did a study years ago that I was part of to try to figure out why the games have slowed down so much. I have my own theory but one of the things that they looked at was the time between innings. Before we put in the new rules the time between innings would drag to 3 minutes or longer. So the thinking was that we could save ½ minute each ½ inning. That cuts almost 10 minutes out of each game. So with these new time limits it actually decreased the average length of game since we started enforcing them.

My personal opinion is that the game takes longer because of how tight the strike zone has become over the past 30 years. Back then you had four primary pitchers and all four of them were pretty good and knew how to throw strikes. There were less teams and I think a much bigger strike zone. Today I think the strike zone's much smaller and pitchers aren't as accurate as they used to be. Sometimes you will see a really quick game when you have two good pitchers that are throwing strikes. When that happens we'll all be out of here in less than 2 ½ hours. I don't think fans mind too much though. Philadelphia fans tend to stay the entire game. I think they just love being at the ballpark and watching them play.

Quotable: "I definitely had more confidence today than I did in my first start of the year. I had a little bit of everything going tonight. I had some changeups early to get outs and then the cutter came into play later and the fastball and things like that. I was able to go hard and soft and that combo did the job." - Adam Eaton on his 7th quality start of the season

Tuesday, June 3rd - Phillies 3 Reds 2 (35-25) 1st Place - 2 ½ GA of the Marlins

Philadelphia - Chase Utley led off the 6th with a double and Pat Burrell followed a batter later with a tie-breaking two-run homerun off of Reds' starter Aaron Harang to break a 1-1 tie ... Utley went 2 for 3 raising his average to .325. He also knocked in his 52nd run of the year ... Adam Eaton (2-3 4.63) allowed 1 run on 3 hits in 6 2/3rd innings for his second consecutive win ... Brad Lidge did it again as he threw his 15th consecutive save. Stuff: The Phillies are 7-1 in this home stand and have won 11 of their last 14 games ... Greg Dobbs had his ML leading 14th pinch hit of the season ... Griffey didn't start for a second consecutive game but did pinch hit in the 8th. Manuel elected to walk him to the loud boos of Phillies' fans, keeping him at 599 HRs, saying, "We didn't want him to hit one." ... Jimmy Rollins stole his 23rd and 24th consecutive base dating back to last season. It is the longest streak in the majors.

The way free agent pitching has performed throughout baseball, Eaton's 3-year, $24.5 million contract isn't much of a stretch, but you get the drift. The right-hander is 2-1 with a 2.29 ERA in his last three starts, including last night's one run, three hit, five strikeout, zero-walk performance. Afterward, Eaton told Phils broadcaster Tom McCarthy that "repetition" has been the key to his sudden turnaround, which has lowered his ERA (4.63) to second best in the starting rotation behind Cole Hamels. Others have pointed to a more aggressive approach, even though better control seems like the obvious factor. Eaton has farther to go before he erases the memory of last season's mess, but to some, this small resurgence isn't unexpected.

Jennifer McNesby settling in to her seat in left center field

With the win, the Phillies moved 2 ½ games up on Florida. Right now the wins are occurring with shocking regularity. Presently, there's barely anything worth complaining about, which Philadelphia fans aren't used to at all. There's nobody to blame when the team wins eight of their last nine. They're healthy, exciting and play the game hard. They have the right blend of pitching to build a bridge from the first inning to the ninth. They've avoided ruinous outings, which has kept them in rhythm. This is getting interesting …

Quotable: "That kind of irritated me a little bit. I know they want to see a home run hit, but they should be pulling for us." - Brett Myers on the fans booing him after he walked pinch-hitter Ken Griffey Jr. who was going for his 600th homerun of his career

<u>Wednesday, June 4th - Reds 2 Phillies 0 (35-26) 1st Place - 1 ½ GA of the Marlins</u>

Philadelphia - *Brett Myers (3-7 5.13) flirted with a no-hitter for 6 2/3rd innings before he walked Brandon Phillips and then gave up a two-out double to Joey Votto to break up the no-no. He retired 13 straight batters to start the game before surrendering a walk to Adam Dunn with one out in the 5th. He gave up a total of 1 run, 1 hit, struck out 8 and walked a season high 6… Reds' starter Edinson Volquez (8-2 1.32) came up just a bit bigger and shut down the Phillies allowing only 2 hits (singles by Geoff Jenkins and Ryan Howard) in 7 innings. Stuff: Eagles QB Donovan McNabb took batting practice before the game. He only managed a one-hopper over the left field fence quipping "(In) Little League, that's gone!" … For a 3rd consecutive game Ken Griffey Jr. sat out with general soreness. He was however able to pinch hit in the 8th but was unintentionally walked by Brett Myers.*

With the 24th pick in the 2008 draft, the Philadelphia Phillies have selected … toolsy shortstop Anthony Hewitt of Salisbury prep school in Connecticut.

According to the scouts surveyed on MLB.com, the 6-1, 195 pound shortstop has a future in the outfield, possibly center field, and earns high marks for having all the things the Phillies typically look for in a position player: a terrific body and great natural strength. The same things their neighbors across the parking lot, the Eagles, look for at the NFL Combine. Hewitt, 19, swings from the right side of the plate and possesses plus power, plus speed and a strong arm – strong enough to play short, in the eyes of scouts. There are questions about his signability due to a commitment to Vanderbilt. Strengths: "Tools galore and perhaps as much upside as anyone in the draft class." Weaknesses: "He's a little raw, and hasn't faced stiff competition in the Northeast."

Brett Myers flirted with a no hitter in to the 7th

The selection appears to be all about power, which is in short supply down on the farm. His offensive tools are said to be "considerable," yet the prospect of another raw talent with a similar skill set as many others along the chain doesn't invoke much rejoicing. "He's a little raw" is something we've read before. As usual on draft day, there's no real reason to get excited until we see how he adjusts to pro ball.

Quotable: "It's my fault. I can't get mad at him. That's like breaking the law and getting mad when the police show up. You can't do that." - 2007 MVP Jimmy Rollins on being benched for lack of hustle by Charlie Manuel

Thursday, June 5th - Phillies 5 Reds 0 (36-26) 1st Place - 2 ½ GA of the Marlins

Philadelphia - *Cole Hamels came back from two consecutive poor starts to pitch a 3-hit, complete game shutout over Cincinnati ... Geoff Jenkins hit his 6th homerun of the season while Ryan Howard and Shane Victorino each had RBI singles ... the Phils' first 3 runs of the game were unearned as the Reds committed 3 errors. Stuff: Hamel's shutout was the 2nd of his career ... The Phils' team pitching ERA is 3.91, 4th best in the NL ... The Phils are now 5-1-1 in their last seven series. They have won 12 of their last 16 games (.750) ... Ken Griffey finally started a game and went 1 for 4, coming close to homering twice but eventually leaving Philadelphia stuck at 599.*

Phillies skipper Charlie Manuel yanked Jimmy Rollins from today's game for dogging it down the line on a pop fly that ended up being dropped. Afterward, Rollins took responsibility for his actions but I suspect this wasn't an isolated incident. J-Roll has been playing with his head down and jogging out plays for a little while now. While many of us have probably ignored it - perhaps because he's reigning MVP, or because half of baseball wouldn't have run out that play - Manuel called him out on it. If he's hurt, it's one thing, but the fact that Rollins took responsibility indicates that wasn't the case.

The truth of the matter is Rollins, for whatever reason, hasn't played with the same level of intensity that he flashed last season. The numbers aren't there, which is understandable, but the lack of effort is not acceptable. With the benching, Manuel sent a message that all the MVPs in the world, the 8-2 home stand and a division title take a back seat to achieving the ultimate team goal.

Jimmy Rollins found himself riding the pine for not hustling

Nevertheless, expect the fallout to be short-lived. Manuel and Rollins aren't the type of men to hold a grudge, and fans can be made to forget if Rollins simply does what he's supposed to. Owning up to his mistake was a good start.

Quotable: "Sometimes you are the hero and sometimes you are the goat. It's a lot nicer to be the hero" - Shane Victorino on his game-saving throw to the plate in the 10th to preserve the Phillies' 4-3 win

Friday, June 6th - Phillies 4 Braves 3 - 10 inn. (37-26) 1st Place - 3 ½ GA of the Marlins

Atlanta - In the wildest game of the season the Phillies eked out a 4-3 victory over the Braves in extra innings ... In what should have been a 2-1 Braves victory, Chris Coste popped up to Braves' second baseman Kelly Johnson with two on and two outs in the top of the 9th, however, Johnson dropped the ball, allowing the Phillies to tie the game at two ... In the top of the 10th the Phils scored two more runs with a pinch-hit double by Chris Snelling, a triple by Shane Victorino that scored Snelling and a double by Chase Utley that knocked in Victorino. The Braves continued to threaten in the bottom of the inning against Brad Lidge as they put runners on 2nd and 3rd with two out. Braves shortstop Yunel Escobar lined a single to center, scoring one run, but Gregor Blanco made a mistake as he tried to score from second on the hit. Shane Victorino gunned him down at the plate for the final out of the game. ... Victorino was the star of the game on the field as well as at the plate as he went 2 for 3 with two triples, two runs scored and knocked in the go-ahead run in the 10th ... Thanks to Shane, Lidge earned his 16th save in 16 attempts this season. Stuff: Tom Gordon's son Devaris was selected in the 4th round of the Major League draft by the LA Dodgers ... the Braves are beginning to falter in the NL East as they are now 3-17 in one-run games and 1-6 in extra innings.

Phillies' scouting director Marti Wolever told the *Bucks County Courier Times* they will shift first-round pick Anthony Hewitt from shortstop to third base and are optimistic they can sign him soon.

For any fan, discussing the draft is a stretch. Only tight-lipped scouts and perhaps a handful of insiders have ever seen guys like Anthony Hewitt swing a baseball bat. At best, the details filter in second-hand from a few vague, short scouting reports written in places like Baseball America. Less than 24 hours after the draft, the information is already obsolete, replaced by better reports taken directly from the horse's mouth. It turns out Hewitt will play third instead of the outfield, as several sources assumed.

Atlanta manager Bobby Cox can't seem to find the right lineup to beat the Phillies

Nevertheless, yesterday's draft sent a clear message about positional priorities and spelled out the Phillies' talent philosophy better than any draft in memory. Five of their first six picks were high school selections, representing the raw talent, big upside qualities they adore.

"As a scout ... this is why you scout because when these [high-ceiling] guys hit, you're not talking about an average major-league player," Wolever told Randy Miller of the Courier Times. "You're talking about a well-above major-league player, and to me that's what you win championships with. To start off with these guys is very exciting."

The Phillies aren't afraid of high risk, because it can often lead to high reward. Cole Hamels was an injured high schooler. Ryan Howard, taken in the fifth round, represented raw power personified. But then there were guys like Reggie Taylor, who was supposed to be the next great five-tool star. Still, guys like Chase Utley and Pat Burrell suggest that a polished college hitter would be the way to go.

The first couple of picks appear to be all about restocking the power supply. Hewitt, 19, possesses what the Phils consider a complete package of strength and speed. They used their next two picks on a pair of 17-year-old California high school outfielders who hit from the left side of the plate. Zach Collier, taken 34th overall, is considered very raw, but is quite strong and expected to get stronger. Anthony Gose, selected 51st, is another "toolsy" player who is compared to Juan Pierre and Corey Patterson.

Quotable: "He's fast. When he gets on it's kind of like an instant run. He's on, and it's second, third, home, 1-0." - Jimmy Rollins on Shane Victorino's speed as he scored from first to put the Phillies ahead 3-2

Saturday, June 7th - Phillies 6 Braves 2 (38-26) 1st Place - 3 ½ GA of the Marlins

Atlanta - In the eighth inning of a 2-2 game, Shane Victorino walked, then raced from first to home on Chase Utley's triple into the right-field corner, scoring the go-ahead run in a 6-2 win over the Braves ... Pat Burrell went 2 for 4, hitting his 15th homerun of the season along with his team-high 17th double ... Jimmy Rollins slugged his first homerun since May 9th ending an 0 for 13 slump. Stuff: Charlie Manuel won his 300th game as a Phillies manager, which ranks him 11th on the team's all-time manager list... Although he went 0 for 4 in the game, Victorino is batting .355 with 22 runs scored in the past 19 games ... the Phils are now at a season high 12 games over .500.

"Andy was a wonderful man. He was just so easy going. He never, never got uptight about anything. In this business there are times when things will change at the last minute and you have to quickly move in a totally different direction and I never once saw Andy get upset all those years I worked with him. He would always come into the booth with a smile on his face and he was such a joy to be around. He was just great." – Harry Kalas on his friend and former Phillies' broadcaster Andy Musser

Andy Musser was bitten by the broadcasting bug early in his life. Born in 1937 in Harrisburg, PA, Musser got his start behind the microphone after winning a sportscaster contest back in 1956. At the time, Atlantic Refinery was a sponsor of Phillies' games on the radio and television and each year they would sponsor a contest where kids 18 and under could come and broadcast one inning on TV and one inning on

Phillies' announcer Andy Musser traded his microphone in for some beer – photo courtesy of Anchor Brewing Company

the radio. Musser submitted his entry and was one of nine kids who were chosen to go to a Phillies' game, tape one full inning and then meet the Phillies' players and the broadcast team. Out of the nine kids who taped an inning, Musser was declared the overall winner of the contest and began what ended up being an illustrious broadcast career that included two World Series (1983, 1993) , two Super Bowls (VI and VIII), one NCAA Basketball Final (1975) and two Masters Golf Tournaments (1969 and 1970).

From 1976-2001 Musser was part of the Phillies' broadcast team. He loved the Phillies and he loved his profession but decided to retire because, as he so eloquently stated, "I had such a tremendous career with the Phillies and I wanted to leave when people still wanted me to stay around instead of them having to ask me to move on. It was time for me to start another chapter in my life. I had a tremendous time with the Phillies, but I just wanted to do other things."

For the past seven years, Andy has been working as a representative for the Anchor Brewing Company. A brewery in San Francisco, CA, Anchor has been making beer since 1896 and has kept Andy happily engaged in his "second" career since he left the broadcast booth.

When I was with the Phillies one of my hobbies when I was on the road was to try different types of beers from microbreweries from around the country. One time when I was in California I stopped by a restaurant that had a new beer that they had just started selling on draft. It was called Anchor Steam. I told the waitress that I'd try it and after I tasted it I couldn't believe how incredible it was. I literally had tasted hundreds of beers and I had never tasted a beer that was that good. That was over thirty years ago.

Come to find out Anchor Steam is made by Anchor Brewing which is owned by Fritz Maytag. He's part of the famous Maytag family out in Iowa. It was his great grandfather that started making Maytag Blue Cheese and the Maytag appliance company. Over the years I became good friends with Fritz and one day he said to me, "When you retire from baseball come and help us out; we don't have that many people on the East Coast and we think we could use you on our team." So I started working for him back in 2001. It's a labor of love, believe me.

I work with all of the distributors on the East Coast. I coach them about our brands and what they offer to the consumer. By far our most popular beer is Anchor "Steam". It got its name from back during the turn of the century when any beer made in California was called a "Steam". We also sell Liberty Ale, Anchor Porter, Anchor Summer beer, which is a wheat beer, and four other unique blends that complete our lineup of beers.

The company is doing quite well. It's an old established company and our sales are up this year whereas the overall beer business is flat. More people are drinking spirits these days so we're very pleased with how things are going.

What do I miss about broadcasting? Nothing. I can't say that I miss anything about it. I mean it was an enjoyable life but it's a young man's life and it was sort of a case of been there, done that. The travel is what really wears you down. The travel was terrible and I really couldn't much handle that any longer.

Actually there is one thing I miss and that's Spring Training. I miss a month of the winter sitting in sunny Florida. That was quite relaxing.

I guess I would step back in if they needed me for a game or two. If it was an emergency of some kind, I suppose I would do it but it helps to know what you're talking about and I'm not sure I would know as much about that ballplayers that I used to know.

The Phillies did have me back for a couple of games the first year I retired. Harry went to the Hall of Fame that year so I stepped in for a weekend, but I have not done anything since. Actually, I was down there and helped to moderate the closing of the Vet ceremonies. But I haven't done a single thing since then.

Something that fans don't know about me? That I'm a believer in Jesus Christ and I try to follow his example of helping others. I believe that when you place your trust in Christ and you put yourself in His hands I believe that it saves you a lot of unnecessary worry. When you realize that there's a greater authority out there than yourself, well you just kind of relax a little bit more.

I'd like fans to always remember me as a pleasant person who always tried to make his fellow broadcasters sound the best that they could. I have great memories working for the Phillies and some really fun times. The fans have always been kind and gracious to me, and I will always be thankful to them for that.

Quotable: "They've been real tough to beat at home, and all three games were real close. We scored runs late in all three games, and I'd say we outplayed them at the back end of all three games."
- Charlie Manuel on the Phils' 3 game sweep of Atlanta

<u>Sunday, June 8th - Phillies 6 Braves 3 (39-26) 1st Place - 3 ½ GA of the Marlins</u>

Atlanta - *Ryan Howard slugged three doubles and knocked in four RBIs while Shane Victorino knocked in another game-winning RBI, which helped lead the Phillies to a three game sweep of the Braves at Turner Field ... Starter Adam Eaton gave up 3 runs in 6 innings ... Chad Durbin (2-1, 1.67) picked up the win in relief ... Brad Lidge pitched a perfect 9th for his 17th save. Stuff: The Phils have won 4 straight and 15 out of their last 19 games and now have the 2nd best record in the NL (Chicago is 40-24) ... It appears Howard's early season slump is officially over; he had bottomed out at .163 on May 7th but since then he is hitting .270 with 9 HRs and 33 RBIs. In his last 18 games, Howard is batting .290 with 24 RBIs.*

Ryan Howard knocked around Atlanta pitching with three doubles and four RBIs

Trade deadline primer: It's still a month and a half away, but it's about that time to start talking non-waiver trade deadline, where the Phillies should be active participants. Seth Everett of MLB.com was a guest of 610-WIP's morning show with Angelo Cataldi and Rhea Hughes discussing the reported availability of problem-ace Eric Bedard. He also reports that Paul Byrd, along with C.C. Sabathia, could be on the block. Both pitchers are free agents after the season, and Byrd - unpopular as he was in Philadelphia - pitched well in the 2007 post-season.

Quotable: "... but it is a great lesson, in my opinion, about the way baseball players ought to act and Senators ought to act and everybody ought to act. We all ought to so-called run it out, with that kind of intensity." - PA Senator Arlen Specter on the Charlie Manuel's benching of Jimmy Rollins

<u>Monday, June 9th - (Off) (39-26) 1st Place - 4 GA of the Marlins</u>

Washington D.C. – *With the Phillies having a scheduled break on their calendar, the Honorable Senator from Pennsylvania, Arlen Specter, took the opportunity to apply a life-lesson from the baseball field to the world of politics ... what follows is a speech that the Senator gave on the floor of the US Senate today.*

"Mr. President, a unique event occurred in a Philadelphia Phillies' baseball game last week. The

Philadelphia Phillies' shortstop, named Jimmy Rollins, who was the Most Valuable Player in the league last year, hit a looping ball into left field--which was an easy ball to catch--and instead of running it out, he ran at a very leisurely pace down the first baseline. The left fielder on the defensive team moved in and, in a very unusual play, dropped the ball. Instead of Rollins getting to second base, he was left at first base.

The Phillies' manager, Charles Manuel, then immediately benched Jimmy Rollins, the most valuable player in the league. He put him right on the bench because he did not run it out. That took a lot of guts, and manager Charles Manuel has been complimented on that, and I renew the compliment here today. But it is a great lesson, in my opinion, about the way baseball players ought to act and Senators ought to act and everybody ought to act. We all ought to so-called run it out, with that kind of intensity.

Senator Arlen Specter talks about Charlie Manuel's benching of Jimmy Rollins in the US Senate – photo courtesy of Arlen Specter

I am an avid squash player, and one of the maxims I have developed over the years is that I am never too far ahead to lose and never too far behind to win. The game is always in play, if you run it out. I think it has some applicability to all facets of life in things that all people do, in terms of the intensity of their activity. And I think we need a lot more of that attitude in the Senate and a sense of urgency to deal with the people's business.

This relates directly to the presentation I made a few moments ago on going back to the rules of the Senate on open debate, open amendment offering, and not filling the tree. But it is a great lesson to have that rule stamped indelibly of "running it out." So I congratulate Charlie Manuel. He took out a key player, whose absence could have been decisive even in that game because of Rollins' hitting and fielding ability. But I think it is a great message and a great symbol for all of us to run it out."

Quotable: "I pretty much stunk!" - Brett Myers self assessment of his pitching performance

<u>Tuesday, June 10th - Marlins 5 Phillies 4 (39-27) 1st Place - 3 GA of the Marlins</u>

Miami – Brett Myers (3-8, 5.34) struggled in 5 1/3rd innings, giving up 5 runs, 7 hits and walking 4. Three of the five hits he surrendered were long balls ...Pat Burrell went 2 for 4 with a homerun (16)... Jimmy Rollins went deep as well for his 5th HR of the season. Stuff: For the third consecutive week, Chase Utley is the leading vote-getter for the NL All-Star team with 1,284,961. Atlanta's Chipper Jones is 175,000 votes behind ...Last season's NL MVP Jimmy Rollins ranks 5th amongst all NL Shortstops with 442,885 votes ... With four extra base hits in today's game the Phillies rank 1st in the NL in that category with 236.

On May 2, 1983 the Phillies buried a time capsule at Veterans Stadium in front of the Connie Mack statue at Broad and Pattison Avenues to commemorate the Phillies 100th anniversary in Major League Baseball. The plan was to leave the capsule untouched until 2083 when the Phils would celebrate their 200th anniversary.

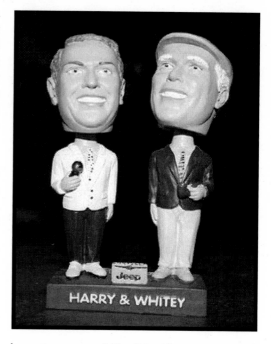

This plan changed when the Phillies relocated their home to Citizens Bank Park and the time capsule had to be exhumed prior to the Phillies imploding Veterans Stadium. When the capsule was dug up they found cracks in it so the Phillies ended up making a new one and decided to add a few new items to the capsule.

According to Scott Palmer and Larry Shenk, the original time capsule from 1983 included a baseball autographed by the entire team, a Mike Schmidt jersey, an autographed Pete Rose bat, the 1983 team media guide and a number of other items. Taking the opportunity to add some more items, the Phils built a new maroon and white capsule with the Phillies logo on the side and decided to add some more items for our great-great grandchildren to enjoy:

- A lineup card from the 125th anniversary game from last week,
- A Harry Kalas and Richie "Whitey" Ashburn bobblehead doll
- A piece of Astroturf from the 1980 Vet Stadium surface
- A Fathers Day giveaway straw hat from the head of Gary Matthews
- A Larry Anderson mask with his baseball card taped onto it
- A small replica statue of Veterans Stadium
- A small replica statue of Citizens Bank Park
- A media guide from the Phillies' inaugural season at CBP
- A Phillies year book and media guide from this season
- Tickets to the final game at the Vet in 2003

Two bronze plaques now mark the location of the burial site of the time capsule out in front of the Phillies' administrative offices on Pattison Avenue. The first plaque is from the original burial of the capsule, the second a new one commemorating 125 years of Phillies' baseball.

Mike DiMuzio, Bill Giles and David Montgomery helped lower the capsule into its new home today where it will sit for another 75 years. Hopefully by that time the team will have added far more than its one World Championship in its first 125 years of existence.

Quotable: "I was all over the place with my command tonight." - Phils' reliever Tom Gordon after surrendering a walk-off grand slam to the Marlins' Dan Uggla

<u>Wednesday, June 11th - Marlins 6 Phillies 2 (39-28) 1st Place - 2 GA of the Marlins</u>

Miami – Cole Hamels and Marlins' starter Andrew Miller threw a classic pitchers' dual only to have Tom Gordon (5-3, 5.19) surrender a walk-off grand slam to Marlins' second baseman Dan Uggla in the bottom of the 9th …Hamels went 8 strong innings, giving up 2 runs and striking out 13 while Miller went 7 innings, giving up 1 run and striking out 7 Phillies. Gordon came into the 9th with the game tied 2-2 but proceeded to walk two batters and give up a single before Uggla's crushing blow … Chase Utley drove in both Phillies' runs. He now has 58 RBIs on the season. Stuff: Prior to today's performance, Tom Gordon had gone 5-1 with a 2.13 ERA over his past 27 appearances …Chris Coste was given permission to miss the game so that he could be with his wife for the birth of their 2nd child, Camryn Marie … The Phils released veteran reliever Steve Kline from their AAA Lehigh Valley team. Lefties had been hitting .341 against him. In addition to his pitching problems, Kline had just been suspended for bumping an umpire in a recent 4-1 loss.

The Phillies have spoiled fans so much lately that to some a two-game losing streak feels like having one's head in a vice. Here's a sampling from an agonizing night in the Beerleaguer peanut gallery.

"Carlos Ruiz is ridiculous. I have supported him for too long. He's horrible at the plate. I know he's the 8-hole hitter, but he really sucks. Not only does he have no plate discipline, he grounds into double plays far too often, I'm sick of him."
– GM-Carson

"Flash was Flush tonight. Arguably the toughest loss of the year but the Phils certainly had some very questionable managerial and player decisions tonight." - MG

"The Phillies always seem to reserve their worst games of the year for Florida. That one was lost unnecessarily in so many different ways, you have

Mitch Williams doing Phillies Post Game Live … when only your upper half appears on TV it doesn't matter what's on underneath

to stop and remind yourself they're where they are in the standings. Manuel managed poorly and Werth pulled one of the most inexcusably bonehead plays I may have ever seen. And yet again they waste a premium effort from Hamels." – RSB

Quotable: "We'll see if we can't get that 43-year-old to throw 2 of the 3 games against them." - Charlie Manuel commenting on having Jamie Moyer pitch against the Marlins for the remainder of the season

Thursday, June 12th - Phillies 3 Marlins 0 (40-28) 1st Place - 3 GA of the Marlins

Miami – *Jamie Moyer (7-3, 4.12) shutout the Marlins for 8 spectacular innings, surrendering only two hits and losing a no-hitter in the bottom of the 6th ... Brad Lidge pitched the 9th for his 18th save of the season ... In a scoreless tie going into the 6th, the Phillies scored 2 runs on a wild pitch and then a throwing error by Marlins' catcher Matt Treanor ... Jayson Werth's 2-out RBI single in the 8th made it 3-0 ... The Phils banged out 11 hits including two each by Rollins, Utley, Burrell and Feliz ... the victory saved the Phils from a three-game sweep by the Fish. Stuff: Moyer retired the first 10 batters he faced and 16 of the first 17 ... He is now 9-0 lifetime against the Marlins with a 3.03 ERA. At Dolphin Stadium, he is 4-0 with a 1.30 ERA ... Marlins' starter Scott Olson, a career .077 hitter, broke up the no-hitter ... with Chris Coste out on "maternity leave", Jayson Werth served as the Phillies' back-up catcher. Werth hasn't caught a game since 1998 and was thankful that he didn't have to do so. Coste will be back with the team tomorrow.*

There are Submarines, Heros, Grinders, Cosmos, Torpedos, Wedges, Spuckies and Zepplins but none of them can beat Philadelphia's own Hoagie. Legend has it that the hoagie was created in an area of southwest Philadelphia called Hog Island. Back during World War I, Hog Island, which today is now Philadelphia International Airport, was once home to the largest shipyard in the world. Italian immigrants working at the shipyard would bring giant sandwiches to work that were made up of various meats, cheeses, lettuce, tomatoes, onions and peppers, which were put between two pieces of bread. These workers were nicknamed "hoggies". Eventually these large sandwiches became known as the "Hog Island" or "Hoggie" sandwich and eventually made its way to what is now know today as the hoagie.

Go to any town in the surrounding Philadelphia

Sal Fogarino's hoagies are out of this world!

area and you will find at least 2-3 stores that can make a hoagie for you. However when you put them all together you can find no better hoagie in Philly than at Planet Hoagie, which is conveniently located right on Ashburn Alley and in various locations across the Delaware Valley.

Winner for multiple years of the "Best of Philly Award" by Philadelphia Magazine for Hoagies, Planet Hoagie is owned and operated by Sal Fogarino: a lover of great Italian foods and of the Phillies.

We opened up the store on Ashburn Alley the year after the ballpark opened so this is our 4th season at Citizens Bank Park. Right now we operate six other stores, some of which I operate (Media, Brigantine and Mount Laurel which is co-owned with Tim Moffitt) and some of which are franchises (Deptford, Norristown and Wilmington).

When we first opened here we primarily sold your basic hoagies but last year (2007) we expanded our menu. We now have chicken cutlet, grilled chicken and wraps. We have over 65 kinds of hoagies that we sell at Planet Hoagie. We don't sell all of them here at the park so what I try to do is change the menu every series. We always have a series special that we name after one of the Phillies players like "The Shane Victorino," which was a buffalo chicken with blue cheese dressing or "The Jayson Werth" which was grilled chicken with sharp provolone, roasted eggplant and spinach. The fans really enjoy them.

During a sellout we'll probably sell 450-500 hoagies. The business is really good here especially when they're winning. Everything we make is fresh, done right here on the premises. So if a customer wanted a "Jayson Werth" with American cheese instead of the sharp provolone we will do that for them. If a customer says "the works," they'll get lettuce, tomatoes, onions, oregano, black pepper and oil on the hoagie.

We'll probably sell anywhere between 28,000 – 35,000 hoagies a season. As long as it's not on dollar dog day, we do really well. Dollar Dog Days are a killer for us and it's not a favorite of the Ashburn Alley vendors. Let's put it this way, if you can buy 7 hot dogs versus one sandwich, what are you going to buy? But the Phillies love Dollar Dog Days. They'll sell 50-70,000 hot dogs in one night and it packs the fans in during games, which might otherwise not be a sellout.

Right now our best selling item believe it or not is the chicken cutlet. Since we introduced it fans have been buying them like crazy. All of our hoagies cost $7.75 each. We don't price them, Aramark does. Everyone has the same price The Schmitter, Tony Luke's, Rick's ...most are $7.75. There's no competition in that respect, but we give more for that $7.75 than the others.

I think we're the most popular vendor with the workers in the ballpark. They all come and they want our sandwiches. Don't get me wrong, Tony Luke's does a phenomenal business; he does 2-3 times what we do, but it's all like Pavlov's dog when people come to the park. They think to themselves, " I got to get a cheese steak". I mean it's in their head. I'll be honest with you, I love Tony Luke Jr., extremely nice kid. But with cheesesteaks, there's nothing to them.

Just a slab of steak and some cheese. I'm not such the big cheese steak person anyway. So my guys eat his stuff; he eats ours.

What makes our hoagies the best in Philly? I think it's a combination of the quality of our products and how we put it together. We use Hatfield products as well as Italian specialties of Satero, Margarite, and other Italian brands. The biggest thing is we cut everything, it's made to order and everything's cut thin. There's no thickness. Our motto is "Thicker is not quicker." It's thin, we pile it on. We're there to fill up the roll so if that roll is fat one day that's your advantage. So we're there to fill it up. If you're going to get a nice sandwich, we can give it to you. We give you value for your money.

Our rolls are from Lanci's bakery. Their heritage is from South Philly. The father of the current owner of the bakery had a store right on 17th & 10th. Lanci's is now in Blackwood, NJ. He has a bakery there that does a wholesale business. All the Planet Hoagie shops use their bread.

One of our trademarks is the sesame seed roll. The bread is a big part of it. It's just like a quarterback on a football team. The beauty of that bread, it's a crusty bread and it's light enough that when you're finished with it, you're not to the point where you need a nap. You feel good. There are some breads out there and they're really good but they're not for hoagies. They're just very doughy and very heavy. By the time they get halfway through it, people are starting to pass out. So we use the rolls and load it up with quality products. It's a good combination and it's not overwhelming. It's overwhelming to look at, but you can get through it and feel good.

Our most famous customers are the guys up in the radio and TV booths. Larry Anderson and that group come here all the time or we go up and deliver to their booth. I'm on a first name basis with him. He's a pretty nice guy. Greg Luzinski's another big fan of our hoagies. At least twice in a series he's sending somebody over to bring food back to him. He's a big fan. Mitch Williams comes here as well. Aramark's also pretty good about using our hoagies when they have celebrities or one of the major networks at the ballpark. They'll send them up to Joe Morgan or whoever's here from ESPN or FOX.

Players love our hoagies as well. One time Ryan Madson and Shane Victorino stopped me and thanked me for sending hoagies down to the players. They told me they really appreciated it and that they loved them. Jamie Moyer actually eats our Italian hoagie after every start he throws here at home.

As a Phillies fan we're all hoping that they go all the way this year. They have a really good team. I hope the pitching holds up, but we'll see. I wouldn't mind selling hoagies in October.

Quotable: "We hadn't been scoring too many runs lately. I guess we were waiting to get some tonight." – Charlie Manuel on the Phils' 20-run performance

<u>Friday, June 13th - Phillies 20 Cardinals 2 (41-28) 1st Place - 4 GA of the Marlins</u>

St. Louis – *Chase Utley, Ryan Howard and Pat Burrell homered back-to-back-to-back in the 1st inning and then continued to tear apart Cardinal pitching for the remainder of the game in a 20 run, 21 hit rout of St Louis ... Six players had a multi-hit game including pitcher Kyle Kendrick who had two hits. Carlos Ruiz led the team with 4 hits while Shane Victorino, Pedro Feliz, and Ryan Howard had three hits a piece ... Kendrick (6-2, 4.54) pitched 7 strong innings only giving up 1 run on 8 hits. Stuff: This is the Phils first time since 1900 that they've scored 20 runs twice in the same season ... the 9 runs that they scored in the 4th inning was a season high for an inning. Their previous high was back on May 21st when they scored 8 runs against the Nationals in the 6th during a 12-2 win ... Ryan Howard hit 2 homeruns and drove in 5 runs. A native of St. Louis, Howard now has a lifetime average of .353 against his hometown team with 8 homers and 22 RBIs.*

The Phillies have certainly made Kyle Kendrick's transition to the Major Leagues as comfortable as possible. After Chase Utley, Ryan Howard and Pat Burrell staked him to a three-run lead with jacks in the first, they continued to pile it on en route to their second 20-run outburst of the season. Howard feasted on home cooking with a two-HR, 5 RBI night, while Carlos Ruiz, who also needed a lift, went 4-for-6 with a pair of RBI doubles.

While the rest of baseball enjoyed the magic of interleague play, the Phils and Cards engaged in an old-fashioned match up that proved to be most memorable from start to finish. The game featured Cardinals' second baseman Aaron Miles pitching a shutout ninth, Howard getting thrown at by the Cardinals and Tony La Russa getting tossed for throwing his sunglasses.

Tony La Russa wasn't too happy with his team surrendering 20 runs to the Phillies

On a night when the offense gorged on poor pitching, the best part might have been Kendrick taking care of business for his sixth win of the season. The 23-year-old also added a pair of hits during a nine-run fourth inning. After one full year of play, Kendrick improves to an understated 16-6 with a 4.13 ERA. What a fine job by Kendrick and by Rich Dubee; Kendrick has been a true portfolio piece for the Phils pitching coach.

Quotable: "(Lohse) knew how to pitch to us. He had a game plan and he did it pretty good."– Charlie Manuel on ex-Phillie Kyle Lohse who silenced the Phillies' bats throughout the day

Saturday, June 14th - Cardinals 3 Phillies 2 (41-29) 1st Place - 4 GA of the Marlins

St. Louis – Kyle Lohse (8-2, 3.77) cooled down the Phillies' red-hot offense throwing a season-high 8 innings while giving up 4 hits and allowing only 2 runs … The lone runs came on a single by Ryan Howard that was then followed by a Pat Burrell 2-run homer in the 4th inning; his 18th of the year … Adam Eaton (2-4 4.57) pitched effectively, going 6 2/3rd innings and giving up 3 runs, but the offense just couldn't put together any real threats after the 4th … For the second consecutive night a Phillies' starter had a two-hit game. Adam Eaton went 2 for 3 with a double and a single. Stuff: The Phils are now 4-8 this season in one run games on the road and 13-13 overall … Kyle Lohse is now 12-2 since last July 25th, with a major league best .857 winning percentage. The Phillies tried to sign Lohse in the off-season to a 3-year, $21 million contract but he and agent Scott Boros turned it down. He ended up signing a one-year contract with the Cardinals for $4.25 million.

Jody McDonald has spent more than eighteen years as a sports talk host in building a reputation and following as one of the most knowledgeable and personable radio hosts in the country. The fact that Jody Mac has staked 15 of those 18 years in Philadelphia is a reflection of his fondness for Philadelphia sports and for the passion that drives the fans here.

Jody's wide-ranging knowledge of sports is quite impressive and is most likely rooted in his love of sports from an early age. While growing up in Yonkers, New York, Jody had a great view of the inner workings of the pro sports world through his father, Joseph McDonald, Sr., who was the General Manager of the New York Mets, the St. Louis Cardinals and the Detroit Tigers. Jody's connection to the past and the perspective that he is able to offer from the sports world is what makes for one of the most interesting and enjoyable radio shows on the airwaves.

950 AM ESPN Radio's Jody McDonald, sports run deep in his family

Not many fans may know that your father was a General Manager. How did he work his way into that role?

Horatio Hornblower story, right up the ranks. In 1962 starting with the math, he was the stat-istician in the booth for their broadcasts. And back and forth between the Mets original radio and television team of Ralph Kiner, Bob Murphy and Lindsey Nelson. After his first year with the Mets, he got into a minor league system worked his way up to the Farm Director position that directed their entire minor league teams. He ended up getting promoted to GM when he replaced Bob Sheffield after he resigned in 1975. So in a total of thirteen years he went from statistician to the Mets General Manager.

So he was a part of the resurgence of the Mets I'm guessing.
Oh yes. He was there when they drafted (Jerry) Koosman, (Tom) Seaver and (Gary) Gentry and all those guys. He was a big part of the minor leagues.

When did your father stop working with the Mets?
He was the GM from 1975-79 and stayed on one year after the team was sold to help out and be Frank Cashen's main assistant. He then left for St. Louis to be with his good friend Whitey Herzog and helped run the Cardinals for three years. Afterwards he moved to the Tiger's orga-nization and ended up being their GM during the 1991 and 1992 seasons.

Since you probably have a good feel for GMs, how would you rate Pat Gillick since he has been with the Phillies?
I'd say slightly above average. He's great with the little moves like how he got Dobbs, JC Romero and Jayson Werth. Not as good with the bigger moves like Freddie Garcia and his starting catcher for 2007 Mr. Barajas. But if you do enough of the little ones, they can add up. You can't always outweigh the bad ones, the big ones, but he's been very good at building a 25-man roster. He just needs to do a little better at the big top of it. There's one thing I will give him credit for, there hasn't been a trade yet that you can say was a terrible trade. A really terrible trade is when the guy you get stinks and the guys you give up are pretty darn good. Like let's say I don't know, Jim Fregosi for Nolan Ryan. Fregosi came to the Mets and he stunk and Nolan Ryan went on to be one of the greatest pitchers in major league baseball. That's a terrible trade. We'll see if Geo Gonzalez ever makes it but I doubt it. All the deals that he's made, what he's given up, nothing has come back to bite him on the other end.

What are his best moves so far?
You know there isn't one great move. They're all little moves. I think Rowand for Thome when people didn't think they could get anything for Thome was a good move. Granted they did have to eat some of Thome's salary but the two years that he got out of Rowand were pretty darn good. They couldn't keep Thome anyway when Howard busted in on the scene. I remem-ber that people thought they would have to eat up more money and get nothing in return for Thome and they only ate part of it. I think that was his first big move and I've got to say it was his best.

What has been his worst move?
That's close between Adam Eaton and Freddie Garcia. I'll say Freddie was the worse move but with the chance that Eaton can lap him because you got another year of Eaton to go. At this point, one win out of Garcia is just terrible. Paying him 10 million dollars and giving him a

spot in the rotation.

The Phillies have grown some high caliber players out of their farm system with Utley, Howard, Rollins and Hamels leading the pack. It would appear that they are doing something right. However now the minor league system is quite thin. Why is that?

Because it's an inexact science. I think they have an ok minor league system right now. I wouldn't call it great. Mike Arbuckle is solid. He's surely not spectacular but if I were to grade the entire system I'd say it's probably about a C+. What they currently have in their farm system now is OK but it's not good enough. They need to improve. I think they realize where they come up short the most is in the pitching department. Hopefully Hamels and Myers are the dawning of a new day. I really do like one of the young kids that they have in Carlos Carrasco. I think he's going to be in the big leagues within the next two years. So the pipeline is improving. Give Arbuckle points for trying. He just needs to get some better results.

Are the Phillies wining in spite of or because of Charlie Manuel?

Charlie gets an A for chemistry and a C- for strategy. Balance that out, it's a B- or a C+. He is what he is. He's the kind of guy that you like to be friends with, have a beer with; you know he's got your back for you. There are times when I just scratch my head and wonder why he's making moves in the game that I just don't understand. But in evaluating managers you got to take everything into consideration. Not just when to pinch hit and when to do a double switch. It's really how hard your players play for you. If they have a no-quit attitude, which I certainly think has been evidenced in this squad, then he's done a good job. Overall, with the tangibles, Charlie's not great. With the intangibles, he's pretty darn impressive.

You grew up as a Mets fan. Do you still root for them?

I don't root against them as wholeheartedly as most Phillies fans do. If the Mets should advance past the Phillies in the playoffs this year I will then root for the Mets, but no I'm a Phillies guy now. You gotta know where your bread is buttered. I root for the Phillies first.

Philly and New York, what's the biggest difference between the fans?

The biggest difference is the biggest problem with each of the two sports towns. In New York, they'll second-guess a champion. The Yankees will win the World Series in six games and I would take a call two days after the World Series and there would be someone saying, "We could have won it in five games if Joe Torre didn't make this move in game #4." I'm on the radio thinking, "You f***g won, shut up!!!" You don't get that here in Philadelphia. When you have championships, which are few and far between, you win one and you buy so much goodwill. Look at Bobby Clark. He's made a living hanging around here and living off of those two championships. Not in New York. Down here in Philly I think the biggest problem with the sports fans is that they think there's no grey area. In New York, you can have a player who's talented and really good but is a bad guy and a bad teammate. You can put out both the positives and negatives in New York and fans will accept that. Down here in Philadelphia, people feel the need to get on one side or the other.

The greatest example believe it or not still hasn't changed in the 18 years since I've been here was the head football coach of the Eagles, Mr. Buddy Ryan. There was a segment of the population who honestly believed that he could out coach Vince Lombardi. There's also a segment of the population that believed this guy is a blithering idiot that should be taken out in the parking lot and shot. Of course the truth is somewhere there in the middle but try to tell the people that are at one end or the other of the spectrum. They can't process through that.

Why do you think Philadelphia fans are like that?
I don't know. Grey area just doesn't work in this town. It's a blue collar, cotton picking town that where you are either in or you're out. They don't see the grey area. New York gets that. But down here they also get the fact that a championship can be pretty special so why don't you cut a guy some slack when you just won the big ring.

What's one thing that the Phillies' fans and listeners probably don't know about Jody McDonald?
That twenty years ago, I was a dynamite basketball referee. I haven't done it in a number of years, but I did a lot of it in college. A bit of refereeing after college …made a couple of extra bucks. I thought I was a phenomenal referee and most coaches would probably tend to agree with me unless they were on the short end of one of my decisions.

Quotable: "I just didn't see the ball. I couldn't find it … couldn't locate it. I got there (to first base) quick enough. I was prepared for the play." - Tom Gordon on his missed catch in the bottom of the 10th that allowed the winning run to score.

Sunday, June 15th - Cardinals 7 Phillies 6 - 10 inn. (41-30) 1st - 3 GA of the Marlins
St. Louis – *The Phillies committed two costly errors in the bottom of the 10th that led to their fourth loss in their last six games. With two-outs and nobody on Chase Utley cleanly fielded a grounder hit to him off of the bat of Rick Ankiel but threw it wide and out of the reach of Tom Gordon who was covering the bag on the play. After Troy Glaus singled, a second grounder was hit to Chase Utley. This time he threw the ball right on target to a covering Tom Gordon, however this time Gordon didn't see the ball and the ball went by him allowing Ankiel to score from second to win the game … Although Gordon (5-4, 5.06) took the loss, Brett Myers once again pitched poorly giving up 6 earned runs in six innings. In 15 starts this season, Myers is 3-8 with a 5.58 ERA … Ryan Howard went 2 for 4 with 4 RBIs (58) and even stole his first base of the season … Jimmy Rollins went 2 for 5 scoring three times and stealing his 13th bag of the year. Stuff: The offense went 4 for 16 with runners in scoring position and left 15 men on base leaving the bases loaded four times during the game … The Phils ended their road trip 5-4 … they batted .271 with 10 HRs and 53 runs scored (5.9 runs/game) while the pitching staff did fairly well with a 3.26 ERA, but only had 5 wins to show for the effort. The team now begins a six game interleague series against the Red Sox and the Angels, two of the best teams in the American League.*

Covering baseball is the most difficult newspaper beat in all of sports. The deadlines are tight and the workload is ridiculous. You practically live out of suitcases and wait around airports for half the year, and while your neighbors and friends are down at the beach enjoying the summer, you get to hang around sweaty ballplayers who would rather be at the beach as well.

This is the life of Scott Lauber, the 32-year-old reporter for the *Wilmington News Journal.* Scott has been the Phillies' Beat Writer since November of 2005. Prior to that, Scott covered the Mets farm system for the Press & Sun-Bulletin out of Binghamton, NY. Originally from Manalapan, NJ, Lauber now makes his home, when he's there, in North Wilmington, Delaware.

Phillies Beat Reporter Scott Lauber ... who's the toughest Phillie to interview?

There are a number of benefits to being a Beat Writer and some pitfalls too. It's funny because when you talk to a lot of people and you tell them what you do, they think that it's awesome and probably the best job in the whole world. I'd prefer doing this than sitting in an office or doing something that I'm not interested in, but that's why I think I got into sports writing. I knew I wasn't going to be able to play for the Yankees or anything and I wanted to work in sports and was kind of told that this would be a great way to do it. It really is a great job. There are worse things in the world then going to a ballpark as your office but the thing I still tell people is that it's still a job. The hours are long and strange. There are a lot of nights, a lot of weekends and a lot of waiting around. Whether it's waiting for the players, planes, taxis, coaches, you do a lot of waiting.

You really don't have the summer to yourself and when your friends are down at the shore you're generally working. The benefit of it is that you get to go do something that people pay to go see. You get to go to baseball games and kind of get a back stage pass when you go, but the pitfall is that it's still a job and you do end up spending a significant amount of time working most of the year.

Of a 162 game season, I'm usually covering 125-130 games a year. That doesn't count Spring Training or playoffs either. I go on every road trip except one of the two west coast trips. I also cover at least 5 out of every 7 home games.

For a 7:05pm game start, I'm generally at the ballpark by 2:30pm. Before I actually leave to go there, I'll take the time to jump on-line and read what all the other papers have written that day. The clubhouse doors open at 3:30pm so I generally catch up on blogging and emails before I go in and talk to the players.

The clubhouse is open from 3:30 to 4:00pm until the players go out for the batting practice and for their stretching. Once the players are on the field Charlie Manuel will meet with the Beat Writers and go over a lot of what happened the game before that maybe we didn't get a chance to get to. He'll then talk about what's ahead, any news that's going on, any injury updates and those sorts of thing. That takes about 15-20 minutes.

At around 5:30pm or so the clubhouse reopens when the players are done batting practice. It then stays open until 6:05pm for a 7:05pm game. So that's another chance for us to get to some of the players that we weren't able to get to earlier. Unfortunately what comes with this job is a lot of waiting. If you don't like waiting around it's definitely not the job for you. You sometimes have to wait for players for a very long time. They have their schedules that they have to keep so if you want to talk to Jimmy Rollins or Ryan Howard or Chase Utley, sometimes you have to wait them out and it can get kind of boring during pre-game preparation.

Once the clubhouse closes, I go back upstairs to the press box and quickly get a bite to eat in the Media Dining area. As soon as I'm done eating, I then start working on my "notebook" article for the next day's paper. The "notebook" is kind of a roundup on what's going on with the team. I like to have a lot of news in there from the information that I find out about during the day. I generally write two stories a night. If it's a busy night, I'll write three.

Once the game starts, I finish up the notebook in the first few innings and then I'll start writing about the game. It's there that you kind of have to master the art of working and watching at the same time.

When the game is over we go down to the Media Room where Charlie will give his post-game press conference. If we're on the road, he will usually do an informal gathering in his office. Once that is done, we'll head into the clubhouse and talk to the players then head upstairs and write the rest of the game story as the clock keeps on ticking before I have to get my story to the paper before the second edition deadline ends.

I send my "Notebook" story to the paper as soon as it's done. Once the last pitch is thrown I'll then send the game story to the paper so that both are ready for the first edition printing of the paper. The first edition of the *Wilmington News Journal* goes to the far reaching areas of Delaware like Kent and Suffix County. Once I come back upstairs from the clubhouse, I usually have until 11:30-11:35pm to get a story with quotes in it for the second edition run of the paper for the central and northern areas of the state. The third edition of the paper is delivered to the areas surrounding Wilmington, up into Delaware County as well as into Philadelphia. The deadline for that edition is between 12:30-1:00am. I think our total circulation is about 125,000 – 130,000 papers a day.

There really isn't enough time to experience writer's block when covering a game. There are some nights that you struggle a little bit more than others but you know that the little clock on your computer keeps on ticking and you have to get something written down on the page no matter what.

I usually find that I struggle when I have more time to write a piece like a feature story or one of our longer Sunday stories. During Spring Training I write a lot of features and I'll find myself staring at a blank screen for awhile; I think that not having a deadline can sometimes be a curse because I usually sit there and think a little too much. It can sometimes be one of the bad habits that you can fall into in this job.

My favorite thing about being a Beat Writer is the writing. You have to enjoy writing as much, if not more, than you enjoy baseball. You are basically tied to your laptop most of the day especially now with the Internet and all the blogging and web updates that we do. Being a Beat Writer is more than just writing your story for the newspaper, it's all the other media that we do as well. That can include appearances on radio talk shows, Comcast, even with bloggers.

My favorite interview of all time was with Ted Williams. In 1999, I was working for a small paper in Concord, NH and they would put on a baseball dinner there every January. That year Williams was the keynote speaker. To make a long story short, Ted was close friends with a State Trooper friend of mine who was able to set me up with a one-on-one interview with Ted the morning of the dinner. I remember going up to Ted's hotel suite and it was just me and him. I didn't even have to ask that many questions. Ted just kept talking and talking and talking. It was great. So for 45 minutes, Ted Williams talked to me about hitting. He gave me quite an education, and it's sort of one of those things where you walk out of the room when you're done and you say to yourself, "I'm never erasing that tape." It was something that I will always remember. To do something like that with a Hall-of-Famer like Ted Williams late in his life was pretty cool.

The worst interview is any one in which an athlete doesn't feel like talking. I remember one time while I was at Boston College I was doing some freelance work for a college hockey magazine and I was asked to do a cover story on the goalie from Boston College by the name of Scott Clemmensen. I had been critical of him over the past few years for various reasons so when I called him up to do this cover story, a cover story that was supposed to be a positive story, he just really didn't want to talk to me. He was aware of some of the things that I had written. Obviously that is an athlete's prerogative. The first few minutes of that interview were pretty tough because I got a lot of one-word answers. He did kind of warm up a little bit after he realized what I was doing and it got a little easier.

I think the toughest Phillie to interview is Chase Utley. He's not a huge fan of being interviewed. He's very careful about what he says. He doesn't particularly like the spotlight being on him. Often times it's like pulling teeth trying to get some type of emotion or response out of him, but Chase likes it that way. So you know when you go to talk to Chase Utley that you are going to be in somewhat of a little battle. As a reporter though that's fine. Sometimes you just have to better understand a guy's personality. The more you get to know Chase the better you understand how you should phrase a question to him so that he feels a little bit more comfortable around you.

And then there are sometimes guys who are just characters. Brett Myers is a character and a lot of the time you know that when you go up to Brett, especially on a day when he is not pitching, he will give you 30 seconds of grief and then he'll answer your questions. There are also some guys like Jamie Moyer who you can ask one question to and then he'll talk all day long because you'll get a fully thought out answer. You have to make sure that when you go to Jamie that you have some time on your hands because it's going to be awhile. It's just the case of getting to know their personalities and getting to know how the guys will react.

Chris Coste is one of the players that I probably get along well with. Myself and the other writers have an easy time talking with him. Brad Lidge is also someone that I think is easy to talk to. He's always available for you, and he's somebody who has great insights and has something good to say about everything. Victorino and Hamels are pretty easy to talk to as well. The Beat Writers that cover the Phillies are lucky because we have a pretty good group of guys who don't mind speaking to the reporters.

My favorite cities to visit on the road are Chicago and San Francisco. Some really good restaurants in both of those towns and they are just fun places to go watch a ballgame.

My least favorite is probably Cincinnati. We usually stay over on the Kentucky side of the river and there's not a lot to do there … just a whole lot of fast food restaurants. Not a whole lot there. I'm not a big Florida fan either. I used to not like going to Atlanta, but I've found out that once you start visiting these cities on a regular basis you end up finding some things about them that you really like.

My favorite hotel is any Marriott in the city that I'm visiting. I'll let you in on a little sports writer's secret. They are the biggest fans in the world of Marriott points. There are probably a ton of 5-star hotels in these cities that I'll never see because they're not Marriotts. My favorite Marriott's are in Chicago and Atlanta. Last year after the season was over I was able to go to Europe with a friend of mine almost exclusively on Marriott points. It does have its rewards.

My favorite restaurant outside of Philadelphia varies depending upon what I'm eating. The Vortex in Atlanta is a really good place for burgers. For barbeque it's Tom Jenkins Barbeque in Fort Lauderdale. I guess though that my favorite dinner on the road would be in Chicago at Harry Karry's. A bunch of us will usually get together and go there at least once when we're in town.

Favorite Stadium: I really like Dodger Stadium. For an older stadium it's a nice place to work. Coors Field has the largest Press Box and a big clubhouse, and it's fairly new so it's one of the nicer ones that we visit.

Least Favorite Stadium: Shea Stadium. Thank goodness this is the last year we have to visit it. The stadium is really old and has a really small clubhouse so when you fit all of those media cameras and beat writers in there it gets kind of tough.

Favorite Media Dining Room: Houston generally has good food in their dining facility. Dodger Dogs in LA believe it or not are pretty good. I think though that Atlanta has the best food. They have a sandwich station there where I can make a quick tuna sandwich and I can quickly get back to work.

Least Favorite Media Dining Room: Washington. It's not as bad now with the new stadium but when they were at RFK it was horrible.

Quotable: "I believe we are destined to play each other in the World Series. We can compete with them any day of the week." - Cole Hamels on playing against the Red Sox

Monday, June 16th - Phillies 8 Red Sox 2 (42-30) 1st Place - 3 GA of the Marlins

Philadelphia – *Ryan Howard continued his torrid hitting, going 3 for 5 with two homeruns (19), a triple and 4 RBIs off of the defending World Champion Red Sox ... Howard is now tied with San Diego's Adrian Gonzalez and Chase Utley for the NL Lead in RBIs with 62 and is tied for 2nd in HRs ... Cole Hamels (7-4, 3.23) pitched like the ace of the staff that he has become, going 7 solid innings and allowing 2 runs on 7 hits for the victory. He has a 1.50 ERA in his last three starts ... Jimmy Rollins continued his hot hitting as well as he went 3 for 5 with a homerun (6) and 3 RBIs. He is now batting .284 ... Pat Burrell and Shane Victorino contributed in the win with two hits apiece; one of Burrell's hits was a triple ... Chase Utley took a 0 for 5 tonight and is now 0 for his last 13. Stuff: The sold-out ESPN game was split 2/3rd Phillies fans, 1/3rd Red Sox fans at Citizens Bank Park ... It was the 17th sellout of the season ... One large banner in the stands read "World Series Preview" ...It was announced tonight by the Phillies that Juan Samuel will be this year's inductee to the Phillies' Wall of Fame ... Even with his recent power surge, Ryan Howard leads the majors with 97 whiffs and still is only batting .224. However, since May 7th, Howard is batting .276 with 13 HRs and 46 RBIs.*

You definitely need a Type "A" personality, be a bit of a class clown, have a certain theatrical presence about yourself, be able to stand up in front of hundreds of people and you have to have no fear if you ever dreamt of being a Phillies Phanstormer. Phanstormers are those boisterous men and women that you see every game springing confetti on the heads of the embarrassed men, woman, boys and girls who are celebrating their birthdays at the ballpark. They do everything from getting 200 people to sing "Happy Birthday" to loading up the Phanatic's hot dog gun. Their job is to entertain the fans.

Phanstormer Dan Rich helping Nicole McNesby celebrate her 21st birthday at Citizens Bank Park

Dan Rich is a Phanstormer and a pretty good one at that. A Southwest Philadelphia native and a Theatre graduate from DeSales University, Rich is an experienced actor who has performed numerous times in children's theatre productions. Today, he is in Section 144, putting the final throws of confetti onto the head of Nicole McNesby who is celebrating her 21st birthday with her cousin Jessica Buchan.

To become a Phanstormer you have to audition with the Phillies. It takes place in February right before Spring Training starts. When I auditioned six seasons ago it consisted of an interview with the Phanstormer managers, Chris Long (Director of Entertainment) and included a bunch of group improv games. I think now they've added a monologue to the process.

I found out about Phanstorming from a fellow co-worker Greg Hammel. He thought that my sense of humor and play might be well suited for the type of work that we do here at the park. After hearing Greg talk about how much fun he had with the job, I figured that I should check it out, and honestly, what better way to spend the summer then at the ballpark!

The heart of Phanstorming is entertainment. Before the game, Phanstormers interact with guests and fans, welcoming them to the ballpark and helping to build excitement for the game. During the game, we celebrate birthdays, assist with engagements, assist in giveaways that happen during the game, assist the Phanatic when he needs any help and interact with fans in between innings.

My favorite aspect of the job is to completely be able to make someone's day. I get to take part in people's birthdays and engagements. I give out t-shirts and amusement park tickets to unsuspecting fans. It's incredible how something as simple as talking to a crying child during the game and giving him a Phanatic temporary tattoo can work wonders.

I think the funniest time I've ever had Phanstorming was during the first opening weekend at Citizens Bank Park. I was standing at the left field gate with another Phanstormer who was armed with bongos and a harmonica. We spent a number of hours improvising rally songs and would get random guests to improvise with us. It was amazing how clever and brave some of the fans were and we did experience some side-splitting moments.

I've had some embarrassing moments as well. One time, they had me dress up as an elf and dance on the dugout with the Phanatic to celebrate Christmas in July. The most embarrassing thing that I've done was sing "Happy Birthday" to a guest under the wrong name. I was singing to the intended receiver, but during the song, I accidentally sung the name of the previous birthday that I performed. Fortunately, the party was very understanding.

My future? I'm obsessed with improv comedy so one day I plan on studying in Chicago and New York City. I've certainly had a lot of practice here over the years doing it with the fans.

Quotable: "We didn't have a whole lot of opportunities and we didn't do anything with the ones that we had." - Pat Burrell on the effective Red Sox pitching

Tuesday, June 17th - Red Sox 3 Phillies 0 (42-31) 1st Place - 3 GA of the Marlins
Philadelphia – Red Sox starter Jon Lester (6-3, 3.18) and relievers Hidecki Okajima and Jonathan Papelbon shut down the Phillies' offense by striking out 10 and scattering 7 hits …Jamie Moyer (7-4, 4.09) threw 5 innings, giving up 2 runs and walking 5 … the Phils' bullpen allowed 1 run and struck out 4 in 4 innings of work …Jimmy Rollins, Jayson Werth and Pedro Feliz accounted for 6 of the Phils' 7 hits … Ryan Howard went 0 for 4, striking out all four times at the plate. Stuff: The Red Sox stole a season high 6 bases off of the Phils … The NY Mets fired manager Wil-

lie Randolph as the team has continued to struggle through the season. He was replaced by Coach Jerry Manuel (no relation to Charlie). The Mets are currently 34-36 and are 6 ½ games behind the Phillies.

Over the last two nights, the in-game discussion revolved around hitting, but on the field, it's been all about pitching: Cole Hamels and the poor outings by Bartolo Colon and Mike Timlin on Monday; and Lester's terrific start tonight. For the fourth time this season, the Phils never touched home, but it was only the second time where the opposing starter had dominant stuff. In other words, Lester isn't the two-pitch enigma known as Tim Redding. He's closer to Cincinnati's Edinson Volquez, making hitters look foolish with a darting fastball, including a nasty cutter inside to right-handed hitters. Odds are that Lester, followed by Hideki Okajima and closer Jonathan Papelbon, who combined for the shutout last night, is how more than one box score will read this October.

Jamie Moyer didn't get the black from home plate umpire Brian Knight, making it a short night for the 45-year-old. Still, Moyer limited the damage to just two runs, keeping his club in the game.

The Mets fired manager Willie Randolph today after the team lumbered their way to a 34-36 start this season

Unfortunately, they could not pull through. Utley went hitless for the fourth game in a row, dropping his batting average below .300 for the first time this season. Afterward, Charlie Manuel said he considered giving Utley the night off, but the second baseman talked him out of it.

Quotable: "Chase is going to be fine. Nobody needs to make a big deal out of it ... I wouldn't even worry about it." - Ryan Howard after Utley extended his hitless streak to twenty at bats.

Wednesday, June 18th - Red Sox 7 Phillies 4 (42-32) 1st Place - 2 GA of the Marlins

Philadelphia – *The Red Sox's first five hitters went a combined 11 for 23 with the much fan-hated*

JD Drew leading the way. Forever remembered as the 2nd overall pick of the Phillies in the 1997 ML Draft who refused to sign for anything less than $10 million, Drew was mercilessly booed each time he went to the plate. It didn't phase him at all as Drew single handedly beat up on the Phils' pitching staff, going 4 for 5 with 4 RBIs … Kyle Kendrick (6-3, 5.06) lasted only 6 innings giving up 6 runs on 6 hits … The bullpen pitched well only giving up one run in the final six innings … Chase Utley went 0 for 4 and extended his hitless streak to 20 at bats. Stuff: The offense continues to struggle, since their 20-run explosion in St. Louis. The team is averaging less than 3 runs per game … Hall-of-Famer Robin Roberts threw out the first pitch today to commemorate the 60th anniversary of his first major league ballgame. On June 18, 1948, the 21-year-old Roberts went 8 innings against the Pittsburgh Pirates, giving up only two runs on five hits but lost the game 2-0.

Was it or wasn't it a measuring stick? Yes, it was. Even with key pieces missing from Boston's lineup, it's a formidable order that rivals any other club in baseball. The Phillies own no book on Jon Lester and Scott Masterson and hold only Cliffs Notes versions on the rest of their staff. It was an excellent test against an unfamiliar foe.

And how did Boston study up on Kyle Kendrick? They didn't need to. They punished mistakes out over the plate. While Kendrick did not achieve his 16-7, 4.33 career mark by starting 35 games against the Toledo Mud Hens, doubts still linger whether he can hack

Even the kids aren't happy with the Phillies' performance

it against this kind of team without the kind of run support he's used to getting. Kendrick isn't blessed with electric cheese; he relies on location, something that went missing today. The six runs he gave up in the ballgame is the most he's allowed as a member of the Phillies.

While losing two-out-of-three to Boston, and winning the first game convincingly shouldn't cause riots in the streets, it should however raise concern over the strength of the Phils' pitching staff. They'll happily go to war in a playoff series with Cole Hamels. Jamie Moyer has been a capable platoon leader in those conflicts too, going perhaps a little deeper into the jungle. But after that, it's a little uncertain; although Philadelphia is a different club than, say, the Dodgers or Angels in they can light up the scoreboard in a hurry and make up for the damage allowed by their starting pitchers. Nevertheless, the Phils feel they need more. According to yesterday's Inquirer, they sent a scout to watch C.C. Sabathia and Greg Maddox duel on Sunday.

Quotable: "It wasn't necessarily that they hit it terribly hard but it was in the right spot. There was a couple balls that, a foot or two closer to the player, we'd be having double plays." Adam Eaton discussing the 12 hits he surrendered to the Angels.

Friday, June 20th - Angels 7 Phillies 1 (42-33) 1st Place - 2 GA of the Marlins

Philadelphia – *The California Angels came into town and pounded starter Adam Eaton (2-5, 4.94) for 6 runs on 12 hits in 5+ innings ... Angels' starter Ervin Santana (9-3, 3.17) completely shut down the Phils' offense, giving up only 2 hits and striking out 9 in 7 innings. The one run he surrendered was unearned... Howie Kendrick (4), Vladimir Guerrero (3) and Garret Anderson (3) led the Angels with 10 hits between them... Chris Coste and Shane Victorino were the only Phillies to manage hits in the game. Stuff: Chase Utley knocked in the Phils' only run of the game but nevertheless went 0-3 and is now hitless in his last six games haven gone 0 for 23 ... The Phils are now 3-7 in their last 10 games and are only hitting .246 as a team during that time ... Guerrero popped his 11th homer of the season in the 1st inning. He now has 29 lifetime homers against the Phillies; the most he has against any team.*

Kenny Gamble and Leon Huff are the architects of the Philly Soul sound. The 2008 inductees into the Rock and Roll Hall-of-Fame wrote and produced some of the best music ever recorded in the 1970s. They single-handedly made Philadelphia the capital of soul music. Gamble and Huff created a tremendous number of soulful hits that even to this day have great appeal to people of all ages, genders and races. They worked with the O'Jays, Harold Melvin and the Blue Notes, the Intruders, the Three Degrees, McFadden & Whitehead, Jerry Butler, Lou Rawls,

From left to right – Kenny Gamble, Jerry Blavet, Teddy Pendergrass and Leon Huff

Dee Dee Sharp, Phyllis Hyman and many others. Their biggest hits, topping both the R&B and pop charts, were jazz singer Billy Paul's "Me and Mrs. Jones"; the O'Jays' "Love Train"; and the Soul Train theme, "TSOP (The Sound of Philadelphia)" by MFSB and featuring the Three Degrees. All totaled, Gamble and Huff have won 5 Grammy Awards, were behind 15 gold singles and 22 gold albums, 8 of which went platinum. It is said that a Gamble & Huff song is played on the radio somewhere around the world every 13 ½ minutes.

Forty-five years after Gamble and Huff launched their careers and created the immortal "Sound of Philadelphia" they continue to give back to the city and in recent years have joined forces with the Phillies to honor Black Music Month. This year Gamble & Huff made their way down to Citizens Bank Park to present singer Teddy Pendergrass and TV and Radio personality Jerry Blavet with the 2008 Phillies' Gamble and Huff Community Partnership Award. With only a few minutes to speak to the multi-platinum duo before they went on the field to present the award along with Ryan Howard, I was able to catch a quick glimpse into their world of music and the Phillies.

What is it about Philadelphia that there have been so many incredible recording artists and musicians that have come from this city?

Huff: I have always thought that Philadelphia was the music Mecca of the world. This city is just full of talent. South Philly, North Philly, West Philly, there's talent and so many different types of music coming from everywhere you look. I think it's always going to be that way. It's always going to be a music Mecca.

Gamble: Well, I think Philadelphia is in a great location. I think American Bandstand had a lot to do with it during the early days when Philadelphia was the center of popular music in America. I think Bandstand was like the MTV of its era. There were also a couple of other TV shows that really dug up some incredible talent. You had the Jerry Blavet Show, the Mike Douglas Show and the Mitch Thomas Show as well. They were all very popular. So you had a lot of television and radio programs here that people grew up watching and listening to, and they just became big fans of music. It was and still is a music city.

Have you always been Phillies' fans?

Huff: Absolutely. I grew up in Camden (NJ). I've always watched the Phillies and have been a fan as long as I can remember. When I was a kid, I remember what a special day it was when the Brooklyn Dodgers and Jackie Robinson came to town. Me and my father would go over to Connie Mack Stadium and just sit and watch him play and also go to other Phillies games over the years. My favorite players growing up were Ritchie Ashburn and Robin Roberts. Now I enjoy watching Chase Utley, Pat Burrell, Ryan Howard and Jimmy Rollins. I like watching the Phillies now more than I ever have.

Gamble: Yea, I grew a Phillies' fan but to be honest I've always been more of a basketball type of guy. Don't get me wrong, I follow them ever year. Hopefully they can go all the way this season.

Huff: I hope they go all the way too. They seem to have a lot of momentum going for them right now. I know that they'll have their ups and downs but I truly hope the Phillies make it to the playoffs and win the World Series. That would be great for them and for the city.

One last question, which songs out of the thousands that you have written is your favorite?

Huff: "Me and Mrs. Jones". I still get chills listening to it when it comes on the radio. We knew it was special as soon as we recorded it. Thirty-six years later people still enjoy listening to it just as they did back when it first came out.

Gamble: All of them. To this day I'm amazed that we were able to even write all of these songs.

Quotable: "Offensively we are going through a drought. Things we did before we're not doing." - Charlie Manuel on the team-wide slump his players are experiencing.

Saturday, June 21st - Angels 6 Phillies 2 (42-34) 1st Place - 1 GA of the Marlins

Philadelphia – *The team-wide slump continues for the Phillies as they only muster 2 runs and 5 hits against a strong Angels' pitching staff ... Brett Myers (3-9 5.51) pitched well through seven innings, giving up only two runs, both solo homeruns to Vladimir Guerrero. However in the 8th, Myers allowed a 2-run shot to light-hitting Erick Aybar. After that, the stumbling Phils' offense couldn't get back into the game. Angels' starter Joe Saunders notched his American League leading 11th victory of the season ... Jayson Werth broke up the shutout in the 7th with his 10th homerun of the year. Stuff: Chase Utley (0 for 23), Ryan Howard (1 for 15), Pat Burrell (1 for 15) and Geoff Jenkins (3 for 27) have practically stopped hitting the ball ... Myers has now given up a ML–leading 23 homeruns ... The Phillies originally drafted Joe Saunders out of high school in the 1999 draft but he declined the offer and instead went to Virginia Tech. The Angels redrafted him in 2002 ... Prior to sitting out tonight's game, Chase Utley had 101 consecutive starts.*

This team stinks.

Following their 6-2 defeat at the hands of the Angels, their fourth in a row and eighth in their last 11, that's basically how it feels to watch this team, even though the standings prove otherwise. The Phils (42-34) still cling to a one-game lead over the Marlins in the National League East, which will disappear entirely if they continue to showcase this latest brand of baseball. Last night featured more light hitting and sloppy all-around play, compromising a rather nice start by struggling right-hander Brett Myers.

Pundits said this week would be revealing, and indeed it has been. Inside the bubble, the Phils looked good; they could over-run the Rockies, the Nationals, the Reds and the Braves. Since then, the schedule built to a crescendo as they faced the class acts in baseball. In doing so, they've fallen flat. The Phillies are definitely not in the class of the Red Sox and the Angels. Any presumed trips to the World Series against these elite teams will most likely result in a similar fashion 4-game sweep like the Phillies experienced back in 1950 against the Yankees.

Vladimir Guerrero banged two solo homers off of starter Brett Myers

Quotable: "I don't know, I don't know. I don't think we swung the bats that well this week. I thought we got fairly decent pitching. The bottom line is we didn't score enough runs." - Chase Utley when asked to explain the Phils' recent demise

Sunday, June 22nd - Angels 3 Phillies 2 (42-35) 1st Place - 1 GA of the Marlins

Philadelphia – *Chase Utley finally broke out of a 0 for 24 slump with a double in the 3rd inning, but the Phillies lost their 5th game in a row and were swept by California in the process. Cole Hamels (7-5, 3.27) pitched well enough to win (7 IP, 3 ER, 0 BB, 4 SO), but the offense could only muster 2 runs on 6 hits ... Jimmy Rollins went 2 for 4 with 1 RBI and 2 stolen bases (16 & 17) ... Ryan Howard knocked in the only other run, his 64th RBI of the year. Stuff: The Phils stole a season-high 4 bases in the game ... With the three-game sweep by the Angels the Phils are now 1-7 in their last eight games. In that stretch of games they are batting .202 and are averaging only 3.1 runs per game ... It is fourth consecutive series that the Phils have lost ... Today's sellout was the 9th consecutive at Citizens Bank Park.*

Prior to the start of the Phillies' 1981 season, General Manager Paul Owens was trying to put the finishing touches on a team that had just won a World Series and who had the serious potential of winning back-to-back titles. With Greg Luzinski spending almost 1/3rd of the '80 season on the bench with a bum knee and with the knee still causing Luzinski problems in the spring the Pope knew he needed to make a move. A week before the season began, Owens traded starter Bob Walk to the Atlanta Braves for Gary Matthews, a 30-year-old outfielder with a career .288 average who had a take-charge attitude, could play left field with speed, possessed an incredible arm and had a penchant of hitting in the clutch. Mat-

Gary Matthews Jr. poses with his father the "Sarge" before the start of the game

thews will always be remembered by Phillies fans for his performance during the 1983 NLCS against the Dodgers. Gary hit .429 (6 for 14) with 3 homeruns and 8 RBIs, earning him the MVP of the series.

After a 16 year playing career and some stops around the league as a hitting coach, the "Sarge" made his way back to Philadelphia in 2006 as a member of the Phillies' broadcast team. Now 58 years old, Gary is able to enjoy the game and watch his son, Gary Matthews Jr., play ball "almost" as good as he did a few decades ago.

I got the nickname "Sarge" from none other than Pete Rose. He gave it to me during the 1983 season for always taking charge of the game. When Rose gave me that nickname he told me, "When a future Hall-of-Famer gives you a nickname, it sticks!" Well, he was right about one thing, the name stuck but he's not in the Hall-of-Fame.

Prior to coming back to the Phillies I was a part of Dusty Baker's coaching staff with the Cubs. After Baker got fired by the Cubs, I joined the broadcast team here and really fell in love with it and the city again. Even to the point that when Dusty was hired by the Reds as their new manager in 2007 he asked me to join him as a coach but I turned it down. This is too much fun.

I still make my home in Chicago in the off-season. My daughter lives there as well as two of my four sons, Delvin and Junior (Gary Matthews Jr.).

Phillies' fans tend to be a bit harder on their team than Cubs' fans. I think it's because they are more used to winning than Cubs fans. I guess their barometer is a little bit higher in judging the guys that they have. One thing that Philadelphia fans expect is that their players play hard every day of the season. They just want you to give 100% each and every time you're in the game. When I played here, I did that every day. The fans really took to me because of that and they do the same today.

It's hard to say how I would have faired if I were playing ball today. One thing I know that a lot of the line drives that we hit back in the 70s would have been out of many of these smaller parks that have been built recently. Conservatively, I would have to say that I could have tacked on 10-12 more homeruns per year in a ballpark like this. Just hitting the ball hard deep in the gap back at Veterans Stadium are gone here.

I stopped playing baseball back in 1987 after the Cubs traded me to Seattle. I think I could have played another three years, but I wasn't able to sign on with anyone after the season. I probably could have gone and played in Japan but I liked being around my kids and I wanted to be around them all the time.

When was the first time I knew Junior could play? You know what; every dad always thinks their kid can play. It's hard to say. My other kids were just as good as or better than Junior was coming up through Little League. I think a lot of it has to do obviously with the talent, but also being at the right place at the right time. You look at Gary Maddox's son (Gary Maddox Jr.). He was really talented and was as good if not better than Junior when they were coming up in the minors. As a matter of fact, in A-Ball they both made the All-Star team. Maddox's son had some injuries while he was in the Diamondbacks' system. At the time, Arizona was rebuilding and they switched over from younger players to all veteran players. He got caught in that mix right there and never made it to the majors.

I talk to Junior constantly throughout the season. It's not always about what he's doing on the field but about what's going on in his life as well. I have the Major League Baseball Extra Innings package so I'll tape his games or come home and watch him when he's playing out on the West coast.

I'll sometimes call him after one of his games and say, "Son, why are you taking those fastballs right down the middle of the plate?" So he knows I'm watching the game and I know he was looking for a breaking ball. So sometimes when he calls me he'll say, "Hey did you see anything in my swing that I'm doing wrong?"

I think a lot of fathers do that with their sons. I know that for a fact. Before he died I played golf with Bobby Bonds and he was complaining about something that Barry was doing at the plate. I said to Bobby, "Man, how can you complain about anything that he's doing?" … so, I think all dads do that.

What makes me the most proud of him? Just the way he goes out and plays the game hard. He plays it the way that it should be played. Thinking about winning first as opposed to personal stats. I'm proud at how he has endured some of the hardships that he's gone through mostly because he is all on his own. It doesn't matter if I played or not, you have to do it all yourself when you go out on the field.

He's had opportunities where he could have gone to Japan, and I was encouraging him to do that, to take the money. This happened when he was still in the minors. He turned the money down and said that he knows he can play in the Major Leagues. He turned it down. It was a smart move by him not to go.

Who has the bragging rights around the Thanksgiving Day table? (laughter) He's catching up. I told him the other day that he's 134 (homeruns) behind! But we have many other talks just like other fathers and dads have.

I have three other sons. My one son Delvin used to play ball but he's now with the White Sox's front office. I also have another son … Danon … he thinks he's a poker player. My other son Dustin, who's Dusty Baker's Godson, says he's trying to find himself, whatever the hell that means. We pretty much let them take their time and do whatever they want.

Junior kind of remembers when I was with the Phillies. He remembers more when I was with the Cubs because he was older there and he remembers when we went to the playoffs. He used to hang out around the dugout with Daniel Cey, Ron Cey's son (LA Dodgers 3rd Baseman back in the 70s and 80s), with Jamie Moyer and Greg Maddox and Ryan Sandburg. As a 10-year-old kid he had the chance to hit against Jaime Moyer during batting practice one day. If I remember correctly, he used to take Moyer deep! You think I'm kidding, but I'm serious. You can ask Moyer yourself.

If it's the bottom of the 9th and the Phillies are winning 4-3 who am I rooting for? Let's put it this way, I want the Phillies to win and Junior to get his hits. That's about as well as I can plan it.

Quotable: "We need another starter. We can use someone else to match up with (Boston's) Beckett and Matsuzaka, or with (California's) Lackey and (Ervin) Santana or Lackey and Saunders." - Phillies GM Pat Gillick when asked what the Phils' top needs were for him in the upcoming trade deadline.

Tuesday, June 24th - Athletics 5 Phillies 2 (42-36) 1st Place - 1 GA of the Marlins

Oakland – *Jamie Moyer (7-5, 4.09) took a 1-hit shutout into the 7th inning but ended up giving up a three-run homer to the Athletics' Emil Brown to spoil a 9 strikeout performance by the 45-year-old lefty ... Pat Burrell connected on his 19th HR of the season and Ryan Howard drove in his 65th run of the year for the only two Phillies runs ... Shane Victorino went 2 for 4 with a run scored and a stolen base ... Geoff Jenkins went 0 for 4 and is now 0 for his last 22 at bats. Stuff: The Phils have now lost a season-high six straight games ... Moyer's 9 K's were the most for him since he struck out 9 against the A's when he was with Seattle back in 2004 ... For the first time in franchise history the Phillies have three players (Utley, Howard and Burrell) with 18+ homeruns before the All-Star break ... They are 2nd in the majors with a total of 105 HRs ... Today marked the first time in the history of baseball that two native Hawaiians from Maui have played together. Shane Victorino and Kurt Suzuki grew up in the same town and even played against one another in high school.*

Jim Jackson is one of the very few broadcasters who have had the fortune of being employed full-time with two of Philadelphia's most popular sports teams. As a play-by-play announcer with the Flyers, Jackson has been with the organization since the 1993 season when he replaced the legendary Gene Hart in the radio booth and has been a fixture within the Flyers' organization ever since.

Jim Jackson shares some laughs with Larry Anderson during the Phillies' Pre-Game Show

In 2007 the future hockey Hall-of-Fame announcer interrupted his long summer vacations, which were spent waiting for the next hockey season to start, by signing onto the Phillies' broadcast team as the Pre and Post-Game host for the past two seasons.

Many fans know me for my play-by-play announcing with the Flyers. What most of Philadelphia doesn't know is that I spent eight seasons as the play-by-play announcer for the Utica Blue Sox of the New York-Penn League (Single "A" team for the Mets). I also did play-by-play for the Trenton Thunder in 2005 and some announcing for the Cal Ripken World Series games in 2006, so I have a lot of baseball under my belt.

1993 was my first year with the Flyers. I've been with them now for 15 years. The transition between hockey and baseball isn't that difficult for me. The sports are completely different, but it's still sports and it's all about wins and losses.

The one thing that I find the most different between the two sports is the approach that each of the leagues takes to their season. The NHL's 82 game season is almost half that of baseball's 162 game season. With hockey there is a bigger emphasis on having to win early and often because of the shorter season. With baseball you can't treat every baseball game like its life and death. You constantly have to look at the big picture across the entire season as a broadcaster, a fan, a GM, the manager or as a player.

I do every one of my Pre-Game and Post-Game shows from Citizens Bank Park. Even when we're on the road. It's quite interesting because it's basically an empty ballpark when the team is traveling. Although the Spanish broadcasting team is here as well so I'm not completely alone.

When the Phillies are at home we do the Pre-Game show from the concourse right behind home plate where all of the fans can watch the show. It's actually a lot of fun. I have a bunch of fans coming by asking me about the Flyers. We also get a lot of them who want to know who our guest is for that night. Once the guest is there and we've started the show they'll huddle around but it's never a distraction. That's what it's about. It's the interaction with the fans.

I literally have a minimum of 162 interviews that I do throughout an entire season. One for every game. Sometimes its difficult finding guests, but I think we do a good job of making it interesting for the fans. There are only 25 players and a handful of coaches on the team so I spend a lot of time scheduling guests for the shows.

My favorite interview so far? Unfortunately we have a hard time getting a Jimmy Rollins or Chase Utley because they're always playing and the Pre-Game show goes on live a half hour before the game starts. If we interview a player we usually have to get somebody that's not in the starting lineup so to answer your question I think my favorite interview has been with Greg Dobbs. I mean Greg Dobbs is one of the nicest guys I've met in any sport, he's a just truly a super guy. I don't want to cut anybody short here because they've all been really good but he was exceptional.

Cole Hamels is another interview that I enjoyed and the fans on the Concourse enjoyed as well. He was fantastic during the interview. When he came onto the show he not only had excellent responses but he seemed to really connect with the fans that were standing around watching the interview. I think the fans can really relate to a guy who's a young stud and who is just such an affable human being. You wouldn't guess it for a kid who's 24 years old but he really has a great presence about himself out in public.

I also do a weekly call-in show on Saturdays with General Manager Pat Gillick. I'm amazed at the access the fans get to a general manager of a baseball team. I mean you won't see that many times in professional sports where the GM is willing to take calls from fans for a half an hour on a weekly basis when things are going well and when things are going bad. Things aren't going too well right now with the team but Pat was there this past Saturday answering question after question.

It's funny, when you're losing and the team is struggling there tend to be more calls to the show. We do screen the callers before they go on the air to weed out the "outer fringe" fans, but Pat doesn't mind us having fans ask him the tough questions. Like a guy called one show and told my producer that he wanted to thank Pat so we put him on the air without any fear. So he comes on and I say, "You're on the air with Pat Gillick…" This guy then just calmly says, "Pat, I just want to thank you for saving me the money I would have spent on going down to the ballpark to watch the team." So you never know what's going to slide through with some of these callers. I mean the calls are passionate but they usually aren't out of line.

A couple of the calls this past week were heartfelt. "I love this team but what are you going to do to improve it?" and others are like, "What the heck is going on?" We had some fan call in who complained that Pat shouldn't have traded Michael Bourn. The caller said Bourn was the next Maury Wills, Vince Coleman and he might have even said the next Ricky Henderson all rolled up into one. Pat handled it well and basically told the fan that Bourn's really fast but he's not going to be a Hall-of-Famer.

Fans still call upset sometimes but he just handles it very calmly, and he didn't seem phased by it at all. But I just don't know if the people here understand how rare it is for a GM to face the fans on a regular basis. I know (Ed) Wade did it with all the turmoil surrounding him at the time but it is still amazing to me that these guys give that kind of access. That's a great thing for these fans. I hope it continues.

I love hockey and baseball. They're so different and I love them for completely different reasons. Hockey I love for the intensity. If you're in a hockey rink, you know what I'm talking about. You may not get it all on TV but the intensity is incredible. These guys are risking their lives every time they're out on the ice. I love that. With baseball it's almost like watching the chapters of a story as they unfold. The intensity is different but the way in which a team scores and wins is so enjoyable. There's a reason why the Phillies are pulling three million fans down here. It's a great sport; it's interesting and most importantly its fun.

Quotable: "We haven't been playing that well. A lot of credit tonight has to go to Kyle. It was good to see that kind of performance." - Chase Utley on snapping their 6 game losing streak.

Wednesday, June 25th - Phillies 4 Athletics 0 (43-36) 1st Place - 2 GA of the Marlins
Oakland – *Charlie Manuel made some major lineup changes while Kyle Kendrick (7-3, 4.59) pitched 8 very strong shutout innings for the longest outing of has career as the Phils shut down the A's and snapped their 6 game losing streak … 1 for his last 29 at bats, Chase Utley was able to break out of his slump in a big way, going 4 for 5 to raise his average to .297… Chris Coste (2 for 3, 2 RBIs) and Pedro Feliz (2 for 5, 1 RBI) also supported the Phillies' attack on offense. Stuff: The Phillies are now 12-1 in Kendrick's last 13 starts. In his 36 major league starts the Phils are 25-11 … This was the Phils' 5th shutout of the season, matching their total for all of last season.*

A's hitters tallied just four hits off Kendrick (7-3), who flaunted "the best sinker he's had all season," according to catcher Chris Coste in a post-game interview. Kendrick, who lowered his ERA to 4.59, shied away from his secondary pitches and instead, kept the ball out of the middle of the plate. He also credited Coste for calling a good game. The San Francisco Chronicle offered a report from the other side: "(Bob) Geren said there was a lot of talk in the dugout trying to figure out what Kendrick was doing, because he wasn't overpowering, but he was moving the ball in and out well. 'The hitters kept coming back saying they didn't get much over the plate,' Geren said."

Charlie Manuel's juggling of his lineup and Kyle Kendrick's strong pitching helped the Phillies get back into the win column

Manager Charlie Manuel juggled the lineup to positive results. The Phils scattered 11 hits and scored all their runs without the long ball. Manuel spread his speed threats evenly throughout the lineup.

With the win, the Phils increased their lead to two games over Florida, who were pummeled by Tampa 15-3. Meanwhile, the Mets (4 games back) and Braves (4.5 back) kept pace with wins over Seattle and Milwaukee.

Quotable: "He pitched one of the better games against us this year if not the best. We got beat by a good pitcher. They out hit us and out pitched us." - Charlie Manuel on the A's Rich Harding

Thursday, June 26th - Athletics 5 Phillies 0 (43-37) 1st Place - 2 GA of the Marlins

Oakland – *The A's Rich Harding (5-0, 2.15) mowed down the Phils' offense, shutting them out for 8 innings while giving up only 3 hits and striking out 11 … Adam Eaton (2-6, 4.86) pitched a quality start (7 IP, 3 ER) but the story of the day was once again the team's lack of offense… Shane Victorino had 2 of the Phils' 3 hits while Pat Burrell collected the other on a triple. Stuff: Harding retired the first 14 Phillies before Victorino singled in the 5th … Jimmy Rollins struck out three times and committed his first error at short in forty games …The Phils are now 3-9 in interleague play this year. They are hitting .221 against AL pitching (15th in the NL) and have scored a total of 41 runs (14th in the NL). Last season, the Phillies went 8-7 against the AL and were one of 6 NL teams with a winning record against the American League.*

There are 7,939 Phillies-related items on eBay today. Many of the items you would probably not spend your hard earned cash to purchase. However there are some items that, if not at least interesting, might be worth a bid or two.

A "scarce" 28" x 22" promotional photo of Pete Rose & his wife Karolyn that reads "Roses in Clover" (advertising an appearance at a Clover retail store) goes for $9.88. No bids ... A black and white 1958 AP Wire Photo of Phillies' outfielder Rip Repulski sliding into second base is up to $7.99 ... An original 1950 Fightin' Phillies felt pennant that reads "National League Champs – 1950" is listed at $395.00. No bids on it yet ... 32 empty Canada Dry soda cans from 1979 that have photos of all of the Phillies on them including McGraw, Maddox, Rose, Schmidt and a host of others for $5.00. I think the aluminum from those cans could probably bring you $7.00 if you recycled them ... A vintage 1964 Game 1 Phillies World Series ticket to Connie Mack Stadium, Section 12, Row 16 , Seat 6; never used for $9.99 ... Six Pat

"Phyllis" – one of nearly 8,000 Phillies-related items out on eBay

Burrell Rookie Cards for 1 penny. That's it? Shipping is $2.98 ...what a pity ... A 1966 Ballantine Beer Phillies Schedule 4" Coaster goes for $39.99. A beer coaster is worth more than Burrell's rookie cards?

A Von Hayes Texaco Oil Company give-away bat goes for $10.99. Maybe they'll do a Five-for-One deal with the bidder? How about a game-used home jersey of Shane Victorino. Currently with 8 bids it's now up to $247.50. I doubt it's real, there are no dirt stains on it ... A Steve Carlton 1973 7-11 plastic Slurpee Cup goes for $4.95 ... A signed Harry Kalas ball that's personalized with "That Ball's Outta Here" has 2 bids and is up to $12.50 ... For the woman who really wants to please her man there is the black Phillies bra and thong set with the Phils' insignia strategically placed on both pieces for $34.99 ... An original 1913 Chicago Tribune newspaper article with an illustration of Phillies' Hall-of-Famer Grover Alexander for $5.99 ... A 1976 Bicentennial game-used Louisville Slugger from none other than fan favorite Jay Johnstone. Seems that the seller personally knew Johnstone who gave it to him after a game in which the left-handed batter put a 6-inch crack in the bat. A steal at $102.50 with 22 minutes left on the bidding.

The most interesting of all the items found today is a 1957 children's book titled Phyllis by author Ted Key (creator of the comic strip Hazel). It's about a sparrow that builds a nest in left field of Connie Mack Stadium. The cover has a ball scooting past the sparrow's nest with the Phillies' left fielder chasing after the ball. That's listed at $11.40. That actually might be worth bidding on. A children's book about the Phillies? Isn't Tom Burgoyne the only guy who does those?

Quotable: "Can I say his job is secure? I don't' know what to say if you want to know the truth. We'd have to find somebody to do his job first I guess." - Charlie Manuel when asked how much longer the Phillies can allow Brett Myers to start.

Friday, June 27th - Rangers 8 Phillies 7 (43-38) 1st Place - 1 GA of the Marlins

Arlington, TX – Brett Myers threw the shortest outing of his career blowing a 5-1 lead in the 3rd inning as the Phils dropped their eighth in nine games. In 2+ innings of work, Myers walked 4 and gave up 5 earned runs ... Clay Condrey (1-1, 4.36) took the loss as he lasted 2 2/3rd and gave up 2 runs ... Pedro Feliz hit a grand slam in the 3rd, his 9th homerun of the year... also hitting homeruns were Jayson Werth (11) and Chris Coste (9). Stuff: Today marked the half-way point of the 2008 season ... After the game, there were serious considerations coming from the Phillies that Myers may be pulled out of the rotation. The team is now 1-11 in the last 12 games that Myers has started. In 17 starts this season, Myers is 3-9 with a 5.84 ERA. He has given up a major league leading 24 home runs ... This was the Phillies' first visit to Arlington, making them the last Major League team to do so.

Myers, who's doing everything possible to force the Phillies' hand regarding his status as a starting pitcher, allowed five runs and four walks in two-plus innings; the shortest start of his career. This latest meltdown came after the Phillies spotted him a four-run lead, following a five-run rally in the third inning that was fueled by Pedro Feliz's grand slam.

It's getting late for Brett Myers to fix this. There's little consistency from start to start. There's nothing to build on, no repetition, none of that. Throw in this latest effort and I have to believe the Phils are ready to face the music and

Brett Myers hit the showers early today as he lasted only 2+ innings

concede that he's not going to be the reliable starter they'd hoped: the guy they counted on in late 2006. That was with 3-4 mph more on his fastball and as a closer. They either trust in Rich Dubee and Myers to solve this problem - starting from somewhere close to square one - or must try something new.

Quotable: "I've said it all along; we've got to hit to win. Our big boys have to hit." - Charlie Manuel after Chase Utley and Ryan Howard combined for two homeruns and four RBIs.

Saturday, June 28th - Phillies 8 Rangers 6 (44-38) 1st Place - 1 ½ GA of the Marlins

Arlington, TX – Facing ex-Phillie Vicente Padilla for the first time since he left the team after the 2005 season, the Phils' offense unceremoniously greeted him with their heavy lumber. Chase Utley (23) and Ryan Howard (20) each smashed 400 foot homers off of Padilla (10-4 4.13) in the 3rd … Utley had a three hit game for the sixth time this year … The pitching staff, led by Cole Hamels (8-5, 3.38) gave up 6 runs but they were able to hold on for the win … Brad Lidge earned his first save (19) since June 12th. Stuff: All of Utley's hits were for extra bases (2 doubles, 1 homerun) … Jimmy Rollins was thrown out at the plate trying for an inside-the-park homerun in the 6th … Brad Lidge is now 19 for 19 in save opportunities, which continues to set a Phillies' record for most consecutive saves to start a season. Al Holland had held the record of 15 straight back in 1984.

Spanish Beisbol broadcaster Danny Martinez's job is to give his Spanish listening audience the play-by-play of each and every game making sure that the 700,000+ Latinos living in the Delaware Valley don't miss an inning with their Phillies.

Martinez comes from an interesting background. He was born and raised in the Dominican Republic until his family moved to New York City in 1971. A standout shortstop in his youth, the Phillies signed him back in the late '70s where he was once one of the team's top prospects.

In my youth I grew up in the Dominican in front of Felipe Alou and his family. His mom lived right across the street from my house. I also lived right near Manny Mota and Cesar Geronimo. I would go watch them play in the Dominican leagues. If we met them after a game and shake their hands then we wouldn't want to wash them because they were such big stars.

We moved to the States when I was 14 years old. I went right to high school as soon as we got there and started playing baseball. There were hardly any Latino teams in Queens back then. I think there were only two. I played against Mets GM Omar Minaya, but there really weren't too many other Hispanics in that area. It was a tough time back then and I ran into a lot of problems with racism. However I tried to make the best of it and I brought all the passion of wanting to play baseball with me from the Dominican.

The Phillies' Spanish play-by-play broadcaster Danny Martinez

I only played about 8 games on my High School team. I couldn't understand what the coach would say. He didn't give me a chance. I couldn't communicate. Playing shortstop you got to know the signs. It just didn't work out.

Coming from another country to the United States and not really knowing the language led to some funny stories. I went to Hooper High School. I needed sneakers for my gym class. I go with my father to the Army Navy store and I see these red, white and blue sneakers. "Wow, this is beautiful." So we go ahead and buy them. Monday comes and I go to my first gym class. I put them on and all that and people starting seeing me and starting cracking up; they're all laughing at me. And I don't know a word of English. I had gym again; I think it was a Friday class. I put my sneakers on again, and then everyone starts cracking up. So we go exercise and I'm running and my feet are hurting and everything. So there's one guy that speaks English and Spanish and I go to him and ask, "Why are they laughing at me?" He said, "Don't you know why? You know what bowling is?" I said, "Bowling? I don't know what bowling is." He goes, "Bowling, you know." and he shows me how one would throw a bowling bowl down the lane. I said, "Oh, boliche." "You got bowling shoes on and you're running in them!" I'm like, "Oh my God, don't tell me that." But they did look good.

Another funny story was I was always late for my science class. One day the teacher calls me over and says, "I don't understand why you're always late when your previous class is lunch. Why are you late all the time?" I said, "Well because, I live three miles away and got to run home and eat and come back." He said, "No! Don't you know that we have a cafeteria here?" I didn't. Back in the Dominican, everyone would go home to eat lunch. I didn't know anything back then.

It took me about 3 ½ years to learn the language. I would watch Big Bird and the Flintstones on TV. That's what helped me. In those days, I'd walk around with a dictionary and I'll be on the subway or in a bus and any word I saw I would look it up or if I wanted to communicate with a teacher. I worked so hard to learn the language.

I did really well playing ball in New York and eventually Dallas Green spotted me playing in a tournament down in Miami in 1977. The Phillies offered me $5,000 to sign with them, which was a lot of money back then. At the same time I was also offered a four-year scholarship to play baseball for the University of Texas. My family needed the money so I jumped at the chance of playing professional ball.

I spent 4 years with the Phillies from 1977 to 1980. I was a shortstop and one of my biggest concerns back then was that the Phillies had Larry Bowa up in Philly. I wasn't sure how I was ever going to make it to the majors.

In 1980 I tore my ACL, and it ended my career. I was 21 years old. I was one of the fastest, if not the fastest, player in the organization and I blew my knee out. The Phillies released me at the end of that year.

The knee still bothers me to this day. It's funny because after I quit playing pro ball I started playing fast pitch softball. I was a pitcher and could throw real hard. About 85 mph. One game, I was throwing a no-hitter and this guy bunted the ball to me. I went to grab it and I tore the ACL in my other knee.

It was tough for me for awhile because I was out of baseball for over 20 years and I loved it so much. I didn't really know what to do. Looking back I probably should have taken the scholarship to Texas so I could have something to fall back on. But, I'm a believer in God. A Christian. I try to tell people about my life and the circumstances I went through because each one of us is on this earth for a purpose and it just wasn't God's plan for me to play in the majors.

Eventually I got involved back in baseball as an agent for ball players. That went fairly well, but then I got involved full time with the Spanish Beisbol Network and I did the play-by-play for the Tampa Bay Devil Rays for 2 ½ years. In 2005, Bill Kulik (Owner of the Spanish Beisbol Network) and I began broadcasting all of the Phillies' games in Spanish.

It's a thrill for me because I signed with the Phillies and now I've finally made it to the major leagues with them. I love it here. I love being around the town, the ballpark and the players. What a great life huh?

Quotable: "Who'd have thunk that the Phils would have the 5th best team ERA in the NL at the halfway point?" - Blogger GoPhilsGo

Sunday, June 29th - Rangers 5 Phillies 1 (44-39) 1st Place - 1 GA of the Marlins
Arlington, TX – In the case of the disappearing offense, the Phils were once again shut down by good pitching but this time it came from a rookie, Eric Hurley (1-1, 3.57), who pitched his first major league win of his career ... Jamie Moyer (7-6 4.13) threw 5 2/3rd innings, giving up 3 runs on 7 hits while striking out 6 ... The Phils' only run came from an RBI single by Ryan Howard in the 6th. Stuff: The Phillies have now lost six consecutive series. The last one that they won dates back to June 6-8 vs. the Braves ... The Phillies finished interleague play at 4-11 ... Although they are 2-4 on this road trip, the team is 22-21 on the road this season (2nd best in the NL and one of only four teams in baseball with a winning road record) ... Unbelievably the Phillies still finish the month of June in first place.

With the interleague schedule complete, it only gets easier, right? Or wasn't this series supposed to be the calm after the storm? I guess it depends whether you think Eric Hurley and the Rangers rival the likes of Boston, Los Angeles and Oakland. In my estimation, the Rangers had nothing, but the Phils had even less this weekend. Highlights of their lone win showed nothing less than Vicente Padilla serving it up on a silver platter. Before that, Brett Myers didn't give them much of a chance. Then today was more of the same from the offense, which isn't hitting the ball well enough to beat anyone from any league.

Charlie Manuel's team only managed an anemic 4-11 record against the American League in interleague play this season

The offense is unwatchable. You have to dig deep to find a stretch when the offense dried up like this. It looks and feels like 2005, when they lumbered along in trips to Seattle and Oakland, then home against Boston and New York. They were just plain powerless. The "June Swoon" was officially in full effect this year.

July - Emotions and Demotions

Quotable: "It's something the bullpen has been doing all season and he came in and shut the door and stopped that momentum." - Shane Victorino on JC Romero and the bullpen as they shut down the Braves

Tuesday, July 1st - Phillies 8 Braves 3 (45-39) 1st Place - 1 ½ GA of the Marlins

Atlanta – *Kyle Kendrick (8-3, 4.58) shut out the Braves for 6 innings before surrendering 3 runs in the 7th, however the bullpen was able to save the victory as JC Romero, Tom Gordon and Brad Lidge held Atlanta's offense to one hit and no runs over the final three innings ... Pat Burrell hit his 20th homerun of the season in the 2nd inning ... The offense exploded for 4 runs in the 3rd capped by a 2-run homer by Shane Victorino. Stuff: Burrell's 20th homerun of the year now gives him eight consecutive seasons of 20 or more homers. Only Mike Schmidt, who holds the franchise record of 14, has done it more ... Victorino had 4 RBIs in the game, a career high ... Starter Brett Myers was sent to AAA – Lehigh Valley to work out his pitching troubles.*

Myers will start Wednesday's game against Scranton/Wilkes-Barre while his replacement will be named tomorrow. In 17 starts, he's 3-9 with a 5.84 ERA, the second highest mark in the National League among pitchers with at least 83 innings. The most damning number: The Phillies were 1-11 in his last 12 starts.

In typical Phillies style, they march to the beat of their own drummer with a stunning move, one that nobody considered. Heck, it's a move that nobody even thought possible. But he deserves it. There's satisfaction in this, seeing a player with his abrasive swagger get knocked down a peg or two. It's almost unprecedented with a player of Myers' status: a veteran of seven seasons, a home-grown player, a first-round pick, someone they committed to financially last off-season, and the guy on the mound when the Phillies won the NL East. It's stunning, and it's bound to send shockwaves through a slumping Phillies' clubhouse. In essence, they're saying, "There's no room for you here, or in our bullpen. You're going to be a starter, and you're

Brett Myers' pitching woes has earned him a trip to the minor leagues

going to do it the hard way." Above all, it's about helping a pitcher who wasn't going to fix it on the fly, but the ramifications are still huge. Take what value he had and throw it out the window. He's J.D. Durbin now, and he'll need to prove himself to earn passage back down the Northeast Extension.

Quotable: "We're trying to put June behind us now, we're in July and right now with the way the offense has been going ... we're getting a couple W's and trying to get the ball going again." - Ryan Howard on getting the Phillies moving in the right direction.

Wednesday, July 2nd - Phillies 7 Braves 3 (46-39) 1st Place - 1 ½ GA of the Marlins

Atlanta – *Ryan Howard and Pat Burrell each hit their 21st homeruns of the season to lead the Phils past the Braves ... Jimmy Rollins went 3 for 4, scoring two runs and driving in his 29th RBI of the year ... Adam Eaton (3-6, 4.79) gave up 2 runs in 5 IP ... the bullpen once again shut down their opponent, limiting Atlanta to one run over the final 4 innings, a homerun by Chipper Jones off of JC Romero... Chad Durbin single-handedly saved the game for the team in the 6th, bailing Eaton out of a bases loaded, no outs jam. Stuff: The Phillies have now won 5 straight games against the Braves and 7 out of their last 11 ... Ryan Howard's 3-run homer in the 3rd now gives him 71 RBIs, the best in the NL and second most in the majors (Josh Hamilton – Texas, has 82). Although Howard is only batting .219 and leads the majors with 115 strikeouts, he is batting .287 with runners on base and .333 with runners in scoring position ... the Phillies called up RJ Swindle to replace Brett Myers. Swindle will be used out of the bullpen until Clay Condrey returns from maternity leave ... Swindle's best pitch? A 59-mph curve ball.*

Call it a marginally better performance than the night before, give or take a few miscues and give or take Atlanta's so-so pitching staff. The Phils got a hit in every inning, and everyone from the starting lineup put one in play except Shane Victorino, who followed a good night offensively with an 0-for-5 game tonight.

Jimmy Rollins was "in the flow." (Chris Wheeler noted that was a phrase Mike Schmidt used to say.) J-Roll tripled, walked, twice singled, stole a base and made two great defensive plays. Last year's MVP becomes the latest player to respond in a positive way to Beer-leaguer criticism. He must be reading,

Linda, Rebekah, Bob and Melissa Buchan enjoy a great start to their 4th of July weekend with another win against the Braves

right? Nah, more than likely, he realized it was time to pick up his head in this winnable division series.

J-Roll was named Chevrolet Player of the Game, but it could have easily gone to Chad Durbin, the bridge that held this game together. On in relief of Adam Eaton, who ran into trouble in the sixth, Durbin worked out of a bases-loaded jam with nobody out, forcing a Jeff Francoeur double play and striking out Mark Kotsay to retire the side. Durbin stayed in for the seventh and retired the side in order. Speaking of "in the flow," that's how Durbin has handled his all-purpose role in the "pen." Whatever they ask, he does. It can't be easy, knowing he could pitch anywhere at any time (but hopefully never in the rotation).

Tonight was a good example of why the Phillies aren't paying Ryan Howard $10M to be Doug Mientkiewicz. The big man stayed back on Jorge Campillo's hanging curve and took it deep for a three-run blast. But in the ninth, he did his best to erase all memory of that, booting two plays and forcing a 28-pitch non-save for Brad Lidge. Lidge managed to escape unscathed by striking out Mark Teixeira to end it. The record won't show it, but it was one of Lidge's best outings of the season.

Myers' AAA Lehigh-Valley line: Five innings, 100 pitches, 60 for strikes, three runs, five hits, two walks, six strikeouts, charged with the loss.

Quotable: "I wanted him to get the shutout, but once he got to 125 pitches, you've got to remember he's got the whole second half of the season. You want to keep him fresh." – Charlie Manuel on pulling Hamels in the 9th inning

Thursday, July 3rd - Phillies 4 Braves 1 (47-39) 1st Place - 2 ½ GA of the Marlins

Atlanta – *Christmas in July came early as the Phillies swept all three games from the Braves and Cole Hamels (9-5, 3.22) came one out away from throwing a complete game shut-out ... Bryan McCann's double with 2 outs in the 9th scored Chipper Jones for the Brave's only run of the game ... Tom Gordon came in to relieve Hamels and on one pitch picked up his 2nd save of the season ... Chase Utley (24), Ryan Howard (22) and Pedro Feliz (10) each hit solo homeruns. Stuff: Howard's homer was the 151st of his career putting him 11th on the Phils' all-time HR list. Willie "Puddin Head" Jones is 10th with 180 ... Howard became the fastest major leaguer ever to reach 150 homeruns doing it in his 495th game. The Braves' Eddie Matthews held the previous record, reaching the mark in his 569th game ... the Phillies rank first in the National League in Extra-base Hits (296), Slugging % (.444) and Intentional Walks (34).*

Chris Wheeler is a lifelong self-proclaimed Phillies fanatic. "Wheels" grew up in the Philadelphia suburbs and regularly went to see his Phillies play at Connie Mack Stadium as a young child. His love of the Phillies continued throughout his youth and into early adulthood. In July of 1971, Chris was able to fulfill his dream of making it to the big leagues when he joined the Phillies as their Assistant Director of Publicity.

Chris Wheeler is now in his 32nd year as a broadcaster with the Phillies

Chris' broadcast career began the day the Phillies clinched the NL East Division Title back in 1976. The Phillies had just clinched the division in the first game of a double header against the Montreal Expos in which Whitey and Harry had to go down to the locker room for the post game celebration and to do some interviews with the players. However that only left Andy Musser and Robin Roberts up in the booth so Wheels was asked to fill in for the second game. The following season, Chris became an official member of the Phillies' broadcast team and is now celebrating his 32nd season in that role. Whether you love Chris Wheeler or hate him, one can't deny his love of the game and his acute knowledge of it. He has taught generations of fans all across the Delaware Valley about how the game of baseball is played.

The first thing I do when I get to the ballpark is prep for the Charlie Manuel Show. I'm usually here by 2:30pm. I've been doing the manager's show now for over 20 years. Once I put my stuff into the office, I'll then go down to the clubhouse and hang out in the coach's room and then go right in with Charlie and talk about the game. After I come out of there, I might go talk to some of the coaches or I might go talk to any of the players that I may want to get some information from. Charlie likes to do the show before he goes out for a little extra hitting practice and before he meets with the media at 4:00pm. We're usually finished with the show by then. That's how I start everyday.

When Charlie and I first start talking, I never know where I'm going with the show. When I come in during the day, I'll think about where the questions should be going. It really depends on what's happening with the team. Sometimes a show is just so easy to do because the game from the night before or some other situation lend themselves right to the questions that I will be talking to Charlie about. Other times you may have lost six or seven games in a row. You don't want to keep beating up on the same stuff so you have to think through how you want the interview with the manager to go.

I've been lucky enough to have a real good rapport with the managers, they trust me. We'll sit there and just do a lot of talking before we even do the show, and I'll get a feel where their head is that particular day. Where they want to go or maybe where they don't want to go or if there is something that they might want to talk about we'll go there.

I started with the Phillies in the Publicity Department in 1971. For a long time I kept the scorebook, the stats, the notes and all that after each game. Till this day, I still spend about an hour after the game logging all the information into a book that I keep. It's just a habit. I use it to go back day-by-day and see what everyone did that day. I keep the pitchers, I keep the hitters, I keep homeruns. It keeps my head in how the team is doing and how individuals have performed. I write all my thoughts on the game down so when I need the information during the game, I have it. It's more or less habit.

I used to keep all of the official Phillies stats and stuff but now Kevin Gregg does it. Greg Casterioto did it, Leigh Tobin did it for awhile. All the PR people get to keep the stats. But for maybe the first, wow, 10, 11, 12 years when I was here I did all that. I don't have all my books starting back in '71, but I have my own scorebooks probably going back about 25 years now.

To really be engaged in a game, I think keeping score is a must for either a broadcaster or a sportswriter. When you go back and write your story or see what happened a few innings back when your broadcasting you want to be able to go back and put things together. You could always go off the play-by-play that they put out during and after the game but in our business you have to keep score. When you're sitting there doing play-by-play, you got to go, "Here's Jimmy Rollins, 0-3, grounded out in the first" … you have to remember all this stuff.

With regards to writing notes in the scorebook I use that for my prep work for the next day. That's all you can do because you don't have the game notes until the next day and all of the stats so I write it down to help me better prepare for Charlie's show and the broadcast. After a game I'll also go home and I'll also continue prepping for the next day. There's a great website called PlayersProfiles.com that I'll go onto if I'm not sure about a player. You can get stories about them; you might find some strengths and weaknesses. I'll use some of it during the broadcast.

When I go down to the coach's room, they'll let me look over the scouting reports if I want. I have a pretty good feel for players once I watch them, but if I haven't seen a guy and I'm not sure about something, I might ask Milt or Rich Dubee or one of the other coaches about something. So if I'm not sure, my philosophy is that I should never ever have somebody come off that bench on the other team and not know something about them.

I can't do Whitey's old act and say, "Tell me everything you know about this guy?" That worked for him but that wouldn't work for us. People would be sitting at home wondering, "Why don't you know that? You're supposed to know that stuff. Don't you do your job?" It's not funny if I did it. So I've always felt that way. You should know something about everybody. So I try very hard to do that.

The cities I like visiting the best during the season are San Francisco and Chicago. But unfortunately we only go there once a year now. It used to be we went to Chicago three times when I first started and San Francisco twice. For obvious reasons we only go once now. To be honest, I like all of the towns we visit. I can't think of a town in which I would say, "Oh, God, I got to go there?!"

The hardest thing about traveling is the wear and tear on your body. They make it as easy as they can for you, with charter planes but when the fans turn off their TV sets at 11:00 pm and we have to go to another city we don't get to bed until 4:00am. That's if everything went right. To me the hardest part is the travel especially as you get older. When I first started I was 25, I'm 62 now so there's a big difference in how you feel. So to me the hardest part is just the travel involved. Like I said, I'm not complaining about anything, it's just time consuming.

My favorite ballpark might be the one in San Francisco. I think that it is so pretty. I really like the view we have from the booth. I always loved Dodgers Stadium too. I've been going there for so long. For a working facility, those are both great. I would probably say San Francisco right now would be my favorite. Candle Stick was not my favorite park, that place was horrible. Being next to the bay it was always too cold and windy. Their new park is much better.

What does it take to be a good announcer? Wow. I can't answer that because I just try to do what I do. I love the game; I'm very enthusiastic. I've been lucky enough to be around great people who help me. I know Philadelphia fans don't want to hear this but the first thing you learn when you get around the game is how little you really do know about it and I've always been a sponge for information. I suck up things. So I had a lot of people who took me under their wing like Larry Bowa, Greg Luzinski. Back in the early '70s, we were all around the same age when I started, and they would help me out. We were together all the time so when I get a chance to go on the air I see things like a player or a field person does. I don't know why, I played ball a lot, but I didn't play at this level. But I'm able to explain them.

When I watch a sport, another sport or our sport, I just want somebody to tell me something to help me understand the game more. That's what I try to do. I have the people that are critics of mine say "I don't need you to tell me that, I know it." Well they probably don't. Number one the odds are you don't know. Number two is we have to think that we have a huge audience out there and maybe somebody's watching the game for the first time and they don't know what the infield fly rule is. So sometimes you have to explain those kinds of things. If that bothers somebody, tough. You know, I can't worry about that; so I've always felt my job is to inform and entertain as best as I can. I have a tremendous enthusiasm for the game. I love it.

I have no preference between TV or radio. But there's different skills involved. Radio's harder to do because you have to paint a visual picture and if you're doing a call on the radio you get very little time to be really coherent in your thought process. Probably what's really helped me to be fairly good at what I do is because I did so much radio when I first started. TV you can be in the middle of something, a guy will foul off a pitch and you can keep talking. People saw it happen. You can't do that on radio. You have to allow your play-by-play guy to say here's the stretch and the pitch. You don't say, "Here's the stretch and the pitch," on television.

Television is much different in that you're constantly being talked to by the people in the truck and you got so many visuals to work with. There are a lot of people who do television now-a-days that still don't understand when something shocking comes up on the monitor you got to say something about it. Even if you're in a middle of a story, you have to address what everybody just saw on their 64" TV because they're looking at the screen and thinking what the hell was that? Some announcers don't have these skills because they were radio people. I believe there's a real skill involved in that. Like I say, you get the producer, director talking to you live. You got promos to read; you got replays to do. It's just busy. People will come in there and hang out with us once in awhile. There's a lot going on in here.

I still keep in touch with some of the old broadcasters who have left. Once in a while, I'll talk on the phone with Bill Campbell and Andy Musser. Tim McCarver and I are best friends. We talk continually; in fact, I talked to him two days ago. I've worked with a lot of guys but the main guys I worked with were Harry, Richie and Andy. You know Whitey's gone, and I still talk to Andy and of course I still see Harry. The four of us were together for a long time.

My favorite all-time favorite Phillie was Richie Ashburn. He was my boyhood idol. In fact, I told him that when we first got together. He never let me forget it. Probably the guy I enjoyed watching the most was Richie, but I'm so lucky because I saw Mike Schmidt's whole career as well. That's tough but I think my favorite was Richie.

One thing that fans don't know about me? That I'm a history nut. I love Civil War History.

I go to Civil War battlefields. I did a great tour about 8 years ago with Tim McCarver from both the point of view of the North and the South. We stood on top of Marines Heights in Fredericksburg, which is a horrible Civil War battle where the Union troops were basically slaughtered. While we were up there McCarver said to me, "If we had been here Wheels, I'd been up here (with the South) and you would have been down there (with the North)." We had a good time. We went to Fredericksburg; we were at Chancellorsville, a lot of different places. I've been to Gettysburg about four or five times.

I'd like people to remember me as a professional who cared about his work. That I spent a tremendous amount of time coming prepared for a game every day. That I respected the fans. I just try to do the best I can, and I also understand that when you do what we do for a living, some people are going to like you, some aren't. They don't know me personally. If they knew me personally, everybody would like me. I can't worry about that. I just feel you try to treat people the way you want to be treated. The only time I have trouble with somebody is if they give me a hard time.

Good years, bad years, bad game, good game, I love being here. I consider it an honor and a privilege to do this. So I'm never going to come in here and not give it 100%. When I start to phone it in then you know it's time for me to leave. But I have not lost one ounce of enthusiasm; in fact, I think more than ever I love this stuff.

Quotable: "I think when 'Happie' got called up he knew the situation and how big this series was coming in. They made the call on the right guy to come up." - Ryan Howard on the immediate contribution by rookie JA Happ

<u>*Friday, July 4th - Phillies 3 Mets 2 (48-39) 1st Place - 3 ½ GA of the Marlins*</u>

Philadelphia – *Shane Victorino's two-out, walk-off RBI single in the 9th was the difference in a tight game that featured the debut of Phils' rookie starter JA Happ and the continued mastery of the Phillies bullpen over the rest of the league ... Happ (0-0, 3.86) kept the Mets off of the board for the first 4 innings but ran into trouble in the 5th as New York took a 2-0 lead ... As they have continued to do so throughout the season, the Phils' bullpen then took over, shutting down the Mets as they allowed just one hit for the remaining 4 1/3rd innings ... Reliever Chad Durbin struck out 6 in 2 1/3rd innings ... Brad Lidge earned his first win as a Phillie ... Ryan Howard (73) and Pat Burrell (53) each had RBI singles off of Johan Santana in the 6th to tie the game at two ... Pedro Feliz hit a two-out double off of Mets reliever Duaner Sanchez, setting up the winning run for Victorino. Stuff: JA Happ became only the 6th starter for the Phillies this year, the lowest number of starters used in the majors ... The Phils are now 5 ½ games in front of the Mets ... Chase Utley is still leading all National League players with 2.6 million votes for the All-Star team.*

With Santana's pitch count at 95, Mets skipper Jerry Manuel elected to remove him despite the fact that he had been dominant except for a pair of Ryan Howard and Pat Burrell RBI singles in the sixth. With Duaner Sanchez on in relief, Pedro Feliz roped a two out double, followed by a Victorino single to complete the dramatic victory, their fourth-straight win since completing interleague play.

Happ allowed two hits and four walks in 4 2/3rd innings, holding the Mets scoreless before running into trouble in the fifth. Before that, he retired 12 of 13 batters. "He has improved a lot since last year," Manuel said afterward. "He had a better fastball. I think a little more seasoning and his command will get a lot better."

But the night belonged to the Phillies' bullpen. With the bases loaded in the fifth, Chad Durbin replaced Happ and struck out Carlos Beltran to retire the side. Durbin stayed on to pitch 2 1/3rd perfect innings, striking out six of seven batters that he faced. Ryan Madson and Brad Lidge worked a scoreless eighth and ninth.

A Phillies' usherette hands out All-Star ballots prior to the game

What a difference a bullpen makes. Turn back the clock to '06 or '07 and they don't win this game. It was a night for Happ to build on, and obviously a great way to kick off the home stand by getting the 'W' in a game started by Santana, who has a 2.48 ERA in his last six starts, during which the Mets are 0–6 and averaging about two runs a game.

Additional Links: David Murphy of the *Daily News* had a great story on the latest trade winds and what the Phillies are doing to dig Carlos Ruiz out from his slump. The Phils are reportedly taking a hard look at AJ Burnett, Eric Bedard and C.C. Sabathia. In reading a couple of stories, reports on the availability of Shane Victorino are mixed. I read somewhere that the team will not consider trading catching prospect Lou Marson, with the suggestion being they view Marson as their catcher of the future.

Quotable: "It's going to happen. I think over the course of 162 games you can't expect everyone to be perfect. I think our bullpen has done an outstanding job for us. It's one of the reasons we are where we are." – Jamie Moyer on the bullpen giving up six runs

Saturday, July 5th - Mets 9 Phillies 4 (48-40) 1st Place - 3 ½ GA of the Marlins

Philadelphia – Jamie Moyer pitched a solid outing giving up 3 runs in 6 2/3rd innings, however the Phils' steady bullpen imploded against the Mets allowing 6 runs in 2 1/3rd innings ... With the Phils leading 4-3 going into the 8th JC Romero quickly gave up two singles and was promptly relieved by Tom Gordon. Gordon struggled with command and uncorked a wild pitch that allowed the runner at third to score and tie the game 4-4. A walk and a two-run double later, Gordon was headed to the showers ... Rudy Seanez gave up the remaining 3 runs in the 9th ... The Phillies only managed 4 hits off of 6 Mets pitchers throughout the night with one of them being Ryan Howard's 23rd homerun of the season, a 3-run shot in the 4th ... Jayson Werth had a pinch-hit single in the 7th to give the Phils a 4-3 lead before the bullpen came apart. Stuff: Phillies' first round draft pick Anthony Hewitt was introduced at today's game, the 24th overall pick of the draft is projected as a third baseman ... After 42 home dates, the Phils rank 5th in the NL in attendance with 1,730,128.

George Herbert Walker Bush served as the 41st President of the United States from 1989 to 1993. Many may not realize this but President Bush was an excellent baseball player. He was the first baseman and captain of his Yale University baseball team and he played in the 1947 and 1948 College World Series. Bush threw left-handed and batted right and during his senior year at Yale he batted fourth and ended the season with a .264 average.

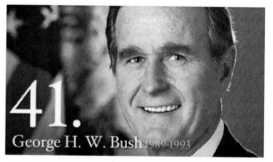

President Bush gives his views of what baseball means to America – photo courtesy Whitehouse.gov

An avid baseball fan, we asked the former President if he would take a few minutes out of his busy schedule to help us celebrate our nation's 232nd birthday by telling us what baseball means to him and to our country.

Mr. President ...

Baseball is appropriately called the national pastime. I think because of all the sports, it's what brings families together. There is something about going to a ballgame with your dad, or a child, that is truly special. Maybe it's because of the slower pace of the game, because it allows you to really visit and enjoy the people you are with along with the game.

I can still remember going to the Polo Grounds and Yankee Stadium with my Dad. Today, I love going to Minute Maid Park in Houston with my grandchildren and sitting with one of baseball's great owners, Drayton McLane. I also love to go to Fenway Park at least once every summer. Like many Americans, when I think "baseball," I also think "family."

My most cherished moment in baseball was when I was captain of the Yale baseball team, and Babe Ruth came to Yale to donate his papers to the college. It was a great moment for me, to stand at home plate with the Babe, and represent our team. Riddled with cancer, he could hardly speak and he died a short time later. I will never forget it.

Quotable: "Wow! That's what an eight hour day feels like." - Jimmy Rollins after a 2 hour 50 minute rain delay and 12 innings of work

Sunday, July 6th - Mets 4 Phillies 2 - 12 inn. (48-41) 1st Place - 2 ½ GA of the Marlins

Philadelphia – Jayson Werth hit a game tying 2-run homer in the 9th to send the game into extra innings but the bullpen failed to hold back the Mets for a second game in a row as Chad Durbin (2-2, 1.80) gave up a 2-run homerun in the 12th to Fernando Tatis that the Phillies couldn't answer. Stuff: Today's game was the Phils' 25th sellout and 12th straight ... Reliever Tom Gordon was put on the 15 day DL with a tender right elbow ... The Phils recalled lefty reliever RJ Swindle to replace him on the roster ... Billy Wagner blew his 6th save of the season on Werth's homerun ... Through the first three games of this series, the Phillies are 22 for 110 (.200 average) with 25 strikeouts and 9 runs scored, leading Charlie Manuel to quip, "I'm definitely concerned with our hitting. We have guys that their averages are down and their production is down. We scored two runs today. We've played (19) games since we scored 20 runs in St. Louis. Since then, we've scored (71) runs in (19) games. That's not too good of a stretch. Can we do better? Yes. We have to catch up."

The $37.5M deal also includes a signing bonus, an awards package, escalators and a club option for 2012, with a buyout.

From the Phillies release: Lidge, 31, is 2-0 with 19 saves and a 0.77 ERA in 35 appearances for the Phillies this season. He has 47 strikeouts in 35.0 innings (12.44 SO/9.0 IP) and has set a club record by converting his first 19 save opportunities of the season. Lidge did not allow an earned run through his first 17 appearances of the season (17.0 IP), which was the second longest by a Phillie to start his career with the team.

The Phils signed closer Brad Lidge at least through the 2011 season

Among National League relievers, Lidge enters play today leading the league in ERA (0.77) and save percentage, has the third-lowest opponents' batting average (.167), ranks fourth in strikeouts per 9.0 innings, tied for fourth in saves, eighth in games finished (31) and tied for eighth in strikeouts. Over the past five seasons (2004-08), Lidge leads all major league relief pitchers in strikeouts (499).

In getting it done now, the Phils avoid the mad scramble they would have faced this fall. That's chest-bump worthy. There's nothing worse than a bidding war for second-rate relievers when the guy you really want jumps ship. History will not have a chance to repeat itself. Among contending clubs, the Phils would have been the most desperate for closer help if Lidge flew the coop. They have no other fallback. He basically forced their hand; he's been so damn good. They realized that a serious contender needs an elite closer. This was a priority. I'm not surprised they had been working on this.

It's a great length for the Phils, and it's a lucrative, incentive-laden reward for Lidge, who's been fantastic. Conventional wisdom, in regards to the Phils, takes another hit today. Pitchers aren't supposed to want to be here. Not today. The Phillies aren't willing to keep up with the rising market value of relief pitching. Not today. This is a nice job by the Phils locking down a core player while the window appears open. It's evidence that they're trying to win now.

But as fans, we're no dummies. Team salary has been locked into that $95-$105M range. With Howard's arbitration win, rising salaries across the roster, and Cole Hamels arbitration looming, they're sure to jettison salary soon. Brett Myers, who earns $12 million next season and is pitching in Triple-A, would be first up. Pat Burrell, a free agent after the season, faces an uncertain future.

It would be foolish not to consider the risks and look back two years from now and cringe at how stupid we sounded. He's been hurt. He was demoted to the seventh and eighth inning in Houston. Relief pitching is mostly a crapshoot. Let it be known that his extension comes at a time when he's pitching for a contract and pitching the best ball of his life.

Quotable: "I said from day one the division was going to be very close, and I also mentioned Florida. I evaluated their team. With the Mets, we're all jammed in pretty close. There are holes on each team, weaknesses on each team. It's right there for us to win. It's going to come down to whoever plays the best." – Charlie Manuel after losing 3 straight to the rival Mets

Monday, July 7th - Mets 10 Phillies 9 (48-42) 1st Place - 1 ½ GA of the Marlins

Philadelphia – *Adam Eaton's lifetime 5-0 record against the Mets didn't provide much help as he was blasted for 8 runs (6 earned) on 10 hits in only 2 2/3rd innings. He is now 3-7 on the season … Clay Condrey (2.1 IP, 0 runs), RJ Swindle (3 IP, 2 runs) and JC Romero (1 IP, 0 runs) were called upon to pick up for the struggling Eaton … Utley (25), Burrell (22), Howard (24) and Jenkins(7) all connected for homeruns … Trailing 10-1 in the 6th the Phils scored 8 unanswered runs but fell short in their rally. Stuff: The Phillies are now 3-7 against the Mets and only 1-8 in their last nine home games going back to last season ... Since the Phillies swept Atlanta in early June they are 9-16 (.360), the fourth worse record in baseball and amazingly they are still in first place ... The rumor mill had it that the Phillies tried to acquire CC Sabathia from the Cleveland Indians but didn't have the talent in the minors to get it done ... Pat Gillick still says that they "have a good opportunity" to acquire a starter before the trade deadline ... Chase Utley and Brad Lidge were named to the NL All-Star Team today. Utley led all NL vote-getters with a final tally of 3,889,602 votes.*

The Phillies game is on one of the two TV sets in the First-Aid room at Citizens Bank Park; NASCAR racing is on the other. A husband and wife, Mets fans from Lancaster County, walk in. The wife is complaining that she has a headache that won't go away. The Mets have the bases loaded with one out. After briefly doing a quick scan of her eyes, an EMT asks her if the Mets should score will the headache go away? She says, "probably!" The husband, however, is fixated on NASCAR. "Alright! NASCAR ... who's winning?" Another EMT jumps in ...

The Mets have now won 8 out of their last 9 games against the Phillies

"You know they did a test, people that watch NASCAR have next to no brain cells in their head and they can only turn to their left." The Mets' husband says, "Well I guess I got less than nothing then!" The EMT says, "And a Mets fan to boot!" The wife is given some ibuprofen and they both head back to their seats to see how the Mets' rally ends.

Welcome to the First-Aid room at Citizens Bank Park. Located directly behind Section 105 in right-center field it provides medical services to all guests that come to the park. Even Mets fans.

Jason Theiling, a resident Emergency Room Doctor at Thomas Jefferson Hospital in downtown Philly, is on-call for tonight's game. He works in the First-Aid room as part of his residency to help provide on-site medical support for all the Phillies' home games.

This crowd is keeping us pretty busy tonight. We are mostly seeing heat-related injuries and stuff like that. Nothing out of the ordinary, just busy.

We had an Aramark employee pass out behind one of the food counters because of the heat. We sent the mini ambulance over to pick her up and we wheeled her over to one of the medical couches that we have here in the clinic. She's doing much better now.

There have been a few one-off problems that we've seen ... one lady who had a panic attack, another fan who came in with an upset stomach. We treated a young woman who fell and scraped her arm, and we had a young boy come in with abdominal pains. Nothing life threatening. We treated them and they should all be fine.

Our primary role with providing emergency medical care is to help ordinary people who come under extraordinary circumstances. In the event that an extreme injury occurs, such as a bat or ball flying going into the stands and striking a fan, we are trained and well prepared to address anything that might occur.

We can handle about 90% of the typical injuries that happen at a ballgame ... we don't have surgery on hand but we can stabilize them, get them into an ambulance and off to Methodist Hospital or Thomas Jefferson Hospital where they can address their need. The good thing is that both hospitals are only about a mile or so away and I personally know the ER staff at both places so it makes it easier when we do have to take a fan to them.

In the course of the interview, an elderly lady walks into the First-Aid room with her husband. She is complaining that she feels very weak. One of the EMTs sits her down and begins to go over her vital signs. She appears to be doing OK but they call her family physician, as it appears that there is some history involved with her symptoms. They talk to her doctor on the phone, and he wants her to get to a hospital. In no time, they take her to the back of the First-Aid room to a waiting ambulance.

The worse problem that I've run into so far was a woman who came in with a heart rate in the 150s. If you are running the bases and your heart rate gets up to 150, it's no big deal. However if you're sitting and watching a ballgame and its 150, that's a big deal. We got her over to the hospital as fast as we could.

The best part about working here is that I'm a huge baseball fan. I grew up in a military family so we moved around a lot, but I'd go see any major league team that I could see in the cities that we moved to and became a fan of those teams. I quickly learned that when in Rome, do as the Romans do. Now that I'm in Philadelphia I really do love the Phillies and enjoy watching them when we aren't too busy in here.

I guess the most important thing that I want a fan to know about us is that we are here and we are well prepared to address any of their needs. They can come to the ballpark and know that if something does happen to them we will be here to take care of them. Even if they are Mets fans!

Quotable: "We're not getting too much from the bottom of our lineup. That's what happens when you aren't playing good baseball … consistent baseball. Last night, we scored some runs, but it wasn't enough. Tonight, we had Hamels pitch a good game and we got shut out. It's kind of how we've been playing." - Charlie Manuel on the hitting woes that his team is facing

Tuesday, July 8th - Cards 2 Phils 0 (48-43) 1st Place - 1 ½ GA of the Marlins & Mets

Philadelphia – *Cole Hamels (9-6, 3.18) gave up two solo homeruns in an otherwise outstanding start by the left hander going 7 innings and striking out 8 … The offensive drought continued as the Phillies were only able to manage 6 hits against Cardinals' pitching … Pat Burrell went 2 for 3 with a double and a single … The Phils hit into 3 double –plays in the game. Stuff: This was the 6th time this season that the Phillies have been shut out. The last time the Phils have been shut out this many times before the All-Star break was in 1990 when they were blanked 9 times … To date the team has been held to one run or less 11 times… Ryan Howard extended his hitting streak to 11 games with a single in the 6th … Brett Myers went 7 1/3rd innings, giving up 3 runs and striking out 6 at AAA- Lehigh Valley. The Phils' plan on bringing him back after the All-Star break… Chase Utley was named as one of eight participants in this year's All-Star Homerun Derby … In other All-Star news, Pat Burrell is one of five National Leaguers who fans can vote for to be the last individual to make the NL All-Star squad. Burrell, who is in his 9th major league season, has never played in the All-Star game.*

"Bryon is a great guy … hard working, gets the job done and sells lots of beer. He's been doing it for a very long time and he is still one of the best we have!"
– Anthony Miller, Head Manager of Commissary

Byron Sharpe is a beer vendor. He wears the bright yellow number "123" jersey as he lugs beer up and down the aisles at Citizens Bank Park. He turns sixty this month.

I have been vending in the stands at Phillies' games for 42 years. That's over 3,000 games in my career. I started back in 1964. I was 16 years old … sold Coca Cola. I didn't start selling beer until 1971. The vendor at the

Byron Sharpe has been vending with the Phillies since 1964

time was the Nilon Brothers. They sold beer in paper cups back then. It was somewhat more difficult to get around the Vet with open containers but I never spilled a beer in all those years. I missed two seasons of selling due to a car accident and was out the entire '72 and '73 season, but I was able to make a comeback and sold beer for the Nilon Brothers until 1985. In 1986, Ogden Food Service took over selling food at the Vet. That went well for about two years until they stopped selling beer in the stands. It was getting too rowdy, and there were a lot of fights. I had to go back to selling Coke until they started allowing beer vendors back into the stands in 2000.

I guess I've sold over a half million beers during my career. For a sellout crowd, I'll sell 10 to 12 cases of Miller Lite. That's about 225 to 250 beers a night. The most I ever sold at a game was 384 beers. It was a multi-rain delayed game a few years ago against the Mets.

We sell Miller Lite for $6.50 a bottle. We get .25 cents a beer plus tips. They also sell Budweiser in the blue and red aluminum cans for $7.00 a bottle but it doesn't sell nearly as well as Miller Lite so I stick with Miller.

A full case of beer weighs about 30 pounds with the beer, ice and the carrier. It's only heavy when you have a small crowd and the fans aren't buying.

Best day to sell beer used to be College Nights. But they got rid of those at the end of the 2007 season. It was the best idea they had come up with since they invented the Phillie Phanatic.

The best place to sell beer at the ballpark is in the right field stands and the sections behind both sides of the dugouts. Lots of thirsty people there.

The most famous person I've ever sold a beer to was Ed Rendell. He was extremely kind and he was a good tipper!

My call? "Ice cold Miller Beer! Cooooold Beeeeeeer! Cold Beer Right Heeeeeeere! Get your Cold Miller Lite!" Miller Lite outsells Budweiser every day of the week. Budweiser has two billboards in the ballpark and I think that management doesn't want anyone to make any definitive statements that might upset Bud, but Miller Lite goes like gangbusters.

I'm the best beer salesman at Citizens Bank Park not only because I've been here the longest but because people relate to me and my work ethic. A guy in his 40's told me that he bought a Coke from me when his father took him to his first ball game when he was five years old. He said that he couldn't buy a beer from anyone else.

The best piece of advice I can give a new beer vendor would be to tell them that the customer is there to see the game and not the vendor so stoop down so people can see the game. They will appreciate that and you will sell a lot more beer.

Players, owners, coaches and stadiums come and go… but I am blessed to have some longevity in this sport. I'm going to do this for as long as I'm able.

Quotable: "J.A. did a great job starting tonight, and we really needed a good start. He does a lot of the things that Cole [Hamels] does, but has a couple more pitches. Cole might throw a click or two harder, and Cole has a Nintendo change up, but J.A.'s got some great stuff. He knows how to pitch and how to hit his spots." - Closer Brad Lidge on rookie starter JA Happ

<u>Wednesday, July 9th - Phillies 4 Cards 2 (49-43) 1st Place - 1 ½ GA of Marlins & Mets</u>

Philadelphia – Ryan Howard hit his 25th homerun of the season in the 8th to give the Phillies a 3-2 lead and Pedro Feliz followed later on in the inning with his own solo shot to put the Phils in front by two runs … Howard ended the evening going 2 for 3 and driving in 2 runs … Rookie JA Happ, making his second start since being called up from the minors, pitched 6 1/3rd innings, giving up only two runs, walking 4 and striking out 5 … Brad Lidge walked two in the 9th but managed to hold on for his 20th save in 20 tries. Stuff: The win snapped a four game losing streak by the Phils … Ryan Howard's 80 RBIs set a Phillies record for most RBIs before the All-Star break. The previous record was 79 by Greg Luzinski in 1975 … Howard extended his hitting streak to 12 games and has now raised his average to .231 after spending most of the season below the Mendoza line. During these past 12 games, Howard is hitting .340 with 6 HRs and 15 RBIs … So that Happ can continue in his starting role during the All-Star break, the Phillies optioned him back to AAA and called up infielder Mike Cervenak.

You might think that the 4th of July fireworks celebrations would end on, well, July 4th. But here in Philly we do things a bit differently and continue celebrating our nation's birth well into the following week. Fireworks at the Phillies' game is a tradition that goes back as long as anyone around the ballpark can remember. Even when the Phillies were in last place you could guarantee that the fireworks games would be sold out.

A member of the Pyrotecnico team sets up the fireworks for the sold out crowd

Behind center field sits the wares of what is going to be one of the largest fireworks setups on the East Coast. Starting at the edge of Phillies Drive and extending almost half way down to the Holiday Inn on South 10th street are hundreds of yellow fireworks mortars being set up by the fireworks team from Pyrotecnico. One of the fastest growing and innovative fireworks display companies in the United States, Pyrotecnico does over 2,000 shows a year, including more than 600 Independence Day celebrations. The man responsible for ensuring the safety and entertainment for tonight's fireworks display is Ken Furstoss, the On-site Producer for Pyrotecnico.

As with all fireworks shows safety is of the utmost importance. The largest mortar shells that we will be using here are our 5 inch shells. The safety zone for those sized shells is 350 feet. Generally, the Phillies shut down Phillies Drive, 10th Street and the parking lots on either side of 10th. All of our staff are certified to handle fireworks and have to go through an extensive screening by the Department of Defense. In the rare event that something does go wrong, my crew and I are completely capable of addressing any problem that comes up.

Tonight we will shoot off about 4,500 shells in 17 minutes. About 5% of the time we will have a "low-break" shell that might burst about 50 feet above the mortars. It happens almost every show but it's not a big deal as long as it shoots straight up in the air. One of the worst things that could happen is that the mortar tubes are knocked to their side and they continue to shoot off. If that did happen we would be able to shut them down almost immediately. That's probably the biggest issue that could occur.

All of our shells come from China. We keep them stored in a magazine in York County, PA. The magazine is built just like the ones in the military so that none of the shells can explode. We literally have tons of fireworks stored there in over 50 magazines. If by some freak of nature they did explode, we would probably be able to see the mushroom cloud from here.

We have all types of shells. Probably well over 2000 different kinds. We have fireworks that will explode into stars, hearts, hats, smiley faces, lots of different things. This one right here is called a multi-colored coconut. It's a five-inch shell. It goes up and it kind of looks like a tree in the background with a multi-colored coconut in the middle and it's played during some of the more summery songs with Beach Boys music. There's about six of them here for tonight.

The Phillies pick out the music each year. When they are done choosing the songs, they will send them over to our Design team who will then begin scripting the show. They focus on the timing, rhythm, size and layering of the fireworks that will give the fans the greatest thrill. Although the show is 17 minutes in length, we will put in between 200-300 hours of our time to create the show and set it up. It's not a small process at all.

When it's time for the show to start, we will do a 30 second countdown on Phanavision to get everybody ready. It's the perfect way to ensure that the fans know that the fireworks are synced up to the music before they start shooting off. The music in the stadium is aligned with our computer so when they press start we're both locked in and we can start the music and the fireworks at the same time.

We really don't sell the shows based upon the length of the shows. We sell on entertainment value. If I wanted to I could stretch this show out for an hour with all the shells that we have. But it's not going to send the crowd away with the same entertainment value and the feeling inside with what we have planned for tonight.

The Phillies want the highest impact for the fans and that's why the length of the show isn't an important issue. Nobody will walk out of here tonight thinking, "Geez, that was only 17 minutes long." They will walk out awed. That's our job. To entertain the fans.

What's a successful show to me? One that gets up in the air and the customers walk away extremely happy.

Quotable: "Find somebody that has produced more runs than him. That's kind of hard. He's lead-
ing the league in homers and he's leading the league in ribbies. Who tops that? That's the name of
the game ... produce runs." - Charlie Manuel on Ryan Howard who drove in 3 of the Phillies' 4
runs

Thursday, July 10th - Phillies 4 Cards 1 (50-43) 1st Place - 1 ½ GA of Marlins & Mets

Philadelphia – Ryan Howard continued his power surge as he homered twice and drove in 3 runs.
His first homerun was a 2-run blast in the 1st. He then connected on a solo shot in the 6th, his 27th
of the year. He now leads the majors in homeruns ... Jamie Moyer (8-6, 3.95) pitched another solid
outing going 7 innings and allowing just one run ... The Cardinals threatened in the 9th when
Ryan Madson walked a batter and then proceeded to give up a hit, but JC Romero came in and
pitched the team out of the jam and earned his first save of the season. Stuff: With Howard leading
the NL in both homeruns (27) and RBIs (83), he will be the first player in 60 years doing so NOT
to make the All-Star team. The last time this occurred was in 1948 when Hank Sauer of the Reds
led the NL with 24 HRs and 64 RBIs.

The Phillies' cleanup hitter is nothing
if he's not unique. His 80+ RBIs sets
a new club record for RBIs before the
All-Star break. At the same time, he's
set to annihilate his own major league
record for most strikeouts in a season.
Here's what we know about Howard,
who is in this his fourth season as a
regular contributor. He can't field and
he'll start slowly. During this time,
other players will need to carry the offense, and Beerleaguer will entertain
a flood of posts on why he should be
traded. He'll become more productive
as the season wears on. Eventually, he'll
get the point where he can carry them,

Fans are hoping that Ryan Howard's offensive output will
continue to keep the Phillies in first place

like last night for example. For the sake of comparison measure him only against himself. He's
a different animal.

Moving on, Happ had an encouraging start; I'd go so far as to call it a very good outing. Charlie Manuel kept him in too long. His command wasn't great (105/60 K/B), but we see that
he can retire batters via the strikeout, and lefties have notched just one hit against him in two
starts. He's poised. He's not afraid to pitch inside to right-handed batters, but his approach to
righties, in general, still needs work.

The ninth inning was more stressful than it should have been for Brad Lidge, but this was a
game the Phillies really needed, so the pressure was on. And how about Clay Condrey striking
out the side in a high-leverage eighth inning? His pitches were actually quite nasty.

Quotable: "We had a lot of chances against them tonight, but we stuck with them. At some point somebody was going to break through. Luckily it was us." - Charlie Manuel on the Phillies' 12th inning walk-off win.

Friday, July 11th - Phils 6 D'Backs 5 - 12 inn. (51-43) 1st - 1 ½ GA of Marlins & Mets

Philadelphia – Jayson Werth hit a single through the right side of the infield that scored So Taguchi from second base for the walk-off win ... Ryan Howard once again proved his worth as the premier slugger in baseball as he crushed his 28th homerun of the season in the 2nd ... Werth and Shane Victorino each had 3 hits in the game with Victorino falling a homerun short of the cycle ... Kyle Kendrick yielded 4 runs on 9 hits in 6 1/3rd innings ... The bullpen only allowed 1 run in 5 2/3rd innings ... Rudy Seanez (4-3, 2.63) picked up the win in relief. Stuff: Howard extended his hitting streak to 14 games ... The Phils' bullpen has been stellar over the last 5 games going 2-0 with a 1.45 ERA (3 ER, 18 2/3rd IP) ... 31-year-old rookie Mike Cervenak played in his first major league game today. He flied out to deep left center in the 11th.

When Richie Ashburn passed away in 1997, it left a void not only in the hearts of millions of Philadelphians but also in the Phillies' radio booth. For 27 years, Whitey and Harry charmed the socks off of a city with their quick wit and humorous stories. Almost a decade later, fans were still able to hear Harry on the radio but the chemistry just wasn't the same with the other announcers as it had been with Ashburn.

Philadelphia's favorite new play-by-play radio broadcaster Scott Franzke

But it appeared that same magic may have begun in 2007 when Phillies' Director of Broadcasting, Rob Brooks, took a gamble and paired up veteran Larry Anderson and new-comer Scott Franzke in the radio booth. The two gelled immediately and fans quickly started falling in love with Phillies radio all over again.

Anderson: *"Lidge has an incredible back-up slider."*
Franzke: *"A back-up slide huh? Well, it's always good to know you have one of those, just in case ..."*

A lot of people say that Larry and I work well in the booth together. I think that's because we have a similar sense of humor. We both like to have fun with the game. I think we both realize that the season is so long that you have to have a little bit of fun with it sometimes. Especially if it's in the 8th inning in a one run game. I don't know, I think we just have a similar idea of what it's supposed to sound like at times. It's nothing that we plan or talk about before hand. Maybe that's what people enjoy.
Franzke: *"Do you have a long Irish heritage?"*
Anderson: *"Sort of ..."*

I grew up in Dallas Texas. I really learned how to do play-by-play by listening to Mark Holtz and Eric Nadel on the Rangers' radio station out there. Holtzy passed away in 1997. Nadel is still there. He's been with the club for 30 years now but they were incredible to hear together. Kind of what Philadelphia experienced with Richie and Harry.

I got the bug for broadcasting in college at Southern Methodist University. I did it as a side job between classes. I'd do the student radio station and play-by-play for SMU's basketball team. I enjoyed it but I wasn't sure how to go about getting a job at it.

Franzke's partner in crime, Larry Anderson, has helped form one of the best play-by-play teams in Phillies' history

When I got out of college I got a job in Prime Sports Radio. It was a startup company. It was just starting when I got there. I did sports talk for 2 ½ years and I used that experience to get a job with the Rangers as one of their Pre and Post-game talk show hosts. But I did the talk stuff and all the while I was doing some high school sports broadcasting on the side. Somewhere along the way, I just got really tired of doing the sports talk radio. I didn't like it. It wasn't for me.

Scott Franzke: *"And stepping to the plate, Andruw Jones. Here comes the pitch from Hamels, and WOOOOOOH and the ball is lined right into the face of Greg Dobbs! And whoa he's not going to make a play!"*
Larry Anderson: *"Yeah, ball hit right to the face of Dobbs, but like we all say, Schmidty would have had it."*

In 1998, I spent a year doing the talk stuff before and after the game, but I also was helping out in the radio booth with the Rangers. Basically, I was just helping Eric keep up with the out of town scores, I'd count pitches for him. I was kind of a statistician and I got to know him and be able to learn from him the entire season. That was the year they said to me, "Look if you really want to try play-by-play you're not going to learn how to do it doing five high school games a year. You won't get anywhere unless you do it ever day in the minor leagues."

The first year I did play-by-play was with the Marlins Class A team. The Kane County Cougars … located just outside of Chicago. It was a great franchise because they had really good attendance numbers. It wasn't like what you would think for A ball. We'd have 10-12,000 fans a game. We were drawing big.

We used to check the Expos attendance against our attendance that's how big it was out

there. It was far enough out in the Chicago suburbs that a family of four that just wanted to see fireworks, a ballgame and didn't want to drive into the city and pay $20 just to park would come out to watch them. I did that for three years starting in 1999 through the 2001 season.

Mets Fans: *"A**-hole! A**-hole!"*
Franzke: *"LA, they talking to you?"*

I went back in 2002 to the Rangers. They made me their full-time Pre and Post-Game host. The only reason I went back to doing that again was because they offered me the chance to do 20-25 games a year as the Number Two radio announcer. They had asked me once before when I was working in Single A if I wanted to come back and do the talk show but I had told them I wasn't interested because I was having too much fun doing the play-by-play.

In the Texas booth I'd do color for the first three innings. In the 4th through the 6th, I did play-by-play and then I'd move back to do color for the final three innings of the game. It was then that I really knew that I could do this job. I enjoyed it and it just seemed natural to me.

I stayed with them from 2002 – 2005. The bad part about it was the first year I got to do 25 games. However, the second year I only did one game. The original plan was that our #2 radio announcer would go and work some of the cable TV games and I would fill in for him. It worked well the first year but then there was a big fight between the cable TV station and the Rangers because they didn't want to pay for the radio guy's salary. So the second year the cable TV station used one of their in-house guys.

The Rangers allowed them to do that because of some other conflict and basically I was at the short end of the stick. They said, "Well Scott, you're kind of SOL … sorry." So for the entire 2003 season, I just did the Pre and Post-Game show. I think I filled in for one game when a guy was sick but that was it. In 2004, I didn't do any games at all, and in 2005, I did a total of six games.

The Phillies hired me to come work for them in 2006. I applied for the job after Tom Mc-Carthy left and went to the Mets. I remember interviewing with Rob Brooks on a Thursday and then I got offered the job the following Monday. I wasn't sure what I'd actually be doing when I applied here, but I got the job and it worked out really well. I initially started out doing the Pre and Post-Game shows and play-by-play in the 5th and 6th innings. Then in 2007, I moved to full-time play-by-play. I work all 9 innings … When Harry comes in he'll do play-by-play in the 4th inning, but I don't get a break during the game. I don't need one.

Anderson: *"Like hell you don't!"*
Franzke: *"Anderson's break? He gets a break by working with me!"*

Quotable: "All we can do to show confidence in someone is by handing him the ball, patting him on the back and saying we have confidence. At some point, you have to help yourself. You have to go out and get it done." – Charlie Manuel on the inability of Adam Eaton to get batters out.

<u>*Saturday, July 12th - D'Backs 10 Phillies 4 (51-44) 1st - ½ GA of the Marlins & Mets*</u>

Philadelphia – With Brett Myers waiting in the wings to make his way back from the minors towards the end of the month, Adam Eaton didn't make much of an opportunity that would ensure his spot in the rotation when Myers returns. Eaton (3-8, 5.71) imploded for the second straight game giving up 8 earned runs in 3 2/3rd innings ... The Phillies only managed 5 hits with Shane Victorino going 3 for 3 with 2 homeruns off of future Hall-of-Famer Randy Johnson. Stuff: It was Victorino's first multi-homer game of his career ... In his last two starts Eaton has allowed 14 earned runs over 6 1/3rd innings. An ERA of 19.89 ... Howard's 14 game hitting streak came to an end as he went 0 for 4... Chase Utley, who is lifetime 0 for 9 against Johnson with 4 strikeouts, was sat down for the game for only the second time this year. Pat Burrell went 0 for 3 against Johnson with one strikeout. It was Burrell's 15th strikeout against Johnson in 25 appearances.

Mark Hayes, age 14, and Francis Wozniak, age 12, have been staked out in front of the player's parking garage on Darian Street since 2:00pm. This is the location to be at Citizens Bank Park if you are trying to get an autograph from one of the Phillies or from the visiting team, which today are the Arizona Diamondbacks.

Autograph hounds Francis Wozniak and Mark Hayes waiting outside the player's entrance for Carlos Ruiz. The sign reads, "Carlos, can we have an autograph? Please.""

The game is quite simple. The players pull up to the gatehouse where Security Guard Kevin Waters watches to make sure only the players and their wives drive into the parking garage and that the kids stay a safe distance away from the cars. The kids stand on the right hand entrance to the gatehouse and patiently wait to see if the player will stop at the entrance or zoom right through into the darkness of the underground garage. If they stop they politely ask the player to sign one of their baseball cards or their notebook. Sometimes the players oblige; sometimes the kids are ignored.

Mark and Francis are from South Philadelphia. This is the second year in a row that they've set out to get as many autographs from the 2008 Phillies' team as they possible can. They are autograph hounds.

"We usually come to every home game as soon as school gets out. But now that it's summer we get here even earlier." said Mark. "Today we got about four autographs. We also got some from the Diamondback players. One of them appears to be Orlando Hudson. I can't tell if it's him or not because I can't read his signature … but he did put the number 8 under his name and we think that's his number." Both Mark and Francis point down to their spiral bound notebooks and show the scribblings of some name with a clear "8" written right beneath the doctor's signature.

"We're really trying to get Ryan Howard and Pat Burrell. Burrell's the hardest to get. We haven't gotten him this year. He doesn't stop. He just drives right through," said Francis. A few seconds later Jimmy Rollins flies through the entrance in a beautiful Mercedes … without stopping … Freddie waves him through.

"We got Jimmy a few weeks ago," said Mark. "We still need to get Burrell, Howard, Cole Hamels, Eric Bruntlett, Carlos Ruiz and Tom Gordon. We pretty much have everybody else on the team including the coaches."

The two kids pull out a number of signed baseball cards wrapped in a rubber band. Each are showing me their prized possessions. Mark begins to rattle off all the players that have signed. "I bought the cards inside the stadium. Here's Chase Utley, Jimmy Rollins, Geoff Jenkins …" He sounds like Dan Baker on Opening Day as he literally reads off every player on the team, plus coaches and the Phillies Phanatic. "So Taguchi signed in Japanese. See here? Pretty neat!"

When asked what happens if a player stops and they already have their baseball card autographed Francis replies, "Well, I have a baseball in my bag. I'll usually have them sign that or just have them sign my notebook."

For the visiting players the routine is a bit different. The team bus actually pulls into a parking area to the right of the gatehouse. Some players take the taxicab to the park but many come on the bus. "The rule is that we can only go into the parking area if a player waves us in. Otherwise Mr. Waters will toss us out of here."

About ten minutes go buy and a taxicab pulls into the visiting player's entrance. Out steps a giant of a man who is immediately recognized by both Mark and Francis as future Hall-of-Famer Randy Johnson. "Mr. Johnson! Mr. Johnson!" they both yell. With the cab about 75 feet away, Johnson looks back at the kids and waves them to come on over to him. Both Mark and Francis take off like a lightning bolt and are standing next to him in a matter of seconds. Johnson bends over and quietly signs both of the kid's spiral notebooks. The kids come jogging back a few seconds later.

"Wow! Randy Johnson. I didn't think we'd get him," said Francis. "He was really nice too," chimed Mark. The thrill of getting an autograph of a player of that stature is just as thrilling today as it was back in the 1930s if one was fortunate enough to get Babe Ruth to sign something or in the 70s if Mike Schmidt stopped for a minute to sign his baseball card for you.

Both kids stare at their signatures with a big smile.

A few minutes later a truck pulls in. Clay Condrey is behind the wheel. Chris Coste is sitting shotgun. Condrey stops to talk to Freddie for a moment and the kids approach the car. "Mr. Coste can you sign my ball please?" said Mark. "Sure," said Coste. Coste quickly signs the ball and then passes it over to Condrey. Clay grabs the pen and signs the ball as well and hands it back to Coste. "Here you go kid," Coste says. "Thank you! Thank you very much!" says Mark. Francis then hands Coste his ball and they sign his ball as well. After they give the ball back to Francis, they slowly pull away and drive down into the garage.

The Diamondback's Randy Johnson calls the kids over to give them an autograph

"Coste is always nice," Mark says. "Nice truck too!" Francis chirps into the conversation. "They all have nice cars," Mark quickly says to his friend. "Utley drives a Mercedes, Ryan Howard drives an Austin Martin, Rollins has about 5 different cars he'll drive to the park. Ruiz drives some kind of Ford. Condrey's from Texas so he drives that nice pickup truck."

Francis then adds in the other players. "Kendrick drives a Beamer, Geoff Jenkins a grey Mercedes. Charlie Manuel drives some type of black SUV. He usually has his wife in there with him."

How about license plates? "Most of them have regular license plates," said Mark. "Last year when I got Jayson Werth's autograph his car had a license plate that said "Werth it."

Almost on cue, Jayson Werth comes flying through the opposite side of the guardhouse and darts into the garage. "He always does that," says Francis. "He doesn't like stopping so he'll go in on the other side so we don't bother him."

Quotable: "I like where we're at. I said coming out of spring training we had to stay close to the lead and we're kind of exactly where I want us to be. Of course, it would be nice if we had a bigger lead." – Charlie Manuel on his team at the All-Star Break

Sunday, July 13th - Phillies 6 Diamondbacks 3 (52-44) 1st Place - ½ GA of the Mets

Philadelphia – *Tied at two going into the bottom of the 8th, Pat Burrell hammers a 3-run homer (23) to cement the victory over Arizona ... Pedro Feliz went 3 for 4 with a homerun (12) and two runs scored ... Jimmy Rollins went 2 for 3, tying the game at 3 on a double in the 7th. He also stole 2 bases and now has 24 on the season... Cole Hamels pitched well enough again for a victory (7 IP, 2 ER, 8 Ks) but the Phillies' offense waited a bit too long for him to enjoy the victory ... Ryan Madson (2-0, 2.77) notched the win with a scoreless 8th inning. Stuff: The win gave the Phils their 3rd series victory in their last 4 attempts, and in turn, they lead the NL East at the All-Star break for the first time since 2004 ... Hamels is on pace to throw 240 innings this year. He has now pitched at least 7 innings in his last 8 starts ... The offense goes into the All-Star break with the 2nd most runs (481) and homers (132), trailing the Cubs (507) and Marlins (135) respectively ... Although he had no RBIs today, Ryan Howard has set the Phillies' all-time mark for most RBIs going into the All-Star break with 84. He beat out Greg Luzinski who had 79 RBIs in 1975.*

Freddie Waters is a 78-year-old former Philadelphia Police Officer who has been in charge of the player's parking entrance since 1991 at both the Vet and now at Citizens Bank Park. He's also been a Phillies' fan his entire life.

I worked at Shibe Park as a kid in the late 1930s and early 40s. I sold papers at Shibe Park. The Daily News was 3 cents, the Inquirer was 3 cents, the Ledger was 3 cents, the Bulletin was 3 cents and all of them had scorecards. For each one you sold you got a penny. Back then you could get into the Knothole Gang and watch a game for free. I'd usually then use the money to buy a hot dog for 5 cents.

There are a few players that I remember from my youth and early adulthood. Robin Roberts, Del Ennis, Richie Allen, Chuck Klein, Schoolboy Rowe, all them guys.

I was a Police Officer from 1970 – 1991. A Traffic Cop. After I retired I started working for the Phillies. They asked me to come work for them. I first told them no because I thought that I'd be chasing kids around all the time but then they told me that I'd be in

Security Guard Freddy Waters waves in another player to the parking garage

charge of VIP parking so I've been doing that at the Vet and right here since it opened. It's a nice job.

For a 7:05pm start all the players have to be at the park by 4:00 pm. They start coming in around noon and then they come in sporadically until 4:00 pm. We've had some players come in after 4:00 pm. Most of the time though, it's the starter for the next night's game. They don't have to take batting practice or run around or anything like that so they're allowed to be late.

The earliest arrival is usually Utley. Most of the time Utley will arrive with Burrell. They usually come together at around noon.

The players sometimes stop for the kids. Most of the time though, they sign on the way out at night or on the field. Very seldom do they stop here because you get 10-15, 20 people out here and the players will drive on through. It holds them up if they stop. Unless it's like what it is now when you got these two kids over here. They'll stop and sign for a kid if there are only a few people but usually they drive right through.

The best signer? Probably Charlie Manuel…he's a nice man.

If the Mets or Yankees are in town we'll get anywhere from 35-40 people standing out here. Most of them come down from North Jersey or New York. On average though, there are usually about 10-15 people here. Today's a light day. I'm not sure why.

I usually don't talk to the players as they drive in. They'll say "hi" and usually just keep going. The only time they'll stop is if they have someone coming to the park that needs to park in the garage. They'll give me their names and I'll write them down. Sometimes when the rookies come in, they're a little afraid and they're a little awed by what's going on, they'll stop and talk to you for a little bit. But after they get a little taste of it, they just fly by too.

Most of the time the players drive in themselves. Some of them, though, get dropped off … their wives bring them and drop them off and then come back later that night to pick them up.

After a few minutes go by Scott Palmer, the Phillies' Director of Public Affairs, pulls up in a beautiful 1967 metallic blue Mustang, sporting a light-colored fedora on his head. He says hello to Freddie and then stops and signs autographs for the kids waiting nearby.

"Now that's a nice car," one of the kids says as Palmer drives away. Freddy agrees saying, "Yeh, I'd take that over Rollins' Mercedes any day."

Quotable: "All my pals were going into the game. I was literally the last man standing. It was the bullpen coach, the catcher and me." - Brad Lidge on the number of pitchers that were used in this year's marathon All-Star game.

Tuesday, July 15th - American League 4 National League 3 – 15 innings

New York – *In what was the last All-Star game in the 85-year-old Yankee Stadium the American League once again beat the National League as the Texas Rangers' Michael Young hit a sacrifice fly in the bottom of the 15th off of the Phils' Brad Lidge to end the 4 hour and 50 minute marathon at 1:37 am. It was the American League's 12th straight All-Star victory and will once again give them home field advantage in this year's World Series. Stuff: Chase Utley started the game at second base and went 1 for 3 with a single. Florida's Dan Uggla replaced him in the 6th inning and went on to set an All-Star record by committing three errors in the game. The first one not even happening until the 10th inning. Brad Lidge took the loss and blew his first "unofficial" save of the year. During the course of the game, he was asked to warm up on six separate occasions, throwing well over 100 pitches in the bullpen. He ended up coming into the game in the 15th inning and threw 2/3rds of an inning, giving up two hits, one walk and one earned run. He ended the game with a 13.50 ERA and the loss. When the game ended, there were no pitchers left in the National League bullpen, which actually caused National League Manager Clint Hurdle to have to ask the Mets David Wright if he could pitch if the game went any further.*

Quotable: "We've been attempting to upgrade our rotation, and we feel like we've done that. We think Joe is a very strong, competitive pitcher that has the mental makeup to pitch productively in a pennant race. He pitches a lot of innings and takes some burden off the bullpen." - Phillies Assistant General Manager Mike Arbuckle after the Phillies acquired Oakland A's starter Joe Blanton

Thursday, July 17th - Did Not Play Record: (53-44) Tied for 1st Place with the NY Mets

Philadelphia – *An off-day for the Phillies as they travel to Florida to begin the second half of the season ... In the process the Phils pick up a solid starter in Oakland's Joe Blanton, however they lose sole possession of first place in the NL East as the Mets (52-44) continued their winning ways, beating the Cincinnati Reds 10-8 for their 10th victory in a row. Stuff: The Philadelphia Medical Examiner's Office reported today that the death of Johnny Marzano was ruled accidental. According to Jeff Moran, spokesman for the Examiners Office, the cause of death was postural asphyxia, or suffocation. Contributing factors that led to his death were blunt trauma and alcohol intoxication.*

Joe Blanton, 27, is 5-12 with a 4.96 ERA in 20 starts for the A's this season. He has a 3.87 ERA in 17 of his 20 starts and is tied for sixth in the American League in innings pitched (127.0), having gone at least 6.0 innings in 16 starts. Blanton has the seventh-lowest run support average in the AL.

Over the past four seasons (2005-08), Blanton, a first-round pick in the 2002 draft, is tied for third among American League pitchers with 752 2/3rd innings pitched. Only Mark Buehrle (766 1/3rd) and Jon Garland (760 2/3rd) have pitched more in that span. Last season, Blanton went 14-10 with a 3.95 ERA in 34 starts with 230.0 innings pitched. He threw two scoreless innings for Oakland in the 2006 American League Championship Series. Blanton is 47-46 in his career with a 4.25 ERA in 122 games (118 starts).

Outman, 23, was 5-4 with one save and a 3.20 ERA in 33 games (five starts) for Double-A Reading. Cardenas, 20, was hitting .309 in 67 games for Class A Clearwater. Spencer, 22, was hitting .249 with six home runs and 41 RBIs in 84 games for Clearwater. All three players were drafted by the Phillies.

The Phillies Majestic Clubhouse Store may have some new jerseys to sell with the acquisition of pitcher Joe Blanton

The Phillies trade their top position prospect for the privilege of going season-to-season with a decent starting pitcher, one that would've required an expensive, long-term deal if picked up on the open market. Following a couple of misfires, the Phils are gun shy about playing that game again. Instead, they maintain flexibility and make a deal for a mid-season non-rental. The Phils pick up about $1.5M on his contract this season and he's arbitration eligible through 2010.

Cardenas goes from being the best, pure hitting prospect in our system to being the best for Oakland, where they'll need to decide whether his future is in the infield or outfield. The redundancy at second base, with Chase Utley ahead of him, is only partially correct. Cardenas' future position is still undecided. Left-hander Josh Outman, who was converted from a starter to reliever in May, will pitch in the majors some day but is in the midst of a lost season spent adjusting to the bullpen. He's deceptive, and he can miss bats. Spencer is a throw-in.

The Phillies get Blanton, and Blanton, to be frank, has been rather bad this season. There are a lot of miles on that 27-year-old arm of his. He tallied 230 innings last season, and he's at 127 so far in '08. The A's have a history of using and abusing their pitchers and why not? They're too expensive to keep. Some, like Tim Hudson, ended up OK. Others have not.

Statistically, Blanton's K rate is down (4.6/G) and his control hasn't materialized like it did in 2007 when he was walking 1.6/G. As mentioned earlier, Blanton's home/away splits are severe (4.63/5.73), and obviously, Oakland's McAfee Coliseum is gigantic. His splits were even worse last season (2.69/5.11). The A's had begun shielding him from as many road games as possible.

When a pitcher falls into that kind of pattern, you wonder if a change of scenery isn't the best course of action. In Philadelphia, he gets a fresh start and better run support. It also doesn't hurt that he'll play against inferior competition, which is exactly what the National League will offer.

Positives: The Phillies will make the playoffs if he can become the "Kentucky Joe" of old. I like the timing of the deal. Wait until the deadline – an injury here, a winning streak there -- and the market could have shifted. I definitely respect how the Phils are no longer interested in screwing around with underachieving pitchers like Adam Eaton, and I like the message it sends to a scuffling club. They can afford to be patient with J.A. Happ. Blanton is a safer option than Happ during the stretch run. And depending on where they need him, Brett Myers can pitch in the rotation or bullpen now that they've added some depth. Or they're clear to trade Myers, save the money and test Happ. They could go a couple of directions. I think anytime a team can trade with another contender for a capable, cost-efficient major league non-rental, it's to be commended, in principle. After CC Sabathia and Rich Harden, Blanton was in that next tier of marginal difference makers.

Negatives: As mentioned, he's a marginal difference maker. Blanton's decline from '07 cannot be ignored, and his workload raises a red flag. His average season is an average season (100 career ERA+). He's been bombed a couple times lately (1-2, 7.41 in last 17 IP) and is now being thrust into a new, high-pressure environment. He's been a much, much better pitcher in low-profile, large McAfee Stadium. Readers of A's blogs are bothered by his weight. Goodbye Adrian Cardenas, who could have been used in a sexier deal or become a starting player for the Phillies some day.

Scouting: Fastball sits about 90-91. Very good 12-6 curveball, secondary slider and change-up. Pitches deep into games.

Quotable: "We have to take care of our own business whether we're 20 ahead or behind. You can rely on other teams to win but if we don't continue to win, it's not going to mean a hill of beans." – Jamie Moyer on the race in the NL East

Friday, July 18th - Phillies 4 Marlins 2 (53-44) 1st Place - 1 GA of the Mets

Miami – Once again Jamie Moyer continued his mastery over the Florida Marlins as he improved his lifetime record against the Fish to 10-0 with a 3.03 ERA in 10 starts. Moyer (9-6, 3.90) didn't allow a base runner until the 4th inning and ended the day with 6 IP, giving up 2 runs … The All-Star break didn't seem to affect Ryan Howard as he punched out his 29th homerun of the year … Geoff Jenkins and Chase Utley both went 2 for 3 in the game … Brad Lidge continued his All-Star form, pitching a perfect 9th for his 21st save of the year. Stuff: Lidge's save was his 24th consecutive save dating back to last season while with the Astros … Harry Kalas underwent surgery this morning for a detached retina in his left eye. He is expected to miss 5-10 days in the television and radio booth.

The latest from Fox Sports' Ken Rosenthal finds the Phillies in pursuit of Colorado outfielder Matt Holliday and closer Brian Fuentes.

"The Phillies were working multiple fronts before, acquiring right-hander Joe Blanton from the A's," Rosenthal writes. "Among the possibilities that reached a standstill: A blockbuster for Rockies left fielder Matt Holliday and closer Brian Fuentes."

"Master of the Fish" Jamie Moyer is now 10-0 lifetime against the Florida Marlins

"The talks probably will not revive, major-league sources said, even though the teams continue to scout each other and the Phillies used different players to obtain Blanton than they would need for Holliday and Fuentes," he continues. "For Holliday and Fuentes, the Phillies probably would need to part with a package of Shane Victorino, left-hander J.A. Happ, Class AA right-hander Carlos Carrasco and Class AA catcher Lou Marson. Holliday would play right field, with Jayson Werth taking over full-time in center, then return to left next season if Pat Burrell departed as a free agent. After that, Holliday, too, would become a free agent." Jim Salisbury of the Inquirer reported that Colorado scouted Carrasco last night in Bowie.

Quotable: "He threw too many balls over the middle of the plate. Yeah, he didn't have his sinker, and that could have been a result (of not pitching since July 11 because of the All-Star break), but that just means you have to go to Plan "B" and Plan "C" … all the way to Plan "Z"." - Phillies pitching coach Rich Dubee on Kendrick's pitching struggles during the game

<u>Saturday, July 19th - Marlins 9 Phillies 5 (53-45) 1st Place - 1 GA of the Mets</u>
Miami – *Kyle Kendrick (8-4, 4.87) suffered one of the worst outings of his young career as he gave up 3 homeruns and 7 earned runs in 4 1/3rd innings pitched … Pat Burrell went deep twice (24 & 25) ending the game 3 for 5 with 2 RBIs and 3 runs scored … Chase Utley had his second two hit night in a row, raising his average to .296. Stuff: Pat Burrell is now tied for third place with Chuck Klein on the Phillies all-time homerun list with 243 … pitcher Joe Blanton was added to the 25 man roster. Reliever Joe Bisenius was optioned to AAA Lehigh to make room for him… The Marlins drew 26,250 fans to today's game and 23,124 at yesterday's game. The first time this year that the Marlins have drawn 20,000+ in consecutive games.*

Bill James defines sabermetrics as "the search for objective knowledge of baseball." In layman terms, there are a bunch of statisticians running around with every baseball stat known to mankind that are finding new ways to answer questions such as "Which player on the Phillies contributed the most to the team's offensive output?" or "How many homeruns will Ryan

Howard hit next season?"

Nobody has a crystal ball but through the use of some well-defined and well-applied statistics, teams are now looking at how Bill James and his team of baseball gurus continue to predict scarily accurate statistics about every player in the majors.

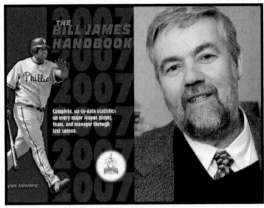

Today, Bill James is the Senior Advisor on Baseball Operations for the Boston Red Sox. It is by no coincidence that the Red Sox have won two World Championships since Theo Epstein

Baseball number wizard Bill James
- photo courtesy of ACTA Sports

brought him on board to apply his nearly 40 years of statistics to his club.

We caught up with Bill at his Kansas home and asked him some questions that the fans in Philadelphia have been noodling around in their heads regarding their beloved Phillies.

The Phillies have a $105 million dollar payroll and have only made the playoffs once in their last 14 years. Have you found any correlation to a team's payroll and their ability to make the playoffs? To win a World Series?
If you mean have I? Personally no, I haven't. I haven't studied that question in that form. But other people have studied that and found the correlation, and I have no doubt that there is one.

One contention as to why the Cubs and Red Sox have only won two World Series titles (both by the Red Sox) is partially due to their small ballparks that favor hitters. Citizen's Bank Park appears to play as a small ballpark that favors hitters as well. Are there any statistics that you've seen that would suggest that small ballparks play a role in keeping teams out of the playoffs?
 It's not a question of statistics; it is a question of what is true. Your real question, if I understand it, is, "Do teams that play in small, hitter-friendly ballparks have more difficulty winning the pennant?" And the answer is, "Yes, they do." In every era of baseball history, a majority of the pennants have been won by teams that played in pitcher's parks.

One quote that we all have heard numerous times over the years is that, "Pitching is 80% of the game." Another one that an old timer just quoted the other day is that, "Pitching wins pennants." Is this statically true? In your opinion what percent of the game is pitching as a whole?
No, it's not true, at all. Baseball is about 38% pitching. Teams that win pennants have strong pitching; they also have good hitting and good fielding. The adage that baseball is 90% pitching actually arose about 1905 or 1906 from something that Addie Joss said … and apologized for saying a week or two later. Addie Joss, who was a Hall of Fame pitcher, took a couple of tough losses. Trying to shoulder the blame for this himself, he said that, "Baseball is 90% pitch-

ing," as a way of saying, "I don't blame anybody else for this. It's up to me to win the game." The initial reaction to this was widespread ridicule. John McGraw did a very intelligent analysis in which he explained that baseball was 30-35% pitching, 15-20% fielding, 35-40% hitting and 10-15% base running. ...very reasonable estimates for that era. Pitching is somewhat more important now than it was then.

Anyway, everybody ridiculed this statement, and Joss realized that he had unintentionally been rude to his teammates, saying, in essence, that what they did didn't really matter. He apologized, and explained that what he had MEANT to say was that the pitching-and-defense side of baseball was 90% pitching, not that the entire game was 90% pitching. But later, as time passed, this misconception passed into the language, and people will tell you now that John McGraw said that baseball is 90% pitching, which is entirely untrue. Connie Mack DID endorse the "baseball is 90% pitching" nonsense, but late in life, after he'd lost his marbles.

That baseball is 38% pitching is still an estimate. The outcome of a given batter/pitcher match up is more determined by the batter than it is the pitcher, and this becomes obvious if you try to simulate the game. The spread of occurrence for every type of event, I think without exception, is greater for different hitters than it is for different pitchers. This means that, in creating a simulation, you have to leave more "space" for batter control than for pitcher control. If you don't, it becomes impossible to replicate the extremes of batter performance.

One way to think about it is that offense and defense are the same thing, only seen from a different angle. Offense and defense are like the two sides of a coin. When the offense succeeds, the defense fails, and vice versa; it cannot be otherwise. Baseball is thus 50% offense and 50% defense. To suggest otherwise is like arguing that the head of a coin is worth more than the tail of the coin.

Of the 50% of the game that is pitching-and-defense, most is obviously pitching. Suppose that the difference between the best pitching-and-defense team in the National League this year will be 250 runs. Most of that difference is accounted for by things that pitchers do. ...strikeouts, walks, and home runs allowed, hit batsmen and hit types . . .that is, ground balls as opposed to fly balls as opposed to line drives. But SOME of that difference is accounted for by fielders. My best estimate is that pitching is about three times as important, in the prevention of runs, as fielding.

If you were a building a team from scratch how would you break down a $100 million payroll to build a 25 man team with an 11 man pitching staff?
Well, I don't know that it's a useful theoretical examination, because it doesn't resemble the real-life problems that teams deal with. But if you could keep the money spent on pitching under $50 million, it would certainly help.

Pat Burrell is an enigma here in Philadelphia. Fans either love him or hate him. He's a decent player with power and has a very good on-base percentage (.389 in 2005, .388 in 2006, .400 in 2007) yet a player that appears to not have performed to the expectations of both management and fans. In your overall evaluation of outfielders in baseball where does Burrell rank? Any particular statistics that jump out at you on Burrell? If you were

to place a yearly salary on a player of Burrell's capabilities what would be a fair salary for that type of player?

You know, I really don't know. I wouldn't want to say something that was unfair to Burrell. A player gets paid more when he's been in the league a number of years, as Burrell has, and most players who have been in the league more than six years are over-paid, if you want to look at it that way. But you have to have them, because nobody's farm system is good enough to win with just the young players they have produced in the last few years.

Cole Hamels has quickly become the Phillies ace in three short years and appears to be a very special pitcher. If he stays off of the DL list what would you project his pitching numbers (W-L, K's, ERA) to be over his career?

It's like asking what a happy meal would be worth if you assumed that the French fries would turn to gold. Assuming a pitcher won't get hurt is silly. All pitchers get hurt. If I were a betting man, I would bet that he wins less than 100 games. But that's not really based on Cole Hamels; it is, rather, based on the average of all young pitchers who show the earmarks of greatness. 70, 80, maybe 90% of them get hurt within their first two or three years.

Same question for Ryan Howard. How would you project his hitting numbers over his career right now?

If he stays healthy, he'll hit more than 500 home runs.

Oh by the way, according to the 2008 Bill James Handbook, Jimmy Rollins contributed the most to the Phillies during the 2007 season by creating 124 of the Phillies' 871 runs … and how many homeruns is James' book predicting that Howard will hit this season? 53. With only 29 homeruns hit so far this season, 53 might seem like a stretch but there's still 2 ½ months left in the season.

Quotable: "Are you serious?" - Jimmy Rollins when he heard that the Phillies are 2nd in the National League in runs scored.

Sunday, July 20th - Marlins 3 Phillies 2 - 11 inn. (53-46) Tied for 1st Place with Mets

Miami – *The offense continues to pull a Houdini each time Phils' ace Cole Hamels shows up on the mound. Hamels pitched another strong outing going 8 innings while only giving up 2 runs on 4 hits and striking out 7. Unfortunately, 2 of the 4 hits were solo homeruns with the second one coming in the bottom of the 8th off the bat of Marlin's outfielder Cody Ross, which tied the game at two … The bullpen held the Marlins scoreless through the 10th but Clay Condrey (2-2 3.73) gave up a walk and 3 hits in the 11th for the loss … Ryan Howard went 2 for 5 with 2 RBIs (87) and amazingly none of them were homeruns. Stuff: Geoff Jenkins left the game in the 6th inning after hitting his shoulder with his bat on the follow through of his swing. He is day-to-day … Mike Cervenak was sent to AAA Lehigh to make room on the roster for Brett Myers. He was recalled from Single-A Clearwater and is scheduled to start against the Mets on the 23rd of the month.*

Following the game, a disgruntled Manual had this to say about a lineup that wasted yet another gem by Cole Hamels: *"We get pitching like that, we've got to win. Our situational hitting is absolutely terrible. Absolutely off the chart, really. It's going to be hard for us to win if situational hitting does not improve. [On Saturday], we hit all those balls down to third base in one inning - absolutely bad hitting. I'm not trying to hurt anybody's feelings, but if I do, if I'm talking about you, that's good. I mean to be talking about you."*

Charlie Manuel continues to look for flaws with his batters as they waste another Cole Hamels gem

For the record, those hitters on Saturday were Jayson Werth, Chris Coste and Jimmy Rollins, since we have no problem naming names here.

Let's take this Manuel rant a step further and throw some players under the bus. I'm getting awfully tired watching Shane Victorino – your No. 2 hitter – sky balls to left field with a man on base. It happened right out of the chute in the first inning. Vic is somehow immune to criticism by fans but the fact is, for all his speed and defensive talents, he doesn't play the game the way it should be played. The Phillies last, best No. 2 hitter was Tadahito Iguchi. He knew how to hit behind the runner. I don't know that anyone on this team understands what that means, especially Victorino.

Maybe it's not Geoff Jenkins fault that he's so one-dimensional, but he is, and it's killing this offense. Jenkins went 0-for-3 and stranded five men on base. He's a big reason why the bottom of the lineup isn't producing against right-handed pitching, where Pedro Feliz – hitless yesterday – is hitting .240. This situation with Jenkins and Feliz represents my worst fears; I wasn't wild about either of these aging signees for this all-or-nothing reason. The 6-7-8 hitters went 1-for-14 yesterday, where Carlos Ruiz continues his tailspin.

Hidden injuries? Chris Coste: 4-32 in July. Big home-plate collision about three weeks ago. Just sayin'. Rollins: Coming up lame in first inning, apparently a knee problem. High ankle sprain earlier in the season. Noticeably less high-motor than in 2007.

Mutual option watch: If Jenkins makes a total of 925 plate appearances in the 2008 and 2009 seasons or 525 plate appearances in 2009, it would trigger a $7.5 million vesting option for 2010. He's currently at 261 plate appearances. If the agreement fails to vest, he and the Phillies have a mutual option for the third year. The contract also includes a six-team limited no trade provision.

Quotable: "I am a small part. It's not me, it's the team" - So Taguchi after his bases loaded pinch-hit double in the top of the 9th knocked in the winning runs

Tuesday, July 22nd - Phillies 8 Mets 6 (54-46) 1st Place - 1 GA of the Mets

New York – An incredible 6 run 9th inning capped by a bases loaded double off the bat of pinch hitter So Taguchi propelled the Phillies over the Mets to regain sole possession of first place. Going into the 9th down 5-2, the Phils could do little against Met's All-Star pitcher Johan Santana. Instead they waited until the 9th and then teed off against New York's motley relief corp ... Joe Blanton, the Phillies' newest acquisition, didn't fair too well in his first outing, giving up 5 runs and 8 hits in 6 innings ... Brad Lidge gave up one run in the 9th but was able to hold on for his 22nd save of the year ... Chad Durbin (3-2, 1.78) picked up the win in relief. Stuff: Prior to his double, So Taguchi was 0 for 16 in pinch hitting appearances. He lead the National League in pinch hitting last season with a .407 average ... Greg Dobbs continued his pinch hitting tear as he singled in the 9th for his 19th pinch hit of the season. It's the most pinch hits in a season since Greg Gross had 19 in 1982 ... Dating back to Aug 27th of last season, the Mets bullpen has a 7.18 ERA against the Phillies.

The Phillies' offense remained ice cold through Santana's eight innings, managing just two runs, including a Shane Victorino solo homer in the seventh. The game appeared to be in the bag for the Mets, who scored five runs off Joe Blanton in his Phillies' debut. Blanton allowed two homers and three walks on a night that featured a few too many hanging breaking balls and untimely mistakes. But it didn't matter. With Santana gone and three outs to play with, the Phils worked a series of good at bats against Duaner Sanchez, filling in for injured closer Billy Wagner. Jayson Werth started it with a single, followed by a two-strike, pinch hit by Greg Dobbs. Shane Victorino would then single to load the bases and knock Sanchez from the game. With Sanchez out, Joe Smith in and the pressure on, Jose Reyes botched Carlos Ruiz's high bouncer and the runners were safe all around. Taguchi would

So Taguchi got his first pinch hit of the season ... and it couldn't have come at a better time

follow with his greatest hit of the season, and at that point fans were whooping and hollering all across the Delaware Valley.

Like a wise man once said: "There will come a time when So Taguchi will help the Phillies." For months, we wondered, doubted and questioned, waiting impatiently for the veteran to deliver. "What purpose does he serve?" Ah, yes. Of course.

Quotable: "I just wish I could have thrown my four-seamer better and for strikes. I felt like I would have gone deeper if that first inning didn't catch up with me." - Brett Myers on his first start since returning from the minors

Wednesday, July 23rd - Mets 6 Phillies 3 (54-47) Tied for 1st Place with the Mets

New York – Brett Myers pitched a shaky 1st but settled in, giving up a total of 3 runs in 5 innings pitched in his first start back since being sent to the minors in June. With the score tied 3-3 in the 6th, Ryan Madson came in and gave up a walk and three hits including a 3-run blast off the bat of Jose Reyes to put the Mets in front for good ... Shane Victorino and Geoff Jenkins hit back-to-back homers in the 2nd to tie the game at two ... The Phillies only managed 6 hits through the course of the game. Stuff: Madson came into the game not having allowed a run in his previous nine appearances that totaled 8 innings of work ... Mets' starter John Maine improved his record against the Phillies to 5-0 in 9 starts with an ERA of 2.54.

After a head-clearing, soul-searching, location-finding, fastball-reviving demotion to the minor leagues, right-hander Brett Myers rejoined the starting rotation against the rival Mets tonight and did a so-so job. Considering that there could have been a story line that showed no improvement whatsoever we'll take today's performance and see if he can build upon it for the remainder of the season.

Injured reliever Tom Gordon may not have been sharp before his June 6 trip to the DL, but his absence means more innings, more mismatches and more heat on the back of the Phillies' bullpen.

Harry Kalas completing his 4th inning radio play-by-play assignment with Larry Anderson and Scott Franzke

Lost in the Brett Myers shuffle was Ryan Madson's three-run sixth inning, which put the Mets ahead for good 6-3. Madson served up a level pitch for Jose Reyes to wail on for a three-run jack, equaling the number of runs Myers allowed through five, no-control innings.

Before last night, Madson had been steadily working his way back into Charlie Manuel's good graces; he had not allowed a run in his last nine appearances and was seeing action in something like a set-up role. The numbers show that his best work has come in high-leverage situations; so last night was definitely something of a rarity, not just for Madson, but for the entire bullpen. We haven't seen many of those "losses directly attributable to the bullpen" that we've complained about in previous seasons.

Realizing it's only one game and the bullpen has been solid, take heed. One of the main dangers of Gordon's absence is that J.C. Romero will continue to be thrust into mismatches. Right-handed batters are hitting .304 against him, and his WHIP is 2.37. We're also starting to see Clay Condrey creep into games like last night, with the outcome still in question. Condrey is fine at what he does, but he doesn't classify as a high-leverage reliever. Meanwhile, Rudy Seanez has become a non-factor, just like his '07 second half with the Dodgers. At 39, Philadelphia will likely be the end of the line for the journeyman right-hander. And it would take a blowout for Manuel to test Adam Eaton.

Quotable: "It's the same thing I do all the time - leave 10 minutes after the bus when I drive myself. You can't change the lights." – Jimmy Rollins explaining why he was late for today's game.

Thursday, July 24th - Mets 3 Phillies 1 (54-48) 2nd - 1 GB the Mets

New York – *The big news of the day was the benching of Jimmy Rollins by Charlie Manuel for getting to the ballpark late for a 12:10pm start. The other big news of the day was the continued collapse of the Phillies' once mighty offensive machine ... Jamie Moyer did his part in trying to win the game, pitching 7 brilliant innings while only giving up 1 run on 2 hits with 6 strikeouts ... The Mets' Oliver Perez kept the offense in check as he threw 7 1/3rd stalwart innings, holding the Phillies' offense to 1 run while striking out a season high 12 batters... JC Romero (4-3, 2.50) relieved Moyer in the 8th and gave up a single and intentionally walked David Wright with two outs. Carlos Delgado then smacked a 2-run double in the gap to knock in the decisive runs as the Mets took 2 of 3 games at Shea ... Jayson Werth hit his 13th homerun of the season to tie the game 1-1 in the 7th ... Eric Bruntlett batted leadoff in place of Rollins and went 3 for 4 ... Chase Utley and Ryan Howard each struck out 3 times each against Perez. Stuff: Oliver Perez has allowed only 1 run in 26 innings for a 0.35 ERA against the Phils this season. Versus other teams his ERA is 5.24 ... The Phils fell out of first place for the first time since May 31st, a span of 53 days.*

On a day that ended with the Mets making it their division to lose, Jimmy Rollins was scratched for showing up late to the game, according to multiple reports. That's twice this season that the reigning MVP has been benched for disciplinary reasons. Are you kidding me? Not even the purveyor of bold, 100-win predictions could have projected that one. His fortune-telling ability must be slipping, along with his interest, apparently.

So much for leadership. It's not what the Phillies wanted from their off-the-field and on-the-field leaders in a crucial series, with the on-the-field leader being Chase Utley, the man who would've been MVP two months ago. Utley went 0-for-4 with three strike-outs, completing the 0-for-11 series as a no-show.

This team has problems, brother. Do they ever. Chief among them: the New York Mets, who were better than the Phillies in approximately 26 out of 27 innings this series. Perez becomes the latest pitcher to set a season high against the vaunted Phillies' offense. A close second: the vaunted Phillies' offense, past the point where dysfunction can be blamed on "pressing." Third, the Marlins. Or the pitching. Take your pick.

Carlos Delgado's bat was the big difference in today's game

So is it inappropriate to use the word "collapse" in July? Because this one is starting to mix in all the wonderful ingredients (comfortable lead followed by controversy, dysfunction, underachieving) that sunk the Mets in '07. Or do we skip all that and say the Phillies just aren't good enough?

Yesterday saw the second rule violation from Jimmy Rollins, just days after a fly ball, no-hustle play over the weekend, the same reason he was benched on June 6. Does it pay for Charlie Manuel to be such a stickler?

If winning is the desired effect, there's some evidence to the contrary that the strong arm of the law has worked for Sheriff Manuel this season. Since J-Roll's first benching, the Phillies have gone 19-22. A handful of players have struggled, including J-Roll (.250), Chase Utley (.243), Carlos Ruiz (.189) and Geoff Jenkins (.143). Highest average during this span, if you ignore ABs, would be So Taguchi's .364. That's .75 batting points higher than your first regular, Jayson Werth (.289).

It isn't just performance. There's been dissention in the ranks. We've read the reports about Cole Hamels' disapproval of his handling after the All-Star break. We've read about Pat Burrell's displeasure over being taken out of games early. Yesterday, J-Roll became the latest player to publicly denounce a Manuel decision. Jamie Moyer would then defend it.

It's not to say the offense has been weakened by a dictatorship. Much of this can be laid at the feet of Brett Myers and Adam Eaton, and a lot of it has to do with the quality of the opposition. But if playing the game right, performance and winning were the desired effect from that first J-Roll benching, it hasn't been the result for Manuel's second-place club.

Better to keep it in-house? On the subject of artificial motivators, it worked in the past at least once. Last season, after the Phils started 4-11, they held a team meeting before a game in Cincinnati. Team leaders, including Moyer, Aaron Rowand and Utley, reportedly spoke out. They turned it around.

One of Manuel's greatest traits is that he's been able to keep problems inside the clubhouse. By all accounts, he's balancing many different personalities. Writers connected to the team maintain he's the only man who could make it work. In his fourth season, some of those seals are starting to crack.

Quotable: *"Look, we know what's at stake. We have to turn this thing around now so we can win the division, win some playoff games and play in the World Series." - Jayson Werth after Charlie Manuel's 20 minute closed door meeting*

Friday, July 25th - Braves 8 Phillies 2 (54-49) Tie for 2nd - 2 GB the Mets
Philadelphia – *Atlanta rookie Jair Jurrjens (10-5, 3.02) continued the dominance over the Phils' offense as he threw 8 shutout innings while only giving up 3 base hits ... Ryan Howard knocked in the Phillies' only two runs on a 2-run homerun in the 9th. It was Howard's 30th of the year as well as his 90th RBI ... Kyle Kendrick (8-4, 4.70) pitched well as he only gave up 1 run in 6 innings ... The Phils were in the game until the 9th inning when Brad Lidge came in and got lit up for 5 earned runs on 4 hits and a walk. Lidge was unable to record an out in the inning in what was his worse appearance of the year. Stuff: The Phillies are now 2-5 since the All-Star break ... With his 30th homerun tonight, Ryan Howard is the 3rd Phillie in history to have 3 consecutive 30+ homerun seasons. The other two are Mike Schmidt and Chuck Klein ... Pedro Feliz did not play because of lower back spasms.*

Fragments today instead of cohesive sentences. A game this bad deserves nothing better. It deserves primal grunting actually, but it's difficult to translate grunting to this page.

Three whole hits off Jair Jurrjens through eight innings. Jurrjens (which sounds like primal grunting) is a good, young pitcher, but the "good pitcher" excuse grows tired. There's good pitching in the league, so step it up. Chase Utley (pictured with wife Jen and kittens) might have been the worst hitter in the lineup. The biggest, RISP ABs fell in his lap again yesterday and he couldn't come through. He's hitting .225 since the 20-run explosion June 13. Short, compact swings replaced by big, sluggish, looping cuts.

The Vizquel-esque season for Jimmy Rollins continues. J-Rolls went hitless. He's not on base, not in the mix and he's not the power-hitter of a year ago, certainly. They were counting on him to be a power guy. Ryan Howard homered with the game out of reach to pad his shallow pool of RBIs and HRs. The team's long search for someone to step up when the key players don't continues. Unreal offense from the star players masked a multi-tude of sins over the years. Guys like Ruiz, Jenkins and Feliz are pure lineup poison, while Dobbs continues to be a big-time platoon option in theory.

The name Aaron Rowand is coming up more and more in conversation. Do they miss the leadership? Probably, but they're missing that bat even more. If this game was played a year ago, they're not silenced through eight innings be-cause someone like Rowand or Rollins would go deep.

Accolades: OK, here's some good news. What do Chase Utley, Pat Burrell and Jason Weitzel have in common, besides

Chase Utley and his wife, Jen, are in Philadelphia Magazine's "Best of Philly" edition along with author Jason Weitzel
- photo courtesy of Philadelphia Magazine

the obvious good looks? We're all Best of Philly winners in the latest issue of Philadelphia Mag-azine. Utley and wife Jen won best champions for a cause, Burrell won Best Phillie and Jayson Weitzel won … best sports blog? No. Best blog? Guess again. In the upset of the season, Best Sportswriter in the city of Philadelphia! "(A) great mix of analysis, detailed info that obsessive Phillies fans die for (including coverage of the minor league system and fairly intelligent com-ments from die-hard fans)." Fairly intelligent? Must have been written during a Mets series. My sincerest thanks to the good folks at Philadelphia Magazine.

Quotable: "What a game. That's my quote." - Jimmy Rollins after the Phils came back from a Brave's 9-run 4th inning and won.

Saturday, July 26th - Phillies 10 Braves 9 (55-49) Tie for 2nd - 1 GB the Mets

Philadelphia – *The Phillies overcame a 6 run deficit after blowing a 3-run lead as the offense awakened from their slumber and erupted for 7 runs in the 5th in an exciting win at Citizens Bank Park ... Greg Dobbs was the hero of the game as he hit the go-ahead 3-run pinch hit homer to put the team ahead for good ... The Braves smacked in 9 runs on the Phils in the 4th off of starter Cole Hamels. Hamels only lasted 3 2/3rd innings, giving up 9 runs (4 earned) on 6 hits and 3 walks... 6 relievers came in to shut down Atlanta for the final 5 1/3rd innings ... Adam Eaton (4-8) got his first win in relief and Brad Lidge pitched a perfect 9th for his 23rd save of the year ... The Phillies cranked out 12 hits in the game led by Chris Coste (3 for 4, 3 RBIs)... Jimmy Rollins and Shane Victorino each had two hits ... Ryan Howard had 2 RBIs in the game (91 & 92).* **Stuff:** *The Brave's Mike Hampton was making his first start since August of 2005. He gave up 6 runs in 4 innings ... Dobb's pinch homerun was his 20th pinch hit of the season which tied him for the franchise record set by Doc Miller back in 1913 ... Today was the Phils' 26th come-from-behind win of the season ... Harry Kalas returned to the broadcast booth for the first time since his eye surgery.*

It takes a lot of courage to ask your future wife to marry you no matter how you propose. But to do it in front of 45,107 people takes nerves of steel. Amanda Tolino and Norm Bauman are getting married! The young couple from Philadelphia, PA, got engaged at today's game in the middle of the 4th inning on Phanavision for everyone to see. A few moments with the young couple ...

Amanda Tolino was definitely surprised when Norm Bauman asked her to marry him at today's game – photo courtesy of Amanda Tolino

Why did you decide to get engaged at a Phillies' game?
Norm: We've gone to a lot of Phillies' games throughout our relationship for 3 ½ years now. I remember earlier seeing other people getting engaged there and I saw Amanda's reaction and she was always very excited. Going to games in the summer has always been important to us. It just seemed like a really nice opportunity to do it with all of her family and my family as well our friends being there together. To have it all on the big screen and to make a big deal of it. It was really fun.

What was Plan "B"?
Norm: I was actually going to go to Frank Lloyd Wright's "Fallingwater" house out in Mill Run, PA, near Pittsburgh where he built a home over top of a waterfall. I was kind of planning to take her there. I had never been there but I knew she had always wanted to go since it's a very beautiful spot. It was my backup plan but it really never got to the planning stages because the plan to do it with the Phillies worked out perfectly so I just continued to run with

doing it here.

How long have you been a Phillies fan?
Amanda: I'm actually a convert. I will say that I am a loyal fan now but I grew up in Northern New Jersey as a Yankee fan. I want to college at LaSalle and when I started dating Norm I didn't have an option to be a Yankee fan. He fully indoctrinated me with everything I needed to know to become a Philadelphia sports fan and especially a Phillies fan. I absolutely love baseball so coming here to get engaged was just really fun because we always went to games together … it was our thing to do and it was just really special.

Norm: My whole life. I grew up in South Jersey and my Dad and my entire family were always Phillies' fans and I just ended up loving the team. My first memory as a Phillies fan was in the early 90s. I've always known all of the players. 1993 was probably the defining moment of my childhood because I'd always go back to that moment with all of these years that we haven't won anything.

What was your immediate thoughts when Norm proposed?
Amanda: Towards the bottom half of the 4th inning I was talking to Norm about a house we had just looked at that we were considering buying and one of the Phanavision camera guys came down and sat in front of us in an empty seat. So I pointed out to Norm, "Hey look, there's the camera guy." I didn't think much about it and I continued to talk to Norm but he's not even paying attention to me. So finally the inning ends and the camera guy turns around and starts pointing his camera at us. I turn to Norm and say, "Hey look, we're going to be on Phanavision!" All of I sudden I hear the wedding music start and I see Norm go down on one knee and I'm just looking at him and thinking, "Is this really happening?!" I knew that we were going to get engaged but I was thinking that it was going to be at Christmas time or something like that and I no way expected him to propose. So he's on one knee and says to me, "I love you!" All I could do was put my hands into my face and start crying.

We still fight about this but he never really asked me the question. He just took the diamond out and put it on my hand. He actually put in my right hand instead of my left because I had my left hand up covering my mouth in shock. Eventually he took the ring off and put it on my right hand. All I did for the next half hour was cry out of sheer joy and shock. It really was my most amazing moment ever.

What was going through your mind as this was transpiring?
Norm: Well, it was somewhat nerve-wracking because I'm sitting there the entire game waiting for it to happen. I know they are going to do it in the middle of the 4th inning and wouldn't you know that Cole Hamels got rocked for 9 runs. The inning seemed to take forever and I'm just getting more and more nervous the entire time. However once the camera went on I didn't feel nervous and I just proposed.

It was amazing. You kind of feel like a rock star being on the big screen and people all over the place cheering for you and right afterwards everyone was high-fiving me. It was just really exciting.

So when's the big day?
Amanda: August 29, 2009

So in your mind how did it all go?
Norm: Planning it was the hardest part and trying to keep it a secret from her was very difficult. I planned this all the way back in February and we share everything so it was hard not saying anything to her and making sure that everyone kept it a secret. It worked out!

Amanda: It was just incredible. Even the Phillies came back and won the game. What more can you ask for?

Lucky with love, lucky with the Phillies this year?
Norm: I'm cautiously optimistic. They're in first place and this was a great come from behind victory. I just hope they can win the division again. Even if they don't, I won my prize!

Quotable: "(Utley) is having some trouble with his (right) hip." - Pat Gillick on Chase Utley's hitting problems at the plate. "I have no idea what you're talking about," - Chase Utley in response to Gillick's comment

<u>Sunday, July 27th - Phillies 12 Braves 10 (56-49) 2nd - 1 GB the Mets</u>
Philadelphia – *Down 5-0 going into the bottom of the 4th, the Phillies scored 12 unanswered runs over the next four innings led by a homerun hitting barrage of Chris Coste (8), Shane Victorino (8), Pat Burrell (26), Jayson Werth (14) and Jimmy Rollins (7)... Ryan Howard went 2 for 5 with 2 RBIs but was unable to join in the homerun festivities ... Victorino had a team high 4 RBIs in the game ... Five separate players had two hits apiece in the game ...Joe Blanton (2 IP 2 ER) and Adam Eaton (2 IP 3 ER) were knocked around early ... Clay Condrey (3-2 3.72) picked up the win with two scoreless innings in the 5th and 6th ... Rudy Seanez got banged around again as he gave up 4 runs (1 earned) as part of a Brave 5 run 8th inning ... Brad Lidge was able to shut the door on the Braves as he closed out the 9th with his 24th save. Stuff: Although Chase Utley denies he has any physical problems his statistics would say otherwise. On April 24th Utley was hitting .385. Since then he is only hitting .257. "He'll work it out. That's part of the game. Good hitters have slumps," Charlie Manuel said ... The Phillies are now 10-2 this season against Atlanta ... Over those 12 games, the Braves' bullpen was victimized for 17 runs over 12 1/3rd innings for a 12.04 ERA.*

David Montgomery is the President and CEO of the Philadelphia Phillies and a General Partner of the team along with Bill Giles, Claire Betz, John Middleton and the Buck brothers (Alexander, Mahlon and William). He has been with the Phillies since 1971 where he started out in their sales department. He took some time from his schedule today to reflect on his philosophies of running a Major League Baseball team while also providing some insights into his life.

What are your primary duties as the President of the Phillies?
Well it varies daily and that's part of the appeal of the job for me. But I see the role of the president as someone who tries to set the tone for the entire organization. I believe the best way that you can relate to fans and employees is to have as much knowledge of their individual experiences as possible. Some of the areas on the operations side of the house are easier for me to understand. I started in ticket sales so I know that area very well but for something like Dave Buck's area in advertising sales I

Dave Montgomery taking time to speak with legendary song writer Kenny Gamble

certainly know an awful lot of our key sponsors but as far as pricing the product, that's his world so to speak. On the baseball side I clearly try to be available for Pat (Gillick) and I try to be a listener. I think it's not the easiest thing for me to listen. People probably told you that I'm somebody that has views and am willing to express them. But I try as much to hear other people's perspectives before letting them know what I may think on a subject. But I try to know as much as I possibly can so I am able to better run the team.

You graduated from Wharton School of Business in 1970. What were the most valuable lessons that you learned at Wharton?
There are unique aspects of running a baseball organization as a business and yet it is like many other businesses. There's branding, there's a sales element, there's the marketing of the club. I think what I learned about sales and marketing at Wharton were some of the things that appealed to Bill Giles when he hired me. Bill inherited a staff that had been with the club from the Carpenter family. He probably brought in one person from the baseball side and one other person on the business side before I joined his team so I would say that the academic training at Wharton probably had some appeal to him. I think from my standpoint that the whole concept of market research where you listen to the customers and try to identify your product with them was a key learning of mine. We for years at Veteran Stadium did something called the "fan experience". We thought that it was important that the employees here didn't go to the game as we usually went to the game around here so we would have people at the office actually drive home and then come to the stadium. You drive to the stadium, see what the commute's like, see what it's like to park, see how somebody treats you when you pull into the parking lot, see how somebody treats you when you buy the tickets, see how they treat you when you walk through the gate. It was a way for us to better understand what the fan was going through and we would then spend a lot of time improving that experience for them.

Have you done that yourself recently or in the past?
I have not. I'll confess I haven't done it here but we've tried to have others in the organization stoke out that information for us. I've lost a little bit of my anonymity so it would be hard for me to do it myself. But one of the things that we're pleased about here at Citizens Bank Park is that we have complete control over the whole experience. At Veterans Stadium we didn't.

Earlier today in this very room we were meeting with our Aramark people going over the numbers and we spent a good portion of the meeting going through what type of feedback were we hearing from customers as far as the food experience here and whatnot. And that to me, regardless of what you're selling, is the most important thing. You have to know how your customers feel. The more knowledge you have of your own product from your customer's perspective, the better able you are to make it better for them.

What would you consider your management style to be?
Well I know what I would like it to be, I'm not so sure it always is. I couldn't say that it's not hands-on in the sense that I do try to be available to people. I do try to have an open door and have anybody that feels they have something to bring to my attention can do so. For the most part our employees are encouraged to use department heads to do address issues, but I do believe that if an employee has a personal matter or something that they think I should know, they will find me accessible.

Who are your favorite leaders of all time?
You know nobody has ever asked me that and I'm not so sure of it. I was a History major and there is good reason to go back through history. I'd rather pick people that I've seen. More recently, as far as being inclusive and a good listener, Pat Gillick. As far as being creative and really open to sort of pushing the envelope, Bill Giles. This one may shock you a little bit but as far as building consensus, Bud Selig. If you are looking at local leadership and people who are great at matching strengths I would Ed Rendell and David Cohen. I just thought that Ed has a real gift with people and David's retention is extraordinary and he was able to handle so much detail when we worked on building this ballpark. To me Ed Rendell was perfect in setting the tone in the city, and when he had somebody like David being able to execute effectively they formed a great team. I remember when Ronald Reagan became President. I thought, "Hmm. I'm not too sure about him." But Ronald Reagan surrounded himself with what I thought were some quality people and he seemed to let them make decisions and it ended up being a good period in time.

Who would you consider to be the one mentor that has helped you most in your career?
Bill Giles would be the person that was a mentor for me in this game. One of the things that I'll be eternally grateful for him doing so as well. When Ruly Carpenter was president of the Phillies, he was very interested in all aspects of the baseball side of operations so he really gave Bill great leeway on the business side decisions. Bill was kind enough to include me in on almost all of them. I've been attending Major League meetings probably since 1974. So I was like 28 years of age or something like that and Bill had me going to all these meetings. That was a tremendous opportunity as a young person. It gave me an opportunity to get a whiff of knowledge about this game that probably few have ever had the opportunity to do. Certainly not at that young age. I mean I wasn't a family member or anything like that. In other words there have been cases where fathers take sons because they own a club to a meeting and all that. But to have that opportunity? I have so much to be thankful for.

Do you feel as though the Phillies are the best organization in baseball? If so, or if not, can you elaborate on that a little bit?
I wouldn't say we're the best at anything. I would say we try to be the best we could possibly

be. Every organization has different circumstances, uniqueness associated to facilities and what not. I'm pleased now that we have an opportunity to have direct communication and direct contact with our fans. When people come to a Phillies baseball game the Phillies are providing the experience, not the city. So if it's a good one, fine. If it's not let's work it and make it better.

One of the nicer things that has happened to us as far as organizational perception is concerned, I think, is that we brought a lot of our game day staff over from Veterans Stadium. And over time some of our organizational habits weren't the best. But from the time we walked in here, and I don't know if it's pride in the facility, a lot of it had to do with training, but we worked hard at training everyone with the whole concept that a fan is our guest. Whoever says hello to them at the gate, whoever seats them, whoever serves them the hot dog, whoever they meet anywhere in the park, we want the fan to have a pleasant experience.

Chase Utley came up to thank our game day staff in their meeting room for the fact that for three years in a row we've been one of the best clubs at generating All Star ballots. That's probably the best example, the concept that we try to make everybody that works here feel that they have a role in the organization that's meaningful.

What are your top concerns right now on the baseball side of operations?
Well I got this fellow who claims he's going to walk away at the end of the year so I guess it would be the situation with Pat Burrell. I get that question often. I mean we're fortunate on the one hand that we have a good core group. To get to that core group we had to take a little bit of a step backwards as far as our player development progress was going.

I would make the analogy that I do often with a college basketball team, you know you've got freshman, sophomores, juniors and seniors. Well if you're playing 5 seniors you may be good this year but what's going to happen next year? If you're playing all freshmen there's usually not enough experience out there to win today. Well right now we're in a situation where we're winning today but we also have to make sure that we continue to build a pipeline for enough young talent so that there's a Chase Utley coming tomorrow. You have to have a core group of players and be able to mix in the other talent around them. We'll see what happens with Pat. We'd love to keep him but we'll have to see where we are at the end of the season.

Who in your opinion is the next Chase Utley in the minor leagues?
Well, I don't think we know who will play at Chase's level. That's pretty high. But we have position players like Lou Marson who's a catcher for us at AA, we think Jayson Donald who's an infielder is going to be a big league player. There's also another AA catcher named Jason Jaramillo, but I wouldn't put the pressure on those guys to be the next Chase Utley.

One of the questions I get all the time around the trade deadline is, "Do you have payroll flexibility to improve the club?" And I say, "Well the cost is really more the talent cost that you have to pay attention to." I mean for us to take on a couple of million dollars more on payroll, that's a lot easier than to mortgage a future by trading a young player for someone you might be renting for two months. I'll give you an example. You don't want to trade John Smoltz for

Doyle Alexander although Doyle Alexander got the Detroit Tigers into the post season. But boy did they miss John Smoltz for all those years. So the real cost of trades is that you just don't want to set yourself back to the point that you don't have any prospects in your system. The key to building a great club are sometimes the less valued moves. Look what Pat Gillick did. He made some wonderful moves to go get JC Romero, which nobody thought was a big deal when we got him and the contribution that Jayson Werth's made, the contribution that Greg Dobbs has made. Sometimes the less valued moves become as meaningful for you as some of the bigger names ones that get discussed almost ad nauseam.

This is where I think Pat has a real advantage as GM for our club because he has universal respect with everyone in the game. He has so many people that he stays in contact with. I mean, he calls another GM, they call back. I'm not saying that they don't for some GMs but my point is that he is so widely respected that other teams want to talk with him.

Is Gillick going to be hard to replace?
Yeah, absolutely. At the same time the one thing he did when he came here was to use the people that we had here in the organization and spent a lot of time with them. When it looked like he was seriously going to consider joining us I said, "Now Pat, are there people that you feel you have to bring with you?" He said, "No. I really would prefer the challenge. I've heard positive things about the people who work with the Phillies. I enjoy more mentoring those people than bringing them in." Since then he's worked with Charlie Kerfeld, Mike Arbuckle, Ruben Amaro, and a number of other guys. I think to a person they would all say that the experience with working three years with Pat has made them better.

Any front runners yet for GM?
No.

Ten years from now what do you think is going to be the most pressing issue to Major League Baseball and how would that effect the Phillies?
Well I think we've done a very good job right now of staying up with new technology and I would not venture to guess what that may look like in 2010. But we're a game that has traditionally received a tremendous amount of exposure from what I would call traditional media. I'll still be reading traditional. I'll be still alive. You'll be writing it and I'll be reading it.

But it's dying...
Well that's my point. And so I give us a lot of credit for major league advance media. The MLB websites are very well received. I look at how we've taken advantage of the ticketing technology that has moved. I mean the biggest thing we used to debate here was what the cutoff date to mail the tickets should be. If you ordered for tonight's game last Friday we put it in the mail Saturday. But if you ordered Saturday and we couldn't mail until Monday and we didn't want to risk not getting the ticket to the fan. Now they bring your credit card up to the ticket booth and give your last name and you slide the card in and out comes your reservation.

We have the advantage of the coverage that we currently get today. We still appeal to a broad spectrum of people and that includes both sexes, that includes all ages, that includes hard core fans, that includes casual fans, that includes as we've seen here in this ballpark young people out to meet and greet who want to just come out for a night of entertainment. So I don't know where all the meters are going to move on all these things in 10 years but to stay relevant and current is always a challenge and you just hope that we stay on top of it.

Bud Selig has truly been a leader in this type of thinking. Over the last 10-12 years we've brought in some very talented people into New York to work for Major League Baseball. By the time your book comes out the MLB Network channel will have launched within some 50 million homes. That will be the opportunity for some of your more hard core fans to get their game information that way. We hope that the fan experience coming here will still be enjoyable enough so that people keep on following the team.

What's the best decision you think you ever made as President of the Phillies?
I think the best thing we did was the research that went into Citizens Bank Park and the time we spent going to other parks and then incorporating the best things into ours. One of the nicest compliments we got as an organization were from the design architects of the ballpark. They told us that they never had another team pay as much attention to sightlines for our fans. We kept asking, "Well can't more people see if the aisle is moved to this side." And the suites, when you walk out of the suites there's 2 seats, the aisle is more in the middle rather than on one side or another because we realize if you're in a suite and you have to step over 5 or 6 people, you're not comfortable doing it. You're more likely to stand in the back. Well let's put the aisle in the middle. Well to do that you had to design the door differently, which in turn meant that we had to create a sliding glass door because we wanted the suites to be open on nice nights, etc. Things we sort of talked about it and decided it was worth the effort.

There's only one flaw I found in the stadium and that's Ashburn Alley which needed to be 20 feet wider.
That's true. Well as it turns out...two or three things I will freely admit that I wished we had caught. I mean we thought we were designing a fairer ballpark for the hitters and pitchers and with the benefit of hind sight, even though we did wind studies, the question we probably should have asked those people was how will the wind influence play at Citizens Bank Park as opposed to the way it did at the Vet. I think the reality is that the prevailing winds come out of the southwest; you won't see it as much when we get into this time of the year but in late May, June and early July the wind is almost always out of the southwest, which aids the hitter.

We probably didn't have 20 more feet to add to Ashburn Alley because of the street. Particularly if we moved the fences back another 8 or 10 feet or whatever it should have been. But we made the modest adjustment we could by moving the fences back a few years ago. It's interesting there's so much talk about our facility as you mentioned even as far as home runs, but I think as we sit here today our home runs home and road...I think they're pretty close. Look, there's not a ballpark that is going to hold Ryan and Pat when they hit them and conversely we have some pitchers that do give them up occasionally. They seem to leave Florida and Washington as much as they do here in Philadelphia. This group of players is always going to be a high home run team. I mean as effective as Cole Hamels pitches, the one thing he does do is give up the home run ball once in awhile. Robin Roberts is the all time owner of giving up gopher balls or something like that. And look at all the wins and effectiveness that he had.

What was the first Phillies game you ever went to?
I first one I have memory was in 1954. Bobby Adams was a third baseman for the Reds. He led off with a home run and Robin Roberts then retired the next 27 in a row. Funny thing about Roberts is that he is the reason why I got the opportunity to talk to Bill Giles. I was coaching out of Germantown Academy and I had the opportunity to coach Robin's sons. So one day I approached Robin and said, I wanted to work in sports, somebody was encouraging me to talk to like the Sixers and I had an opportunity to talk to somebody there and so I talked to Robin and I said "Who would I talk to in baseball?" and Robin said, "Well I'm doing a clinic next Saturday with a fellow by the name of Bill Giles. Why don't you come along and I'll introduce you?" I met Bill on a Saturday. He asked me what I was doing Monday. I had a job interview in the morning so I said to him, "May I come in the afternoon around 2:00pm?" He said, "Absolutely." By 3:00pm I took my coat off and have been here ever since.

If you can sit down with every Phillies fan for five minutes each, what would you tell them?
I would hopefully listen to them. I really would. I've had the opportunity to shape the ballpark experience and to some degree shape the team but the most important thing is that they're here. We do take input seriously. You get it from them. Sometimes you get it in the heat of the moment and it's a little less rational. But we try to do focus groups with season tickets customers. I can't participate as much as I used to but I try to. But then I guess I would emphasize one thing, and that is, as much as they care about winning, we care about it that much and then many times more. You wouldn't be in this if you didn't care that way. But beyond that I think it would be a matter of listening to hear what they have to say and hopefully improving the product for them. They're us. I was lucky enough to be them first and still am. Now I'm lucky enough to have a job where I get to be the ultimate fan.

Quotable: "We make a living by what we get, but we make a life by what we give." – Winston Churchill

Monday, July 28th - (Off) Record: (56-49) 2nd - ½ GB the Mets
Philadelphia – The Phillies are an extremely generous organization. It would seem that almost every home stand the Phillies are raising funds for people or organizations that have true needs. Through their charitable arm of the organization, Phillies Charities, they have raised millions of dollars on behalf of over 150 charities. The largest of which is for the ALS Association. Since 1984, the Phillies have made the ALS Association of Philadelphia its primary charity. At this year's 19th annual Phillies Phestival today a sellout crowd came out to Citizens Bank Park and helped raise a record $758,540. From its humble beginnings when they raised $4,500 in its first year of operations, the Phillies Phestival has now raised over $10.1 million dollars to battle ALS.

Gene Diaz is the Phillies' Director of Community Relations. He and his team help plan, set-up and run numerous charitable and community events around the Delaware Valley for the Phillies. Whether it's for a player's event, a baseball clinic or a community request, Gene and his team help keep the Phillies at the forefront of many of the philanthropic events in the city.

I'm basically in charge of the community activities of the club. One of my jobs is to try to get the players involved in different charities and organizations across the city. The great thing is that we already have several players that are deeply involved in charitable work.

Jimmy Rollins, Jamie Moyer, Geoff Jenkins, Shane Victorino and Chase Utley all have charity events that they run. We work closely with them as their representatives and help them run the event. Rollins and Utley have bowling tournaments. Victorino is having a golf tournament in Hawaii in November, Jenkins had a poker tournament and Moyer has a Celebrity Waiters event where the Phillies players actually serve food to guests in the Diamond Club. Each of the guests pay $250 to be a part of the evening and they literally have

Gene Diaz inviting fans to bid on items that will benefit one of the many charities that the Phillies support

players delivering food to their tables. This year Moyer's event raised over $400,000. For each of these events we will help out with planning, getting them items that can be auctioned off, and financially supporting the event. These five guys alone will raise over $1 million dollars in just these five events.

My department is also responsible for handling all of the donation requests that the Phillies get every year. We get thousands of calls, emails, and letters from organizations looking for donations. We mostly help out by sending autographed items to them that they can use to raise money. So for example if you were running a charitable event we would possibly send you a bat signed by Pat Burrell. That could raise a few hundred dollars for them.

The costs of sending autographed items out can be quite expensive for the Phillies but we're committed to helping the community. Our thinking is that we can take a $12 bat and it gets autographed and send it to a charitable organization where they may be able to get $300 for it. As long as that $12 bat is given back to the community in some manner, we know it is going to be worth it to us and our fans.

We'll also get items signed by players from other teams. I don't do that myself; we usually have a clubhouse guy on the visitor's side that will ask the top players from other teams to sign things when they come in during the season. In turn, the same thing happens to our guys when they're on the road. So we'll auction off those items as well. You'd be surprised at how much money some of these items can raise.

Not everything is just raising money for charities though. We have a number of other programs that we run that will help inner city youth such as baseball clinics. Danny Martinez and Bill Kulik of the Phillies' Spanish broadcasting team had a program this past year where they brought in 200 Hispanic children for a hitting clinic with Milt Thompson. By bringing these kids to the ballpark we're not only helping them with their baseball skills but Danny will speak to them and encourage them to better citizens and to respect themselves.

We will also handle player appearances at local organizations like when they visit the Children's Hospital. Player appearances are a big one. We get asked a lot for players to come to charitable events. They can't do a lot of them because they are playing every day but we do have guys doing clinics or visiting the Little Leagues pretty frequently.

A Quick List of some of the Phillies Players Charitable Contributions in 2008:
- Romero's Rookies: JC Romero purchased $10,000 in Phillies tickets, food coupons and t-shirts for underprivileged kids.
- Lidge's Legions: Brad Lidge purchased tickets, concessions and caps for child cancer patients at Children's Hospital.
- Brett Myers donated $20,000 and raised thousands more during an autograph signing to help a four year old child in his home town of Jacksonville that has Treacher Collins Syndrome, a rare facial deformity.
- Utley's All-Star Animals: A casino night in which Chase and his wife Jen raised $200,000 for the Pennsylvania SPCA.

Quotable: "He was goofing off like usual. In some ways yeah, that's a good sign. Except don't piss the skipper off." - Charlie Manuel after Brett Myers expressed disdain on Manuel pulling him from the game after the 7th inning

Tuesday, July 29th - Phillies 2 Nationals 1 (57-49) 2nd - 1 GB the Mets
Washington D.C. – *Brett Myers (4-9, 5.46) appears to be back to his "ace" form as he allowed just one run in 7+ innings ... Chase Utley gave the Phillies all the runs they needed with a 2-run*

homerun (26) in the 3rd inning ... Utley and Pat Burrell each had two hits in the game ... JC Romero, Chad Durbin and Brad Lidge combined for two hitless and scoreless innings to closeout the game with Lidge racking up his 25th save in the process. Stuff: Adam Eaton was sent down to AAA to see if he can work out his pitching problems down there. Pat Gillick says that he will remain there until the September call-ups ... JA Happ was recalled from Lehigh to take Eaton's place ... Pedro Feliz was placed on the 15 day DL with a stiff back. In six games since the All-Star Break, Feliz is 1 for 21 (.048) ... The Phils recalled Mike Cervanek again to replace him on the roster ... Prior to tonight's win, Brett Myers was 0-6 with a 7.91 ERA on the road ... Wilmington Journal Beat Writer Scott Lauber reported that Jimmy Rollins continues to ignore reporters after games and has made a point of showing up just in time to beat Manuel's arrival deadline. Lauber wrote that, "he affects a body language that indicates he doesn't much care what anyone thinks of it. If his teammates aren't tired of the act, you can be sure the front office is."

A corresponding roster move to fill Eaton's spot on the 25-man roster will be made prior to Tuesday's game against the Nationals. Eaton, 31, was 4-8 with a 5.80 ERA in 21 games (19 starts) for the Phillies this season. His last two appearances came in relief.

The revolving door ushers another veteran to the minors; only this time, the current could make it more difficult for Eaton to spin his way back into the Majors. Best case scenario for Eaton: he performs well and earns his way back when rosters expand in September, but I wouldn't necessarily count on it.

Courier Post Beat Writer Mike Radano questions Phillies' pitching coach Rich Dubee on the decision to send Adam Eaton down to AAA - Lehigh

The Phillies took the three-game series from a thoroughly second-rate Atlanta Braves team yesterday, but questions about the makeup of the pitching staff linger, including the future of a failed starter.

There's nothing like watching live baseball to appreciate the nuances of the game. For example, the fury unleashed upon two grooved Adam Eaton pitches in the fourth inning. You can't appreciate that on television. Watching Kelly Johnson and Omar Infante's blasts carve through the storm-soaked air left little doubt. It's time for the Phillies to free Philadelphia from the Eaton burden.

The back-to-back jacks left an impression on the front office, too, and one can only hope that it's the final impression Eaton is allowed to make in a Phillies' uniform. According to the Inquirer's Bob Ford, the team brass met with the displaced right-hander behind closed doors following the game.

A two-hour rain delay threw a wrench into the Phillies' plans, but even before that, the pitching staff was skewed out of whack. They were using a valuable roster spot just to hold a player in limbo, but Eaton isn't the only pitcher who isn't performing. Rudy Seanez's tenure may have run its course. The veteran served his purpose at the beginning of the season, but is not cut out for the stretch run, where he'll need to pitch back-to-back games every once in a while. Seanez allowed four runs, one earned, as the Braves climbed back from the dead yesterday.

These are questions that could be resolved between now and Thursday's non-waiver trade deadline. I've been saying for months that despite their performance for most of the season, additional bullpen help wasn't a bad idea. Now, they need to do it.

As for Eaton, if I were in his shoes, I wouldn't accept a minor league demotion. But if I was Pat Gillick, I wouldn't give him the option. There's nothing to resurrect. It's time for the relationship to end, plain and simple.

Pitching stuff: It was a crazy, high-scoring game, but Clay Condrey's fifth and sixth innings shouldn't be forgotten. After the Phils tied it up, Condrey kept Atlanta off the board for two innings, earning the win as a result of Pat Burrell's fifth inning homer. Condrey is all right by me; he's done a very nice job in myriad situations this season. ... I would be fine with Happ becoming the new long man and second left-hander out of the pen. His minor league training is over - there's nothing left to prove or learn. Many other teams ease starting pitchers to the majors this way.

Quotable: "(Victorino) hit some balls hard tonight. (His power) might be coming from his lips. He's got a lot of wind to him doesn't he?" - Charlie Manuel after Shane Victorino's 3 hit, 3 RBI performance

Wednesday, July 30th - Phillies 8 Nationals 5 (58-49) 1st - ½ GA of the Mets

Washington D.C. – The Phillies scored 5 runs in the 5th off of the Nationals' Tim Redding to take a 7-2 lead that led to the eventual win that moved them back into sole possession of first place in the NL East ... Jamie Moyer won his 10th game of the season against 6 losses. He pitched 6 innings giving up 3 runs on 6 hits ... Brad Lidge earned his 26th save of the year ... Shane Victorino went 3 for 5 with a homerun (9) and 3 RBIs ... Chase Utley hit his 27th homer while going 2 for 4 with 2 RBIs. Stuff: SS Jayson Donald and C Lou Marson of the Reading Phillies left today to participate in the 2008 Summer Olympics for Team USA in China ... Moyer has now allowed 3 or less runs in 10 consecutive starts ... The Phillies are now 47-0 when leading after 8 innings this season.

Scheduling yourself and your family for a vacation trip is not an easy task. You have to find the best prices to fly your family to your destination. You have to figure out transportation and then make sure you get a nice hotel. You practically need a vacation just for planning your vacation. Now just imagine that you have to plan these "vacations" thirty or so times a year. Oh, I forgot to mention that you to also do it for fifty other people, many whom are millionaires, and you can't screw up … ever!

Welcome to the world of Frank Coppenbarger, the Phils' Director of Team Travel & Clubhouse Services.

From Fans Field To Philadelphia

...With a Few Stops Along the Way

By Frank Coppenbarger
As told to J. Thomas McNamara

This is my 20th season now with the Phillies. Prior to coming here I worked eight seasons with the St. Louis Cardinals as their Assistant Equipment Manager. I started in professional baseball quite early. As a 10-year-old kid, I was the batboy for a Class A farm club with the San Francisco Giants in my hometown of Decatur, Illinois. I've been involved with baseball one way or another ever since. This is now my 39th year in professional baseball.

Frank Coppenbarger has written a book on his travels from Decatur, Illinois, to Philadelphia

I'm not only responsible for running the clubhouses but I'm also in charge of all the team travel. Each season we have 27 series at home and 27 series on the road. There are always 81 home games and 81 road games and we spend 4 to 5 off days on the road. So the team probably spends 85 nights in a hotel during the season. On top of that you spend another two months down in Spring Training. So basically about five months of the year is spent on the road outside of Philadelphia.

When the club flies we charter an entire plane from Delta Airlines. They've been our sole carrier for the last four years. We use a 737-800 (seats approximately 160 seats) and then we use a little bigger plane, a 757-200 (seats 183) when we go out to the west coast.

The planes are pretty nice. As soon as the players board the plane we'll have food and drinks waiting for them so the can eat. Once we take off some players will just go to sleep. Some will watch TV, play video games, use their laptops or sit and talk to everyone. It's a great place for them to relax and be their own selves.

When the team gets on to the plane for the first time each year they kind of claim their seat location on the plane for the season. We don't have assigned seating per se but players generally sit in the same sections of the plane every year.

There was a little issue with some of the players a dozen years or so ago who thought that Harry Kalas shouldn't be sitting in the back of the plane. Usually that's reserved for the veteran ballplayers. But that didn't last very long. We put an end to that issue quickly. To this day Harry still has the last seat in the last row of the plane and he's been back there for the bigger part of over 30 years. I think Harry sits there just because he likes it. I think when he was younger and more the player's age he probably had a few smokes and drinks back there together with them. Sitting back there all of these years I guess he grew familiar with it and decided to make that his own little area.

Usually we will take anywhere between 50-55 people on the charter. The Beat Writers technically can go with us but they don't. We haven't had one in years. I think that's because there is a comfort or a discomfort level on both sides. I think they and their newspapers prefer that they take care of their own flights. Flying for them was never for free. The Phillies would charge the newspapers for the cost of the flight. So if you're going to pay to fly they might as well go when they want to go. In many cases the writers would have to shut their writing down and jump on board the charter because sometimes we leave immediately after the game is done. Maybe it's better for them to knock out their story and fly the next morning so they're not rushing.

Once we get to our destination we'll have two buses waiting for us. Bus #1 is for the manager, coaches, staff and front office types. Bus #2 is only for the players. Usually the rookies are tasked with having to carry all the beverages off of the plane for the veterans. They'll also have to carry the poker chips, the stereos and anything else the veterans can think of them to carry.

At the hotel we always have the keys laid out on tables. One table for staff, one for the players and one for the broadcast teams. Once the players arrive the luggage will be brought to them about 30 minutes after they get into their rooms. It's the first time the players will have touched their luggage since they dropped it off in the morning in the clubhouse.

I don't go out on the town with the players any more. I mean occasionally I run into a guy or something, but not really. Big age difference between us now. On the road, I usually go out with my guys and one or two of the coaches. Wheeler and I will do something sometimes as well, but as you get older you don't want to go out as much. I'm more than happy to go back to the room and have a glass of wine, put my feet up and watch some TV.

Major League Baseball doesn't tell the teams what hotels to use when we travel. Each team is on their own. If a hotel is doing things the way we want them to do it and the rates are good and there's no issues, then it's just automatically the same place year after year. The only problem is if there's a big convention or something like that at a hotel and we will go somewhere else. Knock on wood we've been fortunate and haven't run across that one yet, thankfully. Generally we'll go with a hotel that's got a good location; it's got shopping and restaurants and so forth. Most of the time we stay in the main downtown area.

When we go to play the Mets we take a bus. It's easiest just to get on a bus at Citizens Bank Park and just drive straight up to New York. If you took the train there you'd still have to bus everyone from the train station over to Staten Island and get in all that traffic anyhow.

When we go to Washington we take an Amtrak train. The train is chartered. What they'll do is they will set aside four rail cars that only the team sits in. It's kind of like a plane. There's a big first class car where Charlie, the coaches and Pat Gillick sit. The next car would be a club car. It's kind of like a cafeteria car with snacks and food. The next car is kind of like the coach section of an airplane, smaller seats. That's where some of the players sit. The last car is another snack area and kind of like a club car that has booths and card tables. Most of the guys hang out back there. The players really enjoy the train. I think they'd do it more often if they could.

My favorite city we travel to is Chicago. In Chicago we stay at the Weston. It's a really nice place. I also like the Hotel Nikko in San Francisco. I also like the place that we stay at in San Diego because of the location. It's beautiful there. Sometimes it's not the hotel that you really look for but it's what's close by to the hotel that makes you like it for one reason or another. You look out the window and there's the bay right there in San Diego or the ocean in Miami. Those are nice hotels.

I really enjoy going to Dodgers Stadium. I just think it's just beautiful when you drive in there; it's so picturesque. We were just talking about this the other day. Just the layout, the look of it, the PA guy has got the best voice and the mountains in the background and the palm trees up on the hill up there behind the field. It's beautiful. You really feel like you're a major leaguer when you're there. They don't have the best clubhouse but for a road stadium it's the best.

RFK Stadium was my least favorite to visit when the Nationals moved to D.C. Probably now it's Shea Stadium but now that one's going to be gone as well so I'm glad I won't have to go to either of those places any longer. The amenities in the clubhouse aren't the greatest and they're relatively quite small. It's just not a place that you really want to be in for any length of time.

One thing the fans don't know about me? That I was once a professional baseball player. Back in 1978 I was a clubhouse manager for the Angel's Class A Salina team. One day the manager asked me if I wanted to play pro ball. I said, "Absolutely. Every kid wants to play pro ball." I was 23 at the time and I used to take a lot of batting practice for the heck of it. He said, "You're going to get a chance." I thought he was kidding but a few days later the team had me sign a 1 game contract. That day they put me in as the DH and batted me third. I struck out but I did hit two foul balls. The contract was for $1.00. I'll never forget that.

The most difficult part of this job is being away from your family. I have two kids and they're still fairly young. John is 13 and Caitlyn is 17. It takes a toll on the family life. It is a lifestyle, it really is. It's not a 9-5 job; it is a lifestyle. I don't think if you didn't like it you could survive with the amount of time commitment required. I do like the game but family can suffer from it and you miss so many things. You miss Little League games, dances, recitals and birthdays.

What do I like best about my job? I like to see all the different cities and see what they have to offer. I get out and go do things in towns. I've seen many of the sights in all of the towns that we've visited. A lot of players never do that. They're really missing something because for them it ends quickly. If you ask some of them what it was like in these towns they couldn't tell you. I get out. I try the restaurants out, the nightspots. I guess my favorite part of my job is that it's never boring. It's something different every day. I like the action. I'm not good at sitting around for long periods of time so I've got the perfect job.

Quotable: "I felt like after that first win against the Mets we had something going but we lost the next two and blew a great start by (Jamie Moyer). Then we lost to Atlanta. It's simple, when you hit, you look better and you have more energy. We've started to hit over these last five games." - Charlie Manuel on the Phils' 5-game winning streak

Thursday, July 31st - Phillies 8 Nationals 4 (59-49) 1st - 1 GA of the Mets

Washington D.C. – *The Phils completed a sweep of the Nationals scoring 8 runs on 11 hits while leaving 17 men on base in route to their fifth straight victory ... Kyle Kendrick (9-5, 4.59) pitched effectively going 6 2/3rd innings, allowing just 2 runs on 7 hits ... Jimmy Rollins led the way on the offense, going 2 for 4 with a homerun (8), 3 RBIs and 2 runs scored ... Jayson Werth his 15th of the season in the 2nd inning ... Shane Victorino and Ryan Howard had 2 hits apiece. Stuff: Adam Eaton got smacked around in AAA giving up 4 runs on 5 hits in 3 2/3rd innings ... Since Manuel's closed door meeting, the Phillies are 5-1. They are hitting .331 (57 for 172), scoring 40 runs and hitting 11 homeruns ... After the game Charlie said, "I don't know if the meeting has anything to do with it or not. It's a conversation piece I guess. The fact that you start winning is better." He added, "If we go 10-1 and we lose a couple, believe me, I'll have another meeting."*

The Phillies doubled up on the inferior Nationals 8-4. Kyle Kendrick (9-4) earned the win against a badly flawed lineup. It's just a brutal situation for Manny Acta's club, which has now lost nine in a row. As bad as the Nats are, John Lannan's been decent, so it's not like the Phils lit up a creampuff. Tim Redding isn't a creampuff, either.

I'm pleased with the way they've played this week, but it wouldn't be very "Beerleaguer" of me if I didn't nitpick about something. It was a little unsatisfactory to see Chad Durbin enter the game during an inning that started with the Phils up 8-2. Durbin has become a precious commodity. He's established himself as part of the big three with J.C. Romero and Brad Lidge. Unfortunately, this trio is starting to log some needless innings because parts of the bullpen are starting to crack and the starters haven't pitched as deep. Rudy Seanez has been hit very hard lately and I wonder if he's reached the end of the line.

Of course, the Phillies tried to get reinforcements yesterday at the trade deadline, but came up empty. The market crashed. Buyers universally denied the high asking price for mid-level relief.

Only the Marlins added bullpen help on a day that saw far more losers than winners.

According to reports, the Phils were close to a three-way deal to acquire a fourth-starter type, but details were not revealed. They'll come out eventually. Names like Bronson Arroyo spring to mind. In other words, no one close to the difference makers that relocated to the Cubs and Brewers in earlier deals. Along with the Yankees, who did more with less, and the rebuilding Pirates, who loaded up on young players that can become building blocks or off-season trade bait, they're the four winners in the deadline sweepstakes.

Jimmy Rollins' bat paved the road to victory with a homerun and 3 RBIs

August - Setting the Table

Quotable: "... ah yea. I think at some point we had a good feeling about it (getting Manny Ramirez)" - Pat Gillick as reported by Scott Lauber (Wilmington News Journal) that the Phillies were going after the Red Sox's Manny Ramirez

Friday, August 1st - Cardinals 6 Phillies 3 (59-50) 1st - 1 GA of the Mets

St. Louis – The Phils' 5-game win streak came to an end as Cole Hamels (9-7, 3.37) gave up 5 runs (4 earned) over 6 innings ... Ex-Phillie Kyle Lohse (13-3, 3.73) won his second game of the season against his former team as he threw 5 1/3rd innings, giving up 3 runs on 5 hits ... Pat Burrell drove in 2 of the Phils' 3 runs with a 2-run homerun (27) in the 6th ... The Cardinals' Ryan Ludwick was a one-man wrecking crew as he went 4 for 4 with 2 homeruns, 2 RBIs and 3 runs scored Stuff: Cole Hamels gave up 2 homeruns in the game and has now given up a total of 23 on the season, second in the league only to the Cubs' Ted Lilly (25) and Brett Myers (25) ... Ex-Cardinal So Taguchi got a standing ovation from the St. Louis fans when he came up to pinch-hit in the 7th ... Reliever Rudy Seanez was put on the 15 day DL after injuring his right shoulder after falling on it in last night's game ... 31-year old lefty Les Walrond was called up from AAA-Lehigh to replace him. Walrond's best game of the season with the Iron Pigs was against Louisville when he struck out 17 in a 5-hit complete game shutout.

There's nothing to like about win/loss statistics as a measuring stick for starting pitchers, but in the case of Hamels it paints a portrait of dysfunction from a team and pitcher that seem to be out of sync with each other. When he pitches well the bats go silent. When he's rocked, like last Saturday, they pull through. Hamels hasn't been getting the consistent run support he deserves, but tonight the loss was all his own.

With Rudy Seanez hitting the DL a lot of new faces are popping up in the Phillies' locker room lately

Hamel's fastball and change-up were up in the zone all night long and to their credit, the Cardinals made him pay. For all his talent, Hamels can really get hurt when he is out over the plate as was the case tonight when his fastball didn't move and his hanging change-ups were laid down the middle of the plate for the St. Louis lineup to knock all over Busch stadium. Just a forgettable night for the ace.

Turning to the offense, Charlie Manuel didn't have his best lineup on the field. Starting Eric Bruntlett at third was a mistake against a right-handed pitcher. He's a marginal defensive upgrade over Greg Dobbs at third but not enough to burden the lineup with another weak bat. Bruntlett fanned three times and committed a costly throwing error. It was an awkward game and Manuel didn't play his cards right.

Quotable: "Sometimes as a starter, those at-bats can kind of be the ones that make or break the game. I wanted to make tough pitches and hopefully make something good happen." - Joe Blanton on striking out Albert Pujols to end the 3rd inning

Saturday, August 2nd - Phillies 2 Cardinals 1 (60-50) 1st - 1 ½ GA of the Marlins

St. Louis – *The Joe Blanton trade has started paying dividends. Blanton (6-12, 4.94 on the season /1-0, 4.80 with the Phillies) threw 7 solid innings, striking out 5 and only allowing 1 run ... JC Romero, Chad Durbin and Brad Lidge pitched the final 2 innings, allowing no runs on 1 hit with Lidge getting his 27th save of the season ... All of the Phillies' runs came on solo homers off the bats of Greg Dobbs (4) and Ryan Howard (31) ... The Phils only managed a total of 4 hits against the Cardinals with the other two hits coming on a Chase Utley double and a Chris Coste single ... Ryan Howard walked 3 times in the game, including one intentional pass. Stuff: The Phillies promoted 21-year-old pitching prospect Carlos Carrasco to AAA – Lehigh. He was 7-7 with a 4.32 ERA at AA Reading ... Ryan Howard is now batting .363 with 12 HRs and 32 RBIs lifetime against his hometown Cardinals. Howard is from Wildwood, Missouri, which is about 35 miles west of St. Louis.*

On the verge of being swept by Houston, the Mets have suffered two more injury setbacks. Closer Billy Wagner will undergo a second MRI on his left forearm, while starter John Maine has been placed on the 15-day disabled list with a mild strain in his right rotator cuff. The Mets fell to the Astros 5-4 in 10 innings and are losing 4-0 in the 8th inning as of this writing. Should Houston hold on to win, the Mets will fall to 2.5 games in back of the Phils before the start of tonight's game. Not wishing any bad news to ex-Phillie Billy Wagner but if he goes down for any length of time the Mets are really going to struggle to find someone to nail down his closer role in the bullpen, which can only mean good things for the Phils.

The news on Billy Wagner isn't looking good for Mets fans

Quotable: "He seems a lot more like himself. He wants to get back to the way he's been. He's such a strong-minded guy. He doesn't like reaching out for help but I think going down [to the minors] was good for him. I'm happy for him because we need him. We need him, big-time." – Ryan Madson on his close friend Brett Myers

Sunday, August 3rd - Phillies 5 Cardinals 4 (61-50) 1st - 2 ½ GA of the Marlins

St. Louis – *Down 2-1 going into the 8th, the Phillies exploded for 4 runs capped by a 3-run homerun off the bat of Shane Victorino, his 10th of the year ... Chase Utley hit his 28th homer of the season in the 2nd ... Ryan Howard went 2 for 4 to raise his average to .242 ... Although he didn't get the win, Brett Myers pitched well, giving up 2 runs in 6 innings while walking none and striking out 3. Since his return, he is now 1-0 with a 2.50 ERA ... Chad Durbin (4-2, 1.77) got the win in relief ... In the bottom of the 9th Brad Lidge worked his way out of a bases-load jam to earn his 28th save of the year. He had given up a homerun to start the inning to cut the Phils' lead to one run. Stuff: Since the Jimmy Rollins benching, the Phils are 7-1 averaging 6.25 runs per game with an ERA of 3.68 ... The Mets lost their 5th game in the row and haven't scored in 16 innings. They are 3 games behind the Phils ... Tom Gordon began his rehab assignment in Clearwater. He threw 2/3rd of an inning giving up a 2-run homerun.*

If you've been to Citizens Bank Park you are sure to have seen the Turkey Hill Ice Cream Shuffle game. Usually it's played in the middle half of the 5th inning on Phanavision. Fans try to follow a baseball that is hidden underneath one of the three Turkey Hill ice cream containers. It's fairly easy to follow the ball at the start of the game but as the game speeds up and the containers mix together faster and faster you practically have to be Houdini to know where the baseball is when the game ends.

Rick Chestnut is the genius behind the Turkey Hill Ice Cream Shuffle

The creator of this animation is the Phillies' own Rick Chestnut. Rick Chestnut is the Video Graphics guru for the team who is also responsible for a number of fan favorite videos including the Motrin baseball Bloopers.

I created the Turkey Hill shell game about 3 ½ years ago after Turkey Hill came to the Phillies and asked if we could create an in-game promotion for their *Phillies Graham Slam Ice Cream* flavor. We quickly agreed that a "hidden ball" animation game would be a fun way for Turkey Hill to market their product and a great way to entertain the fans using the animation. .

I created the animation by building the ice cream carton, then the ball and then finally the background. Once Turkey Hill sent me the artwork for their Graham Slam Ice Cream carton I scanned it into my computer and then cut it up in a way that it would fit nicely around the 3-D animation software (3D Studio Max) that I use. One of its functions is to automatically take a regular picture and give it an elastic look and feel. Basically I just put that animation box around the artwork of the ice cream carton that I made and then animate the scene. Most of my animations are done on a pixel resolution of 848 x 480. That's the size of our Phanavision screen. There are literally hundreds of thousands of lights on Phanavision, all of them broken down between red, blue and green lights. With those three primary colors I can create any color in the entire color spectrum.

Once I finished the animations I then created three different endings for the game. During an actual game one of our technicians will choose one of the three animations (where the ball ends up in carton #1, #2 or #3) and then load it into the video system. The fans get a kick out of following the game and hoping that they picked the right container with the baseball underneath of it.

I'm basically a self-taught type of person. With this animation software I didn't have any formal training with it. If there's something that I want to do I'll step back and think through how I can get it done. I'll get a book on it or I'll find somebody who knows something about it. My brother's a computer geek so sometimes I'll call him up and say, "Hey, have you ever done this before or do you know anybody who does this?" I'm always looking for different ways of gaining knowledge. It's just the type of person that I am.

Mark DiNardo (Director of Video Services) is really the one who got me involved with all of this. He's not only responsible for Phanavision but also for all the in-park video and sound. He hired me as an intern back when we both worked across the street at the Wachovia Center. He taught me a lot about producing videos. Once I got the job here doing graphics they really didn't have anyone to do animations so I started doing stuff like this and it took off. .

I really enjoy working here. It's a family atmosphere. The people here are not only your co-workers but they're your friends as well. A good example is someone like (Phillies' President) David Montgomery. He knows my nickname from high school. We were in the draft room one day setting up one of the TVs for ESPN and I had my high school jacket on that says "Juice" on the back of it. David said to me, "Hey Juice. What does that stand for?" and I told him the story about how my classmates in high

Mark DiNardo, Director of Broadcasting and Video Services, keeps the Phanavision team running smoothly

school nicknamed me "Juice" because in Biology class the teacher said a chestnut is a fruit. Well because my last name is Chestnut, my best friend started calling me "Fruit". So one day, I was at lunch with a few of my friends and a guy walks over to the table and he says, "Hey Juice" to me. We all looked at him and I said, "Who's Juice?" He said, "Ain't that what they all call you?" and everyone started laughing and the name just stuck.

After I told David the story, he would call me "Juice" every now and then. I mean that's the kind of atmosphere it is here working for the Phillies. The general manager or the owner, they know your family, your nicknames, where you went to high school, college. They know a lot about you. They take that extra step just to get to know you as opposed to working for somebody else that really don't care. The people here aren't co-workers, they're family.

Quotable: "I don't know if I gave them (the Marlins) a chance (to change their game plan). My command was so poor that it really didn't matter." - Starter Jamie Moyer on being questioned whether the Marlins had to approach him differently after being 10-0 against them in his career

Tuesday, August 5th - Marlins 8 Phillies 2 (61-51) 1st - 1 ½ GA of the Marlins
Philadelphia – Jamie Moyer's perfect record against the Marlins came to a close as the Phils' starter gave up 2 runs on 6 hits while walking 3 in 5 innings of work. He is now 10-7 on the season … The Phils' bullpen weren't their stellar selves either as they gave up 6 runs in 3 innings. J.A. Happ pitched the 8th and 9th giving up 4 runs on 4 hits and two walks … Shane Victorino's 2-run homerun (11) in the 7th accounted for the only 2 runs for the Phils … Jimmy Rollins went 2 for 4. Stuff: Victorino's homerun was actually foul by a few inches. MLB is seriously considering allowing umpires to review questionable homerun calls with instant replay … Adam Eaton continued his march to oblivion in the minors as he allowed 6 runs in 3 1/3rd innings at AAA Lehigh … The Phillies are showing some interest in Cubs' reliever Scott Eyre who was released today. The lefty reliever was 2-0 with a 7.15 ERA with Chicago.

The most famous radar gun scout of all time was the Los Angeles Dodger's Mike Brito. Most old timers would recognize Brito if they saw him. He was the guy that used to stand behind home plate at Dodger Stadium wearing a white Panamanian hat with a huge cigar hanging out of his mouth. Brito was a fixture at Dodger Stadium as he handled the radar gun for over twenty years, tracking the speed of pitchers the likes of Oral Hershiser, Jerry Reuss and Fernando Valenzuela. Unfortunately due to the ever present need to generate more revenues for the team, the Dodgers added additional seating behind the home plate area of Dodger Stadium and replaced Brito with a mounted radar gun. Aah, progress. Nothing in baseball seems to be sacred any more!

In Philadelphia we have our own Mike Brito but he still captures the pitch speed with a manual radar gun. His name is Jon Joaquin. Jon's official role with the Phillies is as the

Coordinator for Fan Development as well as being in charge of the Phillies' Rookie and RBI Programs. One of the biggest kept secrets in the organization is that Jon gets more exposure on TV than anyone else in the organization. That includes Chase Utley and Jimmy Rollins! Take a close look the next time you watch a Phillies' home game. He's "the guy with the radar gun".

When I first started manning the radar gun I used to get calls on my cell phone all the time from my friends. They'd be leaving me messages telling me that they kept seeing me on TV. It's still pretty cool doing it but I don't get as many calls as I used to a few years back. I guess there's a bit of the celebrity aspect to it but I've never been stopped on the street and someone has said to me, "Hey you're the radar guy on the Phillies!"

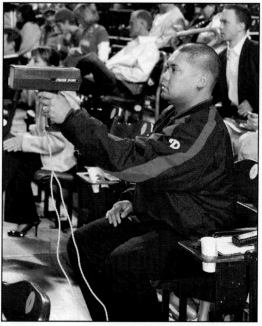

Jon Joaquin's radar gun keeps the fans and the coaches tuned into the pitcher's velocity

The fastest pitcher I've recorded on the radar gun was with Billy Wagner. He used to hit 100mph on the gun all the time when he was with the team. You didn't even have to look at the gun when he did it. You see the blur of his fastball and then hear the loud pop of the catcher's mitt. He was lightning quick. Hitters would just wave their bats at the ball when they were up against him. I don't think they even saw the pitch leave his hand.

The slowest pitcher I ever clocked was with Tim Wakefield of the Red Sox. He was throwing his knuckleball and it was only in the low 60s. He'd then come back with a 75 mph fastball and totally strike the guy out swinging. It goes to show you that anybody can pitch if they have good control and can dramatically change their velocity.

I get to see every pitcher that throws at Citizens Bank Park from April through September and into the playoffs. Probably the most complete pitchers that I've seen that just have incredible control are Jamie Moyer, John Smoltz and Tom Glavin. They might not be throwing some of the hardest things that you've seen, but they really know how to command their pitches and keep the hitters off balance. They basically have pitching down to a science.

The Phillies starting pitching speeds? Brett Myers hits 95 every now and then. I think he hit 96 this year. Hamels is about 92-93 but he has an incredible change-up that really fools the hitters. It's amazing that his arm speed looks exactly the same when he's throwing his fastball. His change-up comes in around 80 or 81mph. That's why he's so good. Moyer's fastball is about 84. Kendrick's hits 93 now and then. Eaton throws about 92.

Brad Lidge throws the fastest out of the bullpen. He has hit 97-98. Madson is the second fastest thrower at 96. Gordon throws about 91.

The fastest visiting pitcher I've seen this year was Matt Lindstrom of the Marlins. He hit 99mph. Joel Hanrahan of the Nationals hit 98 a few times. Papelbon of the Red Sox hit 97. They were quite fast but the funny thing was that the Phils could hit them.

Sometimes it's hard getting the right angle on the pitch because the umpire is in the way. It's a little bit harder doing it here at Citizens Bank Park than it used to be at the Vet because of where we sit but once you get adjusted you can pick it up without any problem.

Radar guns aren't always 100% accurate. You really need to know how to use them properly. That's why it's important to know the type of pitches the pitcher will throw and their usual speeds for each of their pitches. But most of the time the gun is right on.

There are two purposes for the radar gun in the ballpark. One is to capture the speed for the coaches. They get the speed and record it onto their video equipment that's in the video editing room behind the dugout. Sometimes the coaches will go in there during the game to see the velocity of the pitcher. The second purpose of the gun is to let the fans know how fast the pitchers are throwing. Back when Billy Wagner was here this place would go wild when he hit 100mph. Funny thing was the place would start booing if he only hit 99. You have to love Philadelphia fans!

After each pitch I use a walkie-talkie to call the Phanavision Room. I give them the speed of the pitch and the type of pitch that was thrown. They then record it and put it up around the ballpark. In this role, you have to know the types of pitches that a pitcher can throw and be able to recognize them when he throws them. It helps that I was a catcher in high school because you have to watch the angle that they throw, their arm speed, what the pitch does. You have to pay attention to every pitch.

I sit here from the beginning of every game to the very end. The worst game I ever had to sit through was back in April of 2007. It was freezing. I think it was in the high 30s. I had my heavy jacket on and my batting gloves. They didn't do much to help me because it took me forever to warm up after the game.

The best part about this job is that I literally have the best seat in the entire ballpark. You really can't complain. If you love baseball as much as I do this is just the most ideal job you could ever have. I could never think in a million years I'd be sitting here right behind home plate tracking pitches. I have seen some of the best pitchers to have ever played the game like Randy Johnson, Roger Clemens and Billy Wagner. I've enjoyed every minute of it.

Quotable: "Do you think (Arizona's) Brandon Webb cares if they know a sinker is coming? No. ... Now (Kendrick's) isn't that category necessarily but when he has the sinker he can go six scoreless like he did today." – Chris Coste telling reporters what he told Kyle Kendrick before the start of today's game

Wednesday, August 6th - Phillies 5 Marlins 0 (62-51) 1st - 2 ½ GA of the Marlins

Philadelphia – Kyle Kendrick (10-5, 4.22) threw 6 shutout innings tonight giving up 4 hits but walking 5 ... Chad Durbin and Ryan Madson threw 3 scoreless innings in relief for the combined shutout of the Marlins ... Ryan Howard went 2 for 5 on the day crushing his 32nd homerun in the 3rd inning. He now has 97 RBIs on the year ... Eric Bruntlett started the game at third base and went 2 for 3 with a double and a stolen base. Stuff: Rookie Mike Cervenak got his first major league hit ... Kendrick had 9 groundball outs in the game ... Tom Gordon complained of elbow discomfort again and is being shut down in Clearwater.

Kyle Kendrick allowed four hits and five walks but pitched around danger and benefited from some sharp defense. Like he's done many times throughout his short career, he was able do bear down when he needed to. The Philadelphia Inquirer compared him with Jamie Moyer and said they were the unappreciated heroes of the season. It's true, and they're also similar pitching-wise. Obviously, they don't throw electric cheese but although he walked five, Kendrick, like Moyer, can hit the mark when he needs to, and he usually avoids the middle of the plate. For someone who has not yet turned 24, his maturity is perhaps his greatest asset.

Hamels, who's gone off track in his last two starts, could learn a little from Kendrick. Hamels has been overthrowing lately and was tagged for four runs on eight hits and two homers in Friday night's start in St. Louis. Hamels' fastball, which is straight to begin with, was out over the plate all night, as was his change-up. When it happens, he's prone to the long ball.

Mike Cervenak got his first major league hit in today's game after spending 1,088 games in the minors

Hamels' mediocre 9-7 record would look a lot better if he received the kind of run support Kendrick's been getting. Hamels has received only nine runs of support over his last five losses. In those losses, he's posted a 3.25 ERA.

Quotable: "If you can figure why it happens, you come and tell me. When you send Hamels out there like we did today . . . I felt real good about this game, and we can't score. That makes it tough, but that's why we're inconsistent. - Charlie Manuel on why the Phillies never seem to score runs when Hamels pitches

Thursday, August 7th - Marlins 3 Phillies 0 (62-52) 1st - 1 ½ GA of the Marlins

Philadelphia – *Cole Hamels once again threw a quality start giving up 2 runs and striking out 7 in 6 1/3rd innings but failed to get the win as the offense seemed to have taken the night off again. Hamels is now 9-8 with a 3.35 ERA ... The offense could only muster 3 singles and a double off of the Marlins who used a total of 5 pitchers to throw the shutout. Stuff: When Hamels pitches, his team only averages 4.43 runs per game. That ranks him 40th out of 45 pitchers in the NL with at least 120 innings pitched. In Hamel's last 5 losses the Phillies have only scored 8 runs including getting shutout twice ... The Phils are now 5-7 against the Marlins and 4-9 against the Mets, a combined 9-16. Against everyone else they are 55-36 ... The Phillies acquired Cub lefty Scott Eyre for minor leaguer Brian Schlitter.*

Eyre, 36, who appeared in 19 games for the Cubs and has twice been on the disabled list with elbow and groin injuries this season, was let go by the Cubs less than two months after setting the franchise record of 33 consecutive scoreless innings. After his second stint on the DL, he returned to the club July 31st , allowing three runs in just one-third inning. He was let go by Chicago to clear space for Kerry Wood and became expendable due to the acquisition of Chad Gaudin and emergence of Jeff Samardzija. A veteran of 12 seasons with four clubs, he is 23-29 with a 4.42 ERA in 556 games (32 starts) with the White Sox,

Hamels pitched well but the Phils' bats fell silent once again for the Phils' ace

Blue Jays, Giants and Cubs. Over his career, he's held left-handed hitters to a .259 average and .244 average this season. He's in the final year of his contract. Schlitter, a 16th round pick in the 2007 draft, had a 2.22 ERA in 34 games with Clearwater.

With regards to the game, perhaps dominance isn't the right word for what the Marlins have done to the Phils, but it's something close. It's getting hard to ignore how the offense clams up when Hamels is going strong. What's going on there? And their 14-21 record in day games is also bizarre.

This team has issues. Getting shutout at home in a deciding game three against a division rival, with your ace delivering the goods, is pretty unacceptable. First place is still theirs, but this isn't the joyride of '07. Far from it. This business against .500+ teams makes their place atop the NL East just a wee-bit shallow, no? Not only are they starting to become tough to watch, they're uncomfortable to watch. And it stands to reason that it's getting a tad uncomfortable in that clubhouse.

Welcome to the funhouse, Scott Eyre.

Quotable: "We're still in first place. We have to keep looking forward. We dropped one tonight, but we have to keep looking forward." – Jimmy Rollins on the Phillies being shut out two consecutive games

Friday, August 8th - Pirates 2 Phillies 0 – 12inn. (62-53) 1st - 1 GA of the Mets

Philadelphia – After being shut out for the second time in a row, the Phils have now not scored in 23 consecutive innings ... Joe Blanton (7 IP, 1 hit, 0 ER) had his best performance since being traded to the Phillies but it wasn't enough as the offense could only muster 6 hits against the Pirates ... Jimmy Rollins and Shane Victorino both had two hits ... Pat Maholm of the Pirates struck out 10 Phils with 5 of them coming against Utley, Howard and Burrell ... The only scoring of the night came in the 12th off of reliever Les Walrond (0-1, 16.20) when the Pirates led off and combined two doubles to score the first run. Walrond was then replaced by Clay Condrey who then gave up the second run on two infield singles. Stuff: This is the second time this season that the Phils' offense has sputtered to a stop. The first time was a 17 inning drought that ended on May 20th ... The 23 inning dry spell is the longest for the Phillies since a 24 inning outage from September 1-3, 2000 ... The last time the Phils were shut out in two consecutive games was in September of 1999 ... The Phillies sent AJ Happ to the minors to make room for reliever Scott Eyre.

There have been over 2,000 baseball players that have been a part of the Phillies' organization in their 126-year history. Some like 92-year-old Ed Levy, who played for the 1940 Phillies, only appeared in one game as a pinch-hitter. Others like Hall-of-Famer Mike Schmidt, who holds the club record with 2,404 games as a Phillie, were fortunate enough to spend their entire baseball careers with the club. But no matter how short or long a career those players enjoyed, the Phillies' Public Relations team will always remember and honor them as Phillies.

Leigh Tobin is the Phillies' Director of Public Relations. She and Larry Shenk, VP Phillies Alumni and Senior Advisor, are responsible for ensuring that those Phillies are never forgotten. In addition to planning the Phillies Alumni Weekend they are also responsible for building a complete database of all Phillies' players past and present.

One of my roles in this position is to continuously update our list of alumni. Who's alive ... Who's dead ... Where they live. All of that type of information. We really want to get them more involved in the organization and build a legacy around them going forward.

Right now I am trying to put together a complete list of living players so that the Phillies can send them a card each year on their birthday. The bulk of my day is usually spent organizing all of this data, emailing people, calling them up. Just trying to make sure we get in touch with all of them.

Sometimes I feel like I'm a detective trying to track some of these players down. A lot of the times my primary goal for the day is to just make sure that the information we have is up to date. What I'm thinking of doing is taking the current list of players we have and going through my old address list and then working my way back because some of these older guys I'm never going to find.

The alumni program is really growing and we've had great response from the players. We currently bring back one alumni a month and have them do signings in the Hall of Fame Club. We've had players come in like

Leigh Tobin, Director of Public Relations, with Phillies' Hall-of-Famer Juan Samuel

Darren Daulton, Larry Christenson, Mike Rogodzinski, Bob Walk and Rico Brogna.

I've had Lee Elia (former Phillies' manager) call me and thank me for having him come back to the ballpark. He told me, "Don't forget to use me, don't forget to use me." That was nice. Keith Hughes (former outfielder – 1987) was grateful that I treated him like all the other players even though he only played 37 games with us. Going through these lists, we have at least one or two guys who only made a one pinch appearance or two but they are still a part of the Alumni program.

We are working on some programs that I think fans will like. We don't know exactly yet but we might steal an idea from the Blue Jays where they have flashback Fridays. They bring an alumni player back every home Friday game and they kind of dedicate it to the guy. He'll sign autographs for a little bit and they'll do scoreboard features with him.

I like meeting some of the older guys and making them feel important. I know the sun rises and sets with them when they're players, but when they're gone it's got to be an empty feeling. I've done my job if we can make them feel important. It really does make their day. Doug Clemens (of/1b 1966-68) couldn't thank me enough for Alumni Weekend. We had him and Keith Hughes go down and greet people at the gate and they had an incredible time.

When we bring the players back we always make up a jersey for them with an alumni patch on the sleeve. It makes them feel special and I think the fans who remember them really enjoy seeing them again because they probably haven't seen or heard about some of these guys in 20-30 years.

I have a few personal favorites myself. I really like Steve Carlton. I still have the most respect for him. I liked the fact that he said he wasn't going to talk to the media back in the 70s and he stuck by his guns, plus he was a hell of a pitcher. Although I didn't see him pitch, I enjoy being around Robin Roberts as a person. He's a kind man. Rico Brogna is one of my favorite people of all times. My first really favorite player that I worked with was Larry Anderson because he treated me like a person and that made me feel special.

The Alumni program is still in it's infancy but it will continue to grow. I think the Red Sox alumni are proud to be Red Sox alumni. Even the Pirates have a very good program, but not too many teams have good alumni programs. My goal is to not leave anyone out so I'm going to make the whole list of everyone who's ever played for us and try to find them all. I want Phillies' alumni to be proud that they are part of the Phillies' family.

Leigh's list of players include a lengthy number of them that are well into their 90s. Listed below are the ten oldest living Phillies in order of age as of 2008:

1)	Art Mahan	6/8/13	1b	1940	age: 95
2)	Gene Corbett	10/25/13	Inf.	1936-38	age: 95
3)	Stan Benjamin	5/20/14	Inf/of	1939-1942	age: 94
4)	Tommy Reis	8/6/14	p	1938	age: 94
5)	Alex Pitko	11/22/14	of	1938	age: 94
6)	Nick Strincevich	3/1/15	p	1948	age: 93
7)	Freddy Schmidt	2/9/16	p	1947	age: 92
8)	Danny Litwhiler	8/31/16	of	1940-43	age: 92
9)	Ed Levy	10/28/16	ph	1940	age: 92
10)	"Moon" Mullen	2/9/17	Inf/c	1944	age: 91

Quotable: "I wanted to stay in." - Brett Myers on why he went nose-to-nose with Charlie Manuel in the dugout after being pulled in the 8th.

Saturday, August 9th - Phillies 4 Pirates 2 (63-53) 1st - 1 GA of the Mets

Philadelphia – *Finally some runs ... The Phillies banged out 10 hits, 6 of them from the top two positions in the batting order to beat the Pirates ... Jimmy Rollins led the charge going 4 for 4 with 2 triples and 2 runs scored and Shane Victorino went 2 for 3 with a double and 2 RBIs ... Ryan Howard went 1 for 3 and knocked in his 98th RBI of the season ... Brett Myers (5-9, 5.09) con-*

tinued his excellent pitching since returning from the minors going 7 2/3rd innings, allowing only 1 run while striking out 6. Unfortunately the main event with Myers was him going nose-to-nose with Charlie Manuel in the dugout after getting pulled ... JC Romero finished out the 8th and Chad Durbin pitched the 9th for his first save as a Phillie and the second of his career. Stuff: The Phils are batting an anemic .232 in their last 11 games but the pitching staff's ERA is a mighty 2.94 ... Robin Roberts number was officially retired in pre-game ceremonies, this time in front of the fans. Back in 1962 the Phillies invited Robert's out to lunch during Spring Training to a restaurant in Tampa where the Phillies were playing the Yankees. During the lunch the Phils officially retire Robert's number 36 with about 6 people in attendance. So to make it up to him 46 years later, the Phillies invited the 81 year old Hall-of-Famer to Citizens Bank Park for Alumni Weekend to officially retire his number in front of a sold out crowd of 45,060.

Charlie Manuel isn't regarded as the greatest tactician, but he's one of the best at quashing controversy by handling hot tempers and large egos. Manuel and starter Brett Myers, who pitched a fine ballgame, exchanged words after Manuel lifted Myers after 7 2/3rd strong innings. By the time Manuel and Myers addressed the media afterward, the issue appeared to be smoothed over, at least publicly.

Charlie Manuel and Brett Myers went toe-to-toe in the dugout after Manuel lifted Myers in the 8th

"He's fine," Manuel told Michael Radano of the Courier Post. "He just wanted to stay in the game and I like that. There's nothing wrong with that. In fact, if he didn't want to stay in the game, I'd probably be mad."

"It's my fault," Myers said. "It's patched up. We're buddies."

Whatever, dudes. In any event, the Phillies finally gave fans an opportunity to notice how good the pitching has been lately, rather than boo the pants off of the offense. It's Pittsburgh, but the pitching staff has been sharp and largely mistake-free, and early signs show that the minor league demotion worked in reviving Myers' confidence. That's good news for a team that also saw a fine outing by Joe Blanton yesterday, his second quality start in a row.

Quotable: "I'm not going to rule it out if I'm still able to be effective. I have an obligation here that I plan on upholding next year with the Phillies, so I will be back at 46. Hey, 50 is five years away. It's not something I'm ruling out." - Jamie Moyer on the potential of pitching in to his fifties.

<u>Sunday, August 10th - Phillies 6 Pirates 3 (64-53) 1st - 2 GA of the Mets</u>

Philadelphia – *Greg Dobbs' pinch-hit double in the 7th tied the game at 3-3, which was then followed up by a Chase Utley 2-run homerun (29) to give the Phils the lead … The ageless Jamie Moyer threw well again, going 6 innings and giving up 3 runs while striking out 5 … Scott Eyre (3-0, 6.94) pick up his first Phillie win, pitching a scoreless 1/3rd of an inning in the 7th … Ryan Madson pitched the 9th for his first save of the season … The Phillies only had 7 hits in the game, 2 off the bat of Carlos Ruiz, but managed to still squeeze across the 6 runs. Stuff: Dobbs' double was his 21st pinch hit of the season, breaking the Phillies' all-time pinch-hits in a season record previously held by Doc Miller of the 1913 Phillies … Chase Utley broke an 0 for 12 with his homerun. He only batted .182 during the Phillies' 3-3 home stand, going 4 for 22 and leaving 21 runners stranded on base … Pat Burrell went 0 for 17 in the home stand … Ryan Howard went 5 for 24 … Brad Lidge remained unavailable to pitch for a second straight game because of shoulder tendonitis.*

Approximately 10 miles northeast of Citizens Bank Park along the Delaware River in the town of Palmyra lay one of the best kept secrets in all of baseball. The secret source of *Lena Blackburne's Baseball Rubbing Mud.* The mud that almost every professional and collegiate team in the world uses to remove the shine off of their baseballs.

The Pennsauken Creek is one of the many tributaries that feed into the Delaware River. Located on the Jersey side of the river in Burlington County, the creek runs through the towns of Moorestown, Maple Shade, Cinnaminson, Pennsauken and Palmyra

Dan O'Rourke uses mud from New Jersey to rub up the baseballs before every game

where it then dumps its mineral filled waters into the Delaware. Along the way the water pulls just the right amount of deposits from the banks of the creek and dumps it ever so gently just behind the old Pennsauken Drive-In theatre near the Tacony-Palmyra Bridge. It's here that the major league mud lies until it finds its way into the clubhouses of every major league team in baseball.

The story of *Lena Blackburne's Baseball Rubbing Mud* starts way back in 1938 when an umpire complained to Philadelphia A's 3rd base coach Lena Blackburne about the conditions of the baseballs that they were using in the American League. Back then teams created their own mud using water and dirt from the playing field but the mix left the baseballs too soft and vulnerable to tampering. Blackburne took it upon himself to find a solution and set off into the Pennsauken Creek back behind his house in Palmyra, looking for something that would work. What he found in the bottom of the creek was a gritty mud that looked more like chocolate pudding than anything else. He brought it to the park the next day, rubbed it on a few balls and it worked beautifully. Soon thereafter teams began clamoring for the mud so Blackburne started digging buckets of the "black gold" and began selling it to American League teams and a business was born.

Today the mud is still so superior to any other mud on the planet that it is being used to rub up all the baseballs in every major and minor league park in the United States and Canada. Even the Phillies' clubhouse manager Dan O'Rourke would have to agree that the mud is something special. He knows because it's his job to mud up all of the balls for the umpires prior to every home game.

My title is the Manager of Equipment and Umpire Services. I basically have the same job that Phil Sheridan has. He's the manager of the home clubhouse. We both have the same job; the only difference is I also take care of the umpires.

I started working for the Phillies part time in 1985 all the way through 1990. Then in July of 1990, I was offered a full-time position with the Astros and I jumped on it. I was 23 years old; it was full-time with benefits. I just packed and left. I spent ten years with them and then came back to this job when it was offered to me.

Part of my responsibilities include rubbing up all of the balls for every game. At the beginning of each season we get two containers of Lena Blackburne Original Baseball Rubbing Mud. One goes to spring training and when we come back from spring training one is sent here at the beginning of the season. The first two are free of charge but we usually only go through two containers a season. Each of the containers hold about 30-32 ounces of mud.

Frank Coppenbarger taught me how to rub up the baseballs properly. Believe it or not there is somewhat of a technique to putting it on the ball. First you take a couple of dabs of the mud and just get a little bit of water and mix it into your hand. You then take a baseball and rub the entire ball until it is covered. I can usually do three baseballs before I go back and dip again into the container.

The Rawlings balls are very slippery when they are shipped to us. You really have to rub the ball down hard to get the shine off of it. Sometimes the leather on the balls are a bit different and the mud just doesn't take to it well. When that happens you have to stop, apply more mud and really rub it in to the ball hard. You know you've done a good job when the mud dries and it leaves a fine thin layer of grit on the ball.

It's an imperfect science as to the amount of grit you are supposed to have on the ball. I hear about the consistency of the amount of mud on the ball all the time. Pitchers like them dark. I think primarily for the grip. My first year with the Astros, I was in charge of the balls and I met Doug Harvey, the umpire. I was in awe of him. He was probably the best umpire in the game at the time. When he came into the room, I didn't say a thing. He treated me very nice, he called everybody young man. So my ball bag was half the size that it is today. I had it all done and ready to go. He said, "Let me see the balls son." So I showed him the balls. He then dumps them out onto a chair, and I got balls rolling all over the umpire's room. He goes, "Son, come over here and let me show you how to rub a ball." So I'm like alright, OK, it's Doug Harvey I'll listen to whatever he says. He says to me, "Alright, you want a dark ball, I'll show you how to get you a dark ball." He then proceeds to make the balls really dark.

Well the next day Jerry Crawford had the plate. The Astros were playing the Reds and Barry Larkin steps into the box. Strike one goes right by him and he looks back to Jerry and says, "Jerry, those balls are too dark, I couldn't see that." Jerry reached into his bag and said, "Hey, they're all dark today, get in the box."

Before a series starts I'll rub up about 11 dozen baseballs and fill the baseball bag up in the umpire's room. We probably go through 10 dozen balls a game. Once the game starts, I'll come back to the room and knock out another 10 dozen so we'll have them for the next game.

We go through a lot of balls. Think about it, after every inning at least one of the balls goes into the stands so that's about a dozen and a half balls a game. Then there are all of the foul balls and homeruns that end up out of the playing field. When the relievers come in it seems that we go through a lot of balls with them. I guess the batters are protecting the plate a bit more and they foul off a lot of pitches. But when you get guys like Lidge coming in and throwing a hard slider the batters are usually just trying to get a piece of it and they end up fouling a lot of them off.

What's funny is when you're watching the game and you see kids hooting and hollering that they got a ball. All I'm thinking is that's just one more ball I have to rub up.

The most balls we've ever gone through in a single game is about 12 dozen balls. There was a time I remember when we played the Orioles on a fireworks night. I think we played like 14 innings. And I don't think the players came off the field until quarter to one in the morning. I had to keep rubbing up balls all night long.

When I'm done rubbing the balls the mud really gets caked into your hands. I actually have to use a stiff brush to get it off of me. To be honest I really wouldn't say that I enjoy rubbing them up. It's kind of boring so I'll pass the time watching TV while I'm going through them.

Quotable: *"They've got a tough lineup now. Not only Manny (Ramirez), but (Casey) Blake. That gives them more balance in their lineup. That gives them a better hitting team. They're tough." - Charlie Manuel on the Dodgers 4, 5 and 6 hitters that knocked in 7 of the Dodgers 8 runs*

Monday, August 11th - Dodgers 8 Phillies 6 (64-54) 1st - 2 GA of the Mets

Los Angeles – *Kyle Kendrick (10-6, 4.74) was bombarded by the Dodgers as he was only able to make it into the 4th, going a total of 3 1/3rd innings giving up 7 runs on 9 hits while walking 3 … Down 7-1 at one point, the Phillies made a go of it scoring 5 runs in the final 4 innings but weren't able to catch up … Jimmy Rollins and Shane Victorino each had two hits … Chase Utley went 3 for 5 with two RBIs (82) … Ryan Howard went 0 for 5 but did knock in two runs. He now has 100 RBIs on the season. Stuff: Howard is only the second player in franchise history to have three straight 30 HR/100 RBI seasons. The only other to accomplish that feat was Chuck Klein (1930 – 1932) … Kendrick was 2-1 with a 1.45 ERA in his last three starts before tonight, the worst start of his young career.*

If you are an Acrophobiac (have a fear of heights) and an Ancraophobiac (have a fear of wind) or an Aeroacrophobia (have a fear of open high places) you probably wouldn't want to be Brian Walsch. Brian is an electrician at Citizens Bank Park whose job isn't the most difficult in the world, but its close. He's responsible for replacing all of the burned out lights high above Citizens Bank Park.

I was part of the crew that actually helped build Citizens Bank Park. We worked out of the union hall, Local '98 of the IBEW, International Brotherhood of Electrical Workers. At the

Citizens Bank Park has great lighting – But who wants to climb those towers to change the bulbs?

time the ballpark was going up we were working as a subcontractor for all the electrical work that needed to get done here. Once the ballpark was completed and the Phillies were ready to start the season, they were looking to hire maintenance staff so I went through a big interview process with Global Spectrum and ended up getting the job.

There are four of us that are responsible for all of the electricity in the park. All the outlets, all the lighting, all the fire alarms. We also maintain the generators outside that provide the emergency power. We're also responsible for all the street lighting and the parking lots all around the ballpark. We do all the neon work around the ballpark, all the signage on the roof. If it's electrical, we support and fix it.

One of the more interesting things that I am responsible for is ensuring that all of the lights above the field are working. There are a total of six towers. One in left field. Two along the third base line. Two along the first base line and one out in right field. All the towers have three tiers. Each tier contains 33 lights. That's 99 lights per tower. We have an extra tier on the scoreboard tower so there are 132 lights on that tower.

To light the field we use Sylvania 2000 watt Metal Halide bulbs. There are a total of 624 bulbs that, when fully lit, give off 94,000,000 lumens.

A lumen is the amount of light a bulb gives off. If you have a 100-watt light bulb in your house it gives off about 1,500 lumens. So the total lumens in the ballpark would be equivalent to having 65,000 100-watt light bulbs turned on. It's a lot of light.

When a bulb goes bad we have to climb up into the towers to replace them. The towers are about 300 feet above the ground so they are up there pretty high. During the season we probably go up and replace blown bulbs about once every 2-3 weeks.

It's not as simple as replacing a bulb in a lamp in your house. The lights are extremely involved. Often times it's not just a burned out lamp but one of the components of the entire bulb. There are transformers in there, capacitors, you've got all kinds of different control fuses. If you lose a fuse it's the same thing as the lamp going out. There are resistors, different things like that. If a transformer goes bad they weigh about 40 pounds each so we have to lug them up there and replace them. It's a lot of fun.

When we climb up there we always wear a safety harness. The towers have a 70-foot ladder built into them that allow us to go all the way to the top. When we're climbing them you can't carry anything in your hands, so you have to put all of your parts in a backpack and haul it all up along with all of your tools.

If we count two blown bulbs in a tower we will bring everything we need to completely replace both of them. That way we only have to go up once and not keep on going back and forth looking for the right part. The most we ever had to fix at one time in a single tower was four bulbs. That was a heavy backpack.

What's it like up there? It's fantastic. On a windy day the towers sing. You can hear the wind whistling though the towers and it makes a beautiful sound all day long. On a clear day, it's absolutely beautiful. You can see straight through to Center City. You can almost look inside the windows of the high-rises. Our scoreboard tower is so high that you can actually see down into Lincoln Financial Field.

I think fans would really enjoy going up into the towers. On a nice day, you get the beautiful sunshine and a really nice breeze. On days like that I think of all the people that are shoved in their cubicles with their mouse pads and I feel bad for them. That type of job would drive me crazy if I had to sit there all day and look out the window when it's so nice outside. I'd much rather be up on top of one of the towers.

Quotable: "It all evens out. If he keeps pitching the way he's doing we're going to score some runs. It's unfortunate because he's had tough luck." - Pat Burrell on the lack offense the team generates when Cole Hamels pitches

Tuesday, August 12th - Dodgers 4 Phillies 3 (64-55) 1st - 1 GA of the Mets

Los Angeles – *The Dodgers' Andre Ethier singled home the winning run in the bottom of the 9th off of reliever JC Romero (4-4, 2.30) who took the loss in 1/3rd innings of work ... Romero hit Russell Martin to start the inning. Martin was then sacrificed over to second and then scored on a single by Ethier to end the game ... Cole Hamels continued pitching well on a team that doesn't give him run support. He threw 7 innings only giving up 2 runs while striking out 7 ... Reliever Chad Durbin blew a 3-2 lead as he loaded the bases with no outs in the 8th when Casey Blake hit a sacrifice fly to center to tie the game at three ... Chase Utley hit his 30th homerun in the 1st ... Cole Hamels went 1 for 3 with an RBI. He is batting .281 on the season. Stuff: Jimmy Rollins stole his 30th base of the season ... Tom Gordon is officially done for the year with a blown elbow ... Shane Victorino left the game in the 7th with lower back stiffness after striking out.*

The tone of the fans and their mood all point toward waning expectations.

It's getting hard to justify five hours of sleep to stay up and watch the same problems manifest into six hits, three runs and another Cole Hamels loss. How many times can one identify the holes? My apologies if their record, in comparison to where they were at this point last season, does nothing to soothe anxieties over two months of offensive strife and mounting injuries. By October, they may be the team left standing in the National League East. It's very possible. The Mets and Marlins, who trail the Phils by 1 and 1.5 games respectively, have the same number of holes. The Phils need to do whatever it takes to upgrade the offense because the scale

Phillies fans aren't exactly confident that their team is going to make it in to the playoffs

can still be tipped. In the meantime, we endure nights like this. Wouldn't it be nice to just fast-forward to October to see which team successfully backed their rental car into the post-season?

Quotable: "It can be, yeah. There are times, like, it (Philadelphia) is one of those cities. I might catch some flack for saying this, but, you know, they're front-runners. When you're doing good, they're on your side. When you're doing bad, they're completely against you." – Jimmy Rollins with his take on Phillies fans on the "The Best Damn Sports Show"

<u>Wednesday, August 13th - Dodgers 7 Phillies 6 (64-56) Tied for 1st with the NY Mets</u>

Los Angeles – *The Phillies blew an early 6-1 lead as Joe Blanton and the bullpen couldn't keep the Dodgers' offense in check ... Ryan Howard (33), Greg Dobbs (5) and Jayson Werth (16) all hit 2-run homeruns to account for all 6 of the Phillies runs ... Joe Blanton gave up 4 runs in 5 innings pitched ... Chad Durbin gave up 2 runs in 2/3rds of an inning in the 8th to allow the tying runs to score ... Clay Condrey (3-3, 3.71) took the loss, allowing a walk-off homerun to Nomar Garciaparra in the bottom of the 9th . Stuff: Shane Victorino didn't play because of back pain ... Ryan Howard continued his consecutive games played streak to 235 - the longest in the majors ... With the three homeruns today, the Phils lead the NL with 164 ... for the 8th consecutive year the Phillies have at least 6 players with double figures in homeruns. The all-time record for the team is 9 players back in 2004.*

Jimmy Rollins was asked his opinion of Philadelphia sports fans on *"The Best Damn Sports Show Period,"* a rubbish talk show that's syndicated to fill space on Fox Sports and Comcast outlets. Here's what he had to say:

"It can be, yeah. There are times, like, it's one of those cities. I might catch some flack for saying this, but, you know, they're front-runners. When you're doing good, they're on your side. When you're doing bad, they're completely against you." When the show's co-hosts argued that many cities fit that description, Rollins said: "I hear you. But, for example, Ryan is from St. Louis, and St. Louis, it seems like they support their team, they're out there and encouraging." – Jimmy Rollins

Jimmy Rollins told a sports cable show that he thinks Phillies fans are front-runners!

The comments become the latest controversy surrounding the 2007 MVP. These issues are getting lumped together in a dangerous way, and it's a shame. J-Roll has become the new boogieman in town, the latest in a long line of great Philadelphia athletes to become vilified after setting new heights. Less than a year after sailing into third for his 20th triple of the season, capping the club's first playoff berth since 1993, there's a different portrait being painted of him now, mastered by typical Philadelphia fandom.

J-Roll's problems are threefold and should be viewed separately: There were the benchings, which are disappointing, but ultimately, forgivable.

There are the comments about fans, words spoken out of frustration, and the difference between St. Louis, where banjo-hitting reservist So Taguchi received a 20-second standing ovation in their last visit, and Philadelphia, where the cheers are muted and mixed with boos for the best shortstop in franchise history. Sometimes the truth hurts, even if the topic should be taken off the table. Sometimes it pays to have a thicker skin, on both sides of the fence.

Last, but not least, there's his drop-off in production, and by extension, the struggles of the team, and if you want to get to the bottom of fan unrest in Philadelphia, look no further.

"When you're doing good, they're on your side. When you're doing bad, they're completely against you."

Quotable: "We got outpitched, outplayed, out everything. You don't get swept in a series if the other team doesn't outplay you, you know?" - Brett Myers on the Dodgers four game sweep of the Phillies

Thursday, August 14th - Dodgers 3 Phillies 1 (64-57) 2nd - 1 GB the Mets
Los Angeles – *The Dodgers swept all four games from the Phillies pushing them out of first place in the NL East ... Brett Myers (5-10, 5.02) pitched well enough once again for the win (7 IP, 3 ER, 8 K) but the Phillies' offense continued to sputter out on the West Coast ... The Phils only managed two hits off of starter Hiroki Kuroda and reliever Hong-Chih Kuo; a double each by Chase Utley and Jayson Werth ... The lone Phillies run came off the bat of Ryan Howard in the 7th when he hit a sacrifice fly to score Jayson Werth. Stuff: This was the first four game sweep of the Phillies in LA in 46 years ... The offense hit a paltry .194 in the series and are only batting .204 for the entire month of August ... the Dodgers hit .311 in the series ... With the two doubles, the Phils now have at least one extra base hit in 47 straight games.*

Someone must have taken Jimmy Rollins aside and let him know that his comments are causing quite a stir with the "front running" fans back in Philly. So much so that Rollins gave "The Best Damn Sports Show Period" a call again today to clarify his comments. The following is a transcript from the show as Rollins is interviewed by hosts Chris Ross and John Salley ...

Asked if he was surprised about the fans' reaction:

"Actually, very surprised. People take things and use them in whichever way they use, but yeah, I'm

definitely surprised....I don't know who called in and who did what. It's just one of those things. The way, I guess, what front-runner means and the way I think about it is completely different from, yes, than what they're using it... Like I said, they're on your side – they're demanding fans, everybody knows that. When you're doing good, they're on your side. When you're not doing good, they're going to let you know – 'We expect better. We want better. And we want it now.' And I think they feel that by doing that, they can influence the way you play. But when you're giving off that negative energy, it really doesn't."

"And I think that maybe they're like, 'We don't show up,' which is what I guess front- runner means – they're only on your side when you're winning. No, we get 45,000 fans every night. They scream, they cheer and they want a winner. There's no doubt about that. But, as passionate as they are about us going out there and winning and playing well, that's the same passion I feel about them giving us support. Don't get on us when we're down this time of the year, come out and support us."

"There are definitely games, don't get me wrong, where I'm like, 'Damn, you know, we are getting booed and we do need to get booed because we're not doing well.' But there are a lot of times where it makes it harder to play at home when they're against you – or it feels like they're

Jimmy Rollins clarified his "front-running" comments by saying the fans "negative energy (booing)" doesn't help matters

against you. They're never really against you, but it feels like they're against you – they're venting against you and it doesn't help. So, like I said, they show up. You asked about the West Coast, I'm from Oakland, I'm like, 'They don't show up.' That has nothing to do with it."

"The whole thing was, look, here we are in the playoffs, we're at home, we're in first place. There's really nothing to boo about. We're not going to win every game. As long as we win by one when it comes down to the finish. But, go out there and support us. When Carlos Ruiz comes up to the plate, don't boo him because you want (Chris) Coste in the game. This man has a job to do today.

Encourage him to do his job to the best of his abilities."

Asked if he wanted to take any of his original comments back:

"The term front-runner and what it actually means and to what I was using it, what was going through my mind, they weren't accurate. Front-runners is like people who only show up when you're winning. Hey, we're going to cheer you if you win. That's not it about Philly fans. They're passionate. They show up – like I said, 45,000. We've got like 42 sellouts. They announce it every night. That's not what I meant. Like I said, it's the fact that here we are at this point of the year, come out and be supportive. Don't necessarily get on us. We can use that positive energy. And you know that positive energy can lift you, that negative energy can bring you down."

On what he expects the reaction to him will be when he gets back to Philly:

"Who knows? Who knows? We're trying to win games. All we look for is support. If they want to boo me, that's fine. That's fine. It's not going to affect me from doing my job. My job is to go out there and try to win ballgames and I'm going to do my best."

Quotable: "Our offense has been shut down, and I'm still trying to figure out why, but I think before the season is done, we'll go on a hot streak," - Charlie Manuel

Friday, August 15th - Phillies 1 Padres 0 (65-57) 2nd - 1 GB the Mets

San Diego — *With the offense continuing to struggle, Jamie Moyer (11-7, 3.64) was able to lead the team to victory as he shut out the Padres for 7 innings, scattering 3 hits while striking out 2 and walking 2... Ryan Madson and JC Romero combined to pitch a scoreless 8th ... Brad Lidge threw a 1-2-3 9th on only 11 pitches for his 29th save of the year ... 42-year old Greg Maddux (6-9, 3.99) took the loss for the Padres with his only mistake coming in the 7th inning off the bat of Pat Burrell who slugged his 28th homerun of the season. Stuff: Moyer has now pitched 13 straight outings where he has allowed 3 or less runs ... Both Moyer and Maddux were drafted by the Cubs back in 1984 ... This was Burrell's first homerun since August 1st. He is hitting .074 with 1 RBI in his last nine games.*

After an awful series in LA, the Phils finally gave us a chance to decompress, discuss a win and appreciate how good the starting pitching's been. Moyer, who's carried the team as much as anyone, ran his streak to 13 straight starts with three earned runs or less. Aside from Pat Burrell's solo shot, Maddux matched him pitch for pitch, as the savvy vets handled these two struggling offenses. Mix in the work of Brad Lidge, 29-for-29 in save opportunities, and the rest of the pen, last night's 1-0 win embodied how the Phils have gone about business for the last two months.

No matter how grotesque it gets, it's all about the bottom line. After 122 games here are the totals from 1980 and last season compared to where the team is now:

      1980: 65-57, 3.5 games back
      2007: 65-57, 4 games back
      2008: 65-57, 1 game back

Jamie Moyer shut down the Padres
with his 13th consecutive start where he
has allowed 3 runs or less

Quotable: "I wasn't around the strike zone enough. One bad inning really hurt me. My command was off. I was falling behind, walking hitters, then I had to throw strikes... I just have to fight through this." - Kyle Kendrick after having given up 13 runs in his past two starts

Saturday, August 16th - Padres 8 Phillies 3 (65-58) 2nd - 2 GB the Mets
San Diego – *Kyle Kendrick's first three innings went fairly well but then he fell apart in the 4th giving up 5 runs and the lead to the Padres. Kendrick (10-7, 5.01) gave up a total of 6 runs on 6 hits in 3 2/3rd innings while walking 5 ... The offense only managed 6 hits while striking out 13 times in the game. Stuff: The Phils have lost 7 of their last 10 games ... Since scoring 20 runs on June 13th, the Phillies have the worst batting average in the NL at .236 ...They are 12th in runs scored (out of 16 NL teams) with 220 runs, an average of 4.07 runs per game ... Jayson Werth threw out the Padres' Adrian Gonzalez at 3rd base for his 6th outfield assist of the season and the Phillies major league leading 30th outfield assist ... Pat Burrell is 2nd in outfield assists in the National League with 11 ... Geoff Jenkins has 7, Shane Victorino 5 and TJ Bohn with 1.*

Senator Arlen Specter has been a U.S. Senator for the Commonwealth of Pennsylvania since 1980 and is the longest serving Senator in Pennsylvania's history. A native of Russell, Kansas, the Senator moved to Philadelphia fifty years ago to attend college at the University of Pennsylvania. While in school he ended up falling in love with the city as well as falling in love with the Phillies.

I first became a baseball fan while I was about eight years old living in Wichita, Kansas. When I was eleven I was a messenger boy at a big downtown office building, which also had a ticker tape and a pool hall. I would go down there to watch the baseball scores of the games and then go home. When I got home I would turn on the radio and listen to an announcer named Larry Stanley on KSH radio. He would be broadcasting the game and I was always amazed that I already knew what had happened in the game but he was in the midst of

U.S. Senator Arlen Specter follows the Phillies religiously, even when he is in Washington D.C. – photo courtesy of the US Senate

broadcasting it. Later I found out he was doing it off of a ticker tape. He would re-create it the same way as Ronald Reagan did when he worked for the Des Moines radio station. At any rate that was the start of my interest in baseball.

My first remembrance of the Phillies was while reading a Wichita newspaper that had a story in it from one of the Philadelphia newspapers. At that time the A's and the Phils were at the bottom of the league consistently. So one day the Philly newspaper inverted the standings of both team with a little notation that said, "Thought you might like to see the home teams on top for a change." That was my introduction to the Phillies.

I moved to Philadelphia in 1948 and it was a big thing for me to be living in a city with a big league baseball team. The first thing I did was to go out and watch the Phillies play a game. I remembered that they played the Boston Braves. To me it was an exciting thing to be in Shibe Park to watch the Phils.

In 1950, like the whole town, I was mesmerized by the Whiz Kids. I did not see any of the World Series games, I couldn't afford a ticket then. But over the years, I went to see a lot of their games. I lived and died with the Phils in 1964 when they blew the big lead, Johnny Callison's year. I was a big fan of Richie Allen as well. I remember when Richie cut his hand changing a tire on a car or something. I took my two young sons to Temple Hospital to see him.

I go to a lot of games. Whenever the Phils and I are home on a Sunday, I'm at the ballpark. So I'm a die-hard fan. I have MLB on my TV set to watch the Phils down here (in D.C.). When I finish my workday in the Senate, I go watch whomever they're playing. I can't watch them when they play in Los Angeles because I can't stay up that late and still do my job.

My favorite Phillies? Utley, Howard and Cole Hamels. Last year I was in the White House in the Oval Office with President Bush. This was about July I would say. I said to the

President, "I'm on my way to see the Braves play the Nationals tonight, Mr. President." President Bush said, "Well, why don't you bring them in to see me?" I said to President Bush "Would that go for the Phils as well?" he said, "Sure." So the last game of the season, this was the year the Phillies were here playing in Washington. The President invited in Howard, Utley, Hamels, Jimmy Rollins, Myers and Charlie Manuel to the Oval Office to meet with them.

I have a lot of respect for Charlie Manuel. He has a very interesting way of talking. He sort of grunts when he talks. The first time I ever met with Charlie I said, "Why are you pitching Adam Eaton?" When I said that Jimmy Rollins burst into laughter. Charlie said, "Well ah Senator most managers have a #1 pitcher, a #2, a #3, a #4 and a #5." He said, "I got a #1. I ain't got no 2, 3, or 4 and my 5 belongs in the minors." So when he told me that I had a lot more sympathy for Charles Manual, especially when he first took over the team.

I saw the Jimmy Rollins interview on TV about Phillies fans being front-runners the morning after it happened. I think Jimmy's wrong but I can sympathize with what he's saying. I think the players hear the boos and never hear the cheers but I don't think he's right about that at all. I don't hold it against him for saying that though. I've made a couple of bad decisions myself over the years in the Senate and catch a lot of hell when it happens. I can understand the fan's response to what he said. I'm sure he'll catch some hell for it as well.

Philadelphia fans can be pretty tough sometimes. But Ryan Howard went through a long period in April and May where he didn't do too well and the fans didn't get on Howard. We were waiting for him to perk up. I wrote a letter to the Editor of the Inquirer telling fans to give him a standing ovation and I think that picked up his spirits.

It's not a constitutional right or a legal right but fans sort of have a right to express themselves. They pay for the cost of the ticket that they buy and they sit and watch the game and they end up living and dieing with the Phils. I'll bet thousands of people went to sleep the night before last when we had a 6-1 lead. They woke up and were devastated. I'm in Washington, first thing I do in the morning is get the Washington Post and check the sports and I couldn't believe that we'd lose four in a row.

So being a fan is a big emotional investment. That means that booing is a tradition of being disappointed and expressing yourself. I don't think the Philadelphia fans have any apologies to make.

I think the Phillies have got to pick up the pace over the next six weeks. They haven't been showing much fire lately, there's no doubt about that.

It's good to see Myers pitching the way he has. I liked the little incident that he had with the manager. It showed me that Myers has got some fire in his belly and I liked that Manuel stood his ground. Because Manuel has to assert himself in front of the other players. Manuel wasn't bashful about it he did it publicly. I think that kind of a little spat is helpful. They're all trying real hard and I admire and respect that.

Quotable: "I'm puzzled. I stay up late at night thinking about how we can get our offense going. I'll listen to what anybody's got to say. Fans, Cab drivers, President Bush, anybody." - Charlie Manuel after the Phils' 2-1 victory over the Padres

Sunday, August 17th - Phillies 2 Padres 1 (66-58) 2nd - 2 GB the Mets

San Diego – *For the first time since July 3rd, Cole Hamels (10-8, 3.22) won a game with him having to practically do it all on his own. The Phils' ace threw 8 solid innings, giving up only 1 run on 7 hits while striking out 3 and walking none ... Brad Lidge pitched the 9th for his 30th save ... Pat Burrell (2 for 3) hit his 29th homerun of the year, a solo shot in the 6th, to give the Phils the deciding run in the game ... Hamels went 1 for 3 to raise his average to .283. The anemic Phillies offense could only muster 6 hits in the game but made them count as the Phils took 2 of 3 games in the series from the Padres. Stuff: The team batted .190 on the 7 game road trip to the West Coast as they won 2 and lost 5 while falling into 2nd in the NL East in the process ... The NY Mets have won 6 straight games and made a trade with the Washington Senators to obtain reliever Luis Ayala to replace the injured Billy Wagner.*

At the end of each home victory Phillies DJ Mark Wyatt cranks up what has quickly become the signature song of each and every Phils' victory, *"Goin' Back to Philadelphia PA"*. The song, similar to the stylings of Bobby Darin's *"Beyond the Sea"* or Robert Gouley's version of *"You've Got a Friend in Me"* at the end of *Toy Story 2,* is sung by professional singer and Philadelphia native Bobby Burnett.

Bobby started his career in show biz at the age of ten. As a teenager he was a winner of the popular *Arthur Godfrey's Talent Scouts show* on CBS TV. Burnett has a voice and style similar to that of Tony Bennett and Frank Sinatra and once had Tony tell him that he loved listening to him sing. Over the years Bobby has appeared with some of the biggest stars in show business and has been featured in numerous programs including National Public TV, the A&E Entertainment Network and many radio and TV commercials.

Bobby Burnett's "Goin' Back to Philadelphia PA" song is played after each Phillies' home victory
- photo courtesy of Bobby Burnett

I've worked with a number of people over the years.
Arthur Godfrey, Merv Griffen, George Burns, Rip Taylor, Connie Francis, Brenda Lee, Joey Bishop and my very favorite, Bobby Darin.

The song *"Goin' Back to Philadelphia PA"* was written by my good friend and fellow singer/piano player, Robert Barbone. Robert now resides in Colorado Springs, Colorado, but he is originally from the Philadelphia area. A few years ago we decided to produce and record a song for the City of Philadelphia. I asked Robert to help me in this regard and we came up with a non-baseball version of "Goin' Back to Philadelphia",

I recorded that version in the spring of 2005. I sent the song to my entertainment agent Bill Hall. Bill has booked a lot of talent for the Phillies throughout the years like the Flying Wallenda's trapeze act. He gave the song to Dan Baker who in turn gave it to the Phillies' music coordinator, Mark Wyatt. Mark loved the song and started to play it in the spring and summer of 2005 after every Phillies win at the ball park.

Everybody seemed to have liked the original version so much that I decided to make it into a complete Phillies' song. I contacted Bill Hall and got a few ideas on how to approach the song using baseball lyrics. I, in turn, contacted Robert Barbone with this new idea, including my idea of the crowd cheering at the sound of a baseball bat hitting the ball and some other items.

With the new ideas and a complete Phillies baseball approach, I went back into the studio in the winter of 2006 and came out with the new "Phillies" version of the song. That spring I gave it to Mark Wyatt. He loved the new version and they have been playing it after every winning game since the beginning of 2006.

I almost performed the song live in the ballpark back in 2006. Chris Long (Phils' Director of Entertainment) had me sing the National Anthem at the last home game of the year against Houston on September 25, 2006. I also rehearsed the new Phillies' song with the background tracks as we intended to do the song at the end of the game out on the field if the Phillies won. Sadly they lost. It was a sad ride home for me that night but I hope to try doing it again one day soon.

One of my favorite days of the season so far was when Dan Baker invited me to sing the song over at Chickie & Petes right off of Broad Street in South Philly. It was all a part of Dan's *"Summer Nights at the Ballpark"* where he hosts an evening at the restaurant and does the PA announcing of a Phillies' game while they are on the road.

There were literally hundreds of people who were packed in there. When I started singing the song everybody started cheering. As soon as it was done the whole place erupted in a chorus of cheers. It was unbelievable. They even made me sing it a second time. It made me feel so good inside. It's a wonderful song and a great way to honor the Phillies.

The next time you're at the ballpark and the Phillies win hang around for a few minutes after the game and listen to what really is one of the better baseball songs ever recorded.

Lyrics to *"Goin' Back to Philadelphia PA"*

I'm going back to see the Phillies back in my hometown
Back to Philadelphia before the sun goes down
I wanna get back there to the ballpark lights
I gotta see the Phillies what a beautiful sight
Gotta go, cheer them on, help them score some runs
We wanna make the Phillies number one
I want you tell everybody that I'm leaving today

I'm going back to Philadelphia, PA
I'm going home to Philadelphia back to ol' PA
To see the greatest team in the USA
Wanna laugh at the Phanatic doing his thing
Wanna stand up for the anthem and hear the people sing
I love to shout "Its outta here" that's one they'll never catch
I even love to do the seventh inning stretch
I want you tell everybody that I'm on my way
I'm going back to see the Phillies today

I'm going back to Philadelphia I've been living my dream
Back to catch the Phillies they're my favorite team
You know I've been to the east, I've been to the west
But Philly has the team that I love the best
I can live without the Yankees and the Dodgers true
You can keep all of Chicago and the Red Sox too
I'm going back to the place where the Phillies play
I'm going back to Philadelphia PA

I want you to tell everybody that I'm leaving today
I'm going back ... back to Philadelphia PA
Back to Philadelphia PA!

To hear this song in its entirety go on to www.youtube.com and type in "Goin' Back to Philadelphia PA" or go over to www.bobbyburnett.com to read and hear more about Bobby.

Quotable: "It seems to me I hear we're out of it right now, like we're not even close. But the reality is we're a game and a half back with six weeks to play. I feel we're the best team in this division. We just need to go out there and play like it." – Jayson Werth commenting on the division race between the Mets, the Phillies and the Marlins

<u>Monday, August 18th - (Off) (66-58) 2nd - 1 ½ GB the Mets</u>
Should we boo? Cheer? Here's what we do: Hope for a lead-off homer in the home half of the first to neuter the groundswell of displaced frustration being dumped on Jimmy Rollins.

"They're front-runners." There it is, gusting along like a storm cloud, gaining strength by accumulating a week's worth of hype. But tonight, baseball gets in a way of a good story. The first pitch will be thrown and it will blow all that garbage out toward the ocean, just like it always does. Blown out to sea by balls and strikes. Win the game or the next couple, and you're living in a high-pressure system without a cloud in the sky.

An unscripted lead-off shot in the home half would certainly spice up the ambiguity. J-Roll has already served and the ball's in our court. "When you're doing good, they're on your side. When you're doing bad, they're completely against you." A lead-off jack would play like a 155 mph ace. If you've been a wet blanket about the situation, there would be no good way to handle it without looking like a bad fan or front-runner.

Odds are that J-Roll does something mundane with his first AB because mundane is the name of the game. No one knows this more than the players and coaches. This is where fans, bloggers and radio hosts get into trouble. There is no artificial game-day, gut-check rally-cry like football. No artificial motivation necessary. They're in the hunt and can't fall out of the race. It's a grind, and the grind is on their side. We're looking at four below-average seasons from Rollins, Ryan Howard, Geoff Jenkins and Carlos Ruiz, and there's a terrific chance they'll turn it around before it's over, whether we boo, cheer or sit on our hands.

Jimmy Rollins rolls back into town with a number of "front-running" fans that aren't too happy with him

Quotable: "I tell them if you come here and do good, they'll cheer you. If it's not going good they'll boo, that's just how it is." - Jimmy Rollins when asked what he tells players on other teams that may be interested in playing in Philadelphia

Tuesday, August 19th - Phillies 5 Nationals 4 (67-58) 2nd - 1 ½ GB the Mets

Philadelphia — *Trailing 4-1 going into the bottom of the 5th, the Phillies pecked away at the Nationals pitching staff for four unanswered runs ... The offense scored twice in the 5th and then tied it up in the 7th on a Chris Coste sacrifice fly ... Jayson Werth had the game-winning hit as he hit a solo homerun , his 17th of the year, in the 8th to put the Phils ahead for good ... Shane Victorino went 2 for 3 with a double, a triple and 2 runs scored ... Ryan Madson (3-1, 3.11) picked up the win in relief ... Brad Lidge threw another perfect 9th for his 31st save ... Starter Joe Blanton threw 5 innings, giving up 4 runs on 8 hits. Stuff: 44,143 fans had their first chance to "cheer" Jimmy Rollins after his "front-runners" comment in LA, the boos were quite loud ...It was the Phils' 40th sellout in 60 home games... With the loss the Nationals have fallen in 11 consecutive games.*

So it's the first game back in Philadelphia since Rollins made his "front-runner" comment last week in LA. Rollins was asked to make a taped response before the game that was only shown to viewers on TV and not to the fans in the stadium. The good news? The Phillies won.

Otherwise it was more of the same with Jimmy explaining to the media some of his thoughts on the subject and about the fans of Philly.

"*You never know. Some are gonna boo, some are gonna cheer. But I don't care about it. That's the way it is, that's the way it was.*

Jimmy with his mom and dad ... who might use their time here in Philly to remind their son that those "front-running" fans are the best fans in baseball

"*I guess it's a good thing -- it got people talking. It's just one of those things. We're people and athletes and when you make a response about how they feel about certain things it's like, 'How dare you.' But the thing is, we're human beings and we all have the right to say things and they have the right to say something, too, and they have.*

"*The question was asked and that's what it was. It's not like I have an agenda or had an agenda. It was what it was and now I guess it is what it is. People here can take it like they want to take it, but it wasn't a false statement. But it's not like I was trying to take a cheap shot at somebody, either. It wasn't intended that way.*

"*I was speaking for a lot of guys; I wasn't just speaking for Ryan [Howard]. Ryan's had his share [of boos], I've had my share; Pat [Burrell's] had his share. I think Chase [Utley] hasn't been touched yet and hopefully it remains that way and he keeps coming out here and putting up numbers and they don't need do. But there are definitely guys who come back to the clubhouse or you see them from the dugout going to the plate and you see the expression on their face. It's like 'Man, I've got to try to do something; I've got to figure something out.' And they're halfway defeated before they get up there. But basically it's something nobody pays attention to, it's like, 'Go get out of here, you can't play in this city.'*

"*This isn't even nothing to worry about. It's not like I'm getting beat up on. But people are going to like you for one reason and they're going to dislike you for another reason. And if you just want to play the politically correct game you can do that and get away with how you really feel behind closed doors. Sometimes you speak up and make a stance, it doesn't mean you did anything wrong, you just made a point.*

"For every action there's a reaction. Some people are gonna cheer, some people are gonna boo. But at the end of the day, we win and they're all be cheering. And that's what we want. We want to win, they want us to win and they'll all be cheering. But in-game action, we're winning 5-3 and a guy makes an out, that's not something to boo. We're still winning. Let's go out there and score some more runs."

Basically, it's a non-issue. There are far more important matters involving the Phillies right now, like, winning games. The reason people like Rollins so much to begin with is that he isn't afraid to speak his mind. Last year, he thought the Phillies were the "team to beat" in the NL East. He said it. People loved it. Last week, he expressed how he feels sometimes about Phillies' fans. Don't like it? Too bad.

Quotable: "I think I'm more into the game instead of (thinking about) what just happened. I don't really care about the outcome. I just try to be in the right frame of mind. You can't look too much into it and get all caught up in it." - Brett Myers, who improved to 3-1 with a 1.94 ERA in six starts since coming back from the minors

<u>Wednesday, August 20th - Phillies 4 Nationals 0 (68-58) 2nd - 1 ½ GB the Mets</u>
Philadelphia – *Brett Myers (6-10, 4.71) threw his 3rd complete game shutout of his career as he scattered 9 Nationals' hits while walking 1 and striking out 9 ... Greg Dobbs hit a 2-run homerun (6) as part of a 3-run 5th inning ... Chase Utley, Shane Victorino and Chris Coste each had two hits.* Stuff: *Jimmy Rollins went 1 for 4 in the game and is 3 for 24 (.125) since calling the fans "front-runners" ... The shutout was the 8th thrown this year by the Phillies pitching staff ... In the last 25 games the staff have an ERA of 3.29 with 17 quality starts while holding the opposing team to an average of .247 ... The Nationals lost their 12th straight game. The last time they did that was back in 1976 when they were the Montreal Expos.*

Jocelyn Brown watched as Washington's Ronnie Belliard drove a screaming line drive past Phils' third base coach Steve Smith. The ball, barely missing Smith's head, slammed into the tarp along the third base fence and began rolling out towards left field. She immediately jumped into action.

Dressed in white pinstripe shorts and a Phillies' jersey with "Jocelyn" and the number "08" on the back, she quickly leapt off her stool and made a quick hop to her left, making sure that her shoulders were square and centered over the ball. Bent at the waist, Brown let the ball roll into her glove before standing up and turning back toward the crowd.

She walked toward the stands and handed the baseball to a young girl with a pink baseball cap on her head, then sat back down and waited for her next opportunity to track down another foul ball.

Jocelyn is one of seventeen ball girls working for the Phillies this season. She's a die-hard fan who got the itch when she started watching the Phillies as a young child. A Devon, PA, native, Brown is spending this summer driving down to Citizens Bank Park and gobbling up as many foul balls as she possibly can.

Phillies' ballgirl Jocelyn Brown with the National's Ronnie Belliard

This is my second year as a Phillies' ball girl. I love it. I think any one of the girls on the team will tell you it's the best job that they've ever had. I've been a huge Phillies fan my entire life so to get to come out and do this job and to be a part of the Phillies' organization and be on the field is exciting for me.

I was here in 1993 when we won the pennant over the Braves. I was 12 years old then. The game ended late and my parents let me stay home from school the next day. I've been a huge fan ever since.

One of the most enjoyable things that I like about being a ball girl are the appearances that we do where you actually get to go out and be with the fans. I love when I can sit and talk to the kids because they get so excited. I don't think that I'm a big deal but they think that we're a big deal and you should see how much fun we have with them when we're with them.

I also just love sitting on my chair and watching the Phanatic perform. After all these years he still cracks me up. I actually have to keep myself from staring at him during games because I'm supposed to be paying attention to where the ball is going but he's hilarious. It never gets old watching him.

I think the hardest thing about being a ball girl is that you can't please everybody. If you have a ball and you give it to somebody, somebody else gets mad. If you give somebody your baseball card, they want a hug. If you give somebody a hug, they want you to kiss them. It never ends; it just continues to escalate.

Our job is basically to go out and well represent the Phillies. We have fun; we talk to the fans and make them feel like they've had a great time at the game even if they didn't get a ball. That's tough sometimes but it comes with the responsibilities of the job.

Getting balls hit at you is a little stressful too. Pat Burrell once hit a line drive that just missed hitting my head. I was on the third base line and was sitting in my chair and he smashed a ball that zoomed right past me. I was fine though. I'm not allowed to talk about this too much or else they're gonna have us start wearing batting helmets like the coaches.

In this job I have to dress up in a lot in different costumes and it can be embarrassing at times. I was an Egyptian Priestess for the Phanatic's birthday last year. For the past two years we've dressed up in Santa outfits for our Christmas in July celebration. We wear these nice little red sun dresses with Santa hats. They're cute. So before the game this year Scott Palmer, Phillies' Director of Public Affairs, comes up to me and says, "Hey can you come with me for a minute? I want you to help us with a promotion."

So I go with him out onto the field dressed in my Santa Outfit and he gives me a Cole Hammel's bobblehead to hold in my hands. He then tells me that he wants to film a promotional video to show the fans the bobblehead and let them know when we would be giving them away to them. Well little did I know that when I come out onto the field all of the Phillies players are taking batting practice. So now it's just me, my Santa outfit, a bobblehead, the camera guy and the entire Phillies team on the field.

So the next thing I hear are all of the players who start teasing me and they begin yelling things like, "Ho, Ho, Ho!" I'm totally embarrassed. Scott then tells me to bounce my head around like the bobblehead and try to make my head swivel all over the place. So I start doing that and all the players are laughing and I was just completely embarrassed. The promo ended up going well and I'm sure people found it amusing. I know the players did!

One question that I get asked a lot is whether I'm on the first base or third base side of the field. We usually switch back and forth. It depends on whether a ball girl has friends or family here or just what their personal preference might be.

I actually like being on the third base foul line the best. Most girls like the first base side because it seems to be closer to the action and the players. I feel like I have more room to move around when I'm on the third base side.

I haven't had any marriage proposals yet. I've gotten other things proposed to me that aren't as nice, but no marriage proposals yet. It's funny, people say all sorts of things to you and make all sorts of comments, some of them are funny and some of them are annoying, but I've had people come up to me and say, "I'm such a big fan of yours." And that to me sounds ridiculous, like, "How do you know who I am?" but you know, fans are fans and I guess they like the ball girls as well as the ball players.

Twenty-five years from now I think I'm going to most remember running out onto the field once the game starts. They play a video and a song that pumps everyone up and we run out to our seats at the same time the players run to their positions. It's the most exciting feeling. You have 40,000 fans and you're running out onto the field with your favorite players. That's probably what I'll remember the most, just that feeling.

Quotable: "He's got home runs and he's got RBIs, but it seems like he's really had to fight to be consistent. He has to really fight hard to find his swing and keep his swing." – Charlie Manuel on Ryan Howard's prolonged hitting slump

Thursday, August 21st - Nationals 4 Phillies 3 (68-59) 2nd - 2 ½ GB the Mets

Philadelphia – *Carlos Ruiz hit a 2-run homer in the bottom of the 7th to put the Phillies on top but reliever Ryan Madson (3-2, 3.38) wasn't able to nail down the win as he gave up two RBI singles in the top of the 8th to put the Nationals in front. Madson gave up a total of 4 hits in 1/3rd innings to blow his second save of the year ... Jamie Moyer pitched 6 2/3rd, giving up 2 runs (1 earned) while striking out 4 ... Chase Utley and Shane Victorino each had two hits for the 2nd night in a row ... Ryan Howard continued his hitting slump going 0 for 4 with 3 strikeouts. Stuff: Ryan Howard has a total of 5 hits in his last 50 plate appearances (.100 average). During that time he has struck out 21 times and is on a pace to strike out 213 times this season. He has 167 so far this year. Howard set the record last year for most strikeouts in a season with 199 ... Pat Burrell is 10 for 60 (.167) in August.*

They came within six outs of nailing down a sweep, couldn't hold it; it happens, but it happens less when you score more than three runs, which the Phils can't do. I'm pretty set on taking out my frustration on Ryan Howard and Jimmy Rollins today, who did nothing this series. Others have worked out the projected strike-outs and Howard stands to whiff 213 times, compounding problems for a team struggling to even put the ball in play. Howard's unsightly .791 OPS tells the story of a cleanup hitter who's been perpetually out of sorts all season, and we could say the same thing about Rollins, who's hitting .261 and

Carlos Ruiz's 7th inning homerun wasn't enough as Ryan Madson couldn't hold the lead

has just three hits and a run in his last eight games. J-Roll has 56 runs this season, fifth on the team, after crossing home 139 times in 2007.

Afterward, Jamie Moyer, the only player who would reportedly talk to the media, spoke of players putting too much pressure on themselves. I believe him. The tight play is reminiscent of the pre-Aaron Rowand Phils, who still scored runs, but seemed to get tight for long stretches. But never this long. The Phils have scored three or fewer runs in 52 of their 127 games, which is a rate of 41 percent. Recent futility has come at the hands of cellar-dwelling Pittsburgh, San Diego and Washington. Take away unreal opening months from Pat Burrell and Chase Utley and you wouldn't even call this an average offense. And it's a joyless group to watch. The tension is palpable. You start to wonder whether Charlie Manuel's alleged ability to get these guys to loosen up is overrated. I've decided that Manuel is a motivational non-factor. I can't get around what many of the beat writers said about

Rowand, that you couldn't put a price on his presence. And I'm just a little tired of sloppy defense. Chase Utley and Howard have taken backward steps this season.

Quotable: "It's the good teams that are strong-minded that get past that (tough losses). All it takes is one break, one bloop hit. You never know how you will get back on track, but we are going to get back on track. The tables will turn when we get those breaks. That's when we're ready to roll." – Chase Utley prior to today's game

Friday, August 22nd - Phillies 8 Dodgers 1 (69-59) 2nd - 2 ½ GB the Mets

Philadelphia – Chris Coste went 2 for 4 with 4 RBIs, a homerun (9) and 2-runs scored as the offense pummeled Dodgers' starter Greg Maddux for 7 runs in 5 2/3rd innings. Ryan Howard (34) and Chase Utley (31) also went deep for the Phils ... Greg Dobbs went 2 for 3 and scored 2 runs ... Starter Kyle Kendrick (11-7, 4.87) appeared to have righted his pitching as he threw 5 2/3rd innings giving up 1 run on 3 hits ... Chad Durbin (1.1), Ryan Madson (1) and Scott Eyre (1) threw the final 3 1/3rd scoreless innings. Stuff: Geoff Jenkins left the game in the 4th with a hip flexor ... The win snapped a 6 game losing streak with the Dodgers ... Greg Maddux was making his first start with the Dodgers after being acquired in a trade with the Padres on Thursday.

Finally making it to the big leagues is a dream that only a few people can actually say they've ever accomplished. Some, like Chase Utley, are destined for stardom and spend only a year or two in a club's minor league system before getting called up. Others languish in the minors their entire careers and never get the call. Then there is Chris Coste.

For eleven seasons Chris hustled and hit his way through numerous independent, Mexican and Venezuelan league games before he finally got the call to join the Phillies in the spring of 2006. In his book "The 33-Year-Old Rookie", Chris documented the long and hard fought struggle of finally realizing his dream of making it to the majors. One of the most interesting aspects of Chris' book isn't so much where he played and how he hit the ball, but how he and his wife Marcia walked through the sometimes difficult process

Chris Coste's wife, Marcia, has been an integral part in the life of the "33-Year-Old –Rookie"

the entire time arm-in-arm. Not only as husband and wife, but as best friends.

Chris and I will be married 12 years come this October. I've probably known him for at least twenty years. I met him in the 11th grade. I really didn't know him too well before we started dating but I just thought that he was really cute.

We had a Sadie Hawkins dance at our school where the girls can ask the guys out to the dance. I had one of my girlfriends ask him to see if he would go with me. So one day she passed him a note that said, "Would you want to go to a dance with Marcia?" and he passed it back and he said, "Sure." We've been with each other ever since.

I've been around baseball since we started dating. In high school I used to go to all of his games and I've been with him throughout his entire time in the minors so I've seen lots and lots of baseball games. Believe it or not I really do like the game of baseball. Especially when Chris is playing.

In all the 11 years that Chris was in the minors, I always knew that he was going to make it. That's why I was always so positive with him. I always told everyone that I met, "If you just come watch and see him play, you will know that he is going to make the big leagues." Our phrase was always, "Good things come to those who wait." We said that every year, so I guess the older we got it paid off.

In May of 2006 Chris finally got called up to the big leagues. It was surreal. I found out while I was at a going away party that our families were throwing for Casey and I, before we left to be with Chris in Scranton, PA (Chris' AAA team). Chris actually called from his car as he was driving down to Philly right in the middle of the party and he said, "I just got traded." and I said, "To who?" and he said, "The Phillies!"

When he said that to me I just started yelling and then crying for joy. Everyone at the party started cheering and crying as well and after that the party really took off... it was so much fun.

Chris had about three hours to get to the game after he found out he was called up. Because we were in Fargo, we weren't able to be there but we have mlb.com on our computer at home so we all left the party and came back to our house to watch him on our computer.

We had about 20 people standing behind me while we watched the game on the computer. A few times they showed Chris on TV, sitting in the dugout. Every time we saw him we were like, "There's Chris, there's Chris, there's Chris!"

We were fortunate enough to be able to be at the first game that he actually appeared in a game. I think it was on May 26th against Milwaukee. He pinch-hit in the bottom of the 9th for one of the pitchers. When he came up everyone in the stands was cheering for him. He lined out to center field on the first pitch but just seeing him in his outfit and seeing that he finally made it to the big leagues after all those years was pretty cool.

What I most like about being a baseball player's wife is just being able to be beside Chris and watch him do something that he has always wanted to do his entire life. I love seeing the people from back home and the people here in Philadelphia being so happy for him. Personally, it's been fun since he made it with the Phillies. Being able to come to this stadium and be a part of this whole world is fantastic.

I think the biggest surprise that I've experienced between the minor leagues and the majors is that there are a lot more fans up here and a lot more attention given to the players. I love being in Philadelphia. There's a lot more culture here than in Fargo, but North Dakota is home. I've grown up there and lived there my whole life. Both of our families are there. We have a lake home in Minnesota, which is only an hour drive. Not as much to do in North Dakota but they have good schools, good people. But you know being in Philadelphia people asked me if I would move here and I would move here in a minute. That's how much we like it. And Chris loves it; I love it.

I think Phillies' fans are the best. Since I've been here they've been really nice to me, really nice to Chris, really warm and welcoming. Chris and I think they're the best fans ever. I mean 40,000 people in the stadium almost every game. I can't even imagine how that's gotta feel as a player. That's just unreal. They've been great; they've been really, really great to us. Every one is always gracious.

I've literally seen no negatives about being in the majors. Absolutely none. I mean it's all good, I don't know how there could be any negatives. This is a dream come true for us.

Chris' book is doing well. No one has bought the rights to the book yet to make it into a movie. A lot of speculation but Chris thinks if it ever comes to that it would be nice to do that later in life. He would rather just be in the big leagues playing baseball right now instead of having to worry about the other things that come along with trying to make a movie.

Who do we want to play us in the movie? A lot of people ask me that question. For Chris he always says Matthew McConaughey. I'm thinking Matt Damon. And for me I would have no clue, really. I don't…It would have to be some blonde actress. I don't know, maybe Kate Hudson. I don't know. That's a hard one.

Quotable: "It's great to put runs on the board like we did yesterday and today, hopefully we can repeat it tomorrow. It's something where when we get the middle of the lineup hot, we can go out and compete and win a lot of ballgames. It doesn't change how I pitch but this is a team game and when we hit on all cylinders it's a very good thing." - Cole Hamels who was ranked 45th out of 51 National League starters who have thrown at least 120 innings when it comes to run support.

Saturday, August 23rd - Phillies 9 Dodgers 2 (70-59) 2nd - 1 ½ GB the Mets

Philadelphia – *Pat Burrell smacked his 30th homerun of the year as he went 3 for 5 while tying a career-high 5 RBIs to lead a 10-hit offense outburst over Los Angeles ... Chase Utley went 2 for 3 and scored 3 runs ... Ryan Howard and Shane Victorino each had 2 RBIs in the game ... Cole Hamels (11-8, 3.20) finally got some run support in his win as he goes 7 innings, giving up 2 runs on 5 hits while striking out 5 ... Scott Eyre and Rudy Seanez pitched a scoreless 8th and 9th for the bullpen. Stuff: Burrell (30), Howard (34) and Utley (31) have combined for more homeruns (95) than 5 of the 30 MLB teams ... Geoff Jenkins was put on the 15 day DL with a right hip flexor strain ... The Phils called up INF/OF Andy Tracy from AAA-Lehigh to fill his spot ... Phillies' minor leaguers Lou Marson and Jayson Donald won Bronze Medals for the Team USA Baseball Team. Donald led the US team in batting .381 (8 for 21) while Marson had the 3rd best average on the team at .308 (4 for 13).*

You know you've made it in your career if someone has taken the time to make a bobblehead of you. Paul Sr., Paul Jr. and Mikey of *American Choppers* each have one. Philly's own Jim Cramer of *Mad Money* fame has one of his own. His even talks! "Booyah!". Heck, even 610 WIP's Howard Eskin has his own bobblehead with him decked out in one of his fur coats. Whether you like bobbleheads or hate them, bobbleheads are here to stay ... as long as they keep packing the fans into the ballpark.

Scott Brandreth is the Phillies' Director of Merchandising and is the man responsible for getting all of those bobbleheads made for giveaways throughout the year. The 2008 season has two bobbleheads planned. One for Jamie Moyer and one for MVP Jimmy Rollins

This season's first bobblehead was one of Jamie Moyer. Officially we called it the "Jamie Moyer NL East Division Champion" bobblehead. It had a circle base with Jamie throwing off the mound with a little plaque that has a logo on it honoring the Phils winning the NL East last season. Believe it or not it was the first bobblehead ever made of Jamie in his 22-year major league career.

Times have changed in the bobblehead business since this vintage 1960's Phillies' bobblehead was made

The first thing we do after we decide which bobbleheads we will be giving away during the season is to gather photos of the player. We then start to consider what pose we'd like him in; whether it be someone fielding, hitting, pitching, running, we like to mix it up. Even within the pose, we consider how we want to portray the player; finishing a home run, sliding into a base or in case of Jamie's bobblehead this year, in the middle of throwing a pitch. We usually send the manufacturer of the bobbleheads a headshot, a side shot, a body shot and a back shot of the player.

We understand that we're never going to be able to exactly duplicate the player. The face will never be quite there, but it's going to be close. If you look at the evolution of the bobblehead, it started with just one pudgy guy with a big head either holding a bat if he was a hitter or wearing a glove if he were a pitcher. Today everyone is moving towards the bobble figurine. It's supposed to resemble the player much closer. For some players, like Ryan Howard, you want to make the figurine thicker to match his body build. For Chase Utley you want it to be skinnier. The point is to make it look like them as much as possible.

It takes a total of about 90 days from start until the time they are delivered to us. We spend about 30 days in development going back and forth with sculpts of the head and body and with designs. It then takes about 60 days or so to then get them delivered to us so it's about a three to four month process.

All of the bobbleheads are sponsored by a corporation. The Phillies actually incur the costs of making them. We do get paid by the sponsor for a promotion but it doesn't necessarily add up dollar for dollar to completely cover all of the costs of the bobblehead.

Bobbleheads and figurines are probably our most popular giveaways. We almost always sell out those games. We had the Jimmy Rollins MVP bobblehead on June 4th and that game was sold out towards the beginning of the season. We did the "Flyin Hawaiian" figurine of Shane in July for kids 14 and under, and we just did a Chase Utley bobblehead on July 20th for all fans. All of those games sold out as well. We try to place the bobblehead giveaways on dates that don't usually attract a sell-out crowd. Usually like a mid week game or against a team that doesn't draw as big as the Mets or Red Sox.

Probably one of the biggest surprises we ever had was with the Larry Bowa bobblehead that we gave away in 2001 on the last day of the season. It was the second bobblehead that we ever had done, and we didn't add it to the promotion calendar until late in the season. I think we had 18,000 walk-ups to that game at the Vet. It was insane. We ended up running out of them and had to give fans tickets and some coupons for them.

We've given a number of bobbleheads and figurines over the past seven years. Our first ever was a bobblehead of Pat Burrell in May of 2001. In 2002, we had the Phanatic and Jimmy Rollins. In 2003 we gave away a Harry Kalas and Richie Ashburn bobblehead, a Steve Carlton 1980 World Champs bobblehead , a Mike Schmidt 1980 World Champs bobblehead and a Phil and Phyllis (the original mascots) on the last day of the season. In 2004, we had them made for Randy Wolf and Mike Lieberthal. In 2005, we just gave figurines of Thome, Abreu and Rollins away. We didn't do bobbleheads that year. In 2006, we did bobbles for Chase Utley and Ryan Howard. In 2007, we did bobbleheads for the Phanatic , Howard and Cole Hamels and did a hula figurine with swivel hips for Shane Victorino.

My favorite bobblehead of all time was the one of Kalas & Ashburn in 2002. It's still a big collectible. People on eBay are still getting a lot of money for them. I've been pushing the idea of doing figurines of the Phils' four Hall-of-Famers (Roberts, Ashburn, Carlton and Schmidt) but we haven't moved forward on any of them as of yet.

Quotable: "I was hitting in the cage early in the game to make sure I was ready. You know, you have a man at second (and third) with two outs, I'm just trying to put the ball in play and get a good swing." - Pedro Feliz, who entered the game as a part of a double switch in the seventh inning, discussing his walk-off 3-run homerun in the 11th

Sunday, August 24th - Phillies 5 Dodgers 2 - 11 inn. (71-59) 2nd - ½ GB the Mets

Philadelphia – *Pedro Feliz provided heroics twice in the game as he tied the contest at 2 in the 9th on a 2-out RBI single and then followed that up with a 3-run walk-off homerun (13) to end the game in the 11th . Feliz, who entered the game in the 7th, went 2 for 3 with 4 RBIs ... Shane Victorino went 2 for 4 and scored 2 runs ... Starter Joe Blanton pitched 6 solid innings, giving up 1 run on 6 hits while striking out 4 ... Chad Durbin (5-2, 1.98) picked up the win in relief. Stuff: For the 4th time this season , and 3rd time this month, the Phillies were featured on ESPN's Sunday Night Baseball ... Jimmy Rollins continues to struggle at the plate as he is mired in a 4 for 48 slump (.083)... The win, coupled with the Mets loss to the Astros, pulled the Phils to within a ½ game of the NL East lead.*

After two lopsided wins, the Phillies scratched and clawed their way to victory, and now the positives are piling up in innumerable ways in what's become a well-rounded 5-1 home stand. Credit Victorino, Feliz and the pitching staff for making Los Angeles pay for leaving this one on the table. The Dodgers squandered a number of golden opportunities, including a bases-loaded, no-out chance in the 10th. Somehow, Phillies' pitching wriggled out of jams and kept it close long enough for the offense to make something happen in the home half of the 11th. Cue Manny

Chad Durbin, pictured here with his wife signing an autograph, picked up the win in relief

Ramirez, whose nonchalance in left allowed Victorino to reach second on a fairly routine base hit, putting immediate pressure on the Dodgers. Besides Victorino and Feliz, the offense couldn't mount much of an attack, while the Dodgers seemed to be threatening all night.

Victorino, who's been their best hitter since the All-Star break, continued to ignite the offense and pester the opposition. Here's a guy who was supposed to start only 125-135 games in center just to keep him fresh. Today, he's the one guy who absolutely must be on the field. Feliz delivered the big blows after starting the game on the bench. On a night where the heart of the order was taken out of the equation, they needed someone like Feliz to step up. The gloves were outstanding. The Phils received a workman-like start from Joe Blanton, who survived a shaky first inning to pitch six innings, allowing one run. The relievers outlasted the Dodgers pen before giving way to "Last Call" Condrey.

Quotable: "I'm pitching now I'm not just throwing. I'm not saying "This guy can't hit my curveball" and throwing six curveballs until he gets a hit. You have to have that feeling of how to pitch and I didn't have it earlier in the year. I'm starting to feel comfortable out there whether guys are on base or not." - Brett Myers who extended his scoreless-inning streak to a career-best 16 innings

Monday, August 25th - Phillies 5 Dodgers 0 (72-59) 2nd - ½ GB the Mets

Philadelphia – Brett Myers (7-10, 4.49) extended his scoreless-inning streak to a career high 16 innings as he shut out LA over 7 innings to help the Phils sweep all four game from the Dodgers ... JC Romero and Clay Condrey scattered 4 hits over the final two innings to help nail down the shutout ... Jimmy Rollins broke out of his extended slump in a big way, going 3 for 3 with 2 RBIs and hitting a double and a triple in the process ... Chase Utley and Pedro Feliz each had two hits ... LA's Manny Ramirez went 0 for 4 in the game (2 for 14 in the 4-game series) and left 7 men on base. Stuff: Myers is now 3-1 with a 1.94 ERA since coming back from the minors ... This was the Phils' first 4-game sweep of the Dodgers since 1985 at Dodger Stadium. It was their first ever 4-game sweep at home ... Rollins had his first extra base hit since August 12th ... The Phils are now a season-high 13 games over .500 for the third time this year.

Larry Bowa goes off: "If you can't get up emotionally and mentally when you're two or three games out of first place, you need to find another job, another occupation," Bowa told the Los Angeles Times. "That's what I see. I've seen teams play like this when they're 30 games out. There's no excuse for it. It's not one person. It's all of us. It's everybody that puts on a Dodger uniform. We should all be embarrassed by the way we played the last four days."

From the opposite dugout (LA Times Dodgers Blog): "They loaded the bases in the first, had men on first and third in the second, first and second in the fourth, a man on third in the fifth, loaded them again in the seventh, got them to second and third in the eighth, and, just to round things out, had men on first and third in the ninth. You can't win if you don't score. Dodgers lose 5-0 in Philadelphia, and if you had to pick a game to serve as a microcosm of the 2008 season, Monday's game is as good a choice as any. I'm leaving out those boring innings where, like, only one guy got on, because I figure by now you've already popped an artery in your forehead."

LARRY
BOWA
PHILADELPHIA PHILLIES   **SHORTSTOP**

Larry Bowa wasn't too happy with the Dodgers' performance after today's shutout

Quotable: "If we go onto win the division, this will be the game to look back on. Whether we won this game or lost it, it wasn't going to make or break the year, but the way in which we won it reinforces the fact that the Phillies are never out of the game, regardless of the score." – Chris Coste on the Phillies' dramatic come from behind win that allowed them to take sole possession of first place.

Tuesday, August 26th - Phillies 8 Mets 7 - 13 inn. (73-59) 1st - ½ GA of the Mets

Philadelphia – Trailing 7-1 going into the 5th, the Phillies scored 4 runs in the 5th and then pecked away at the Mets' bullpen until the bottom of the 9th when Eric Bruntlett tied the game at 7 with a double to right center to score Jayson Werth ... Shane Victorino led off the bottom of the 13th with a triple which forced the Mets to walk the bases loaded. One out later, Chris Coste hit a ball to deep center that allowed Victorino to score the winning run ... Jimmy Rollins continued hitting the ball, going an incredible 5 for 7 with a homerun (9), 3 RBIs and 3 stolen bases ... Ryan Howard went just 1 for 6 but his one hit was a 2-run homer in the 5th; his 35th homerun of the season and 110th RBI ... Jayson Werth went 3 for 5 ... Chris Coste came in to pinch hit for Dobbs in the 8th and managed to go 4 for 4 for the remainder of the game, including the game winning hit in the 13th ... In total, the Phillies banged out 19 hits ... Jamie Moyer got rocked for 6 runs in 3 innings ... Clay Condrey gave up one run in the 4th but then the bullpen shut down the Mets for the remaining 9 innings while only surrendering 2 hits (both by Ryan Madson) ... Rudy Seanez (5-3, 3.38) picked up the win, throwing a 1-2-3 13th inning. Stuff: The Phillies used 23 players and the Mets 21 players in the course of the game ... This was the Phils 9th win in the past 11 games ... The 3 IP by Moyer was his shortest outing since June 16, 2005 when he was with Seattle ... The Phils had a season-high 6 stolen bases in the game.

Here it is, the kind of game that separates the wheat from the chaff.

What a great win and unenviable task. The beat writers had to shovel 10 pounds of s*** into a five-pound bag on deadline last night and they did a tremendous job of it. Meanwhile, I exercised my blogger rights by deferring to this morning, hoping a cup of coffee and a passable night of sleep would aid in making heads or tails of the wildest win of the season. Five hours of sleep and two cups later, making sense of it is beyond hopeless. There's just too much.

Comcast's Leslie Gudel interviews Jimmy Rollins ... Rollins went 5 for 7 with 3 stolen bases in today's game

Baseball doesn't get any more entertaining than this. Even Metsblog seemed to agree. At 13 innings, the Phillies wrapped it up before it became a true war of attrition. Tonight's starter, Kyle Kendrick, was warming in the pen if it went to the 14th and it's unclear whether Kendrick is a go for tonight's 7:05 ET start. The rest of the pen is largely spent and they can ill afford another short outing. For what it's worth, Kris Benson is tonight's scheduled starter for the Iron Pigs, who are at home. They'll need to finesse a roster move if reinforcements are needed.

To the game, we start with Jamie Moyer and Pedro Martinez, who took the mound ages ago. It was Moyer's shortest outing as a Phillie, a three-inning story in-and-of itself. The Mets seemed two steps ahead of Moyer, unloading for six runs and a pair of homers. On the opposite side, Pedro was decent until hitting a wall in the fifth, when Jimmy Rollins and Ryan Howard tagged him for a pair of two-run blasts. The rally started when Clay Condrey doubled to lead off the inning, the first in a series of improbable moments. Pedro finished with five ER but eight Ks, a product largely due to the Phils chasing balls up and out of the zone.

With the score 7-5, and with the Phils already into their third inning with Condrey, both teams calmed things down by settling in with their middle relief. Scott Eyre, one of many unsung heroes, took the ball from Condrey midway through the sixth inning and would rattle off 1 2-3 shutout innings. (Condrey departed after 2 1-3 good innings, allowing the final run for the Mets). After Eyre, the always reliable Chad Durbin finished the eighth cleanly.

The Mets' bullpen, the Crux of Queens, wasn't as spotless. The Phillies started pecking away in the eighth when Carlos Ruiz signaled to left off Duaner Sanchez. Then, Mets manager Jerry Manuel went left-left with Pedro Feliciano matching up with Greg Dobbs. Charlie Manuel countered with his first tactical triumph of the night, pinch hitting Chris Coste for Dobbs. Coste singled, which brought Jimmy Rollins to the plate with a runner in scoring position. J-Roll singled and scored Ruiz from second. The Mets would escape without further damage, making it 7-6.

Now Manuel had a decision to make: keep Coste in the game to replace Ruiz and stick Eric Bruntlett at third for the ninth, or preserve Bruntlett and fill third some other way. In an unexpected move, Manuel inserted Ruiz at third and replaced Durbin with Lidge. The gamble worked: Lidge worked a groundout to short, strikeout, strikeout, making Ruiz a non-factor.

The payoff happened in the 9th. With the Phils down to their final out, Jayson Werth singled to center off temporary closer Luis Ayala, bringing up the pitcher's spot. Representing the final man off the bench, Manuel called on Bruntlett, who was preserved for such an occasion. With the game on the line, Bruntlett smacked a game-tying double to deep right, sending it to extras. For the Mets, it was their 22nd blown save of the season. You have to go back to May of 2003 to find a bigger lead blown by New York.

One by one, the relievers took their turn in extras. Ryan Madson worked two innings, escaping danger. J.C. Romero and Rudy Seanez, the eventual game-winner, followed with scoreless frames. On the other side, Madson-foil Aaron Heilman threw 60 pitches over three frames, well beyond his usual limit. The Phillies would have the best chances, but with fatigue setting in, nobody was able to rise to the occasion.

It took the highest-motor player on the field to deliver a breakthrough. In the home half of the 13th, Shane Victorino lined a triple down the right-field line against the last reliever standing, Scott Schoeneweis. After Jayson Werth and Bruntlett were intentionally walked, Myers hit for Seanez. Myers, who was told not to swing (and look like a goober doing it), worked the count full before striking out looking. Finally, at 12:20 a.m., Coste delivered the game winner, giving the Phillies the win and lifting them back in front of the NL East. I'd like to list everyone who contributed to this total team effort, but there's no way to include Pat Burrell, who went 0-for-7 with four strikeouts, stranding 10. That's his worst game this season if not his entire career. Heroes, in no particular order, include Bruntlett, who picked a swell time to deliver his 10th extra-base hit of the season; Coste, who went 4-for-4 off the bench; and Charlie Manuel, for his finest tactical hour as Phillies' manager. No question about it, the unbreakable bullpen—Condrey, Eyre, Durbin, Lidge, Madson, Romero and Seanez. Rollins—get kudos for a 5-for-7 night, spraying hits everywhere including the right-field seats. Werth is noteworthy, for taking advantage of his opportunities against right-handed pitching and making a great play, cutting off a ball down the line in right and gunning down David Wright at second. The defense indeed made some key plays.

Quotable: "I'm down there for a reason, and that's to be used whenever Charlie wants me to be used. I know that I need to be ready. Tonight I just went out there and didn't get it done." - Brad Lidge on his performance and on being brought in during the 8th inning for only the 2nd time this season

Wednesday, August 27th - Mets 6 Phillies 3 (73-60) 2nd - ½ GB the Mets

Philadelphia – *Leading 3-2 going into the 8th inning New York scored 4 times with 2 outs in the inning as Rudy Seanez and Brad Lidge were not able to hold off the onslaught of Mets' hitting ... Seanez (5-4, 3.82) took the loss, going 2/3rd of an inning and giving up 2 runs on 2 hits including Carlos Delgado's solo homerun (his 2nd of the game) to tie it at 3-3. Carlos Beltran followed Delgado's homer with a single, which led Charlie Manuel to bring in Brad Lidge to try to shut New York down. It didn't work as Lidge gave up an RBI double to Daniel Murphy to put the Mets in the lead and then a 2-run single to Brian Schneider to complete the comeback for the Phils' rivals ... Kyle Kendrick pitched 5 innings, giving up 2 runs on 8 hits ... Ryan Howard's 2-run homerun (36) in the 1st and Jayson Werth's solo shot (18) in the 2nd led to all the Phillies' runs. Stuff: Coming into the game the Phils' bullpen had the best ERA in the NL at 3.05 ... It was Lidge's first appearance pitching prior to the 9th inning since his first game on April 6th ... Since July 24th, the NL East lead has gone back and fourth between New York and Philadelphia four times ... Jimmy Rollins had 2 stolen bases in the game for a season total of 36. As a team, the Phillies now have 107 stolen bases and have only been caught 20 times for an 83.4% success rate, which ranks #1 in the majors ... To help out with the Phillies' depleted bullpen from Tuesday's game, the team called up pitcher Andrew Carpenter from AA-Reading and sent Andy Tracey back to AAA. Carpenter was able to make his major league debut in the 9th, as he pitched one inning giving up no runs on 1 hit while walking 1 and striking out 1.*

Rob Brooks is the Director of Broadcasting for the Phillies. He's the architect and the leadership behind the Phillies' television and radio teams. I caught up with Rob to get some insight on the Phillies new lineup this year and to get some of his personal thoughts.

One of the comments that we constantly hear is that Scott Franzke and Larry Anderson make a great team on radio. Why do you think that is?
When I first read Scott's resume one of the things that struck me that he included in it was that he understands that while the game of baseball is of primary importance it also supposed to be fun for the audience. He grew up listening to the Texas Rangers and there were a lot of seasons when they were out of the race at the All-Star break so the radio team there had to bring some-

Rob Brooks is the man in charge of the Phillies' Radio and TV Broadcasts

thing more than just the game story because the game story was usually dismal. Scott's not opposed to having fun while he's on the air while he's still respecting the game at the same time. With Larry, he's just a natural. He knows the game of baseball; he's naturally funny and he's just fun to be around. The two of them together do a pretty good job of making it sound like they are just two guys who are sitting around at a bar talking about the game and having a fun time doing it.

Do you direct them as to what they should be saying during a broadcast?
No, I mean we talk a little bit about certain performance aspects like making sure you give them the score and stuff like that, technical stuff. But I kind of let them go and do their own thing. It's real live interaction. What you hear those two guys saying on the radio is pretty much what we hear with them in the office.

Right now you have Scott and Larry going all nine innings of the radio broadcast and then have Harry Kalas come in and do play-by-play in the 4th inning. Why did you move to that group of broadcasters for the radio?
A couple of years ago we used to have Scott, Harry and Scott Graham do play-by-play throughout the game and then mix in Chris Wheeler and LA doing color. It got to the point that that you basically needed a scorecard to tell who was supposed to be on during the game. I mean people who were supposedly in charge of setting the schedule used to say, "What inning is he on?" It was really difficult for any of the guys to get a rapport with each other during the game. The play-by-play guy had to change-up his rhythm with each of the color guys that came in; we just weren't creating any bonds with the team and the listening audience. If you want to get a bond going you have to let them sit in the booth and have time to grow that relationship.

So basically you are trying to build and grow that relationship now?
We're in the process of rebranding our broadcast teams. All the rotating makes it difficult to establish that brand. We had a great team for a lot of years in Harry and Whitey. The great Whitey Ashburn just passed on and Mr. Kalas is 72 so he's not going to do this forever. Nobody does it forever. So we're in the process of sort of rebranding all of our broadcasts. We wanted to create a separate radio team and give that an identity. Even with the television team our identify today is Harry Kalas. At some point in time it will be something else. The fans ultimately want to turn on the game and hear their friends tell them about the game.

Many Phillies' fans don't realize that you also have a radio broadcast team that do all of the Phillies' games in Spanish. How much input do you give to the Spanish Beisbol Network?
In terms of direction not a ton. Bill Kulik technically runs that entire operation. He contracts with us for the rights to broadcast the games in Spanish. I interact with those guys a lot because that's something that I really want to see succeed. So I'm talking to Bill all the time about sponsorship stuff. If there are ways that we can help that along. The other day they had the Frankford High School baseball team here. Juan Ramos came to me and said "I'd really like to do something special for these kids." So we got JC Romero and went up and talked to JC and made sure JC was gonna come up and talk to them. So we brought

him up here in the press box and they got lucky and ran into Keith Hernandez when they were up here. I actually ran into Frankford's coach, Juan Namnun afterwards and he said "I really appreciate the time you gave those kids. A couple of the guys on the team wanted to know what it takes to become a baseball broadcaster." So it's great to have the Phillies involved with the Latino community and having us get engaged with them. I really want to see the Spanish Beisbol Network succeed.

You do you spend your time most of the game?
I spend a lot of my time in my office watching and listening. We spent the past couple of years working on addressing the radio team so I'm pretty comfortable with where they're at right now and who they are. However like I said, television is in a transition period. We have a first year play-by-play guy in Tom McCarthy. I have a great history with Tom, we're friends, we were co-workers here. But this is his first year doing television and we've added a new role to the team with him being a sideline reporter, which we haven't done in a long time. So we've added a number of elements to our television broadcast. So I would say that I give a little bit more attention to the television team. It's very jarring for a lot of people here in Philadelphia because we've essentially done our television broadcast the same way for a lot of years and with the same people. So now all of a sudden Tom brings a different energy to the job and it's something new so it's been jarring to the fan's ear. Add him to the mix with Harry, Chris and the Sarge and it's a very different rhythm. It's going to take some getting used to for the fans.

*Quotable: "… but if he tells me he's done I'm not risking anything by sending him back out there."
– Phillies' pitching coach Rich Dubee on Hamels telling him he was done throwing after the 7th inning*

Thursday, August 28th - Cubs 6 Phillies 4 (73-61) 2nd - 1 GB the Mets
Chicago – *For the second night in a row, the Phils' bullpen blew the lead and the game … With the Phils leading the Cubs 4-1 going into the bottom of the 8th, Ryan Madson gave up a homerun to pinch-hitter Mike Fontenot to bring the Cubs within two. Madson then proceeded to give up a double and a single and was promptly lifted for Chad Durbin. Durbin (5-3, 2.19) walked Derrick Lee to load the bases and then served up a grand slam to Aramis Ramirez to put Chicago in the lead … Cole Hamels wasted another solid outing going 7 innings, giving up 1 run on 5 hits while walking none and striking out 6 … Chase Utley went 3 for 5 … Jayson Werth went 2 for 3 with two doubles. Stuff: Cole Hamels leads the National League with 195 2/3rd innings pitched this season … Andrew Carpenter was sent back down to AA-Reading before the game and the Phillies recalled lefty Fabrio Castro.*

They call it baseball's greatest hit. However it wasn't executed on the field of play or even in a ballpark. Take Me Out to the Ball Game is celebrating it's 100th anniversary this year and is considered to be the third most often played song in American history after Happy Birthday and the Star Spangled Banner.

On May 2, 1908, the song was copyrighted by 29-year-old Jack Norworth, an actor and a monologist (one who performs a dramatic monologue) who reportedly had never been to a baseball game. As legend goes, Norworth was riding on the subway car as it took him past the Polo Grounds near Central Park in New York City and saw a sign that said "Baseball Today – Polo Grounds". When the words came to him he began writing them down and out of it came the song that we've all come to know and enjoy.

"Take Me Out to the Ballgame" celebrates its 100th anniversary this season

The song actually starts out with a verse that most have never heard which tells the story of a woman who loved baseball and who wanted her boyfriend to take her out on a date to a ball game …

Katie Casey was baseball mad
Had the fever and had it bad
Just to root for the hometown crew
Every Sou – Katie blew
On a Saturday her young beau
Called to see if she'd like to go
To see a show but Miss Kate said no
I'll tell you what you can do –

Take me out to the ball game,
Take me out with the crowd.
Buy me some peanuts and cracker jack,
I don't care if I never get back,
Let me root, root, root for the home team,
If they don't win it's a shame.
For it's one, two, three strikes, you're out,
At the old ball game."

The song became an instant hit. Four months after it was published it jumped to the Top 10 charts and was one of the most popular songs of 1908. It was recorded by numerous singing groups and was even the title of a 1949 MGM film starring Frank Sinatra and Gene Kelly.

Interestingly enough, Hall-of-Fame broadcaster Harry Carey is credited with being the first person to start singing the song during baseball games back in the early '70s. In 1976, White Sox owner and marketing genius Bill Veeck noticed that fans were singing along with Carey during the 7th inning stretch. The next day, Veeck had a microphone put into Carey's booth and broadcasted it throughout the entire stadium. The rest is history.

After Carey's death in 1998 the Cubs kept up the tradition by bringing in varied types of people to sing the song to their fans. A list of those who have sung the song at Wrigley include Bill Murray, Kenny Rodgers, Mike Ditka, Ozzy Ozbourne and tonight, the Sarge, Gary Matthews.

Matthews, a former Cubs player and coach, found out about the request a week prior to the Phils coming to town. Mike Radano of the Courier Post reported that Matthews was heard saying that he prepared for it by listening to his Luther Vandross songs on his iPod. The Sarge said, "Larry Anderson said they're dipping low in the barrel if they're asking me to do it . I'll be OK. I know the words and I'll be fine."

Matthews was fine. In fact, he actually had his grandson Denver help sing along with him. Luther Vandross he wasn't, but the Cubs fans seemed to enjoy their former star player and coach enough to give him a big ovation at the end. Phillies' fans will be relieved to know that Matthews remained loyal to the team and didn't say "Root, root, root for the Cubbies" but remained silent and held the microphone out to the Cubs fans to let them do their own singing. Way to go Sarge!

Quotable: "We have to play better. They got the big hit at the right moment. We get ahead of them, but it's a one- or two-run lead. That's not enough to hold (the Cubs). They're dangerous. That's kind of where it's at." - Charlie Manuel on the Cubs come from behind victory, the lack of clutch hitting and the Phils' third blown game in a row

Friday, August 29th - Cubs 3 Phillies 2 (73-62) 2nd - 2 GB the Mets

Chicago – The bullpen got tagged with their third consecutive loss in as many nights as the Cubs' Alfonso Soriano hit a solo homerun in the bottom of the 7th off of Clay Condrey (3-4, 3.58) for the Cubs 39th come-from-behind victory of the season. However, a missed call at first base had the potential to change the complexion of the game for the Phillies. With the scored tied 2-2 in the 7th, the Phils put runners on the corners with two outs for Ryan Howard. Howard hit the ball sharply to Cub's first baseman Derrick Lee, who knocked it down toward second base. Lee grabbed the ball and tossed it to first where umpire Chris Guccione called Howard out. On the replay, Howard was clearly safe. The run didn't score, the Phillies didn't take the lead and the inning was over ... Chase Utley was 1 for 4 with two runs scored ... Pat Burrell was 2 for 4 with one RBI (76) . Stuff: The Phils' bullpen has had a lot of work this season. Chad Durbin has thrown 74 innings which is the second most in the NL. Ryan Madson is sixth with 68 1/3rd innings. Clay Condrey is thirtieth with 59 1/3rd innings ... The Phillies acquired outfielder Matt Stairs from the Toronto Blue Jays in exchange for a player to be named later. To make room for Stairs, the Phillies sent Fabio Castro back down to AAA- Lehigh.

Stairs was hitting .250 with 11 home runs this season for the Blue Jays. A veteran of 16 seasons, the New Brunswick, Canada, native has had a solid career, hitting .266 with 252 home runs with 10 different clubs, most of his action coming against right-handed pitching. Stairs was designated for assignment after Thursday night's 3-2 loss to Tampa Bay. Playing in the American League since 2004, he's been used primarily as a designated hitter and corner outfielder, but can also play first. He's under contract through 2009 and is set to make $1 million next season. The Phils will reportedly send a prospect to Toronto.

Raise your hand if you knew this day would come, Matt Stairs in red pin-stripes. And wouldn't this be a fitting last move for Pat Gillick? Here's Stairs, a 5-9, 210-pound bundle of AL obscurity, a no-frills professional hitter who's ancient and available after the non-waiver deadline. And he's Canadian to boot, eh?

It's actually similar to the Jeff Conine acquisition of '06 in many ways, another move that came after the non-waiver deadline. Like Conine, who was also 40 at the time of the trade, Stairs fills a

Pat Gillick thinks he may have found the last piece to his playoff puzzle

void as an extra outfield bat, one that grew even larger when Geoff Jenkins landed on the DL. They also absorb next year's contract, just like Conine. I'm not worried about that; they moved Conine the following spring with relative ease. It's also similar to the Conine situation in that he's added during the throes of a Pat Burrell slump.

With Jenkins out for an undetermined amount of time, Stairs, who's a Jenkins clone only with a worse glove, could jump into the starting lineup as early as this series against right-handed pitching. He still possesses good power against righties; all 21 of his home runs last season came off right-handed pitching. (Has there ever been a team with so many lopsided splits on one roster?)

After missing out on Mark Kotsay, I like this utilitarian addition.

Quotable: "You could see how big it was by my emotion. I got a headache from that. You want to respect your opponents, but in that situation, it's tough to control." – Reliever JC Romero who screamed (and cursed) his way off of the mound after striking out three to work himself and Brett Myers out of a bases loaded jam

<u>Saturday, August 30th - Phillies 5 Cubs 2 (74-62) 2nd - 2 GB the Mets</u>

Chicago – *Outfielder Jayson Werth had a monster day, going 3 for 4 with 2 homeruns (19 & 20) and 4 RBIs (53) ... Brett Myers (8-10, 4.40) gave up a lot of hits again (11) but only gave up 2 runs in 7 innings. He walked none and struck out 8 ... JC Romero saved Myers and himself out of a bases loaded jam as he struck out three batters in a scoreless 8th ... Brad Lidge came in and threw a perfect 9th, striking out two in the process for his 32nd save of the year ... Jimmy Rollins went 3 for 5 with a double ... Chase Utley went 2 for 4 with 1 run scored ... Ryan Howard hit his major league leading 37th homerun of the year in the 8th . Stuff: Werth has a league-best 13 homeruns against left-handed pitchers... The Phils' 10 total hits only came from four players Werth (3), Rollins (3), Utley (2) and Howard (2) ... It was reported by beat writer Scott Lauber that JC Romero's mother (Gladys Romero) called JC after the game and scolded him for using not-so-nice words after he struck out the side in the 8th.*

All sorts of things turn up at Citizens Bank Park's Lost-and-Found department: Besides the hundreds of hats and cell phones that are recovered each year, wallets, crutches, even dentures, have been found.

Debbie Bruner, Manager of Guest Services, is in charge of cataloging and hunting down the rightful owners of these items. When she's not helping fans sift through a dozen or so bins of clothes looking for a mis-placed denim jacket, she's sleuthing her way to connecting a fan with one of their lost items.

The Phanatic hams it up with the author and his wife

What we basically do is collect all of the lost items that fans find and turn into us as well as the items that our Game Day staff finds during the game or after the game is over. Most of the time the items that we receive are turned in at the end of the night. One of the things that the hosts and the hostesses do is walk down each of their rows and check for any items that were left behind. If they find anything they bring it to us on their way out at the end of the night.

Once we get an item turned into us we will log it in onto our lost & found list. If the item is easily traceable to its owner we will contact them and make sure that they get it back. If not we will hold onto the stuff for ten games and wait to see if anyone comes to claim the item.

We probably get 10-12 items turned in every game. If no one claims the item we donate everything to a charity. If its items like clothing we will donate it to Good Will. If it's a pair of glasses we will give them to the Lions Club. We track down a lot of the cell phones to the rightful owners, but what's still left and isn't claimed we end up giving to Women Organized Against Rape for their 911 program. The baseball gloves that aren't claimed are donated to the Philadelphia Boys Club or to our own RBI baseball program that we have here for intercity youth.

The weirdest thing that was ever turned in was a pair of dentures. You would think someone would say, "Hey, I had my teeth before the game started and now I don't have them. Maybe I left them at the ball park!" Nobody ever claimed them.

You'd be surprised at some of the things that have been turned in. We find medication, cameras, Blackberry's, baby shoes, car keys, crutches, credit cards, a single flip-flop. We actually had someone turn in a pair of pants. Now try to figure out the guy who left the stadium without his pants on. That must have been a tough game.

The top five items that we get turned into us would be:
1. Jackets/Sweat Shirts
2. Cell Phones
3. Umbrellas/Ponchos
4. Baseball hats
5. Wallets

We also get people who come to us that have lost something but it was never found. The saddest one I remember was a lady who lost her diamond engagement ring about two years ago. They had just gotten engaged at the ballpark and I don't know, I guess she was showing the ring and it was a little too big for her finger and it flopped off. They couldn't find it anywhere and it was never turned in. I felt really bad for the couple.

Every once in a while we will get lost children. Someone will bring the kid here or the kid will come here themselves. We'll take a description; try to get as much information out of the kid as we can. Some of your smarter 7 or 8 year olds actually know their mom and dads cell phone numbers; we'll call their phone and bring them right over. We have the proud honor of never having lost a kid. We always bring them and their parents together.

We had one night where one kid was lost twice. Then the kid came back a couple of weeks later and he got lost again and you know why? Because, he enjoyed the gifts that we gave him.

Quotable:" Playing everyday has been good for me. It's a good spot, a good club and it's good to be loved. - Jayson Werth who is hitting .342 with 6 homeruns and 15 RBIs after starting 21 out of the last 23 games

Sunday, August 31st - Phillies 5 Cubs 3 (75-62) 2nd - 1 GB the Mets

Chicago – *Jayson Werth follows up a 4 RBI game yesterday with a 3 RBI game today, going 2 for 4 and hitting his 21st homerun of the year. He now has 56 RBIs on the season ... Ryan Howard went 3 for 5 with a double and an RBI (114) ... Chase Utley and Shane Victorino had two hits each ... Jamie Moyer (12-7, 3.80) pitched effectively as he threw 5 1/3rd innings giving up 2 runs ... Brad Lidge pitched a perfect 9th again for his 33rd save of the year. Stuff: The Phillies called up four players for the September roster expansion. Olympic Bronze Medal winner Lou Marson will be put onto the roster in addition to outfield speedster Grey Golson. Pitchers Adam Eaton and JA Happ will also be joining the team. Eaton ended up his stint in the minors going 8-7 with a 3.60 ERA after being sent down to AAA-Lehigh ... Pat Burrell ended August as he began it, struggling. He hit .188 with just 4 homeruns and 12 RBIs for the month. In the Cubs' series he was 3 for 17 with 1 RBI... Charlie Manuel tied Larry Bowa for 10th most victories as a Phillies' manager with 337 wins.*

It's been quite easy to pick on Ryan Howard this year, but think about what would happen if you replaced him with a higher-OBP, lower-power first baseman like, say, Derek Lee or Mark Teixeira. While both those guys are having better years than Howard, you would definitely lose a large number of RBIs if you put them in the Phillies' lineup instead of Howard. On the other hand, you would get a big boost in OBP. The problem is, after Burrell, there's no one in the lineup to drive those runs in. For most of the year, Jenkins was in the 6th spot and, after that, comes the black hole.

Rookie catcher Lou Marson is one of four players the Phillies initially called up for September

It just might be that, for this year, Howard has been a better fit for the Phillies' dysfunctional lineup than a lot of other first baseman who are actually having much better all-around seasons. But, going forward, my concern about Howard is that the 2009 version will be much like the 2008 version -- only without the flukishly high numbers with RISP. If that's the case, then his RBI totals will go down considerably and he will become a huge drain on the lineup.

September – Destiny
…and in all places Philly

Quotable: "(Kendrick) doesn't have a good look about himself right now. He doesn't look like he wants to be out there to get people out. It's like bad stuff is going to happen, and generally if you have that bad look, bad stuff is going to happen. He's got to get a better look about himself. He's got to get more confidence." - Rich Dubee on Kyle Kendrick's poor effort against the Nationals

<u>Monday, September 1st - Nationals 7 Phillies 4 (75-63) 2nd - 2 GB the Mets</u>

Washington D.C. – *Kyle Kendrick (11-8, 5.06) pitched erratically, allowing 6 runs on 8 hits in 4 innings of work as the Phils' September home stretch starts out on a bad note as they fall 2 games behind the New York Mets ... The offense only mustered a total of 4 hits in the game ... Jimmy Rollins went 1 for 4, hitting his 10th homerun of the season in the 9th ... Ryan Howard went 1 for 4 and knocked in his 115th RBI. Stuff: Kendrick has a 9.14 ERA in his last five starts ... The Phillies were no-hit by Tim Redding through 4 innings who has mastered them this season. With the exception of a 7-run outburst on July 30th, Redding has dominated the Phils, going 3-0 with a 1.38 ERA in his four other starts against them... The Nationals have won 7 straight games.*

Today's game wasn't pretty. This Kyle Kendrick situation is most unwelcome. Kendrick allowed six runs on eight hits and three walks against the predominantly right-handed Nats' lineup. I'm inclined to give the struggling right-hander the benefit of the doubt because he's the owner of a 21-12 record and a reasonable 4.53 ERA, but his command has been dreadful. He's been touched for six or more runs in three of his last five starts and a total of five times since July 19th. You have to wonder if yesterday forced the Phillies' hand. The question becomes whether they skip his next scheduled turn at Shea or if they replace him in the rotation entirely. They're running out of time.

Burrell started the month on the bench after hitting just .181 in August

On a day when the Mets added a million pitchers to their arsenal of beleaguered relievers, they went into Milwaukee and won 4-2, pushing their lead to two games in the National League East. Meanwhile, the Phillies were in the process of being no-hit by Tim Redding into the sixth inning. Three of the Phillies' four runs were basically given away by walks and a hit batsman.

Continuing with the offense, one question that came up during the radio broadcast was pinch hitting Carlos Ruiz with the bases loaded. Larry Andersen wondered if Greg Golson should have been used. I'm wondering if Lou Marson should have been used. On a day when Chris Coste started, Ruiz should be used strictly as a defensive replacement. That's the joy of expanding your bench, being able to sit offensive non-entities like Ruiz. Shielding rookies like Marson from those types of match-ups is a hallmark of Charlie Manuel's style. I'm not a great fan of that, particularly with the season Marson had in the minors.

Speaking of the September call-ups ("fantasy baseball," as L.A. calls it), shortstop Jason Donald is reportedly on his way, as are lefty Les Walrond, infielder Mike Cervenak, and first baseman Andy Tracy, who will join the club today. I have a sneaky suspicion the rookie position call-ups will factor in minimally, while the pitchers, J.A. Happ in particular, will play a significant role. Adam Eaton also returns after going 0-5 with a 7.02 ERA in seven minor league starts. To compare, minor league journeyman Kip Bouknight, who is basically the same age as Eaton, was released July 3 after posting a 3-8 and 6.95 ERA at Reading. It's absolutely incredible how the Phillies can't get over it.

After finishing August with a brutal .181 average, Pat Burrell started on the bench. Burrell has watched his career year become career average. However the veteran left fielder took the benching with a touch of humor after being told that he would not be playing today saying "I'm still available to come in defensively late in the game."

Quotable: *"We'll probably make a decision after tomorrow's game or tomorrow sometime. I want Hamels on the Mets. The reason is like we've talked it's a two game swing. At this time of year, we need to win some games over New York." – Charlie Manuel on the likelihood of Cole Hamels pitching his next start versus the Mets after a solid outing over the Nationals*

Tuesday, September 2nd - Phillies 4 Nationals 0 (76-63) 2nd - 2 GB the Mets

Washington D.C. – Cole Hamels (12-8, 3.01) shut out Washington over 7 1/3rd innings while limiting the Nats to 5 hits, walking 3 and striking out 6 ... JC Romero and Chad Durbin came in to close the 8th while Brad Lidge pitched a scoreless 9th in a non-save situation ... Jimmy Rollins went 2 for 3 with 2 runs scored and 2 RBIs (52) ... Pedro Feliz went 2 for 4 with 1 run scored. Stuff: Today's shutout was the 10th thrown this season by the pitching staff ... The Phillies are now 63-0 when leading after 8 innings ... To help get the offense going, Jayson Werth batted 3rd for the first time this season. He went 1 for 3 with a single.

Here's a long-overdue salute to Cole Hamels, top five National League pitcher for my money, league leader in innings pitched (203) and batting average against (.218). He's the owner of a lights-out 174/46 K/BB ratio. In other words, behind Tim Lincecum, Sabathia and Johan Santana, nobody else provides the steady dominance Cole Hamels has delivered.

Cole earns my vote in two categories: Most Valuable and Most Underrated Phillie. With up-and-down seasons from Chase Utley, Ryan Howard, Jimmy Rollins and now Pat Burrell, Hamels outshines them all as the player they've been able to count on most. Nobody evokes the same level of trust. Nobody is achieving the same level of excellence. He's excelled in every area but wins, which is entirely on the offense. Yet again, the bats managed a pedestrian four runs in last night's 4-0 victory, allowing a weak Nationals team to hang in when they should

have been put away. Not to dimin-
ish the job Brad Lidge has done, but
you hear more about the possibility
of a Brad Lidge Cy Young award than
Hamels, who's logged roughly four
times the innings as Lidge with similar
results to scale.

Another reason why Hamels has been
overshadowed is that he hasn't been
matched up in any marquee games
against the Mets. The last time he faced
them was April 18, which is a travesty.
The Phillies have yet to name a starter
for Sunday night's game at Shea. Their
choices include Kyle Kendrick, J.A.
Happ or Hamels. Get serious. It's an
easy choice. They have to showcase
their best pitcher in the final three
games against the team they're trailing.

Cole Hamels won his 12th game of the season

Quotable: "We have three games with (New York), so it's still there for us. I think we better win on Friday and I don't want to go farther ahead than that. We can't get ahead of ourselves." - Charlie Manuel on the dwindling chances the Phils have on winning the division

Wednesday, September 3rd - Nationals 9 Phillies 7 (76-64) 2nd - 3 GB the Mets

Washington D.C. – *Ryan Howard went 2 for 4 with 2 homeruns (38 & 39) and 4 RBIs (119) but it wasn't enough as the Phillies' pitching staff blew 3 leads during the game and dropped 3 games behind the NL East leading Mets ... Joe Blanton pitched a rocky outing only going 4 innings while surrendering 4 runs. He walked 3 and struck out 2 ... Ryan Madson held the Nationals at bay for 2 shutout innings until the Nationals exploded for a run in the 7th and 4 runs in the 8th ... Chad Durbin (5-4, 2.69) took the loss after giving up 4 runs in only 2/3rd innings of work ... Chase Utley went 1 for 3 with a 2-run triple ... Jimmy Rollins and Pat Burrell had 2 hits each. Stuff: Greg Golson appeared in his first major league game as a pinch runner in the 8th. He promptly stole 2nd base for first career steal ... Shane Victorino had a night off as he fights through a 5 for 36 slump.*

I wonder what happened to the young player who used to earn praise for being both a big man and such a nimble, capable defender.

For all his successes, Ryan Howard's glove remains one of the single, biggest disappointments

of the last few seasons. Baseball America once named him "Best Defensive
Power Prospect" in the Eastern League
and I'm fairly certain he received similar accolades while playing in the International League.

His agility is still decent, and his mo-
bility isn't the real problem, either.
Think how he tracks down balls in foul
territory; he's actually quite capable. It's

Ryan Howard has been an MVP at the plate, but one of the worst fielding first basemen in baseball this season

the mental part, the flash decision making, followed next by his arm accuracy and quickness,
evidenced by the number of plays that just gobble him up. The bottom line is he has the tools
to be better than he is. Unfortunately, one just doesn't get the sense that he takes much pride in
it. It's just one more thing for the Phillies to bring to the arbitration table if the two sides can't
agree on a new contract after the season, and they have every right to do it.

*Quotable: "That's definitely his best game of the year. I think he had a stretch like this in my first
year (with the Phillies), but it's more noticeable now because he went to the minor leagues and this
was an important game for us." - Charlie Manuel on Brett Myers' 0 run, 10 strikeout performance
against the first place Mets*

Friday, September 5th - Phillies 3 Mets 0 (77-64) 2nd - 2 GB the Mets
New York – *Brett Myers pitched a monster game against the Mets as he and Brad Lidge combined
on a 5 hit shutout of New York. Myers (9-10, 4.19) looked like an All-Star as he threw 8 scoreless
innings, walking 2 and striking out 10 ... Lidge closed out a somewhat shaky 9th as he yielded
2 hits but was able to keep both runners from scoring for his 34th save of the year ... The offense
only managed 4 hits but made them count when they needed them ... Chase Utley 0 for 4 in the
game had an RBI groundout in the 1st ... Greg Dobbs finished the scoring when he connected off
the Mets' Mike Pelfrey for a 2-run homerun (7) in the 7th inning. Stuff: Myers is now 6-1 with a
1.55 ERA since his return from the minors ... The 10 strikeouts for Myers was the 11th time in his
career that he threw double digits in Ks ... The Phillies signed fan favorite Tadahito Iguchi for the
remainder of the season. He was released by the Padres on September 1st.*

Considering what's at stake, a strong case can be made that Myers just finished the best start
of his career. Don't bother reading the opposite angle because there was nothing the opposition could do. From first-pitch strikes to a devastating curve to finish it, it was good morning,
good afternoon, good night for Mets hitters. This is the new cool and collected Myers... one
with poise and a plan. It's inconceivable to think that the pitcher we saw tonight was trying
to find his way in Double-A just weeks ago. Make it three out of the last four starts where he's
pitched shutout ball, contributing to the third-lowest post-All-Star ERA in the league. With

the win, the Phils pull to within two games of the NL East lead and wait on Mother Nature to decide when the series resumes.

Prior to the game, Phillies' Hall-of-Famer Mike Schmidt sent an email to the Charlie Manuel hoping to fire up the team over the last month of the season. Manuel printed the email and posted in the locker room for everyone to read before the game. It simply read, *"One pitch, one at bat, one situation, think "small" and "big" things result, tough at-bats, lots of walks, stay up the middle with men on base, whatever it takes to "keep the line moving" on offense, 27 outs on defense, the Mets know you're better than they are, they remember last year. You guys are never out of a game. Welcome the challenge that confronts you this weekend. You are the stars. Good luck. #20"*

Mike Schmidt sent Charlie Manuel an email before the game encouraging the Phillies to be tough

Quotable: *"It is a successful series, but it did get away. Unfortunately, we don't play them anymore going down the stretch. The [deficit] is always a lot when you're not playing them. But we're sitting on the door to two ways in [to the playoffs]: one team that we just played, and the other team that's ahead of us in the wild card we're playing [this weekend (Milwaukee)]. We have quite an opportunity, definitely."* - Jimmy Rollins on the Phils' chances of making the playoffs after taking 2 of 3 from the Mets

<u>Sunday, September 7th - Game 1: Phillies 6 Mets 2 / Game 2: Mets 6 Phillies 3 (78-65) 2nd - 2 GB the Mets</u>

New York – *In the first game of the double header, Jamie Moyer (13-7, 3.64) pitched 7 shutout innings while Greg Dobbs continued his power streak, smacking a 3-run homerun (8) in the 3rd to put the Phils up 6-0 in the 4th. He was 2 for 4 in the game with 2 runs scored ... Carlos Ruiz went 3 for 4 with an RBI (24) and a run scored ... The win temporarily put the Phils 1 game behind the Mets for the NL East lead.*

In game two of the twin bill, Cole Hamels (12-9, 3.12) pitched a rare poor outing as he gave up 5 runs (4 earned) on 9 hits while walking 1 and striking out 6 in 5 innings of work ... Ryan Howard belted his 40th homerun of the season. He ended the game 2 for 4 with 2 RBIs (121) ... The Mets' Carlos Delgado had another big game against Phillies' pitching as he went 3 for 4 with 2 homeruns and 4 RBIs. Stuff: Baseball Prospectus reports that the Mets have a 77.3% chance of winning the NL East while the Phillies have a 22.5% chance of winning the division.

I suspect that many conversations around Delaware Valley water coolers start with "Look at it this way..." So that's how I'll start today's recap. Look at it this way: After this weekend, the Phillies could have been 6 games back, 4 back, 2 back, or in a tie for first. They got the second best option. Still, justification like that is a telltale sign that one didn't get what one wanted. The Phils had an opportunity to erase the Mets' lead entirely. Deep down it doesn't feel like a series win or loss for either side.

Last night represented a huge sigh of relief for the Mets as Carlos Delgado almost single handedly saved the season for the Mets. He's not the National League MVP, but the New York media will do their part to float his name. The fact is, there isn't anyone contributing more offensively to a contending team down the stretch, so if that's what you look for in an MVP, look no further than Delgado.

The Phils split the doubleheader but still remain two games behind David Wright's Mets

It wasn't a good night for the men in red. Hamels never settled in after the catcher interference call, the first in a series of weird and unfortunate plays. The drumbeat to run Cole Hamels out of town continued on 610-WIP. I believe the word they used was "soft." His ERA fell to a limp 3.12, but Mister Softie managed to stay ahead of Johan Santana for the league lead in innings pitched. I would have liked to see what Hamels would have come up with if the last time he faced the Mets wasn't five months ago. Expect Mister Softie to carry the team on his back the rest of the way.

Quotable: "It's going to come down to the last week. We just have to take care of ourselves and we'll be all right." – Jayson Werth who cranked a 3-run shot in the 7th to give the Phillies all the runs they needed for the win

Monday, September 8th - Phillies 8 Marlins 6 (79-65) 2nd - 1 ½ GB the Mets

Philadelphia – *The Phils moved within 1 ½ games of first, hanging on to defeat the Marlins back at Citizens Bank Park ... Leading 5-4 going into the bottom of the 7th , Jayson Werth hit a 3-run homerun (22) with two outs in the inning to give the Phils the breathing room they needed for the victory ... Joe Blanton (7-12, 4.86) gave up 4 runs in 5 innings ... The bullpen ran into some trouble in the 8th as JC Romero gave up 2 runs in 1/3rd innings as the Marlins came within two ... Ryan Madson and Scott Eyre however were able to stop the bleeding quick enough before the Fish were able to tack on any more runs ... Brad Lidge pitched a scoreless 9th to earn his 35th save ... Jimmy Rollins went 3 for 5 with an RBI (54) and 2 runs scored ... Ryan Howard continued his hitting ways in the month of September as he went 2 for 4 with 2 RBIs (123). Stuff: Blanton is now 1-0 with a 5.58 ERA in his last 6 starts ... With the win, the Phillies moved a half game closer to the Mets and are only 3 ½ games behind the Brewers in the NL Wild Card race.*

On January 31, 2006, Samuel Anthony Alito Jr. was sworn in as the 110th U.S. Supreme Court Justice, replacing the retiring Sandra Day O'Connor. During his inauguration onto the highest court in our country, President George W. Bush said, "Judge Alito has demonstrated that he is eminently qualified to serve on our nation's highest court, and America is fortunate to have a man of his integrity and intellect willing to serve." What the citizens of the Philadelphia area might not have realized during Justice Alito's inauguration was that it marked the first time in the history of the United States that a Phillies' fan sat on the bench of the U.S. Supreme Court.

US Supreme Court Justice Samuel Alito is a huge Phillies' fan

In a rare in-chambers interview, Justice Alito, born and raised in Trenton, NJ, sat down and gave a brief look into the life of a Phillies' fan who just so happens to have one of the most powerful roles in our nation.

I first became interested in the Phillies when I was around 5 years old. My mother has a picture of me in a little Phillies' uniform and I was just about that age. I was born in 1950 so it was the mid-50's. Richie Ashburn and Robin Roberts were my favorite players.

I met Robin Roberts recently, which was a real thrill for me. I actually met Richie Ashburn very briefly when I went down to Dream Week back in 1993 or 1994. My wife surprised me and signed me up for a week down in Florida where fans get to play baseball with some of the old ballplayers. Richie stopped by one afternoon and I loved seeing him and being down there. It was great.

My earliest memories of being a Phillies fan? Well my father often took us to doubleheaders because we got to see two games for the price of one. We had a particular spot down the first base line out toward right field where we would always try to sit in Connie Mack Stadium. I remember sitting there and looking up at that big wall they had in right field with the Ballantine Beer logo.

There were also times when we would go to doubleheaders on Sundays. Those games were always touch and go as to whether they would be able to finish the second game because back in those days there was a Philadelphia law that required games to stop I think it was either at 6:00 or 7:00 at night on a Sunday. Once you hit the time the game had to stop whatever inning they were in.

One of my most vivid memories was the first night game that I went to in 1957 or 1958. I went with my father so it was just my father and me. I remember walking into the stadium in the evening and the Phillies were playing the Reds. The field looked entirely different at night; it was like a new world to me. I can still remember seeing the Red's Ted Kluszewski. He had these massive arms and this was back in the days before baseball players used to pump iron or whatever else they did there for a while. But he just looked gigantic and I think he actually hit a home run against the Phillies that night; it went out over the right field fence.

When I'm in session I still watch as many games as I can. My son and I are both big baseball fans so we signed up for the MLB cable package so we can see all their games. When they come to play the Nationals, I'll usually go to a few of the games. We went to two of the games last week and it was the two that they lost. Not happy games. Usually I'll try to go to Citizens Bank Park a number of times a season. So far though I've only been up twice but I've seen them here in Washington about five or six times this year.

My most interesting legal cases regarding Major League Baseball? It's funny you should ask that because I had to give a lecture this spring here for the Supreme Court Historical Society. It's an organization devoted to the history of the Supreme Court where they publish a journal of articles about the history of court. They invite each justice when he or she joins the court to give a lecture on some aspect of court history and so I had to pick a topic and I picked the Federal League baseball case in 1921.

I think it was probably one of the biggest Supreme Court cases involving baseball. It was one that held the position that baseball isn't subject to the Sherman Anti-Trust Statute It has quite an interesting history related to the federal baseball league that folded in 1915. I couldn't say whether or not that particular case is something that I could ever see changing because it could one day possibly come before us again. However, what happened was that when this case came up in 1921 the understanding of the Commerce Clause of the Constitution and the Anti-Trust laws was quite different from what it is today. And the court held that baseball was not commerce, it was not interstate commerce, they reasoned that the teams travel from state to state to play their games, but when they did what they actually get paid for doing which is playing a game they were doing it in one place, they were not doing it in interstate commerce. That was the way they understood the law to be at that time. And then the issue has come again in later cases and the court has said that it wasn't going to overrule the earlier precedent whether they would have reached the same result or not. Either way, Congress can change the law if it wanted to.

The only other Justice that I know who is a big baseball fan is Justice (John Paul) Stevens. He's a very avid Cubs' fan. In fact he claims that he was at Wrigley Field during the 1932 World Series when Babe Ruth called his shot and then hit a homerun on the next pitch. He says he was there. Now I think 200,000 people say they were there at that game, but I believe him. He's a very avid Cubs' fan, he goes and he'll watch the games. So he's hoping this is the year for them to win the World Series.

How do I think the season is going so far? Well I was asked at the beginning of the year what my prediction was and I predicted the Phillies would win 93 games. I don't think they're going to get to 93. I still have hope. It's unfortunate they don't have any more games against the Mets so we're going to have to rely on somebody beating the Mets.

I've been a Phillies' fan now for over fifty years and I really like this team. My favorite players are probably Utley, Howard and Hamels.

How would I fix the Phils' currently hitting woes? I don't know. I've been wondering if Chase Utley is hurt. I know there's been speculation about it. He doesn't seem to me to be swinging exactly the way he did earlier in the season when he was putting up MVP numbers. So I don't know if there's anything that can be done about his situation. If I were to make one change right now it would be to stay away from hitting Utley and Howard back to back.

I understand why Charlie usually slots them in together, but I'm finally seeing him make some changes in the order and seeing that he has separated them a few times. I think that's a good move because it makes the team too vulnerable to the left-handed relief specialist late in the game. You have a critical spot in the game and if you've got Utley and Howard coming up the other team is always going to bring in their left-hander. But if you separate them with a right-handed bat in between them then it could protect you against that.

I'm hopeful that they'll make the playoffs this year. My son follows all sorts of sophisticated baseball statistics and he says that the odds say the Phillies have about a 30% chance of making it either as the NL East champ or as the Wild Card. Let's just say that I'll be watching all the games and hoping that they can pull it together.

Quotable: "We'll talk about our pitching. We'll try to figure out the best possible way for us to go."
– Charlie Manuel on Kendrick's spot in the rotation

Tuesday, September 9th - Marlins 10 Phillies 8 (79-66) 2nd - 2 ½ GB the Mets

Philadelphia – *In an attempt to try to get him back on track, the Phillies trotted Kyle Kendrick out to the mound to see if he could solidify his #5 spot in the rotation. It didn't work. Kendrick (11-9, 5.44) lasted only 1 1/3rd innings, giving up 7 runs on 6 hits and walking 2 … JA Happ relieved Kendrick and gave up 3 runs in 3 1/3rd innings … The remainder of the bullpen pitched 4 1/3rd scoreless innings … Down 9-1 going into the bottom of the 4th, the Phils did make a run at it as they scored 7 but were unable to catch the Marlins as they fell 2 ½ games behind New York … Ryan Howard went 2 for 5, hitting his 41st homerun of the season while driving in 2 more runs (125) … Jimmy Rollins went 2 for 4 while stealing his 42nd base on the season. Stuff: Kendrick is now 1-4 with a 11.35 ERA in his last 6 starts … Rollins now has 290 lifetime steals which ranks him 4th on the Phillies' all-time list behind Billy Hamilton (508), Ed Delahanty (412) and Sherry Magee (387) … Geoff Jenkins was activated off of the 15 day DL.*

Fans from Campbell Soup saw a great comeback but the Phillies fell short

The pitcher who once succeeded by pitching within himself is now his own worst enemy. Kendrick lost it, and there's no getting it back. Not this season. Last night was rock bottom in the short career of the 24-year-old right-hander, the one who established an impressive 21-13 career record without being blessed with blazing stuff. Kendrick fell to 1-4 with an 11.35 ERA in his last six starts, toppling into the wrong side of the fine line he's walked since setting foot in the majors. Keep the sinker down, throw strikes and don't be afraid to pitch to contact: three guiding rules to make or break his success. Easier said than done for a pitcher who's lost his cool.

In the second act, the Phils scratched back, while scoreboard watchers noted that the Nats pulled ahead of the Mets 6-5. The big inning occurred in the sixth, thanks to RBIs from Shane Victorino, Greg Dobbs and Matt Stairs. But with runners at first and third, the scoring stopped. Here's where the second-guessing starts. Stairs, possibly the slowest runner on the team, stayed in the game and ended up on third, despite a bench loaded with speed. Jayson Werth flied out to right and Stairs didn't score. Had it been Greg Golson and not Stairs, there's no doubt he scores to make it 10-9. The Phils would then blow another chance in the eighth when Werth couldn't drive So Taguchi home from third. Meanwhile, Carlos Delgado turned the tide once again for New York, helping the Mets edge the Nats 10-8.

Some might suggest this will be remembered as the night the season turned for the worse. Others believe their fate will be determined at the conclusion of their weekend set with Milwaukee. We'll just have to wait and see.

Quotable: "We'll talk about our pitching. We'll try to figure out the best possible way for us to go."
— Charlie Manuel on Kendrick's spot in the rotation

Wednesday, September 10th - Marlins 7 Phillies 3 (79-67) 2nd - 3 ½ GB the Mets

Philadelphia – *Post season hopes are beginning to be wane ... The Phils tied the game in the 5th 3-3 but were unable to hold back the Marlins' offense nor put any more runs on the board as they fall 3 ½ games behind the Mets in the NL East ... Brett Myers (9-11, 4.22) took the loss, giving up 4 runs in 7 1/3rd while striking out 9 and walking 1 ... Chad Durbin gave up 2 runs in 1 IP while JC Romero got tagged for 1 run in 1/3rd inning of work ... Ryan Howard continued hitting the long ball as he socked a solo shot, his major league leading 42nd, in the 2nd inning. It was his 126th RBI of the year.*

For a team that just got out-pitched, out-hit and out-managed in a key best-of-three, Charlie Manuel's post-game press conference, aired live on Comcast SportsNet, could have been uttered by a sage manager who's gliding into the playoffs easily, pulling all the right strings and bending minds as the great Philadelphia Phillies' dynasty reaches for more glistening hardware to place upon the mantle. Instead of urgency, or trepidation to face the fire after managing this series so foolishly, the fourth-year boss seemed downright casual about his club digging themselves into a hole they might not escape. "You

Charlie Manuel doesn't appear to be too concerned as the Phillies fall further behind the Mets in the standings

never know when you're going to get hot," he resolved, referring to their upcoming series against the Wild Card-leading Brewers, who by the way won today.

You never know. You never know for example when Chase Utley will summon the supernatural power to heal the injury he's obviously hiding. Or the day when none of Manuel's star players are mired in some sort of major crisis creating slump. Or when the multi-year search for a capable set-up man would end with a clear victor. Perhaps one will fall from the heavens.

In the world of Phillies' baseball, there's always tomorrow. Eternal tomorrow. And tomorrow, Manuel will ask his 45-year-old starter to start the digging, pitching on short rest.

Quotable: "What's the squeeze sign?" – Asked by Carlos Ruiz to Charlie Manuel as he walked to the plate in the bottom of the 8th. Manuel put the squeeze on and Ruiz executed it perfectly knocking in Jimmy Rollins from third base.

Thursday, September 11th - Phillies 6 Brewers 3 (80-67) 2nd - 3 GB the Mets

Philadelphia – With the more likely scenario of obtaining a Wild Card seed in the playoffs than the NL East, the Phils took their first step toward that goal by defeating the Brewers in the first of a four game series. Milwaukee is in first place in the Wild Card race and now only lead the Phillies by 3 games … Ryan Howard continued slamming opposing pitchers as he launched his 43rd homerun of the year, a 2-run shot in the 1st. Howard ended up going 2 for 3 in the game, scoring 2 runs and knocking in 3 runners. He now has 129 RBIs … Jimmy Rollins and Pedro Feliz each went 2 for 3 … Carlos Ruiz had a double and 2 RBIs (26) … Jamie Moyer (14-7, 3.68) threw 5 2/3rd innings, giving up 3 runs on 4 hits while striking out 5. He was tagged for two homeruns in the game … The bullpen threw 3 1/3rd shutout innings as Brad Lidge nailed down his 36th save, throwing a perfect 9th inning. Stuff: Charlie Manuel put on the squeeze play with Rollins at 3rd and Ruiz at the plate in the 8th. According to Elias Sports Bureau, it was only the second squeeze play ever called by Manuel as manager of the team. The squeeze worked which gave the Phillies an important insurance run in the game …Ryan Howard is hitting .329 in his last 20 games with 10 homeruns, 25 RBIs and 11 walks.

Other standouts of the game included Ryan Madson, who pitched two shutout innings of relief, and Carlos Ruiz, who answered back after a two-run Milwaukee sixth with a RBI double in the home half. Chooch then added a successful suicide squeeze in the eighth to cap the scoring for Philadelphia. Moyer proved ageless once again as he beat Ben Sheets. Unfortunately it's only worth one win and there's little reason to soak it up since they need to sweep the Brewers or at worse win 3 of the 4 games. With the win,

John Heath, Nancy Wescott and Jen McNesby discuss the Phillies' Wild Card chances

the Phils trail the Brewers and idle Mets by three games, but the Mets hold a four-game advantage in the loss column. This should come down to the wire. Hang on tight.

Quotable: "Jimmy's the catalyst. When he goes, we go." - Ryan Howard commenting on Rollins 3 for 5 day

<u>Saturday, September 13th - Phillies 7 Brewers 3 (81-67) 2nd - 2 ½ GB the Mets</u>

Philadelphia – *Following an unexpected night off because of the Phils' second rainout this month, the Phillies scored 5 quick runs in the first two innings as Cole Hamels (13-9, 3.11) and the bullpen shut down the Brewers to move two games behind the Wild Card leaders ... Hamels threw 6 1/3rd innings, giving up 2 runs on 6 hits while walking 3 and striking out 6 ... The offense combined for 9 hits with Jimmy Rollins leading the way as he fell a triple short of the cycle. Rollins went 3 for 5 with a homerun (11), 2 runs scored and 2 RBIs (56) ... Chase Utley went 2 for 4 with an RBI (94) ... Ryan Howard continued his torrid month, going 1 for 3 with 2 RBIs (131). Stuff: The NY Mets split a double header with the Braves, leaving the Phils only 2 ½ games behind the NL East Lead ... There were 45,105 fans in the park for the team's 46th sellout this season.*

Let's put ourselves in the Brewers' shoes for a moment. You've just lost 9 of 12 and the first two games of a four-game set against your closest Wild Card adversary. You feel terrible, battered, beaten, and you have to play two more against a Phillies team that's starting to get their swagger back. You've been stuck in a Philadelphia hotel forever, and after this, you're off to Chicago for another tough series. You're in baseball purgatory, and the ghosts of past failures are beginning to swirl.

But alas, you face Joe Blanton in the early game, and if there's any better way to illustrate why Brett Myers should be starting the first game, not Blanton, I'd like to hear it. Since joining the Phils, Blanton has been mediocre at best and particularly poor in the early innings. Philadelphia has the momentum, but that's only as good as your next starting pitcher, and Blanton hasn't been getting

The Phillies celebrate Latino Family night with song and dance

it done. Milwaukee will send Dave Bush to the hill, and Bush has actually been a pretty good road pitcher lately. The Brewers have to like their chances.

So if you're Charlie Manuel, why not hit them with a sledgehammer and start red-hot Myers in the first game? If he takes care of business, you've won the series and the pressure falls squarely on the road team's shoulders to salvage their dwindling Wild Card lead in a do-or-die nightcap.

Quotable: "When you're struggling, things never seem to go your way." - Milwaukee manager Ned Yost after the 4-game sweep by the Phillies.

Sunday, September 14th - Game 1: Phillies 7 Brewers 3 / Game 2: Phillies 6 Brewers 1 (82-67) 2nd - 1 GB the Mets

Philadelphia – In the first game of the double header, the Phillies came back from a 3-1 deficit to score 2 in the 6th and 4 in the 8th to pull the team to within one game of the Wild Card Lead and 1 ½ games behind the Mets who lost again to the Braves … Ryan Howard hit a 2-run homerun (44) in the 6th to tie the game 3-3. He ended up going 2 for 3 with 2 runs scored and 2 RBIs (133) … In the 8th Pat Burrell hit a tie-breaking single to put the Phils ahead … Shane Victorino's 3-run homerun in the 8th then sealed the victory for the Phils on the center fielder's only hit of the game … Joe Blanton survived a shaky 1st but settled down to throw 7 innings while giving up 3 runs … Scott Eyre (4-0, 4.43) got the win in relief.

In game two of the double header, Brett Myers (10-11, 4.06) threw an incredible 2-hit complete game for the victory, surrendering only one run, a homerun to Prince Fielder in the 7th. That completed the 4-game sweep of the Brewers … Shane Victorino went 4 for 4 … Jimmy Rollins went 2 for 2 with 3 walks and 2 RBIs … Pat Burrell went 1 for 3 hitting his 31st homerun. Stuff: With the sweep, the Phillies are tied for the National League Wild Card lead and only 1 game behind the Mets for the NL East lead.

Myers used just 95 pitches to erase the Brewers Wild Card lead, completing successful short-rest bookends that began with Jamie Moyer's effective outing on Thursday night. Although Myers dominated, the Brewers will spend a plane ride to Chicago looking at themselves in the mirror. Everyone from the entire free-swinging offense to their egghead manager will try to pick up the pieces. Starter Jeff Suppan also had nothing tonight, and in hindsight, voting for the doubleheader and generally looking ahead to Chicago didn't pan out so well for the Brew Crew.

Offensively, Jimmy Rollins doubled out of the chute, and when Jimmy's in the mix, the Phillies usually win. J-Roll was on base all five times, setting the table for an offense that also saw Shane Victorino reach base in each of his at bats and Pat Burrell clout an atom bomb to left, his 31st of the season and first homerun since his five-RBI outburst on Aug. 26th.

On Wednesday, this thing looked close to over. I gotta say, I like where they stand.

The Phillies swept the Brewers and are now tied for the Wild Card lead and only one game behind the Mets

Monday, September 15th - (Off) 82-67 2nd - ½ GB the Mets

Philadelphia – *The Phils gained ground on the spiraling Mets after the Metropolitans lost again, this time to the Washington Nationals 7-2 … Ghosts of their historic 2007 collapse seem to be coming back to haunt them.*

On September 14, 2007, the Phils were 5 ½ games behind the Mets prior to beginning a three game series at Shea. A complete sweep of the series later and the Phils were only 2 ½ games behind and on their way to completing a historic run of capturing the 2007 NL East pennant.

Fast-forward a year later. After a four game sweep of the Brewers and a Mets' loss today, the Phils are tied for the Wild Card lead and only ½ GB of the Mets.

Is it really happening again? Our friendly neighborhood bloggers up in New York seem to be sensing that something's amuck. MetsBlog.com is run by Matthew Cerrone. It has been rated one of the most popular sports blogs on the Internet. On average, the site draws 35,000 fans a day. For any Phillies fan that really wants to get a kick out of watching Mets fans suffer, MetsBlog.com is the place to be.

Cerrone's recent musings on the Mets winning the NL East this year hit a snag as the Mets seem to be starting up their late season swoon again. It started last week when Cerrone decided to ask readers of his blog whether or not he should begin posting a Magic Number for how many games the Mets needed to win the NL East. The Magic Number went up and the Mets started going down.

Mets fans on the site started howling, saying that Cerrone jinxed the team and they are now potentially in harms way of the Phillies. Below is an excerpt of Cerrone addressing his readers on why he just removed the Magic Number from the site.

Is Mr. Met and the rest of the team possibly looking at another colossal collapse?

"I removed the Magic Number, because a) it is essentially meaningless when up a half-game in the standings with 13 games left, and b) because I can no longer waste hours upon hours of my day dealing with e-mails like the this:

"SO U PUT UP THE STUPID @#$%& MAGIC NUMBER AGAIN AND WHAT HAPPENS? METS BLOW 2 @#$%& GAMES ONE IN THE 8TH AND NOW ONE IN THE 9TH ... THE FANS VOTED NOT TO DO IT AND U JUST DON'T GIVE A FLYING @#$%& YOUR A COMPLETE @#$%& I HOPE THEY DON'T MAKE THE @#$%& PLAYOFFS SO U CAN LIVE WITH IT FOREVER! YOURE NO BETTER THEN BARTMAN ... U CAN TAKE YOUR @#$%& WEBSITE AND SHOVE IT UP YOUR @#$%&."

Anyway, I do not believe in jinxes. I do, however, believe in hard work and getting things done during the day, which has been nearly impossible when having to field e-mails like the above over and over and over again. So, while I realize that the majority of this site's readers wanted the Magic Number to be posted, my inbox needs break. I hope you understand."

It's times like these that make a Phillies' fan smile. With regards to the race for the playoffs, you can see the Phillies surging and can almost smell another Mets collapse in the air. Brett Myers seems to be getting that same feeling. After his two-hitter yesterday he said, *"It kind of felt like last year. We just went out there and had some fun. The offense came out swinging, the starting pitching was good. That's what wins championships. Hopefully we can keep it up."*

Quotable: "Chemistry counts and attitude definitely comes into play. If you get too many guys that are complacent or don't buy into what you're trying to do, then you can have problems. For 2 1/2 seasons, our attitude and chemistry definitely are things that drive us. Last night, we got down three runs, and I went out to change the pitcher. Two or three guys said, 'We've got enough to come back and win. Let's hold 'em.' That kind of tells you how they think." - Manager Charlie Manuel explaining why it seems like the Phillies usually find their stride in September

Tuesday, September 16th - Phillies 8 Braves 7 (84-67) 1st - ½ GA the Mets

Atlanta – *The Phillies make another comeback in the race for the NL East as they jump over the Mets and are a ½ game up with only 11 games to play ... Down 7-4 going into the 7th, the Phils put two on the board in the 7th and two more in the 8th for their 37th come-from-behind win of the season ... Ryan Howard continues to make his case for MVP of the National League going 4 for 5 with a homerun (45), a triple and two singles. He drove in 4 runs and now has an amazing 136 RBIs ... Jayson Werth joined in as well as he went 3 for 4 with 3 runs scored, a homerun (23) and 2 RBIs (64) ... Shane Victorino went 3 for 5 with an RBI (56) ... Jimmy Rollins continued his hot September as well as he went 2 for 5, one of them his 34th double of the season ... In total the Phillies banged out 14 hits ... Pat Burrell went 0 for 5 with 5 strikeouts ... Jamie Moyer got banged around for 6 runs in 5 2/3rd innings. He walked 4 batters and struck out 6 ... Ryan Madson (4-2 3.16) got the win in relief ... Brad Lidge walked the bases loaded in the 9th but managed to not let any runs score and earned his 37th save. Stuff: The Phillies are 7-0 in Atlanta this year... Ryan Howard is hitting an incredible .396 this month with 8 HRs and 22 RBIs ... The Mets panic has officially begun as Mets manager Jerry Manuel held a 15 minute meeting before today's game ... The Brewers fired manager Ned Yost today.*

No hit has made more noise this season. No at bat has been better. If the Phillies can run with the lead they've just reclaimed, Howard will become more than just an emerging MVP candidate. In a game that featured Gregor Blanco batting in the 9th inning with the bases loaded and two outs against a dangerously erratic Brad Lidge, each team leaving 10 men on base, a three-for-four night from Jayson Werth, including his 23rd home run, an 0-for-5 night from Pat Burrell, with five, jack-squat strikeouts, and Ryan Madson mastering his most important assignment in ages, No. 6 transcended it all. Right now, Howard is the best.

Mr. September, Ryan Howard went 4 for 5 and helped propel the Phillies back into first place

In other hip-hip hurray finals, the Nationals blanked the Mets 1-0, the Cubs beat the Brewers 4-3 and it was the Marlins over the Astros 5-1.

Quotable: "We've got character on our team. We've got a lot of guys who love to play. If you want to know the truth, the biggest reason I came back on this job was the players we had." - Charlie Manuel before today's game

<u>Wednesday, September 17th - Phillies 6 Braves 1 (85-67) 1st - ½ GA the Mets</u>

Atlanta – *The Phillies won their 6th straight game as rookie AJ Happ (1-0, 4.24) pitched 6 shutout innings to win the first major league game of his career. Happ only gave up 3 hits while walking 1 and striking out 2 ... Clay Condrey gave up the team's only run in the 9th but by that time the damage had already been done by the Phils' offense ... The team jumped on the Braves early with 4 runs in the 1st and then ended the evening by tacking on 1 in the 8th and their final run in the 9th with a pinch-hit homerun by Matt Stairs (12). Stuff: The team is now a season-best 18 games over .500 ... Stairs' homerun with the Phils' 200th of the season which leads the National League and is only behind the Chicago White Sox in the majors who have 216. This is the fourth straight season of 200 or more homeruns for the team.*

Last week, Jason Weitzel was given a chance to live the life of a Reading Phillie as part of Baseball Fantasy Day at FirstEnergy Stadium.

Putting bat to ball instead of pen to paper is every sportswriter's worst nightmare, but who has time for self-degradation when you're having so much fun? Contest winners, United Way sponsors and yours truly were treated to the full Reading Phillie experience last Thursday: locker rooms; custom uniforms; two hours of batting and fielding practice with five ex-Phillies, including John Kruk, Gary Maddox, Greg Gross, Ricky Botallico and Eric Valent; followed by a nine-inning game in front of the wincing gazes of friends, family and concerned citizens. Our team won 17-12. I played third, doubled and struck out in my

While the Phillies remained in first, author Jason Weitzel (Beerleaguer) batted 17th for the Reading Phillies

triumphant return to the diamond. I hit 17th in the lineup. Was it Bill James who called the 17-hole hitter the most important? The last time I stepped onto the field was 16 years ago. Comparatively speaking, a 16-year layoff meant I was in the prime of my career next to other participants.

My purpose for being there was to spread the word for our Reading Eagle partners and to observe. The first thing you notice is how much baseball hurts your hands. Relays to first pummel your mitt, glancing swings rattle your nails. These hands, conditioned to fondle a computer mouse, aren't long for the bronzing of baseball.

The next thing you notice is that the infield, which looks as silken as liquid chocolate when raked, actually contains microscopic death shards designed to rip holes in your flesh. In baseball, the worst mistake you can make is to fall to the ground. The infield grit will tear you, metal spikes impale you, and fences skewer you.

Finally, you gain an instant appreciation for a professional player's ability not to drift off into outer space during hours of batting practice. A generous amount of a ballplayer's career is spent shagging balls and watching teammates hit in the cage. Including spring training, it works out to roughly 200 batting practice sessions a season. These usually occur during the hottest hours of the day. The rest of their time at the park is divided among signing autographs, doing interviews and watching video. Getting back to my earlier point from the previous thread, no wonder players keep such an even keel over a 162-game season. Our dugout needed two buckets of Budweiser just to make it once through the lineup

Quotable: "At the first of the year he carried us. He cooled off a little, but he might be picking it up at the right time." - Charlie Manuel on Pat Burrell's huge 2-run homerun

Thursday, September 18th - Phillies 4 Braves 3 (86-67) 1st - ½ GA the Mets

Atlanta – Pat Burrell's 2-run homerun (32) in the 6th broke a 2-2 tie to help lead the Phillies to a 3-game sweep over the Braves ... Cole Hamels (14-9, 3.10) gave up 2 runs on 6 hits in 6 innings of work ... Brad Lidge earned his 38th save of the year, throwing a perfect 9th while striking out 2. His ERA is 1.98. Stuff: The Phillies ended up the 2008 season a perfect 9-0 at Turner Field ... Burrell's homerun was the 250th of his career. Five of them coming against Atlanta this season ... Now 19 games over .500, this is the most games that the Phils have been over .500 since June 26, 1995 when they were 37-18.

Owned! It starts with the pitching, which is what this series was all about. Cole Hamels might have been sub-par by his own standards, but he still earned a quality start with six innings of two-run ball. He actually lowered his ERA to 3.10 without having his best stuff. The lethargic Braves tacked on an unearned run off Ryan Madson, but that was it. J.C. Romero and Brad Lidge pitched scoreless frames to close it out. For Lidge, who was much better tonight than Tuesday, the All-Star closer improved to 38 for 38 in save opportunities.

Offensively, they hit the ball hard all night, but managed just four runs. The big blow came off the bat of Pat Burrell, who belted a Mike Hampton hanging breaking ball into the left-field seats for a two-run shot, marking his 250th career tater. For the second game in a row, the Phils got on the board early. Jayson Werth continued to earn his everyday keep with a run-scoring double in the first inning. Ryan Howard drove him home to collect his 138th RBI of the season. All-in-all, the story

Pat Burrell connected for his 250th career homerun

boils down to total domination over the Braves at Turner Field, paced by their arms and a ridiculously good 2.74 season-series ERA.

Quotable: "It was obvious what I was trying to do. The harder I went with it, the further they hit it. It was just one of those nights." – Brett Myers on how he tried pitching to the Marlins' hitters

Friday, September 19th - Marlins 14 Phillies 8 (86-68) 2nd - ½ GB the Mets

Miami – Brett Myers got bombed for 10 runs in 4 innings as the Marlins play spoilers and send the Phils back to 2nd place in the NL East ... Myers (10-12, 4.46) got tagged for 5 runs on 5 consecutive hits in the 1st but then settled down until the 5th when Florida broke out a 6-run inning ... The offense did put 8 runs on the board, including homeruns by Greg Dobbs (9), Ryan Howard (46) and Shane Victorino (13) ... Howard had 3 RBIs in the game and now has 141 on the season ... Jimmy Rollins went 2 for 4 while Greg Dobbs went 2 for 2 ... Jayson Werth was 1 for 5, striking out 4 times. Stuff: The loss dropped the Phillies to a ½ game behind the Mets in the NL East, However they are now in first place for the NL Wild Card lead 2 games in front of the Brewers ....The Marlins have won 9 straight games and are only 5 GB the Mets for the division lead to tighten up the NL East race.

The Phillies have reached 86 wins, which matches the prediction many Beerleaguer bloggers issued at the start of the season. Most people said they'd finish somewhere in the 86-90 range, but what they didn't predict was just how good the pitching would be. The offense would be a given. The pitching would be the wild card. It's been the opposite.

The Phillies' 3.88 ERA matches the pitching-rich Angels for fifth-best in baseball, and they trail only the Dodgers and Cubs in the National League. It's a dazzling improvement over 2007 (4.73) and 2006 (4.60). At best, the Phils have been just an average, park-adjusted staff over the last five seasons, and in the previous two, they were borderline brutal (There was a point in '07, before he took one off the leg against Colorado, when Kyle Kendrick gave the Phillies the best chance to win in the starting rotation. Good times).

Quality starts have become so standard; they're easily taken for granted. They have 83 of them. They also have 11 shutouts, second in the NL. They are 73-0 when leading after eight innings, a testament to Brad Lidge and a vastly improved bullpen. Consider the dimensions of Citizens Bank Park and it makes their performance this season even more exceptional.

The reason is simple: their staff is rubbish-free and healthy. Gone are the likes of Jose Mesa, Brian Sanches, J.D. Durbin and others. Even Adam Eaton can't buy his way back into the mix.

Included are improvements like Scott Eyre, Chad Durbin and Lidge. The company line about Brett Myers, how he was both the biggest off-season and mid-season acquisition, proved to be on the mark. Then you have guys like Jamie Moyer showing us that you can teach old dogs new tricks. He's allowed less than one home run per game, which is off the hook.

Indeed, there have been hiccups, like the 8th inning of many games, Kendrick's fall and Myers' first half implosion, but nothing has compared to the turmoil of previous seasons.

Quotable: "We sweated every bit of it. It seemed like a long mental test." - Charlie Manuel on a close 3-2 win over the Marlins

<u>Saturday, September 20th - Phillies 3 Marlins 2 (87-68) 1st - ½ GA the Mets</u>
Miami – *Tied 2-2 in the 6th, Greg Dobbs stroked a two-out single to get Ryan Howard home from second base to give the Phils the win and move them back into first in the NL East ... The offense scored an unearned run in the 3rd to give them a 1-0 lead but the Marlins answered with two of their own in the bottom half of the inning. Shane Victorino then tied the game back 2-2 in the next inning with his 14th homerun of the season ... Joe Blanton (8-12, 4.79/ 3-0 with the Phillies) stuck out 9 Marlins in 5 innings and only allowed 2 runs ... The Phillies' "four horsemen" Durbin, Romero, Madson and Lidge only gave up 3 hits and no runs over the final 4 innings ... Lidge earned his 39th save of the year while striking out the side. Stuff: The Phils have won 8 of their last 9 games ... Ryan Madson has now pitched 10 2/3rd scoreless innings ... With Victorino's homerun the Phillies have tied their franchise record of hitting homeruns in 16 straight games. They also did it in 2002 and in 2006.*

Have you ever heard of Manetho? How about Herodotus? Josephus? How about Rich Westcott? Manetho was an Egyptian historian that wrote the History of Egypt, Herodotus was a Greek researcher that wrote The Histories of the world, Josephus was best known for his histories of the Jews during the time of Jesus Christ. Westcott? Rich Westcott is by far the preeminent historian on the Philadelphia Phillies.

Westcott is the author of over 19 baseball-related books including nine of them on the Phillies. Among them include The Phillies Encyclopedia, Tales from the Phillies Dugout and his most recent one The Fightin' Phils: Oddities, Insights, and Untold Stories. I spent some time with Rich to talking about his books and his many experiences over the years.

Of all the books you've ever written which one was your favorite?
To be honest they were all my favorite. I'm finding it hard to pick one because each has a special appeal to me. If you are making me choose then I would probably have to say The Phillies Encyclopedia because it covered the whole history of the team from its inception up through 1983. .

How long did it take you to complete the Encyclopedia?
Well let's see, I started watching the Phillies when I was 8 years old so from then on...Actually, to be serious, coauthor Frank Bilovski and I researched it for about a year and a half and we were able to use our ample years of experiences and observations throughout the entire book.

Which of your books have sold the most copies?
The Phillies Encyclopedia. It's in its third edition and I think we've probably sold at least 20,000 copies. It's funny, you never know, some of them sell well, some of them don't. I thought that the book I did on the '93 Phillies (Phillies '93 – An Incredible Season) would sell well because that was such a popular team. It didn't sell worth a damn.

What are you currently working on?
Another book about the Phillies. It's basically thirty-three chapters of oddi-

Phillies' historian Rich Westcott is THE expert on the Phillies

ties, untold stories, things like that. A lot of things fans wouldn't know about. There's a story about the Phillies having the first female scout in baseball, a player who was with the CIA and a famous evangelist that was once a Phillie. Lots of stories like that.

Throughout your writing career I am sure you have done hundreds, if not thousands of baseball interviews. Are there any interviews that stand out in your mind as some of your favorite?
I've done some interviews that I've really enjoyed. I interviewed Al Kaline while I was driving him from Wilmington to the Philly airport and I interviewed Ted Williams on the Baseball Broadcast Show. All of these experiences kind of fed into this whole thing of writing books but far and away my favorite interview was with Hall-of-Famer Warren Spahn.

A friend of mine was running a car show in Ocean City, NJ and Spahn was making a personal appearance there for him. When I found out that Spahn was going to be there I had asked my friend if he could let Warren know that I would like to interview him for one of my magazines. Spahn said "Sure, absolutely.", so after the car show he told me that we could go back to his hotel and he would give me the interview. So the car show didn't get over to really late and the deal was I would pick him up at the car show and drive him back to his hotel. I would bring along a six pack and then we would do the interview. So we didn't get out of there until 10:00pm and 4 ½ hours later we wrapped up our little interview. It was by far the longest interview I ever had and as a result it was the longest story I ever wrote of these interviews.

We went from A to Z beginning with his childhood all the way up to his final game and everything after his Hall of Fame induction. We talked about a 16 inning game he once pitched… his two no-hitters and his winning 300 games. He just had one experience after another that he talked about all night long. As I say it was a fascinating interview. For me it was head and shoulders above all the others.

I was amazed at all the details that were in the encyclopedia. Of all the research you've done on the Phillies which one do you believe is the most underrated of all time?
Easy, Ed Delahanty. He's the most underrated because no body ever knows anything about him or writes anything about him and yet, he was one of the greatest players, maybe the greatest player in Phillies history. We're talking about a guy who played with the Phillies from 1888 to 1901 and hit over .400 three times in his career. He has the 4th highest batting average in baseball history at .345. He won a batting title with the Phillies, he won a home run crown, he won 3 RBI titles. He was the second player ever to hit four home runs in one game. I mean you can go on and on about this guy, he was a Hall of Famer but no one ever hears of Ed Delahanty.

Did he spend his entire career with the Phillies?
No. When the American League was formed in 1902 he jumped to the new league and played with Washington and won a batting title there. His life then came to an early demise in 1903. There are various stories about his death but the most reliable ones say that he was put off a train because he was drunk and was bothering a couple of passengers and he wound up going off a bridge washing down Niagara River and over Niagara Falls to his death. A guy wrote an entire book about this and there's always been speculation about exactly what happened. But he was still in his 30's and playing ball for the Senators when it happened.

Growing up as a kid who were your favorite players?
My favorite position player was Ted Williams and my favorite pitcher was Robin Roberts followed by a guy named Ewell Blackwell. Ewell Blackwell was a side arm pitcher who had a couple of very, very good years with the Cincinnati Reds back in the late 40's, early 50's. The only reason that he was high on my list was because I was a pitcher as a kid and he wrote a book called the "Secrets of Pitching". I still have that book. As kid I read it religiously and I tried to learn everything I could from that book. And so automatically Ewell Blackwell was one of my favorite players for no particular reason other then that book.

What is your earliest baseball memory growing up?
My earliest memory was when my dad; my dad and my grandfather were both avid fans and from the time I was about 2 years old I think I heard their stories about the Phillies and the Athletics. In fact my grandfather was the first one who ever told me about Ed Delahanty. And they would tell me about the Baker Bowl and my dad would tell me about Shibe Park. So I was kind of raised with a baseball background and ultimately I guess it led to my love of baseball.

Being that you know the Phillies better than anyone else, who are the all-time best players at each position?

Not taking into consideration the players currently playing with the team my list would be as follows:

1B – Dick Allen – No way "Crash" can be left off this team. (Actually, he played more games at first than he played anywhere else.) One of the Phils' most spectacular hitters. He averaged 30 homers a season during his first six years.

2B - Nap Lajoie* - Had a .338 career BA. More prominent as an American Leaguer where one season he set a record by hitting .426. But he was originally a Phillie, and played in five seasons with the club, never hitting below .324.

3B – Mike Schmidt* - Michael Jack's clouts went "outta here" 548 times. He won or tied for eight home run titles, and in 11 seasons hit over 35. Was a three-time MVP. Plus, he won 10 Gold Gloves. The best all-around 3B in baseball history.

SS – Larry Bowa – His glove was where ground balls went to die. One of the game's finest defensive shortstops. He had a career fielding percentage of.980. One year, Bo fielded .991 with only six errors. As a hitter, he got on base a lot, too.

C – Bob Boone – For all-around talent, no Phils' backstop was better than Boonie. Defensively, he could catch, throw, and handle pitchers with considerable skill. Also a respectable hitter, he went above .280 three times.

LF – Ed Delahanty* - As they said in his days, Big Ed could really swat that old pill. He owns the fourth-highest batting average (.346) in ML history. He hit above .400 three times with the Phillies. Arguably, the club's greatest hitter of all time.

CF – Richie Ashburn* - Hard to believe, Harry, that he was originally a catcher. Moved to CF, he made the greatest defensive play in Phils' history with throw in 1950. Won two batting titles, led the NL in hits three times and in putouts nine times.

RF – Chuck Klein* - A classic slugger, one of Phillies' finest. Won four home run titles, a Triple Crown, and an MVP. Went .386-40-170 in 1930 with 158 runs. No slouch in the field, either throwing out 44 runners one year for a Major League record.

RHP – Robin Roberts* - Consider this: he once threw 28 straight complete games. Phils' winningest right-hander, he won 234, including 20 or more six times. Led the NL in starts six times, in complete games and innings pitched five times each.

LHP – Steve Carlton* - Lefty may have been silent in the clubhouse, but he wasn't quiet on the mound. The ML's second-winningest left-hander, he won 241 with the Phils, plus four Cy Young Awards. Among all-time leaders in strikeouts.

RP – Tug McGraw – You gotta believe the Tugger is tops. Colorful hurler saved 94, won 49,. and pitched in and finished more games than any other Phils reliever. And then there was that unforgettable finish in the 1980 World Series.

Manager – Gene Mauch – The man knew more about baseball than even Abner Doubleday. A master strategist, innovation was his middle name. Won (and lost) more games than any pilot in Phils' history with mostly weak teams. And 1964? Don't blame him.

*Member of the Hall of Fame

Quotable: "Our timing on stuff is tremendous right now." – Brad Lidge after third baseman Greg Dobbs left the game with a leg cramp and was replaced by Pedro Feliz who jumped in a hit a 2-run homer in the 8th

<u>Sunday, September 21st - Phillies 5 Marlins 2 (88-68) 1st - 1½ GA the Mets</u>
Miami – *On the last road game of the regular season, the Phillies made a huge step towards the post season as Jamie Moyer and 5 pitching changes helped nail down the win. With the Phils up 3-2 going into the 8th, Pedro Feliz hit a clutch 2-run homer (14) to give the bullpen some breathing room late in the game ... Chase Utley had a homerun (32) and 2 RBIs (99) ... Jimmy Rollins went 3 for 5 with a run scored and a stolen base (45)... Moyer (15-7, 3.78) gave up 1 run in 6 innings while walking 1 and striking out 4 ...Brad Lidge earned his 40th save. Stuff: With the Mets loss against Atlanta today, the Phils' "magic number" to win the NL East is 6. To make the playoffs its 4 ... Jayson Werth ended the series going 1 for 14 with 8 strikeouts... On the 6 game road trip, Pat Burrell was 3 for 24 ... Utley's homerun was his first since August 22nd ... With his 40th save of the year, Lidge tied Steve Bedrosian for fourth on the Phils' all-time list for most save in a season ... The Phillies ended their regular season road record at 44-37.*

Time to celebrate ... celebrate that the season series with Florida is over. What a pain. Seriously. The Phils didn't play particularly well, but scratched out two-of-three with a 5-2 win yesterday. Call it "The Bad Lighting Series" or perhaps "The Mound Conference Series." "Is it just me or do the Phillies seem to have an inordinate amount of meetings on the mound?" asked one reader via e-mail. "There are constant meetings between catcher-pitcher (both Ruiz and Coste) and then meetings with the infielders all present. Then Dubee will come out for a meeting. This can happen 3-4 times in an inning, sometimes even during one at-bat."

Good teams know how to win ugly, which seems to be how every series in South Florida unfolds. Credit stuff like defense, stable starting pitching and a bend-but-don't-break bullpen, all the stuff that teams who've been there before can execute down the stretch (Wait ... so the Phils are one of those teams now?) Greg Dobbs made another outstanding play in the 7th to limit the damage on a bullet down the third-base line. It's amazing how many times the bullpen worked out of jams. Then they received a huge pinch homer from Pedro Feliz to supply a three-run cushion. But even before that, Jamie Moyer comes up big down the stretch yet again, allowing one run in six innings to earn his 15th win of the season.

Meanwhile in Atlanta, the Mets were victimized with another late-inning bullpen collapse, blowing their 16th save since the All-Star break. And in Cincinnati, Milwaukee dispatched the Reds 8-1 in a must-win for the Brew Crew. A combination of four Phillies wins or Brewers loses punches Philadelphia's ticket to October.

Chase Utley hit his 32nd homerun and knocked in his 99th RBI on the season as the Phillies pulled 1 ½ games in front of the Mets

In another season of peaks and valleys, the Phils have won nine of 10, and a look in the rear view mirror finds two scuffling teams in the Mets and Brewers. The Phillies are on top, but the way good fortune shifts in the blink of an eye; the only thing truly worth celebrating this morning is kicking Florida to the curb.

Quotable: "I don't scoreboard-watch because we control our own destiny. I don't think anybody realizes how much fun this could be."- Reliever Scott Eyre after his third victory since being acquired by the Phillies

Monday, September 22nd - Phillies 6 Braves 2 (89-68) 1st - 2½ GA the Mets

Philadelphia – *With the score tied 2-2 going into the bottom of the 8th, the Phillies' Pat Burrell hit a 3-run homerun (33) that put the lid on the win for the Phils, whose magic number is now 4 for the NL East as the Mets lost to the Cubs 9-5 ... JA Happ continued his sensational September, pitching going 6 2/3rd innings while only giving up 2 runs on 5 hits ... Scott Eyre (5-0, 4.30 – 3-0 with the Phillies) picks up the win in only 1/3rd inning of work in the 8th ... Shane Victorino went 3 for 4 with a triple (8) ... Chase Utley went 1 for 2 and knocked in his 100th RBI of the year. Stuff: The Phillies are now 4-0 when Happ pitches … The team is 14-2 against the Braves with two games remaining against them … Chase Utley is only the 3rd second baseman in the history of baseball to have four consecutive 100 RBI seasons. Jeff Kent (6 yrs 1997-2002) and Charlie Gehringer (5 yrs 1932-1936) were the other two.*

Credit Rich Dubee and the rest of the Phillies' decision makers for going with Happ, making the 5th starter issue moot. Another nice job for the 25-year-old southpaw. The Phils hold off a benign threat using a hodgepodge bullpen. Tonight was all business against a much weaker Braves team, wiping their hands of it like a playoff team should.

Things are looking mighty good.

Pennant Update: The Cubs dumped the Mets 9-5. With six to play, the Mets cling to a one-game lead over the Brewers in the National League Wild

Phillies reliever Scott Eyre is now 3-0 since joining the Phillies

Card race. The Brewers open a three-game set against the Pirates tomorrow. With the win, the Cubs clinched home-field advantage through the NLCS.

Quotable: "I can't for the life of me understand why Phillies' fans hate the Mets so much when all we do is put a smile on their faces every year!" - Mets fan who called into WFAN Sports Radio in New York

Tuesday, September 23rd - Braves 3 Phillies 2 (89-69 1st - 1½ GA the Mets

Philadelphia – *Trailing 3-1 in the 6th, Ryan Howard led off with a rare triple, which was then followed by an RBI double off the bat of Pat Burrell. However, the Phils couldn't muster any more runs against the Braves bullpen, which allowed no runs or hits over the last three innings of the game… Braves' starter Mike Hampton baffled the Phillies offense for 6 innings giving up only 2 runs while striking out 4 … Cole Hamels (14-10, 3.09) pitched effectively going 7 innings but ended up being on the short side of the runs as he gave up 3 runs (2 earned) while striking out 7. Stuff: The Phillies' magic number remains at four for the NL East title as the Mets beat the Cubs 6-2 … The team handed out the Paul Owens Awards to their top minor league prospects. JA Happ was honored as the team's top minor league pitcher. Lou Marson was named the top position player … The Phillies ended their consecutive homerun streak today. They had hit at least one homerun in the past 18 games prior to today's game.*

Over the past 38 years, Phillies fans have come to know Harry Kalas better than they probably know many members of their own families. How he grew up in Napperville, Illinois, and how he started his baseball broadcasting career in Hawaii with the Hawaii Islanders when he was stationed there serving the US Army. Kalas broke into the major leagues with the Houston Astros in 1965 and was eventually hired by the Phillies when they moved to Veterans Stadium in 1971. From spring to early fall, Harry is the background voice that cascades throughout our house or while we are driving our cars down to the shore. However what most Phillies fans don't realize is that nationally Harry Kalas is widely known across the United States as the voice of the NFL.

Harry Kalas is more widely known across the United States as the voice of the NFL and Campbell's Chunky Soup than he is as the Hall-of-Fame broadcaster for the Phillies

Once the Phillies' season is over what type of work do you do during the off-season?
Well I do a few things that keep me busy. I broadcast weekly NFL football games across the country for Westwood One radio and I do a lot of work with NFL Films over in Mount Laurel, NJ, where I do Inside the NFL and I narrate all of the highlights of the games each week. NFL Films usually starts plugging me into their schedule as soon as the season is over but they called me this past week and I said to them, "You're going to have to wait until late October this year." So I don't start either of those jobs until after baseball is over.

When you are working for Westwood One Radio are you traveling every week across the country?
I never know where they are going to send me until about 7-10 days ahead of time. Hopefully I get a lot of Eagle games so I won't have to travel that much or they will give me one of the New York teams, Washington or Baltimore. If the games are within driving distance of my home I can drive there on Sunday, do the game and be back that night.

You used to be the voice of Campbell's Chunky Soup. Do you still do a lot of commercials?
Yeah, I do some. I recently did a movie trailer which I hadn't done in the past. It's for a movie that is coming out titled "Leatherheads" with George Clooney.

Did you go see the movie?
I have not seen it yet but I will make it a point to go see it soon. .

As you travel around the country particularly on the football side, do you run into people who know you as an NFL person more so than a Hall-of-Fame baseball announcer?
I will occasionally get people who run into me outside the Philadelphia area and stop me when I'm talking and say, "I know you." But they really don't. They recognize my voice because of NFL films. I was very fortunate to get involved with NFL Films in the mid-70's. Steve Sabol was listening to a Phillies game one day and liked what he heard and called me and said "You know, you have the kind of voice that would work with our films. Why don't you come in for an audition?" Of course, in those years, John Fecenda was doing the narration. Well they liked what they heard and they started having me do bits and pieces in their films while John was the primary narrator. John was such a wonderful man. Truly my mentor. Steve took John and I to the Super Bowl in 1980 in New Orleans when the Eagles played Oakland. So I got to spend the entire weekend with John. He was so nice to the people of Philadelphia that were there for the game. It was just such a wonderful experience to spend all that time with him. I certainly learned a lot from John about narrating football.

How long have you been with NFL Films?
Well, you know, as I said, I've been doing bits and pieces since the mid-70's. So, um, 30 years.

When you prepare for a football game how does that differ for you then when you're preparing for a baseball game?
Well I have a spotting board that I use for football games that helps the broadcaster identify the players quicker. Each Wednesday before the next game the NFL teams send out their latest news releases and stats so I take some time to fill out the information so that I'm ready for the game on Sunday. For baseball, since it's a day-to-day thing, you're daily preparation is not nearly as much as preparing for a football game. I spend hours and hours preparing for a football game making sure that I have all the information I can about the players. During the game, the teams provide a "spotter" for the broadcaster. Spotters are very important to your broadcast because if they're really good they will point out the defensive player who just made the tackle or the offensive lineman who just made a great block. If you don't have a good spotter, it really is going to hurt your broadcast.

Any particular reason why you choose to continue to work in the off-season? Is it just for pure enjoyment?
I really enjoy calling football games. I like it. It's a lot of fun. I actually enjoy doing play-by-play all the time.

How do you like spending your time away from the ballpark during the regular season with the Phillies? What are some of the things that you do?
I pretty much stay at home; I've had my kids throughout my broadcast career, so spending time with them was important to me. All the kids are out of pocket as of this year. My youngest son Kane is at the University of Miami, so he's away at college. So now I spend a lot of time with my beautiful wife. I like to be at home. After a game I like to just get back and relax at home.

How close do you live to Citizens Bank Park?
I live in Media, PA. It's great because my house backs up to Ridley Creek State Park and it's

such a beautiful area, but living in Media I'm only about 25 minutes from the ball park. 30 minutes from downtown Philadelphia and yet I got deer walking around in my backyard. It's really great.

What's one thing that Phillies' fans probably wouldn't know about Harry Kalas?
That's a tough one ... I would say it's probably the time when I was in high school and trying to save money for college I worked as a Gandy Dancer for the railroad. Do you know what a Gandy Dancer is? Never heard of it. There was a song written about Gandy Dancers (a pause ... and then Harry breaks into song) "They dance on the ceiling and they dance on the wall at the Gandy Dancers ball." A Gandy Dancer is a person that works on the railroad tracks and replaces the old railroad ties with new ones. It's tough labor, it really is, one of the hardest jobs I've ever done.

How long did you do that for?
I did that for one entire summer. It was difficult. It was an interesting crew because the crew chief of our crew was a very religious man. He would read scriptures from the Bible as we were working. When I say we, it was a five man crew and the other four were guys from Mexico that didn't speak any English so I was the only one who knew what he was saying.

So he just preached the Word of God to you all summer?
Yeah. So I was the only one that really understood him.

Do you ever go back to visit Naperville these days?
I was back this year when we played in Chicago. My high school had their 54th class reunion. Unfortunately I missed the 50th because I was doing ball games so they kind of arranged this so it would be there when the Phillies were playing in Chicago. It was really special. I saw people that I haven't seen in years and it was really nice.

In your opinion, what does it take to be a good play-by-play announcer?
I always tell young people that are seeking jobs as broadcasters that the most important thing is preparation. Before the game starts, make sure that you know all you can about the team and the players on the team. Not just what they're doing now but their background, that sort of thing. I always considered preparation as a main key to delivering a good sportscast.

Do you prefer working on TV or radio?
I really enjoy them both. Years ago the Phillies wanted me strictly to do TV but I said, no I broke in on radio and I want to at least keep my hand in it. So I'm still doing the 4th inning on radio every game, but I just didn't want to totally give up radio because that's how I started.

How do you want to be remembered to the fans of Philadelphia fans?
Just as a person that they enjoyed listening to, that called the game that they loved. Really, you hope that you've been able to keep the audience with you when you're calling games and that they enjoy the experience of listening to it.

Quotable: "It wouldn't be the Philly way. No matter what sport, we don't make it easy" – Jimmy Rollins on how Philadelphia teams never seem to do things the "easy" way

Wednesday, September 24th - Braves 10 Phillies 4 (89-70) 1st - 1½ GA the Mets

Philadelphia – *Brett Myers (10-13, 4.55) struggled again as the Braves broke the tie game open with 6 runs in the top of the 5th inning to give the Phillies their second loss in as many days. Fortunately for the Phils, they still remain 1 ½ games in front of the Mets who lost again to the Cubs 9-6 ... Myers never did seem to be able to right himself in this game as he gave up 6 runs (4 earned) on 10 hits in only 4 1/3rd innings of work ... The rest of the bullpen didn't fair as well either as they gave up an uncommon 4 runs in 4 2/3rd innings ... Chase Utley hit his 33rd homerun of the season in the 3rd while Ryan Howard followed with one of his own in the 4th; his 47th of the year ... Pat Burrell is starting to get his swing back as he went 2 for 2 with 2 runs scored and 2 walks. Stuff: Ryan Howard committed a huge error in the 5th inning that led to 4 Braves runs. It was Howard's 18th error of the season, which is worst amongst all first basemen in the majors ... The Phillies set a single season attendance mark tonight of 3,288,316 as 41,430 came out to see the Phils make a run at the playoffs ... A telling tale; Chase Utley had a total of 21 homeruns in his first 59 games of the season and was being touted as the sure MVP of the National League. However over the past 100 games, he has only been able to hit 12 with whispers of a season-long hip problem being the cause of his hitting demise ... The magic number still remains at four for the NL East title.*

Meanwhile at Shea Stadium, the Mets squandered opportunities galore in a 9-6, 10-inning loss to the Cubs, dropping them into a tie with the Brewers in the National League Wild Card race. The Mets let a four-run lead built on Carlos Delgado's grand slam slip away and went five straight innings where they stranded a runner at third, scoring just once during that span on a bases-loaded walk. The Cubs would eventually catch up to the Mets' bullpen (Luis Ayala) for three runs in the 10th. Elsewhere, the Brewers beat the putrid Pirates 4-2. The Phils maintain a 1 1/2 game lead over the Mets in the National League East with a day off tomorrow and the Mets wrapping it up with the Cubs, weather permitting.

Nobody said a pennant race was easy. Myers resembled the lost soul who was demoted to the minors before the All-Star break. It was painful to watch. One can only wonder whether the short-rest complete game took a toll. He had no command of his fastball again, and frankly, even Myers wanted My-

The Mets are on the verge of another late season collapse ... Phillies' fans can't help but think it couldn't happen to a better team in baseball

ers out of this one. His latest struggles are a major setback for a club gaining confidence in his ability to anchor a playoff rotation.

The game at Shea was as poorly pitched as they come, and the blown scoring chances, particularly in the ninth, came back to bite the Mets. They also hit into a share of back luck with runners in scoring position (the double play liner back to Derrek Lee, for example). I needn't mention the Mets' bullpen.

Quotable: "It's all up to us. If we can't get it done it's our fault." - Charlie Manuel on the prospects of making the playoffs

Thursday, September 25th - (Off) (89-70) 1st - 1 GA the Mets

In 2008, Jimmy Rollins decided he no longer wanted to be a power threat. He wanted to be a leadoff hitter instead.

Originally, this story was designed to pose the question: Is Jimmy Rollins, nearing the age of 30, slowing down? I wondered this as I watched J-Roll go 1-for-11 against Atlanta, showing little pop in his bat, continuing what has generally been considered a disappointing encore to his brilliant season a year ago.

In reviewing J-Roll's '08 follow-up, 'disappointing' may not be the right word. Instead, call it a very 'different' season for the reigning MVP. Because of injury and less production throughout the lineup, he's seen 162-less plate appearances than 2007, when he finished with a ridiculous 778. He has 19 less home runs than '07. His OPS (.780) represents a significant drop from last year's career-high .875.

While some signs like his massive drop in power suggest he's slowing down, many others reveal the opposite. Aside from an excellent defensive season, he's already tied his career high in stolen bases with 46, matching the mark set during his rookie year. He's been successful in 93.9 percent of his attempts, which is stellar. And while his triples are down, he's roped 36 doubles, just two less than a year ago.

Then there's this little nugget: His K/BB ratio is an outstanding 55/55. No other season comes close. With two more walks, he will match his career high and he could finish with the highest on-base percentage of his career. He's sitting at .346 now. His career high of .348 was set in 2004.

It's strange, but it's like Jimmy spent his entire career ignoring some of the rules of a leadoff hitter, never quite fitting the mold and behaving, to some degree, like a power hitter. Then when he develops into a legitimate power threat, as he did in 2007, he does a total 180 and converts into the quintessential table setter.

One could argue that 2008 has been Jimmy Rollins' best approach at performing the duties asked of a leadoff man. That was, after all, his original purpose.

Quotable: "I like our position, but I'll like it a lot better when we're two up with one to play. That would be good. That's when I'll crack champagne, dance and sing and everything." - Charlie Manuel on clinching the NL East Division Title

Friday, September 26th - Phillies 8 Nationals 4 (90-70) 1st - 2 GA the Mets

Philadelphia – Ryan Howard cracked his 48th homerun of the year, a 3-run blast, in the 1st and it was all downhill from there on out as the Phils beat the Nats and the Mets lost to the Marlins, reducing the Phillies' magic number to 1, which guarantees the team at least a tie for the NL East Title ... Joe Blanton (9-12, 4.69/ 4-0 4.20 with the Phillies) threw 6 inning giving up 4 runs (only 1 of them earned) on 5 hits ... The bullpen pitched 3 shutout innings, limiting the Nationals to only 1 hit ... The offense pounded out 10 hits that included a 2 for 4 day with Howard, a 3 for 4 day for Chase Utley and a 2 for 5 day for Jayson Werth ... Howard had 4 RBIs in the game and now has 146 this year ... Utley had 3 RBIs and has 104 on the season Stuff: Ryan Howard's month of September has been one to remember. He now is hitting .349 with 11 homeruns and 32 RBIs. The 32 RBIs broke the Phillies' record for most RBIs in the month of September which was held by Gary Matthews who had 31 back in 1981. An entire season for some, Howard's resurgence this month as the premier power hitter in baseball has propelled him to the top of the National League MVP list of candidates ... Jimmy Rollins set a career high stealing his 47th base of the year. This even after missing a month of baseball early on in the season ... This is the first time since 1993 that the Phillies have hit the 90 win mark in a season and only the 12th time in the 126 year old franchise's history that they have done so.

Maybe it's the way that he immediately puts his guests at ease that makes WPHT 1210 AM's Michael Smerconish one of the best talk show hosts in the nation. Maybe it's because his guests sense that his questions are refreshingly upfront and honest that allows them to drop their guards and have a friendly chat with a host that has a few hundred thousand listeners behind him.

Born and raised in Doylestown, PA, Smerconish has made his mark both locally and
nationally. He's a frequent guest fill-in for
Bill O'Reilly on the O'Reilly Factor and on
the Glenn Beck Program. He is also the author of three best selling books and will be
launching his fourth book "Morning Drive:
Things I Wish I Knew Before I Started
Talking" in 2009. Being the flag ship station of the Phillies, Smerconish frequently
interviews the players, manager, coaches
and executives of the team on the morning
drive to work. He lives and breathes Phillies
baseball just like the rest of us.

**I've never known anything different than
being a Phillies' fan.** I have spent my entire life in a 50-mile radius of Philadelphia
so all I know is this area and the only team
that I have ever rooted for has been the
Phillies.

*Nationally syndicated radio talk show host
Michael Smerconish, pictured with his son Wilson,
is a dye in the wool Phillies' fan from birth*

**My first memory of the Phillies is the day
that my father took me to Connie Mack
to see a Phillies-Dodgers game.** There was
a guy playing for the Dodgers who's name was Tom Haller. Haller's father was an umpire and
a friend of my father knew him quite well. So my first time at the ballpark I end up meeting
a major league baseball player. I've got a stained and frayed black and white photo to show
for it.

My favorite player growing up? Well I always imitated Willie Montanez the way that he
would catch the ball at first base. You remember that maneuver where he would snap his glove
down to his side after he caught the ball? I'm not saying he's my favorite, I'm just saying Willie
Montanez was a guy I would imitate. When we would play waffle ball you would always want
to be Steve Carlton. I remember fondly the "Yes We Can" era with Larry Bowa and Dave Cash.
I remember the Bull fondly.

**I also remember that when I was in 6th or 7th grade Dick Allen, who really played just
before my time, moved into Upper Bucks County.** A group of friends and I once went out
on a bike hike where we rode five miles out of Doylestown to see Dick Allen's farm. It was a
really cold day and we rode all the way to his house. When we knocked at the front door Dick's
wife answered and told us that he wasn't home but she welcomed us into their house. I think
she felt sorry for us.

I've been very lucky in just having a number of good Phillies experiences. I remember Bob
Boone came to the Gino's in Doylestown to make a personal appearance and my friends and

I went down to see him there. When I was in Law School I remember that I ran into Steve Carlton after he pitched his last game as a Phillie. I was living in the smallest apartment and he was living in the biggest apartment in the same apartment building and I rode the elevator with him. I remember that he had a bag from Downey's where he must have gotten some takeout food from them. I mean I'm just loaded with funny instances of having these chance encounters with different guys through the years.

I've got to tell you my favorite Phillies' story and it's very much on my mind because I'm doing some public speaking this week and I always tell this story which sort of relates to all my different careers. In the fall of 1980, I was a freshman at Lehigh University. Ronald Reagan and George Bush are the Republican team, running against Jimmy Carter and Walter Mondale. I had just arrived on the Lehigh University campus and I'm living in a hellhole of a dorm called Taylor Hall. Funny thing is it's since been renovated and it's now so beautiful they put the Eagles there when they go to Pre-Season practice. Anyhow, the Hall has 150 guys, one phone, no Internet or cell phones back then. Nothing. I'm all caught up in the Reagan-Bush campaign and mistakenly I think that others at the University are caught up in it too. So I'm trying to organize people politically on campus and I'm having a real rough time doing it so I decide that the way I'm going to break through to everyone is to throw a keg party for all the Reagan-Bush supporters. So I throw together this shindig and I buy 3 half kegs of beer. I end up picking October 16, 1980. Well that was right during the Phillies-Royals World Series. So nobody comes to my party. And I don't mean that a couple of people come ... I mean nobody came to the party. It was a total embarrassment. I end up taking the kegs of beer back to my freshman dorm where the guys who were doing what I should have been doing, which was watching the Phillies, were enjoying the game. The irony is that a couple of days later I got a telephone call from George Bush's staff. They want to know if my club can provide some of the support services for a personal appearance that Bush was then about to make. Well I had no club, my club was a disaster but I now went back and recruited all the guys I served beer to who are watching the Phillies' game and we all worked on the visit for George Bush together. So I learned my lesson, never compete with a Phillies' game.

It really wasn't until the team moved to Citizens Bank Park that my passion for the team was renewed. I'm in a fortunate position now because of the radio station relationship with team. Each of the past five years, I've gone down to Clearwater to Spring Training and now not only does my father meet me down there but I bring my own sons along with me as well. They've had these extraordinary experiences of sitting on a cold March morning at the Tiki Bar in left field and watching their father interview Chase Utley or Charlie Manuel or Cole Hamels. One of the big benefits of my job is to be able to give them those experiences but who am I kidding, I love meeting them as well.

Over the past couple of years I've done my program on Opening Day from McFadden's at Citizens Bank Park and Charlie Manuel has stopped by to talk with me. I do have my own set of four season tickets that I pay for myself along with a few of my friends. They're fabulous seats right behind home plate. So I'm a paying customer and I'm legitimately there because I want to be there but I'm also being able to take advantage of some of the perks of being on the radio station that broadcasts the Phillies.

Charlie Manuel has been my favorite interview so far this year because I think I have a good rapport with him. I mean I base this on the fact that John Brazer of the Phillies said to me, "You're lucky to be getting Charlie; he won't do any other radio right now except your show." And when he's on the program he's always very expansive with me. Probably because he drops his guard. I'm not out to hurt him. I like the guy. I've spent a decent amount of time around him and I get a kick out of having him on and with all the things that he says.

I have a particular rooting interest for Jamie Moyer because we're contemporaries and because when I was at CB West he was at Souderton. Back when I was in school everyone knew his name. Everybody was, "Oh, yeah Jamie Moyer ... you have to see this guy pitch." What I like about him and what I like about this team is the nucleus is so good but I also think that they are such decent guys. I mean that Ryan Howard to me is a big teddy bear. I love Jimmy Rollins' intensity. I feel the same way about Utley. I was one of the guys who were really disappointed when Aaron Rowand left town, but now Shane Victorino steps in and if there's one guy who embodies this team it's him. He's such a hustler, such a never die attitude.

I really think we're going to go all the way this year. It's strange, I just have that feeling with the way the team is playing and how we're hitting and pitching. You never know but this might end up being a very special year for the team and for all of the Phillies" fans.

Quotable: "I was just so excited they made that play I wanted to run out and hug them. "Honestly that's the way it is and I wouldn't want it any other way." - Brad Lidge on the incredible game-saving double play started by Jimmy Rollins to end the game and win the NL East Division Title

Saturday, September 27th - Phillies 4 Nationals 3 (91-70) 1st - 2 GA the Mets

Philadelphia – *The Phillies are the National League Eastern Division Champions!!! Leading by two runs going into the bottom of the 9th Phils' ace reliever Brad Lidge came into the game, struck out the first batter he faced, and then proceeded to give up a walk and 3 hits. With one out and one run already across the plate and the bases loaded, the National's Ryan Zimmerman hit a screaming ground ball up the middle. Jimmy Rollins dove to his left, caught the ball and flipped to a waiting Chase Utley at second base. Utley turned and rifled the ball to Howard for the niftiest, and most important, double play that anyone in Philadelphia can remember. And just like that the crowd of 45,177 erupted and the team celebrated their second consecutive NL East Division title ... Jamie Moyer (16-7, 3.71) picked up the win and Lidge earned his 41st save in 41 opportunities to set a new Phillies' record. Stuff: With his 16th win of the season, Jamie Moyer tied Phil Niekro for the most wins ever by a 45 year old pitcher ... The Phillies are now 78-0 when leading the game after 8 innings ... a large banner was held up in left field that summed up the determination of the city: "World Series or Bust".*

With one out in the inning, Ryan Zimmerman smashes the ball up the middle where a diving Jimmy Rollins makes an incredible diving catch on one hop...

Chase Utley takes the quick flip from Rollins for out #2 of the inning and then rifles the ball ...

to an awaiting Ryan Howard for out #3 and the 2008 NL East Title

The Phillies celebrated back-to-back National League East titles after clinching the division on the second to last day of the season, but unlike 2007, their sights are already set on the next order of business.

I've been looking forward to today's game all season. I revel in its meaninglessness, its absence of consequence. I'm legitimately excited to see today's bench-emptying lineup card. This is one game where the only thing I honestly care about is that the team plays hard and has fun, just like they used to say in little league.

The good people at Comcast SportsNet covered virtually every second of yesterday's post game revelry, and about an hour into the show, I came to the conclusion that I was happier about the Phils clearing my Sunday schedule than a successful defense of the National League East. That's not to undervalue the intense grind that started in mid-February, but the way I see it, you finish with 91 wins, a 3.90 team ERA, a perfect closer, a 45-year-old 16-game winner, a home run and RBI champ, you better be in. Watching the celebration, the view from my oversize loveseat painted a subdued portrait of a division winner. The "team of necessity" celebrated out of necessity, too. Listen to Charlie Manuel and he'll tell you the main reason his club was swept in the '07 NLDS was they got too caught up in the euphoria of finally making it and anything that happened in October was practically viewed as a bonus. That won't be the case here.

To the game, the only thing missing was that it happened in game 161 instead of 162. The final play was given a proper storybook treatment by Phil Sheridan of the Inquirer, who correctly identified it as one of the all-time great defensive plays in Phillies' history. He also recognized the play Carlos Ruiz made on the bounce over his head. Aside from the 9th-inning defense, Jamie Moyer rises to the occasion yet again in a big game. Moyer has become a Philadelphia treasure that needs to be kept under lock and key.

Quotable: "You guys have been unbelievable" - Chase Utley to a sold-out crowd of 44,945 cheering fans

<u>Sunday, September 28th - Phillies 8 Nationals 3 (92-70) 1st - 3 GA the Mets</u>
Philadelphia – *After celebrating the night away, the Phillies rested their starters and gave the bench players and their future stars a chance to play before the start of the NLDS ... The Phillies swept the Nationals behind a 13 hit attack by their "second" team ... So Taguchi led the way going 3 for 5 with a triple, double and a single while knocking in 3 runs ... Rookie Lou Marson made the most of his first major league start by going 2 for 4 with his first career homerun and 2 RBIs ... Eric Bruntlett and Tadahito Iguchi both went 2 for 5 on the day ...Kyle Kendrick started the game for the resting Cole Hamels and gave up 3 runs in 4 innings of work ... Les Walrond (1-1, 6.10) got the win in relief. Stuff: The Phillies set their all-time attendance mark as 3,455,583 fans came through the turn stiles this season which included a record 50 sellout games ... The Phillies ended up*

48-33 at home this year with them going 18-6 in their final 24 home games.
Eighty-nine wins clinched the division for the Phils in 2007, but cleared the calendar for the Mets to book October tee times in 2008.

PHEW!
PHILLIES CLINCH DIVISION TITLE!
Ticket punched for 2008 postseason!

Yesterday at Shea, the Mets season ended appropriately, with the jerry-rigged bullpen letting up the game-winning runs in another last-day, season-ending loss to the Marlins, while in Milwaukee, mid-season pickup C.C. Sabathia proved to be the missing piece for the playoff-bound Brewers.

In fairness, it seems the 89-win Mets haven't been extended nearly the same Big Apple courtesy as the 89-win Yankees for battling through injuries. At times, you would look at the Mets' lineup, with guys like Marlon Anderson starting in left and retreads like Nelson Figueroa on the hill, and wonder how they were hanging in at all. Guys like Fernando Tatis could easily be playing for the unaffiliated Long Island Ducks.

Nevertheless, relying on broken-down veterans like Pedro Martinez and others to turn back the hands of time was a risky proposition from the start. Although the Mets held a 3 ½ game division lead as late as Sept. 10, they were relying on Carlos Delgado to stay unconscious and the bullpen to produce using smoke and mirrors.

While the Phils and Mets can boast a comparable nucleus of home grown talent, they separate in terms of supporting cast. In the end, the better team got hot at the right time, while the flaws of the weaker team were exposed. There was no collapse. The better team won.

Monday, September 29th - A City in Celebration Just Waiting for the Playoffs to Begin

WPHT 1210 AM's Michael Smerconish was able to catch up with Phillies' Manager Charlie Manuel after the Phils clinched the National League Eastern Division Pennant. The following is a cut of Michael's show as he interviewed the skipper today after winning the NL Eastern Division title for the second year in a row.

Smerconish: As interesting as we all find the 2008 elections, this is the story of the hour in Philadelphia and the man of the hour is Phillies' skipper Charlie Manuel. What a privilege to welcome him back to the program. Hey Charlie congrats on the NL East.

Manuel: Hey Mike, how about that man.

Smerconish: Hey Charlie I have to say this Pat McClune is the assistant managing editor of the Philadelphia Daily News and on a day in March when you were down there in Clearwater we played a game on the radio and he said, "How many wins?" and I said, "92." I should have bet the house on it. I hit it on the button.

Manuel: Yeah, it's great. It took every one of them too Michael.

Smerconish: It always seems to Charlie, especially with this team. Doesn't it?

Manuel: It sure does, I mean it seems like we never do anything easy but at the same time, you know what Michael? (In) Spring Training I figured that our league was going to be really close and I figured we were going to go right down to the end. Also I figured the Atlanta Braves were going to be in there. They had a lot of trouble with their pitching this year but they got 3 or 4 big starters that got hurt and we're lucky they didn't make it through but at the same time Florida and the Mets they stayed right there and our division was very solid and good.

Smerconish: I remember back in the outset of the season you just brought Brad Lidge to town and he was coming off surgery. If you had said to me that he would save, what was the final number, 41 games? I don't know you would have been shocked at that number, right?

Manuel: Actually I know exactly what you're talking about because when I first saw Brad Lidge after we had signed him he was kind of on crutches and he was walking around with kind of like a soft cast on his leg and I thought to myself, "Man, that's my closer?"

Smerconish: (Laughter) Go bring back Billy Wagner! ... Hey Charlie you know what occurs to me is because you're down there in the dugout you don't get to hear what happens on the radio can I play you 30 seconds of what went down on Saturday night when you won it? Because I think you'll love Harry Kalas and Larry Anderson. Is that alright?

Manuel: Yeah, please go ahead.

(At this point, Mike Smerconish plays the Harry Kalas/Larry Anderson radio commentary as the Phillies clinch the NL East Division.)

Smerconish: It gives me goose bumps Charlie just to hear it again a couple of days later.

Manuel: You know something Michael that's just unreal. When Zimmerman hit the ball and I first saw it I thought to myself that the ball is going through. I mean it was just that quick. I'm standing there but I think it's going through. You might not believe this but in the four years that I've been here that might have been the first time I ever felt like I had a big lump in my stomach. Zimmerman hit the ball and Rollins totally caught it and we turned it into a double play it seemed like lump just went away.

Smerconish: I watched you just sort of taking it in down there in the dugout after they won the game. You were reluctant to go out onto the field. What was running through your mind?

Manuel: You know what; I thought that all of the season and all of the meetings that I've had and the times that everybody has been together. And I felt like that was a definite moment for my players to like enjoy it by themselves, you know leave them alone and let them go out there and have fun on the field, jump, holler, scream, pour champagne, scream at the crowd, whatever. Seriously that was exactly what was going through my mind. In fact I was kind of at a loss for words really.

Smerconish: When the bases were loaded and there was one out, I said to my sons, "There is no way Charlie is pulling Brad Lidge because Lidge has gotten him so far." I figured I knew you well enough to say "He's gonna let Lidge ride this storm out."

Manuel: You know I just stood there and I thought to myself there's no way Lidge is going to come out of the game but, "What the heck he can get anyone he wants out there."

Smerconish: You set your rotation for the playoffs. It's gonna be Cole (Hamels) tomorrow afternoon and then Brett (Myers) and then Jamie (Moyer).

Manuel: Right, exactly.

Smerconish: I guess there's really no mystery in terms of that order. Everybody would pretty much assign it the same way.

Manuel: Brett pitches much better at home than when he's been away this season. He's thrown a shut out against them (Milwaukee) the last time out. Jamie's been pitching about every four days and Jamie's hot. And also I like Jamie pitching in Milwaukee. There's a dome there, it's gonna be full of people, there's gonna be loud noise. And I think Jamie is a pro, He's the guy that can handle that.

Smerconish: In other words, he's seen it all in his 45 or so years so we'll let him go and deal with the dome.

Manuel: Exactly. I know he's been there because we played him before. You know like when I was over in Cleveland he pitched a big game in Seattle with the Mariners and I know he can play Milwaukee. It's gonna be loud because of the dome and everything. Plus he's pitched there and he knows everything about it and also he's got a hot hand.

Smerconish: How much do you know about (Milwaukee's) Yovani Gallardo?

Manuel: I know he's got a good arm and I know he's had surgery on it this year, but he's got a good arm, good fast ball, good breaking ball, change-up. He's a pretty good pitcher Michael.

Smerconish: I mean this is a guy who's been out there, who's seen very limited action right?

Manuel: Yeah but he's pitched enough around. He's got more major league experience than you think he has if you want to check on him and look him up. He's pretty good. And the injuries that kept him from pitching straight through, this guy has got big arms.

Smerconish: Hey Charlie, you had a long time to think about the .172 batting average against Colorado last season. What was the lesson you took away from that?

Manuel: I think that one of the lessons I take away from it, and also I tell our players all the time, is the fact that Colorado has young pitchers that threw hard and basically we're fastball hitters. We were impatient. We tried too hard and also Colorado had a lot of left hand pitchers and they tried to offset our lefties. I think that we learned from that and I think , also like now if you noticed, that's when I play with my lineup a little bit more and split up Howard and Utley. Especially if a team has two or three left hand relievers and that's kind of how we do it. In Milwaukee they've got CC and he's going to pitch twice. I had CC as a rookie in Cleveland.

Smerconish: I didn't know that.

Manuel: Yeah I was the guy that brought CC to the big leagues and I really had to fight to get CC to bring him up, he was young and he won 17 games for us. I know a lot about CC. CC is a tremendous talent but at the same time like if we can get some run production like we can be like, we can score on CC.

Smerconish: Hey Charlie this is a tough town I don't have to tell you that, but you must be feeling the love because I've been down there for a couple of games recently when those "Charlie, Charlie, Charlie" chants have broken out.

Manuel: I was telling somebody the other day when they were asking me about how does it feel to hear your name and know that they're pulling for you. You know I said it all along if you remember that once that they got to know me and the fact that we can win some games especially with divisions and have a shot and go to the World Series. Our goal is to win the World Series and I've said that all along. Anytime that you can become a winner or be part of a winner I think that you know people have gotten to know me over these last 4 years and also they like the way our team players and who our players are. The players are the ones that always make the managers good. And I think from that standpoint and how much the fans love our team and our players I think that they definitely get to know me and evidently they're happy with the way I do my business.

Smerconish: One final question for Phillies' skipper Charlie Manuel, this is a personal question. I split my season tickets with a bunch of guys, ok? So the playoffs are obviously in demand we have 4 seats. I have 2 of them for tomorrow and my 12-year-old son is in 7th grade. First pitch is at 3 in the afternoon. Now how am I supposed to handle this because I said to my wife, "We're not fooling anybody if we say he's got a doctor's appointment at 3 in the afternoon tomorrow." So my mindset is to send in a note to say, "We're blessed that we have Phillies tickets and I'd like to take my son out of school and go down to the ballpark." What does Charlie Manuel think I should do?

Manuel: I think you should send a note or call the teacher and ask her and say, "Hey look I want to do that. My son and I have to go to the game tomorrow we have tickets and it's more important to him if he goes."

Smerconish: Can I throw your name into the mix?

Manuel: Yeah sure, why not. If it helps you of course.

Smerconish: I got Charlie's personal blessing for this?

Manuel: Yeah, right.

Smerconish: Hey man this could not happen to a nicer guy and I wish you all the best for the second part of the season.

Manuel: Thank you.

October - C.C., Manny and the Rain ...

The National League
Divisional Series

NLDS - Game 1

Quotable: "He was great! He just went out there and was Cole Hamels. He mixed up his fastball and his change-up, threw a few curveballs. That's what he does." – Ryan Howard on Hamel's masterful 3-1 victory over the Brewers

Wednesday, October 1st - Phillies 3 Brewers 1 - Phillies Lead Series 1 -0

Philadelphia – *The Phils took advantage of a misplayed ball by Brewers' centerfielder Mike Cameron to score 3 runs in the 3rd, which was all they needed as Cole Hamels completely dominated the Brewers' lineup. Hamels (1-0, 0.00) allowed only 2 hits and a walk over 8 innings while striking out 9, as the Phillies took the first game of the series ...Brad Lidge came into the 9th and allowed one run on 2 hits and a walk, but he eventually closed the door shut to get his first save of the playoffs and the first Phillies victory in the postseason in 15 years. Stuff: Hamels became only the 2nd pitcher in the Phillies' history to pitch 8 shutout innings in post season play. The last pitcher to do it for the Phillies also happens to be the last pitcher to win a postseason game for the Phils. Curt Schilling shut out the Toronto Blue Jays in Game 5 of the 1993 World Series 2-0 on October 21, 1993 ... Speaking of the Phils' last World Series, Mitch "The Wild Thing" Williams threw out the first pitch and hit the backstop on the throw.*

Cole Hamels threw 8 shutout innings against the Brew Crew

Cole and a batch of gift runs in the third inning made the difference for the Phils in a game contested by two anxious offenses that combined for just eight hits. Brad Lidge came on to close out the ninth and made it an adventure, striking out the potential go-ahead run with men on second and third to end the Brewers' threat, giving the Phillies their first post-season win in 15 years and a 1-0 edge in the series.

Cole was the shining light in a game that featured far more bad than good. The 24-year-old ace took another step in elevating his status as one of the elite pitchers in the game, building on last season's October taste test to notch his first-career playoff win. Similar to their four-game sweep, the Brewers' offense looked uncomfortable the entire game. They had no idea what was coming, and didn't bother sticking around very long to find out, taking their hacks and taking a seat. Cole had them by the neck and squeezed.

To the offense, Chase Utley laced a double to center than got caught in the wind and fooled center fielder Mike Cameron, dropping out of his outstretched glove and allowing two unearned runs to score. It was the big blow, but it wasn't the best at bat. That honor goes to Shane Victorino's bases-loaded walk, staying patient with Yovani Gallardo's breaking pitches. Otherwise, it was a dangerously quiet afternoon for the Phils' offense, which suffered from a couple of bad right/right match-ups, particularly Jayson Werth, who went 0-4 with three strikeouts. Lots of jitters from everyone but Cole, but Cole was all that mattered today.

NLDS - Game 2

Quotable: "It's definitely big to get that win off of Sabathia, knowing that he's been lights-out since they got him at the trade deadline. But we can't take anything for granted." - Shane Victorino after touching Sabathia for a grand slam in the 2nd inning

Thursday, October 2nd - Phillies 5 Brewers 2 - Phillies Lead Series 2 -0

Philadelphia – Shane Victorino's first career grand slam off of CC Sabathia was part of a Phillies' 5 run 2nd inning that gave the Phils all the runs they would need for the win ... Brett Myers had a rough 1st inning in which he gave up a bases loaded walk but was able to work out of the jam and then shut down the Brewers offense through the next 6 innings. Myers (1-0, 2.57) pitched 7 innings, allowing 2 runs on 2 hits and 3 walks while striking out 4 ... Ryan Madson and JC Romero pitched the 8th, surrendering only 1 hit ... Brad Lidge pitched a perfect 9th for his 2nd save of the playoffs as the Phillies took a commanding 2-0 lead in the best of 5 series. Stuff: Sabathia only last 3 2/3rd innings allowing 5 runs on 6 hits ... The Phillies tied two postseason records in the game – most doubles in a game (6) and most extra-base hits in a game (7).

With the score knotted 1-1, Victorino's bases-clearing blast capped an inning for the ages that featured a capacity Citizens Bank Park crowd rise in anticipation over a two-out Brett Myers at bat. A star on the bump and at the dish, fans roared every time Myers fought off a Sabathia pitch and watched as he shimmied a key walk. With his pitch count rising, Sabathia followed by walking Jimmy Rollins to load the bases for Victorino, who received a slider up in his wheelhouse and didn't miss. For many a young Phillies fans, savor it as the greatest post-season hit you've ever seen live, and for the Flyin' Hawaiian (3-for-4 with a walk, a pair of doubles and the slam) that's two-straight games where you delivered the best at-bat of the ballgame my brother.

The Brewer's CC Sabathia could only last into the 4th inning against the Phillies' potent offense

Back to Myers, who settled in after a shaky start to pitch seven strong innings, allowing two while striking out four. There's hesitation in heaping ridiculous praise upon Myers, who was great but unworthy of the same glowing copy Cole Hamels received. If the Phils take this series, it's mainly because the Brewers have been absolutely terrible. Mike Cameron, Prince Fielder and Corey Hart have been particularly atrocious, and many a Brewer missed a Myers mistake tonight.

While the yips have crippled Milwaukee's offense, the Phils are playing it cool. The jitters are completely gone at this stage of the series. They're running wild on the bases. Their defense has been sharp; Chase Utley has had a very nice defensive series. They're taking good at bats and running deep counts. Their approach to C.C. was generally excellent, chasing him after just 3 2-3 innings with his count at 98. The Phils came within inches of blowing the game open, but J-Roll's line smash was hit right at Fielder at first. They're getting two-out runs and the right-handed bats of Pedro Feliz and Jayson Werth clicked in a big way tonight.

With the pressure piled on Milwaukee, the Phils are in great shape to put Milwaukee's life-support season to rest and move on to the NLCS.

NLDS - Game 3

Quotable: "Yeah, I'm concerned about it, but I don't know what you can do right now, especially this time of the year." - Charlie Manuel on Howard, Utley and Burrell's combined 4 for 28 in the first three games of the series

Saturday, October 4th - Brewers 4 Phillies 1 - Phillies Lead Series 2 -1
Milwaukee – The Brewers jumped on Jamie Moyer early in the first scoring two runs on two walks, a wild pitch, a sacrifice fly by Prince Fielder and a single by Bill Hall ... Moyer (0-1, 4.50) took the loss as he went 4 innings, giving up a total of 2 runs on 4 hits and 3 walks ...Ryan Howard went 2 for 4 and knocked in the Phillies only run of the game ... Jayson Werth went 2 for 4 with a triple and a double ... the Phillies loaded the bases in the 9th but Pedro Feliz's double-play groundout ended the threat.   Stuff: Moyer became the 2nd oldest pitcher to start a postseason game at 45 years, 321 days. The oldest ever was Jack Quinn of the Philadelphia A's who started against the Cubs in the 1929 World Series. Quinn was 46 years, 103 days old ... The win was the first for the Brewers in postseason play since 1982.

Tonight, Phillies fans experienced what this series has looked like from the other side, witnessing an ugly, poorly played loss from start to finish.

It started with Jamie Moyer, who struggled with Brian Runge's strike zone right out of the chute. Moyer took the loss, lasting just four innings and walking three and letting up two first-inning runs against a patient Brewers lineup. Moyer's problem was that he wasn't throwing first-pitch strikes. After two miserable games, the Brewers' offense decided they were going to make the opposing pitcher work for it. By the time Moyer figured it out, he was at 60 pitches.

It ended even worse. Down 4-1 with the bases loaded and nobody out in the ninth, Pedro Feliz grounded into a double play on the very first pitch from Solomon Torres, shades of the approach Milwaukee had the first two games of the series. On the play, Shane Victorino was called for interference at second, and Ryan Howard, who scored on the play, was forced back to third and the run was taken off the board.

Prince Fielder knocked in one of the four Brewer's runs in the Phillies first loss of the postseason

Nevertheless, each team had chances. The Brewers probably had more. It was a trap game, and the Brewers, losers of seven straight to the Phils, were due for one. The Brewers were focused at home, the Phils went into a shell, and after Moyer was taken out, the game wasn't entirely managed with a Game 3 victory in mind. At least that's how it seemed. Otherwise, several of Charlie Manuel's moves made no sense. That's it for the summary. For a hint at what I'm also thinking about, Beerleaguer will go to bed searching for meaning as it relates to a certain left fielder's past, present and future.

NLDS - Game 4

Quotable: "Jimmy (Rollins) came out of the gates and really set the tone, he gave us some momentum early." - Starter Joe Blanton on Rollins lead-off homerun in the first inning

<u>Sunday, October 5th - Phillies 6 Brewers 2 - Phillies Win Series 3 -1</u>
Milwaukee – *The Phillies got all 6 of their runs from homeruns, including two by Pat Burrell. Burrell had an incredible day as he went 3 for 4 with 2 runs scored and 4 RBIs ... Jayson Werth hit a solo homerun in the 2nd after Burrell's 3-run jack ... Jimmy Rollins led off the game with a solo homerun that took the loud Brewers crowd quickly out of the game ... Greg Dobbs went 2 for 3 ... Joe Blanton (1-0, 1.50) pitched an incredible outing going 6 innings, giving up only 1 run on 5 hits*

while striking out 7... Ryan Madson pitched the 7th and 8th giving up 1 run ... Brad Lidge closed out the game in the 9th and led another celebration from the mound as the Phillies beat Milwaukee three games to one in their National League Divisional Series. Stuff: Rollin's lead off homerun was the 2nd of his career in the playoffs ... The Phillies will now meet the LA Dodgers in the NLCS for the first time since 1983.

Yesterday, following another grim performance, I searched for meaning as it related to the career of Pat Burrell. Would he even connect for a post-season hit? One could only wonder. Would he ever make the kind of October impact the Phillies envisioned when they made him the first pick overall in the 1998 draft? The outlook wasn't good.

Today, he answered. When history is retold, it will be the much-maligned left-fielder who put his team on his back in Game 4 and carried the Phillies to their first playoff series win since 1993. Burrell awoke from a two-and-a-half-month hibernation for a 3-for-4,

Shane Victorino's first career grand slam in Game 1 was the table setter for the rest of the series

two-homer, 4 RBI afternoon, including the fatal three-run blow that launched the Phils into the league championship series to face the Los Angeles Dodgers.

Like the first two games, they won it with pitching. Turn back the clock to the middle of the season and you'll find a pair of NL Central clubs in Chicago and Milwaukee setting their sights on the Fall Classic thanks to a pair of blockbuster trades. The Brewers made the biggest splash of any Major League Baseball team with their deal for C.C. Sabathia. Victorino made Sabathia's Game 2 debut a failure. He's going home. The Cubs responded to Milwaukee's move by getting Rich Harden from the Athletics. The Dodgers knocked him out after four innings last night, shattering the Cubbies' dreams with a quick three-game sweep. Harden is going home.

Then there's Joe Blanton, considered by some as a second-rate mid-season acquisition, who out-dueled Sabathia, Harden, but most importantly, Jeff Suppan, leading the Phils in a no-nonsense clincher. The big right-hander was in complete control, challenging the Brewers with strikes, allowing five hits while striking out seven. In my eyes, he was every bit as good as Brett Myers, if not better.

Yesterday, following another grim performance, I searched for meaning as it related to the career of Pat Burrell. Would he even connect for a post-season hit? One could only wonder. Would he ever make the kind of October impact the Phillies envisioned when they made him the first pick overall in the 1998 draft? The outlook wasn't good.

Today, he answered. When history is retold, it will be the much-maligned left-fielder who put his team on his back in Game 4 and carried the Phillies to their first playoff series win since 1993. Burrell awoke from a two-and-a-half-month hibernation for a 3-for-4, two-homer, 4 RBI afternoon, including the fatal three-run blow that launched the Phils into the league championship series to face the Los Angeles Dodgers.

Like the first two games, they won it with pitching. Turn back the clock to the middle of the season and you'll find a pair of NL Central clubs in Chicago and Milwaukee setting their sights on the Fall Classic thanks to a pair of blockbuster trades. The Brewers made the biggest splash of any Major League Baseball team with their deal for C.C. Sabathia. Victorino made Sabathia's Game 2 debut a failure. He's going home. The Cubs responded to Milwaukee's move by getting Rich Harden from the Athletics. The Dodgers knocked him out after four innings last night, shattering the Cubbies' dreams with a quick three-game sweep. Harden is going home.

Then there's Joe Blanton, considered by some as a second-rate mid-season acquisition, who out-dueled Sabathia, Harden, but most importantly, Jeff Suppan, leading the Phils in a no-nonsense clincher. The big right-hander was in complete control, challenging the Brewers with strikes, allowing five hits while striking out seven. In my eyes, he was every bit as good as Brett Myers, if not better.

They got help from others. Jimmy Rollins, who had a good series, led off the game with a solo home run. Suppan would later give up consecutive homers to Burrell and Jayson Werth, who also had a good series. Ryan Madson and Brad Lidge finished it off for Blanton.

More to come. Hopefully, much, much more to come.

A look back at the five most important plays of the National League Division Series between the Phillies and Brewers finds Shane Victorino headlining two of them.

Only in a game as great as baseball could a walk and a grand slam represent the best two plays in a series. Let's go to the list, in descending order.

Honorable mention: Brad Lidge strikes out potential go-ahead run Corey Hart with men on second and third to end the Brewers' ninth-inning threat in Game 1, giving the Phillies their first post-season win in 15 years and a 1-0 edge in the series.

No. 5: Shane Victorino forces a bases-loaded walk to make it 3-0 in the third inning of Game 1, staying uncharacteristically patient with Yovani Gallardo's breaking pitches. The Phils would struggle with RISP for most of the series.

No. 4: Brett Myers induces a Hart double play ground out with the bases loaded to limit the damage to one run in the first inning of Game 2.

No. 3: Pat Burrell connects for a three-run jack off Jeff Suppan to put the Phillies up for good in the third inning of Game 4. Burrell added one for good measure in the eighth.

No. 2: In front of thousands of roaring fans, starter Brett Myers fights off C.C. Sabathia to force a key walk to keep the two-out rally alive in Game 2.

No. 1: Victorino makes his first-career grand slam count in a big way, sending Sabathia's eye-high slider deep into the left-field seats to complete the five-run, second-inning rally that was aided by Myers' walk. With Sabathia erased, the series balance shifted heavily in the Phils' favor.

Fittingly, Shane was also involved in the lowest point of the series, receiving an interference call in the ninth inning of Saturday's ugly Game 3 loss.

The National League
Championship Series

NLCS - Game 1

Quotable: "I thought maybe when Furcal threw the ball away, that was kind of a turn for us. Utley hit the homerun ... tied the ballgame up. That got us going." – Charlie Manuel on the turn of events that led to the Phils' victory in the 6th

Thursday, October 9th - Phillies 3 Dodgers 2 - Phillies Lead Series 1 -0

Philadelphia – *The Dodgers jumped out to an early 2-0 lead however the Phillies battled back in the 6th inning when shortstop Rafael Furcal was charged with a throwing error that allowed Shane Victorino to get on base. A few moments later, Chase Utley hit a 2-run homerun to tie the game at two. Two batters later, Pat Burrell lined a homerun into the left field seats to give the Phils all the runs they needed to take Game 1 away from Los Angeles ... Cole Hamels (1-0, 2.57) pitched a superb game as he threw 7 strong innings giving up 2 runs while walking 2 and striking out 8 Dodgers ... The bullpen kept the door closed for the final two innings as Ryan Madson threw a scoreless 8th and Brad Lidge nailed down his first postseason save of his career in the 9th ... The Phillies only managed a total of 7 hits in the game with Chase Utley (2 for 4), Pat Burrell (2 for 3) and Carlos Ruiz (2 for 3) accounting for six of them.   Stuff: Utley's homerun was the 1st homer of his postseason career... It was Burrell's 4th postseason career homerun ... Former Phillies' player and manager Larry Bowa received a nice ovation from the crowd of 45,839 fans in pre-game introductions ... Best sign in the crowd was hoisted out in left-center field, "Hair Today, Gone Tomorrow" ... This is the Phillies 7th League Championship series in their 126 year history and the fourth time that they have played the Dodgers in the NLCS (1977, 1978 and 1983).*

Tonight, an October star was born. His name is Cole Hamels.

Baseball never seems to work out the way it's supposed to. Except, of course, for last night, an unqualified template for how the Phillies would manage to win their games according to many. Pitch great and hope for a big inning. That's exactly what happened. Conventional wisdom said the Phils needed to win Cole's Game 1 in both the Division Series and the NLCS and did just that, squeezing out a pair of three-run innings to achieve victory in both games.

The ace did all the rest. In 15 innings, Hamels has allowed just two runs while fanning 17. His combined inning tally sits at 242.1 and you'd never know it. He's also 24 and you'd never know it. Once again, a Phillies starter escaped danger in the first and settled in. Using mostly fastballs in the first, Hamels struggled with his command and got into trouble, missing on a pitch to Manny Ramirez that Manny cranked to within a few feet of the center field camera deck. It was one of only two real mistakes Hamels made, the other being a pitch that was easily elevated to the outfield for a sac fly later in the ballgame. Luckily, nobody told Manny that left-center field, the deepest and

Manny Ramirez watches Pat Burrell's homerun land in the left field stands in the 6th

darkest part of the Citizens Bank Park, is a no-fly zone. Everyone knows the short porch in left is the preferred flight pattern for right-handed hitters.

NLCS - Game 2

Quotable: "I'm not a very good hitter, I just get lucky occasionally. I'm baffled by it. I would've rather pitched better." - Brett Myers after his 3 for 3, 3 RBI performance against the Dodgers

Friday, October 10th - Phillies 8 Dodgers 5 - Phillies Lead Series 2 -0

Philadelphia – *Brett Myers shaky performance on the mound was made up for by an unbelievable performance at the plate. Myers, who lasted only 5 innings giving up 5 runs on 6 hits and 4 walks while getting the win, went 3 for 3 with 3 RBIs and 2 runs scored. In a season in which he batted .069 with a total of 4 hits and 1 RBI, Myers' performance left Dodgers starter Chad Billingsley quipping, "It's crazy!". Billingsley only lasted 2 1/3rd innings giving up 8 runs (7 earned) on 8 hits and 3 walks ... The other hitting stars for the Phillies included Shane Victorino who went 2 for 5 with 4 RBIs and Greg Dobbs who had 2 singles and scored 2 runs ... Manny Ramirez continued hitting in the playoffs going 1 for 4 with a homerun in the 4th off of Myers ... After Myers left the game the bullpen shut down the Dodgers through the final 4 innings allowing only 2 hits ... Brad Lidge closed out the 9th for his second save of the series while walking two but then striking out the side to end the game. Stuff: Charlie Manuel's mother passed away prior to the game. Manuel didn't speak to reporters in the post game press conference ... After the game Shane Victorino found out that his grandmother had passed away as well back home in Hawaii ... 45,883 fans were packed inside Citizens Bank Park to cheer the Phils on as they now leave for La La Land.*

Shane Victorino continued his torrid "Victober" with a two-run single, two-run triple and a highlight-reel catch in the seventh. While Myers was a star at the dish, he labored on the bump, allowing five runs and four walks over five frames, including a three-run shot by Manny Ramirez to cut the Phillies' six-run lead in half. To the delight of a sold-out Citizens Bank Park crowd, that's where the score would stay thanks to four shutout innings by the

Brett Myers more than made up with a poor pitching performance going 3 for 3 in Game 2

bullpen highlighted by Ryan Madson's brilliant eighth. Brad Lidge turned the ninth into another adventure, but he struck out the side for his 48th-straight save.

Myers' game will never be forgotten, but neither will the work of several others. Victorino has been a delight this entire post-season and has been the Phillies' best overall player for months, period. I loved the look of the Carlos Ruiz double into the gap that got it all started in the second. Old-school Chooch. The job of both bullpens cannot be overstated. Just when the game appeared to be slipping away, Chad Durbin worked a scoreless sixth; J.C. Romero was as nasty as I've seen against the left-handers Ethier and Loney. And then there was Madson, who dialed it up to the high 90s and absolutely annihilated Jeff Kent, Rafael Furcal and Russell Martin in a huge spot in the eighth.

Something smells, and it's coming from the lockers of Myers and Victorino. It smells like destiny.

NLCS - Game 3

Quotable: "I think it's over. I'll squash it." – Shane Victorino when asked if the high and inside pitch to his head by LA starter Hiroki Kuroda would bleed over to the remaining games in the series.

Sunday, October 12th - Dodgers 7 Phillies 2 - Phillies Lead Series 2 -1
Los Angeles – The Dodgers quickly jumped out on top of Jamie Moyer for 5 runs in the 1st inning led by a bases clearing triple off of the bat of Dodgers' second baseman Blake DeWitt … Moyer took the loss, lasting only 1 1/3rd innings giving up 6 runs on 6 hits while the bullpen looked solid once again giving up a total of 4 hits and 1 run over the final 6 2/3rds innings …The Phillies scattered 7 hits with Ryan Howard going 2 for 4 with 1 run scored … Hiroki Kuroda got the win for the Dodgers as he went 6 solid innings giving up 2 runs on 5 hits. Stuff: At 45 years of age, Jamie Moyer became the oldest player to ever start a league championship game …the 56,800 fans in attendance at Dodger Stadium was the largest crowd ever for a baseball game in the history of the stadium.

The Dodgers went on the attack right out of the chute and made quick work of Moyer, who allowed five runs on five hits and a hit batsman in the first.

Then in the second, Rafael Furcal greeted him with a first-pitch home run, making it three hits coming on one of his first pitches. It was reason enough for manager Charlie Manuel to give him the hook, lifting him before Manny Ramirez and the buzzards could get a second crack at him.

The dirty little secret so far in the post-season is that the Phillies' offense hasn't been very good, and tonight was no exception. Dodgers pitching held the Phils down, including a 0-for-8 from the top of the order. Jimmy Rollins is now 1-for-13 with 6 strikeouts in the NLCS and has suddenly turned into a complete wimp at the plate. The bad at bats were shared by almost everyone on a night when tempers flared and the Dodgers retaliated for Friday's throw by Brett Myers behind Manny Ramirez' head. The benches cleared after Shane Victorino was buzzed by

Hiroki Kuroda, and Ramirez needed to be restrained from going after ... pick someone ... but order was restored and the game passed quietly after the second, which was good news for Dodgers fans who wanted to get that extra early jump on traffic.

The Phils used five pitchers after Moyer, including the playoff debut of J.A. Happ, who allowed a run on three hits and two walks over three innings.

Dodger Stadium was host to Game 3 of the NLCS, the first time since 1983 that the Phillies have played a Championship game in the City of Angels- photo courtesy of Leslie Gudel

"Squashed." That's how Shane Victorino put it when Fox's Ken Rosenthal stuck a microphone in his face and asked about the conflict of interest that caused Hiroki Kuroda to throw over his head. Vic said "squashed" before brushing off reporters moments later by refusing to talk any further about this issue, presumably since he answered the question once and felt that once on national television was enough for anyone. Vic was right.

If the pitch that buzzed Vic was intended to keep the Phils on edge the rest of the series, the Dodgers failed to account for one important principle: that a baseball game is a painstakingly long process and a seven-game series is even worse. Read the reports and it sounds like sheer chaos unfolded last night at Dodgers Stadium. In actuality, the game finished at such a lethargic pace that it couldn't have been a better atmosphere for a rookie like J.A. Happ to experience his first taste of the post-season.

If the tension wasn't squashed the first time, a couple of big, control right-handers in Derek Lowe and Joe Blanton will sit on it tonight. If Game 3 embodied the intense extremes of playoff baseball, expect cold feet in Game 4, as the two sides struggle to live up to the title-fight billing the series received today.

NLCS - Game 4

Quotable: "My whole career, even back in the early days, my approach was try to hit the ball out of the ballpark." – Phillies pinch hitter Matt Stairs after launching a 2-run blast in the 8th that put the Phils on top for good

Monday, October 13th   - Phillies 7 Dodgers 5 - Phillies Lead Series 3 -1

Los Angeles – With the Dodgers leading 5-3 going into the 8th, Shane Victorino and Matt Stairs each homered to cap off an exciting come-from-behind victory for the Phillies ... The Phillies pounded out 12 hits over the course of the game with Chase Utley leading the team with a 3 for 5 performance ... Carlos Ruiz continued his hot hitting in the playoffs, going 2 for 3 and raising his League Championship average to .417 ... Ryan Madson picked up the win with 1 2/3rd scoreless innings in relief ... Brad Lidge pitched a 4-out save to earn his 3rd save of the series. Stuff: The Phillies now have 9 homeruns in 8 playoff games with those homers accounting for 17 of their 35 runs scored ... Shane Victorino's homerun was his 11th RBI of the postseason, a new Phillies record beating out Lenny Dykstra's 10 RBIs in 1993 ... Chase Utley made an incredible diving catch in the 6th inning that doubled off Rafael Furcal at second to end a huge Dodgers rally. If the ball got through, the Dodgers could have easily continued to pour on the runs and end up tying the series.

The Dodgers led 5-3 and were five outs away from pulling even in the best-of-seven series when Victorino, the clear catalyst this entire post-season, deposited a two-run shot into the right-field bullpen to tie the game 5-5 in the top of the 8th . Not to be outdone, Stairs, who was acquired by the Phillies after the trade deadline for a situation just like this, stepped to the plate. Two batters later with a runner on and two out, Stairs crushed a Jonathan Broxton 3-1 fastball into outer space. The late-inning heroics erased a multitude of earlier sins by the Phils, including a series of managerial misfires and some all-around shoddy play. But in the end, it will be Dodgers' manager Joe Torre who could be forever second-guessed if the Phillies can deliver just one more win in their next three tries.

Shane Victorino, talking to ex-Los Angeles 2nd baseman and Phillies' first base coach Davy Lopes, set a new postseason record with his 11th RBI of the playoffs

NLCS - Game 5

Quotable: "I guarantee you my mom is watching right now. The last time I talked to her she said to me, 'Pray for me.' Then she said, 'Charles Jr., I'm going to pray for you. You're going to win these games and you're going to go to the World Series.' ... That was the last thing she said to me." - Charlie Manuel on his mother, June who passed away after Game 2 as he spoke to Comcast's Leslie Gudel after the Phillies won the National League Championship.

Wednesday, October 15th - Phillies 5 Dodgers 1 - Phillies Win Series 4 -1

Los Angeles – *The Phillies are going to the World Series! For the first time since 1993 and only the fifth time in their 126 year history, the Phillies have won the National League Championship and will play either the Tampa Rays or the Boston Red Sox for the World Championship ... thanks primarily to their stud ace Cole Hamels. Hamels threw another gem of a game, giving up one run, a homerun by Manny Ramirez in the 6th, and a total of 5 hits to win his second game of the series as well as the NLCS MVP award ... Jimmy Rollins got the party started with a lead-off homerun in the top of the 1st which not only silenced the crowd of 56,800 fans but instantly took away any head of steam that the Dodgers had built up for themselves prior to the start of the game ... Ryan Howard went 3 for 4 with an RBI and one run scored, ending the series with an average of .300 ... Ryan Madson and Brad Lidge pitched the 8th and 9th innings. Stuff: Including the playoffs, the Phillies are now 86-0 when leading after eight innings ... Earlier in the day Geoff Jenkins' wife had a baby ... in the same hospital that Chase Utley was born ... Cole Hamels has proven to be Philadelphia's Mr. October so far giving up a total of 3 runs in 22 innings while tallying three victories. He will be the Phils' game 1 starter for the World Series.*

After the game, Charlie Manuel was overcome with joy as he not only talked a lot about his mother's passing, but how happy he was for the city of Philadelphia saying, "This is for the city for Philadelphia. We have one more step, one big step -- then we're going to make a grand parade." As in past championship years, fans from all over the Delaware Valley poured out onto the streets and begin celebrating what many hope will result in the parade down Broad Street.

Geoff Jenkins and Ryan Howard celebrate after winning the National League Championship
– photo courtesy of Leslie Gudel

The World Series

World Series - Game 1

Quotable: "If you want to take the wind out of the sails you shut the cow bells up and get some home runs. That will do it -- except in Citizens Bank Park. If you hit enough there, they ring a bell. They ring the Liberty Bell." - Charlie Manuel on Utley's first inning homerun that silenced the annoying cow bells by the Tampa fans

Wednesday, October 22nd - Phillies 3 Tampa Bay 2 - Phillies Lead Series 1-0

Tampa – After a six day layoff, the Phillies collectively shook off their rust while Cole Hamels once again proved himself as one of the premiere pitchers in baseball, shutting down the Ray's explosive offense on 5 hits and two runs to lead the team to their first World Series victory in 15 years ... Chase Utley hit a two-run homer to deep right in the top of the 1st, knocking in Jayson Werth who had walked to put the Phils on top 2-0 ... In the top of the 4th, Carlos Ruiz hit a fielders choice to shortstop that allowed Shane Victorino to score the winning run from third ... Tampa Bay rallied for one run in both the 4th and 5th innings, but Hamels kept them at bay through 7 innings ... Ryan Madson pitched a perfect 8th as did Brad Lidge in the 9th to earn his first save of the World Series. Stuff: Hamel's held Tampa's 2-3-4 batters hitless for the first time this post season ... with the win, the Phillies became only the 2nd team in World Series history to have a 6 day rest and win the first game of the Series.

Hamels, Madson, Lidge and Chase Utley, who greeted Scott Kazmir with a two-run first-inning homer, represented some of the standout stars in the Phillies' biggest win in 15 years. Pedro Feliz contributed two hits and robbed B.J. Upton of a bases-loaded smash and turned the twin killing to keep the early lead in place. Rays outfielder Carl Crawford would get to Hamels with a solo shot in the fourth inning and standout performer Akinori Iwamura, who went 3-for-4, doubled in Jayson Bartlett in the fifth to complete Tampa's scoring.

Hamels improved to 4-0 in four postseason starts and helped hold Tampa's 2-3-4 batters hitless. For Lidge, make it 47-for-47 in 2008 save opportunities.

To go into the Orangina Sunny ThunderDome ... that stupid bubble, that dumb turf, its monster truck rally

Charlie Manuel liked the way Chase Utley silenced the Rays' cow bells

lighting, those kickball rules, that Little League World Series camera angle, the "ring your bell if you've been a fan for 15 minutes" crowd ... to go there and stop the buzz in the way Hamels, Madson and Lidge did was unbelievably clutch.   Nothing was hindering these pitchers to-night, and I loved Utley's snap homer to get it started in the first. Very quietly, Utley is sneaking past Shane Victorino as the Phils' most valuable hitter this post-season.

Yes, this was a huge win, and the Phils are three wins away, but if the offense doesn't improve, they'll lose this series. They can't count on two runs from Tampa. If not for the pitching, this isn't just a loss, it's a brutal loss. Watching these post-game shows, they're talking about how they won, and thus, didn't look rusty. They looked plenty rusty. Ask anyone who's ever seen Jimmy Rollins play the game of baseball whether he looked rusty at the plate tonight. Jayson Werth flicked two doubles. He looked rusty. Chris Coste, the choice at DH, couldn't catch up with fastballs. He still looks rusty.

Then there's Howard who struck out three times with runners in scoring position. He can't use rust as an excuse. It's so bad for Howard that Ray's manager Joe Maddon finally had the guts to do what opposing managers probably toyed with doing all season: walk Utley to bring up the cleanup hitter. Lefties fed him a steady diet of low-and-away slop, and as usual, he couldn't resist. But I digress. Three mores wins and this town will explode.

World Series - Game 2

Quotable: "That might be one of our sloppiest games all year." – Charlie Manuel first loss of the World Series

Thursday, October 23rd - Tampa Bay 4 Phillies 2 - Series Tied 1-1
Tampa – *Brett Myers pitches effectively but the Phillies offense and inconsistent play in the field al-lowed the Rays to come back and tie the Series at one game apiece ... Myers went 7 innings giving up 4 runs, 3 earned, while walking 3 and striking out 2 ... JC Romero pitched a scoreless 8th ... Although the Phils did bang out 9 hits (two each by Howard, Victorino and Ruiz), they didn't put a run on the board until the 8th when pinch-hitter Eric Bruntlett hit his first postseason homerun of his career ... Carlos Ruiz scored in the 9th on a throwing error by "Eva" Longoria for their only other run of the game. Stuff: It was the Phillies' first World Series loss since Mitch Williams threw that fateful pitch to Joe Carter back in '93 ... the Phils were 0 for 19 with runners in scoring position until Shane Victorino's single in the 4th moved Ryan Howard to third. It was the second longest 0-fer to start off a World Series. The 1966 Dodgers started off their World Series going 0-22 with runners in scoring position against Baltimore ... they ended up losing the Series four games to none.*

There's debate over the quality of Brett Myers' start. I fall in line with those who believe My-ers pitched just fine. Considering the quality of the Rays' offense, playing at home where they have the best record in baseball, Jayson Werth's error in right, the lousy effort at the dish and certainly the incompetent officiating. The game could have unraveled into a real mess, but to his credit, Myers changed it up and settled down. Myers went seven innings, allowing three earned, which could have easily been less because of the officiating gaff. Tampa scored three of their runs without the ball leaving the infield. Afterward, Myers credited Carlos Ruiz with changing strategies and calling a good game.

Ruiz, by the way, came to play this series.

The problem of course is that no one else has. I keep going back to rust, because it's obvious to this observer that someone

BJ Upton went 2 for 4 and helped the Rays tie the Series at one game apiece

like Jimmy Rollins, for example, isn't in sync. His swings are long. He's behind high heat. He hasn't connected for a hit, but more importantly, he's not on base to create something. He reached on a fielder's choice yesterday, the first time he's reached base, and that was followed by a Werth single. That potential rally was murdered by Werth's base-running gaff, the second of two killer mistakes by the Phillies' right fielder.

The official tally of offensive ineptitude goes one-out, second-and-third in the second. Nothing. That one featured perhaps the worst at bat of the night in Greg Dobbs taking three strikes without swinging the bat in a situation where a walk actually hurts because it puts the double play in order. You're the DH. Swing the damn bat. Then Ruiz leads off with a double in the third. Jack squat. First-and-third, one out in the fourth. Zippo. First-and-third with two outs in the sixth. Nada. Pedro Feliz represented the final out in three of these innings, stranding six. He actually ended the eighth as well.

Additional thoughts: Howard's 2-5, 1 K, 3 LOB night has to be the most celebrated mediocre night in history if you watch these post game shows. His double was off a pitch up a little and the other hit had eyes that beat the shift. ... The dirty little secret about Werth is that his glove is wildly overrated, as we saw tonight. Sometimes, Werth can look awfully raw; he now has 16 strikeouts in the postseason. ... People are jumping on umpire Kerwin Danley, and rightfully so. In a World Series, you can't be that incompetent. He rang up Baldelli, who clearly offered at the pitch and Danley clearly called it when you watch the instant replay. Then Danley lied about not calling it. Then, the blunder is compounded by the first-base ump who also makes the wrong call! Keystone Cops, they umped like clowns.

Nevertheless, to revisit the headline, as ugly as it's been, the Phils have set the pace and return home with the series tied tomorrow night, weather permitting.

World Series - Game 3

Quotable: "It might have took a little squib roller down the third-base line, but at the same time it's better to be lucky sometimes than to be good," - Phillies manager Charlie Manuel on Carlos Ruiz's 9th inning dribbler down the third base line to knock in the winning run

Saturday, October 25th - Phillies 5 Tampa Bay 4 - Phillies Lead Series 2-1

Philadelphia – *Carlos Ruiz's infield single in the bottom of the 9th knocked in the winning run and put the Phillies one game up on the Rays ... Jamie Moyer kept the Rays stymied for 6 1/3rd innings, allowing only 3 runs while striking out 5 ... Chad Durbin (1/3rd, 0 runs), Scott Eyre (1/3rd, 0 runs), Ryan Madson (2/3rd 1 run) and JC Romero 1 1/3rd innings 0 runs and tagged with the win) did an incredible job keeping Tampa off of the bases and allowing the Phillies offense to squeak out a run in the 9th as Eric Bruntlett scored the winning run ... Jimmy Rollins finally started hitting, going 2 for 4 and Carlos Ruiz went 2 for 3 to raise his World Series average to .500. Stuff: Ruiz's single was the Phils' first walk-off hit in the playoffs since Kim Batiste's single in Game 1 of the 1993 Series ... The game was delayed 91 minutes due to the continuing bad weather in the Philadelphia area and didn't start until 10:06pm, the latest start in the history of the World Series ...the game did not get done until 1:47am ... Hall-of-Famer Steve Carlton threw out the ceremonial first pitch of the game.*

Nearing 2 a.m., and in the final moments of a 3-hour, 41-minute marathon, a swinging bunt in the bottom of the ninth goes down in history as one of the biggest hits in Philadelphia sports history. Call it "The Little Squib that Did".   In a game that featured solo homers by Ruiz, Chase Utley and Ryan Howard, his first of the postseason, the game was decided with small ball once again. Six of the nine total runs came via small ball tactics: ground outs, infield hits, stolen bases, hitting behind the runner, a sac fly ... that's been the story throughout much of this World Series.

The dramatic finish erased a multitude of little sins, blunders and a blown call that could have proved disastrous for the team's championship hopes. Instead, fans can forget all about them and focus on the many positives from Game 3, includ-

Tampa's outfield could do nothing but watch as the Phillies took a one game lead in the Series

ing a razor-sharp outing by Jamie Moyer, who hit the bull's-eye all night long and pitched Tampa's power threats perfectly. The Rays continue to struggle against left-handed pitching. Cole Hamels, Moyer, Scott Eyre, J.C. Romero: success, success, success, success.

Offensively, Chooch (Carlos Ruiz) continued his October transformation into a legitimate threat and possible series MVP, while Utley picked a key time to launch his second home run of this series.

Here's how it happened in the ninth: With the game even, Eric Bruntlett, into the game as Pat Burrell's defensive caddy, was hit by a pitch to lead off the ninth, then reached third on a wild pitch and misfire to second by Rays' catcher Dioner Navarro. With Bruntlett on third and nobody out, Rays' manager Joe Maddon ordered intentional walks to Shane Victorino and Greg Dobbs to set up the double play using a five-man infield. Ruiz would then fight off Grant Balfour's high heat for the winning nubber down the third base line, representing the one and only time that the Bruntlett/Burrell speed swap truly paid off this season.

World Series - Game 4

Quotable: *"A championship is the only way to fully reverse that thought of how the Phillies are portrayed. If we get that (last) game, I believe we will be happy, the city will be happy, there will be a big parade." - Jimmy Rollins following the Phils game 4 victory leaving them one win away from a World Championship.*

Sunday, October 26th - Phillies 10 Tampa Bay 2 - Phillies Lead Series 3-1
Philadelphia – *The bats finally came alive with Ryan Howard leading the way ... Howard almost single-handedly destroyed the Rays pitching staff as he clobbered two homeruns and knocked in 5 as the Phils combined for 10 runs on 12 hits (Howard 3 for 5, Rollins 3 for 5, Werth 2 for 4, Pedro Feliz 2 for 4), including a homerun by pitcher Joe Blanton, the first homerun by a pitcher in World Series play since 1974 when Ken Holtzman hit one for the Oakland A's ... Blanton picked up the win as he gave up a stingy 2 runs on 4 hits ... the bullpen was clutch once more as Durbin, Eyre, Madson and Romero combined for 3 scoreless innings, surrendering only 1 hit. Stuff: Best sign of the night from the crowd of 45,903, "Bell?" (showing a picture of a Tampa cow bell) "This is a Bell!" (then showing a picture of a huge Liberty Bell) ... The Phils were 4 for 14 with runners in scoring position in the game versus the 2 for 33 they were the previous three games ... The Rays big bats (Evan) Longoria and Carlos Pena) are a combined 0 for 29 in the Series with 15 strikeouts! ... The Saint Petersburg Times reported after the game that Tampa's manager Joe Maddon suggested that Joe Blanton "may" have had "something" underneath the bill of his cap during the game. Blanton suggested that it was "just dirt from the ball" ... Maddon's response? "Umm, I don't think so".*

Forget his tight slider, pinpoint control and Mickey Mantle-like bat, Joe Blanton's best stuff tonight was between his ears. In a game in which the Phils' bats were the stories for the daily newspapers around the country, the real story tonight and for this entire series has been the pitching, catching and coaches plan as to how they would attack the Ray's offense the entire series. Even in the Game 2 loss the rotation stayed cool and stuck to their pre-game plans. After tonight's game, Blanton became the latest pitcher to praise the game calling of Carlos Ruiz, keeper of the scouting blueprints that have kept Tampa's 3-4 hitters without a base hit this entire series. That's the story. Not the ducks left on the pond by the Phillies' offense, not the blind officiating by the umps and certainly not the "curious dark spot" on Kentucky Joe

Blanton's bill.

Before Game 1, I used the words reliable, tough and dependable in describ-
ing the Phils' starting rotation. Words
that may have raised eyebrows in comparison to Tampa's staff, considered
the deeper of the two units. Well, the
45-year-old, the minor league demotee
and Kentucky Joe, who drew a collective trade deadline 'meh' from everyone, have kept the focus, pitching in
games they've dreamt about pitching
their entire lives.

*A happy fan in left field who caught one of Ryan Howard's
two homeruns in the game*

Tampa hasn't played good baseball, but
they're still dangerous. Step away from the national stage and it's a four-game slump that would
be considered innocuous if this series was being played in May. But facing elimination, and a
million miles from more cowbells, the Rays are all alone with the feet of America's sixth-largest
city standing on their throats.

World Series - Game 5 … Part I

*Quotable: "We'll stay here if we have to celebrate Thanksgiving!" – Commissioner Bud Selig com-
menting on when the "rain delay" would stop and play for Game 5 would resume.*

Monday, October 27th - (Game "Suspended") Game Tied 2-2, Bottom of the 6th
*Philadelphia – Under deteriorating conditions, play was halted one out after Tampa Bay tied the
score on an RBI single by Carlos Pena in the top of the sixth and was officially suspended 30 minutes
later … The Phils scored all their runs in the first on a bases-loaded single by Shane Victorino, but
once again, they continued to come up empty with runners in scoring position … Cole Hamels'
lasted six innings, allowing two runs and striking out three. Stuff: The unprecedented suspension
of the game was played in a virtual downpour from the fourth inning on … Phils' Groundskeeper
Mike Boekholder and his crew literally dumped tons of dirt onto the infield to fill in all the puddles
that were forming around the diamond during the last three innings of the game but alas the rain
won … after the game was suspended Bud Selig held a news conference in which he told reporters
that he, the GMs and the managers made a decision two days prior to the game that a World Series
game would not be won by a team due to the regular rain rules of baseball … When play resumes the
Phils will have their 9-1-2 hitters up in the bottom of the 6th … when that will be will be anyone's
guess … Best sign off the night? "World Series Championship or Bust".*

Game 5 (Part I) of the World Series was suspended due to the rain

Are there lessons to be learned from last night? Sure, but no one's listening. They'll do everything possible to jam the rest of Game 5 into conditions that read like this: "Mostly cloudy and windy with rain tapering off. Lows in the lower 30s. West winds 15 to 25 mph. Gusts up to 40 mph in the evening." An unfortunate turn of events to say the least. Fans may not want to hear it, but with a 3-1 series lead, a great pen and 12 outs to play with, the Phils are still in decent shape to wrap it up in five. That's what this team must remember when they step back on the field tomorrow against a Tampa team that was basically given CPR by Mother Nature and Major League Baseball. But of course, the forecast for tomorrow is even worse.

The first weather suspension in World Series history fouls up the Phillies' possible championship clincher. Why am I not surprised?

The mood in Philadelphia shifted just as quickly as the autumn weather. Gearing up for glory (at one point, 10 outs away from glory) deteriorated into bewilderment and anger directed toward everyone and everything, from Major League Baseball to *Fox Television*. Indeed, the two are in cahoots regarding the ridiculousness of 8:30 p.m., East Coast, late-October baseball.

Early forecasts hinted at mist, a playable condition. The first few innings were played in these conditions. But those forecasts changed during the afternoon; the heavy stuff would hit Philadelphia head on. So Bud Selig weighed the odds, gambled and lost.

It's the rigidity of baseball that has this observer most upset. Even shifting the start time to 7 would be impossible, when it should be so simple. All because of television, which thirsts for 8 p.m. to 11 p.m. Fox knows that old, impotent men, who wouldn't miss the World Series for anything, represent a broader market with deeper pockets than kids with bedtimes. The demographic who buys domestic beer, cell phones, iPods, satellite television, the Honda Fit and everything else Fox hocks during the World Series doesn't have a problem with games that end near midnight. In golf, for example, they wouldn't think twice about postponing a Major in questionable conditions. The demographic, consumers of luxury cars and mutual funds, is completely different.

Ramifications: Charlie Manuel and Joe Maddon have some decisions to mull over. When play resumes, the Phils will send a pinch hitter to the plate against right-hander Grant Balfour, who's still on the mound for Tampa. The Phils could go left/right with one of their big bats, but it's likely Maddon would counter with David Price. Manuel could call on someone like So Taguchi to lead off the inning as a way to get some speed on the bases for Jimmy Rollins and Jayson Werth, and preserve his big lefty bats that would certainly be minimized by Maddon.

Tampa's 3-4 hitters finally come through: Lost in the blame is the fact that Tampa's 3-4 hitters, Carlos Pena and Evan Longoria, finally came through with big hits. Under miserable conditions, Pena's RBI hit in the sixth, to drive in B.J. Upton, was the best execution the Rays had all series. It absolutely saved them

World Series - Game 5 ... Part II

Quotable: "We're the World Series Champions! ... Hard to Believe!" – Charlie Manuel in an interview with Comcast's Leslie Gudel after the Phillies win their first World Series Championship in 28 years

<u>Wednesday, October 29th - Phillies 4 Tampa Bay 3 - Phillies Win Series 4-1</u>
Philadelphia – *Nearly 50 hours after the start of Game 5 the Phillies were finally able to put their claim to destiny and win the World Series ... Geoff Jenkins got things rolling quickly as he pinch-hit for Cole Hamels to restart Game 5 and crushed a double to right-center field . Jimmy Rollins sacrificed Jenkins over to third base and Jayson Werth followed with a single to center to knock in the go-ahead run ... Tampa tied the game in the top of the 7th with a Rocco Baldelli homer to left off of reliever Ryan Madson ... In the bottom of the 7th, the Phils scored their final run of the World Series as Pat Burrell doubled and was pinch-ran for by Eric Bruntlett. Victorino grounded out to second, moving Bruntlett to third and then Pedro Feliz sent the crowd of 45,940 to their feet as he singled to center to knock in the game winning run ... Brad Lidge closed out the game and series by striking out Eric Hinske and sending Phillies' fans around the world into delirium. Stuff: President Bush called David Montgomery after the game to offer his congratulations to the team and the city ... Harry Kalas serenaded the fans in the after-game celebration with his rendition of "High Hopes" ... Cole Hamels was named MVP of the World Series after going 1-0 with a 2.77 ERA in two World Series starts ... Best sign of the night? "Mitch (Williams), You're Off the Hook!" ... The parade down Broad Street is scheduled for Friday starting at Noon. At long last ... a championship parade!*

Brad Lidge strikes out the Rays' Eric Hinske for the final out of the World Series

Brett Myers celebrates the Phillies first World Championship since 1980

Fans in Section 144 celebrate their team's first World Series victory in 28 years

After the parade Charlie Manuel steps up to the mic to thank the fans of Philadelphia
– photo courtesy of Nicole McNesby

Epilogue

24 hours have past since Carlos Ruiz tackled the kneeling Brad Lidge and the ensuing pile-on of the newly crowned World Champions of baseball. The specter of disbelief still looms. Twenty-eight years without a title isn't enough time to guess how this day would feel, or prepare for how things would change. I suspect I will become a better observer of the Phillies because of this, and appreciate this team with untangled clarity. It's already happening; all the nuances from last night are burned to memory as if they've always been there. But to limit this fresh outlook to baseball is to sell oneself short of a golden opportunity for transformation. Is it possible to become a better person because of this, or become happier in deeper, more meaningful ways? There's no better time to find out. It's a good idea to step outside for some air and go to a parade.

- Jason Weitzel

Memories from last night brought back long forgotten ones from 1980. As an 18 year old kid fresh out of high school I can vividly remember the screams of joy, the jumping around the living room couch and the subsequent run to downtown Main Street in Maple Shade, NJ, where my brother Jeff, and my friends Mark Oman, Bill Leahy, Al Marlow, Paul Mortimer, Wayne Sawyer and Joe Alvarez all joined in the celebration of a thousand other fans in the Phillies' very first World Series Championship. Twenty-eight years have gone by and there have been so many changes in our world, but the satisfying joy of winning the World Series remains the same. How else does one explain a 46 year old man jumping, screaming and hugging every one in sight at Citizens Bank Park without any excuse except for the fact that his team is once again the World Champions? Twenty-eight more years from now I will be 74. Hopefully by then we will have celebrated more than just this year's triumph. Even so, I guarantee you the feeling of seeing your team win the World Series once again will fill you with that same feeling that you felt in 1980 and now in 2008. Wow ... We're the champs!!! Pack the kids and lets head on over to Philly and see that parade we've all been waiting for!

- Michael McNesby

In Memory of Harry Kalas

On April 13, 2009 the Philadelphia Phillies and millions of their fans lost a treasure and one of the most distinctive voices in all of sports when Harry Kalas suddenly passed away as he prepared for his Phillies broadcast in Washington, D.C.. For almost four decades we had the privilege of listening to one of the greatest voices to have broadcast the game of baseball. An inductee to the Baseball Hall of Fame in 2002, Harry was an institution unto himself. His kindness as a man and his voice as a broadcaster will be missed for as long as we remember the Voice of the Phillies.

"To be sure in Philly, there might be some boos; because you passionate fans, like the manager hate to lose. Your reaction to the action on the field that you impart; Spurs us as broadcasters to call the game with enthusiasm and heart; We feel your passion through and through; Philadelphia fans, I love you." -A poem written by Harry Kalas that he read during his induction into the Baseball Hall of Fame in 2002.

About the Authors

Michael McNesby resides in Mount Laurel, NJ with his wife Jennifer, his son Michael Ryan, his daughter Nicole and their dog Daisy. He graduated from Maple Shade High School in 1980 and went on to serve in the United States Air Force as an Airborne Cryptologic Linguist (Hebrew) from 1982-1988. As an Air Force Reservist, Mike also serviced in Oman, the United Arab Emirates and Saudi Arabia during Operation Desert Storm in 1991 and 1992. Mike graduated with a B.A. in Information Systems Management from the University of Maryland in 1988 and currently works at Campbell Soup in Camden, NJ.

Jason Weitzel is the proprietor of the popular Phillies blog Beerleaguer.com and was named "Best Sportswriter 2008" by Philadelphia Magazine. He is a writer, editor and graphic designer with the Reading Eagle Newspaper, Reading, Pa. He and his wife, Maribeth, live in Philadelphia.